AQA GCSE
German
Foundation

Andy Holland, Helen Kent, Sabine Leitner, Wanda Marshall, Ben Merritt, Lisa Probert

Pearson

Published by Pearson Education Limited, 80 Strand, London, WC2R 0RL.

www.pearsonschoolsandfecolleges.co.uk

Copies of official specifications for all Pearson qualifications may be found on the website: qualifications.pearson.com

Text © Pearson Education Limited 2024
Edited by Pearson and Newgen
Designed and typeset by Kamae Design
Original illustrations © Pearson Education Limited 2024
Illustrated by Beehive Illustrations (Afua Bediako, Tamara Joubert, Andy Keylock, Daniel Limón, Mauro Marchesi, Andrew Pagram) and Newgen KnowledgeWorks
Cover design by Kamae Design
Cover photo © Shutterstock: Mistervlad
Audio recorded at Chatterbox Studios, London, with thanks to Rowan Laxton

Written by Andy Holland, Helen Kent, Sabine Leitner, Wanda Marshall, Ben Merritt and Lisa Probert.

Additional material written by Carol Mulingani.

The rights of Andy Holland, Helen Kent, Sabine Leitner, Wanda Marshall, Ben Merritt and Lisa Probert to be identified as authors of this work have been asserted by them in accordance with the Copyright, Designs and Patents Act 1988.

This publication is protected by copyright, and permission should be obtained from the publisher prior to any prohibited reproduction, storage in a retrieval system, or transmission in any form or by any means, electronic, mechanical, photocopying, recording, or otherwise.

For information regarding permissions, request forms and the appropriate contacts, please visit https://www.pearson.com/us/contact-us/permissions.html Pearson Education Limited Rights and Permissions Department.

Pearson Education Limited is an exclusive trademark owned by Pearson Education Limited and/or Pearson or its affiliates in the United Kingdom and/or other countries.

Unless otherwise indicated herein, any third party trademarks that may appear in this work are the property of their respective owners and any references to third party trademarks, logos or other trade dress are for demonstrative or descriptive purposes only. Such references are not intended to imply any sponsorship, endorsement, authorisation, or promotion of Pearson Education Limited products by the owners of such marks, or any relationship between the owner and Pearson Education Limited or its affiliates, authors, licensees or distributors.

First published 2024

28 27 26 25 24

10 9 8 7 6 5 4 3 2 1

British Library Cataloguing in Publication Data

A catalogue record for this book is available from the British Library

ISBN 978 1 292 468785

Copyright notice

All rights reserved. No part of this publication may be reproduced in any form or by any means (including photocopying or storing it in any medium by electronic means and whether or not transiently or incidentally to some other use of this publication) without the written permission of the copyright owner, except in accordance with the provisions of the Copyright, Designs and Patents Act 1988 or under the terms of a licence issued by the Copyright Licensing Agency, 5th Floor, Shackleton House, 4 Battle Bridge Lane, London, SE1 2HX (www.cla.co.uk). Applications for the copyright owner's written permission should be addressed to the publisher.

Printed in the UK by Bell & Bain Ltd, Glasgow

Acknowledgements

We would like to thank Vicki Baxter, Sarah Bench, Kate Bonail, Gillian Eades, Gabriela Hallas, Andy Holland, Helen Kent, Monika Lee, Sabine Leitner, Stephen Lyons, Wanda Marshall, Antoinette Meehan, Ben Merritt, Lisa Probert, Frances Reynolds, Judith Rifeser, Mario Rogic, Elizabeth Weatherup, Melissa Weir, the teams at Newgen and Kamae, and everyone else involved, for their invaluable work in the development of this course. We would also like to thank Rowan Laxton and the team at Chatterbox Studios: Daniel Alexander, Phoebe Shepherd Gartner, Britta Gartner, Emilia Kreutzmann Gravioto, Lara Marie Straka, Finn Humphrey, Leo Peithmann and Damien Saini. Andy Holland would like to thank his husband, Michael, his mother, Nicole, and his fellow authors, Sabine and Ben. Sabine Leitner would like to thank her fellow author, Wanda. Wanda Marshall would like to thank her husband, Joe. Ben Merritt would like to thank his wife, Abi, and his daughters, Molly and Matilda. Lisa Probert would like to thank her husband, Roy.

The author and publisher would like to thank the following individuals and organisations for permission to reproduce photographs:

123RF: Stillfx 6, Grebeshkovmaxim 6, Olga Popova 7, Seventyfour74 8, Ssilver 34, Cathy Yeulet 35, Mrivserg 38, Imagesource 43, Carballo 46, Zinkevych 60, Akz 86, Dmitrii Shironosov 86, Dmbaker 87, Brainsil 91, Famveldman 94, Ifong 96, Goran Bogicevic 99, Ratchanida Thippayos 111, Ian Allenden 112, Olegdudko 120, Anandkrish16 120, Dglimages 123, Zoltan Tukacs 132, Iriana88w 136, Aphaspirit 164, Kubko 166, Stanciuc 170, Katarzyna Białasiewicz 180, Cathy Yeulet 180, Kubko 182, Milkos 185, Epicstockmedia 190, Dmitriy Shironosov 190, Iakov Filimonov 221; **Alamy Images:** MBI 10, Galinast 13, Canetti 14, Jürgen Fälchle 14, Stockbroker/MBI 14, Henning Kaiser/dpa/Alamy Live News/dpa picture alliance 30, Science History Images 30, Björn Deutschmann 30, Adam Stoltman/Alamy Live News 36, Kpa Publicity Stills/United Archives GmbH 38, Panther Media GmbH 38, Martin Meissner/Associated Press 56, GERO BREOLER/dpa picture alliance archive 56, Karl F. Schöfmann/imageBROKER.com GmbH & Co. K 56, JEAN-CHRISTOPHE BOTT/Associated Press 57, Blickwinke 57, Classic Collection, Shotshop GmbH 80, Idp french collection 109, Dieddin alsoub 120, Intense Images 132, Dpa picture alliance/dpa 134, Mark Kanning 134, David South 136, Dpa picture alliance 161, Panther Media GmbH 186; **Getty Images:** Westend61/Westend61 6, Stuart Fox/Gallo Images ROOTS RF collection 10, Jan Wlodarczyk/Aflo Images 10, Oliver Rossi/Stone 13, Ozgurdonmaz/iStock/Getty Images Plus 13, Kali9/E+ 14, Liudmila Chernetska/iStock/Getty Images Plus 18, Kammata/Moment 19, Andreas Rentz/Staff/Getty Images Entertainment 31, Stefan Matzke - sampics/Contributor/Corbis Sport 36, SolStock/E+ 41, John Eder/Stone 45, Valeriy_G/iStock/Getty Images Plus 46, Halfpoint Images/Moment 46, William87/iStock Editorial/Getty Images Plus 57, Adamkaz/E+ 60, Rob Lewine/Tetra images 60, Aflo Images/Aflo Images 60, Counter/DigitalVision 68, Sergio Mendoza Hochmann/Moment 73, Simonkr/E+ 80, Westend61/Westend61 80, Lumi Images/Pupeter-Secen/Collection Mix: Subjects 80, Jasmin Merdan/Moment 80, SDI Productions/E+ 80, MarsYu/E+ 86, Erik Isakson/Tetra image 90, Solskin/DigitalVision 100, Alexander Spatari/The Image Bank Unreleased 104, Joe daniel price/Moment 104, Feng Wei Photography/Moment 105, SerrNovik/iStock/Getty Images Plus 107, Habitante Stock/Moment 112, Amazingmikael/iStock/Getty Images Plus 112, Juergen Sack/E+ 113, Yellow Dog Productions/DigitalVision 115, Kzenon/iStock/Getty Images Plus 118, Eva-Katalin/E+ 124, Nikada/E+ 132, © Marco Bottigelli/Moment 132, iStock/Getty Images Plus 134, Juan Algar/Moment 134, SeventyFour/iStock/Getty Images Plus 134, SolStock/E+ 142, Kolderal/Moment 148, Nicolas Micolani/iStock/Getty Images Plus 151, NurPhoto/Contributor/NurPhoto 156, SolStock/E+ 158, Skynesher/E+ 158, Deepak Sethi/E+ 159, Moorefam//iStock/Getty Images Plus 160, luoman/E+ 160, Shaifulzamri/Moment 160, Maja Hitij/Staff/Getty Images News 161, NurPhoto 164, Peter Cade/Photodisc 180, AleksandarGeorgiev/E+ 180, Joos Mind/Photodisc 180, Mgstudyo/E+ 180, Westend61/Westend61 180, Willie B. Thomas/DigitalVision 180, iStock/Getty Images Plus 183, SolStock 186, Vitaliymateha/iStock/Getty Images Plus 188, Sturti/E+ 188, Yacobchuk/iStock/Getty Images Plus 217; **Pearson Education Ltd:** Jon Barlow 34, Handan Erek 32, Jules Selmes 80, Gareth Boden 82, MindStudio 96, Jules Selmes 109, Gareth Boden 123, Jules Selmes 134, Jon Barlow 140, Gareth Boden 142, Lord and Leverett 186, Studio 8 197; **Red Cross:** International Committee of the Red Cross/Thierry Gassmann/ICRC 164; **Save the Children:** © Save the Children 164; **Shutterstock:** Hybrid Gfx 6, KALABUKHAVA IRYNA 6, FamVeld 6, Shutterstock 6, Mariusz Szczygiel 6, Treter 6, M_Videous 6, Karkas 7, Billion Photos 7, Africa Studio 7, NYS 7, Darren Baker 9, CarlosBarquero 10, Sky Designs 11, Tele52 11, ShutterStockStudio 14, Rafael Ramirez Lee 15, Fizkes 16, Prostock-studio 17, Motortion films 17, Dan Rentea 21, Legenda 23, Rawpixel.com 25, LStockStudio 25, Shutterstock 26, Archideaphoto 30, Sky Designs 32, Insta_photos 34, Zoia Kostina 34, Ground Picture 37, Praszkiewicz 38, WB Television/Netflix/Kobal 38, Moviestore 38, Fizkes 38, Ground Picture 40, Eastimages 42, Shutterstock 46, FrameStockFootages 49, Iren_Geo 49, Marino Bocelli 50, David Irlweg 56, FooTToo 56, Isopix 56, Photo Veterok 57, Stokkete 57, Frank Uffmann 57, Darren Baker 62, Andrew Rybalko 64, Heide Pinkall 64, Kobby Dagan 65, Wavebreakmedia 67, AJR_Photo 71, KarepaStock 72, Tom Wang 75, Sirtravelalot 75, PeopleImages.com - Yuri A 76, WAYHOME studio 82, Sianc 82, Estudio Grafico Ve 83, Pixel-Shot 85, Panitanphoto 86, Elena Shashkina 86, Samuel Borges Photography 86, Iakov Filimonov 88, Shutterstock 91, Blend Images 96, Wavebreakmedia 97, JaySi 99, S-F 104, Visions-AD 104, Alexey Fedorenko 104, R.M. Nunes 104, Trabantos 104, Nate Hovee 107, Peter Stein 108, RossHelen 110, Antonio Guillem 112, Altug Galip 113, Stephen Bridger 118, Zurijeta 121, BorisR 132, Martin Furtivo 133, Christian Kaehler 134, Kootzz 134, SARYMSAKOV ANDREY 136, Alpay Erdem 136, Grand Warszawski 136, Atlaspix 136, DGLimages 137, PointImages 137, Altrendo Images 138, Sky Designs 138, PETROV ARTEM 142, Arts Illustrated Studios 143, Saiko3p 147, Momint 149, Syda Productions 151, Ground Picture 152, LeStudio 156, Stefano Garau 156, Shahrul Azman 158, Vladimir Toropov 160, LifetimeStock 160, Reisegraf.ch 160, Stella sophie 164, Olesya Kuznetsova 165, Julinzy 165, Pro-Stock Studio 167, Martin D. Vonka 167, Motortion Films 168, Piyaset 170, Elwynn 170, Rich Carey 170, Wang An Qi 171, Daisy Daisy 172, DPiX Center 173, Prostock-studio 175, Connel 175, Shutterstock 180, Viktoriia Hnatiuk 180, Oliveromg 182, Daniel M Ernst 185, Bbernard 185, Spitzi-Foto 186, Shurkin_son 186, Daisy Daisy 188, Aerogondo2 189, Marcia Bressanin 189, Anyaivanova 190, Science photo 191, Stella sophie 191, Davide Zanin Photography 199, Syda Productions 199, Rawpixel.com 200, Wavebreakmedia 211, MaxFrost 213, Amy Myers 217, Ppa 218, Shutterstock 225, Fizkes 230, Ground Picture 233, Prostock-studio 233; **World Health Organization:** ©World Health Organization/Pierre Albouy/WHO 2024 164.

Notes from the publisher

Pearson has robust editorial processes, including answer and fact checks, to ensure the accuracy of the content in this publication, and every effort is made to ensure this publication is free of errors. We are, however, only human, and occasionally errors do occur. Pearson is not liable for any misunderstandings that arise as a result of errors in this publication, but it is our priority to ensure that the content is accurate. If you spot an error, please do contact us at resourcescorrections@pearson.com so we can make sure it is corrected.

Inhalt

Kapitel 1 Zurück zur Schule!   Theme 1: People and lifestyle

Kulturzone Meine Schule, deine Schule — 6
- Understanding the school system in Great Britain and in the German-speaking world
- Using articles and plural nouns

Einheit 1 Welche Fächer hast du dieses Jahr? — 8
- Talking about your school subjects
- Using the present tense
- Using *weil* to give and justify opinions

Einheit 2 Was trägst du in der Schule? — 10
- Talking about school uniforms
- Using adjectives with nouns
- Describing a photo

Einheit 3 Sind Schulregeln wirklich nötig? — 12
- Talking about school rules
- Using modal verbs: *müssen, dürfen, sollen*
- Using opinion phrases with *dass*

Einheit 4 Schultage: die beste Zeit deines Lebens? — 14
- Talking about special events at school
- Using the perfect and imperfect tenses
- Practising the *w* sound in German

Einheit 5 Austausch geht auch online! — 16
- Describing school life
- Using the present tense with a future time phrase
- Practising the 50-word exam question

Grammatik 1 — 18
Grammatik 2 — 20
Lese- und Hörtest — 22
Mündlicher Test — 24
Schreibtest — 26
Wörter — 28

Kapitel 2 Endlich mal Freizeit!   Theme 2: Popular culture; Theme 3: Communication and the world around us

Kulturzone Kennst du diese Musiker? — 30
- Learning about German-speaking musicians
- Giving opinions

Einheit 1 Was machst du gern in deiner Freizeit? — 32
- Talking about your free time
- Expressing preferences
- Using frequency phrases with correct word order

Einheit 2 Was machst du online? — 34
- Discussing how you spend time online
- Using separable verbs in the present tense
- Practising the *sch, sp* and *st* sounds at the start of words

Einheit 3 Das Leben als Star — 36
- Discussing the pros and cons of celebrity culture
- Asking questions
- Practising the role-play section of the exam

Einheit 4 Wie war der Film? — 38
- Expressing preferences about films and TV shows
- Using the imperfect and perfect tenses together
- Practising the *eu* sound in German

Einheit 5 Hast du Pläne? — 40
- Using the future tense to describe plans for the weekend
- Understanding the 'time – manner – place' rule
- Practising the *ä* sound in German

Grammatik 1 — 42
Grammatik 2 — 44
Lese- und Hörtest — 46
Mündlicher Test — 48
Schreibtest — 50
Wörter — 52
Grammatik: Wiederholung Kapitel 1–2 — 54

Kapitel 3 Meine Welt, deine Welt   Theme 1: People and lifestyle; Theme 2: Popular culture

Kulturzone Feste in der deutschsprachigen Welt — 56
- Describing festivals and cultural events
- Giving opinions and justifications

Einheit 1 Wie ist deine Familie? — 58
- Describing family members
- Using possessive adjectives
- Using relative pronouns

Einheit 2 Deine Beziehungen — 60
- Saying how you get on with people and why
- Using pronouns and possessive adjectives in the dative
- Using qualifiers and intensifiers

Einheit 3 Wer ist dir wichtig? — 62
- Discussing people who inspire you
- Using two time frames together: past and present
- Word order with *da* and *weil*

Einheit 4 Wir haben gefeiert! — 64
- Describing a family celebration in the past
- Practising word order
- Using time phrases

Einheit 5 Partyzeit! — 66
- Discussing a party
- Using two time frames: past and future
- Using *in* + accusative or dative

Grammatik 1 — 68
Grammatik 2 — 70
Lese- und Hörtest — 72
Mündlicher Test — 74
Schreibtest — 76
Wörter — 78

Inhalt

Kapitel 4 Bleib gesund!
**Theme 1: People and lifestyle;
Theme 2: Popular culture**

Kulturzone Ich liebe Sport — 80
- Learning about favourite sports in the German-speaking world
- Using comparative adjectives and adverbs

Einheit 1 Willst du fit und gesund sein? — 82
- Talking about healthy lifestyles
- Revising modal verbs
- Practising a role-play about health and fitness

Einheit 2 Es geht mir nicht gut — 84
- Talking about accidents and illnesses
- Using modal verbs in the imperfect tense
- Using *vor*

Einheit 3 Was möchte ich verbessern? — 86
- Talking about good and bad habits
- Revising present, past and future tenses
- Pronouncing umlauts

Einheit 4 Gute Tage, schlechte Tage — 88
- Talking about wellbeing
- Using *wenn*
- Pronouncing *-ig* at the end of words

Einheit 5 Das finde ich wichtig! — 90
- Talking about what is important to you
- Understanding questions in different tenses
- Writing about lifestyle and wellbeing

Grammatik 1 — 92
Grammatik 2 — 94
Lese- und Hörtest — 96
Mündlicher Test — 98
Schreibtest — 100
Wörter — 102

Kapitel 5 Meine Gegend
Theme 3: Communication and the world around us

Kulturzone Wo spricht man Deutsch? — 104
- Learning key facts about German-speaking countries
- Revising the comparative

Einheit 1 Wo wohnst du? — 106
- Describing where you live
- Using prepositions followed by the dative
- Using a variety of adjectives with intensifiers and qualifiers

Einheit 2 Wie fährst du? — 108
- Discussing transport in your local area
- Using prepositions with the accusative
- Using correct word order with *weil* and *obwohl*

Einheit 3 Wo gehst du gern einkaufen? — 110
- Discussing shopping habits
- Using compound nouns
- Using plurals of nouns

Einheit 4 Mein idealer Wohnort — 112
- Describing an ideal place to live
- Using a range of tenses
- Using *ich möchte*

Einheit 5 Bei mir zu Hause — 114
- Describing your home
- Using prepositions with the accusative and the dative
- Working out the meaning of compound nouns

Grammatik 1 — 116
Grammatik 2 — 118
Lese- und Hörtest — 120
Mündlicher Test — 122
Schreibtest — 124
Wörter — 126
Grammatik: Wiederholung Kapitel 1–5 — 128

Kapitel 6 Schöne Ferien!
Theme 3: Communication and the world around us

Kulturzone Im Urlaub und unterwegs — 132
- Learning about German-speaking travel destinations
- Using adjectival endings after the definite article

Einheit 1 Wo fahren wir hin? — 134
- Describing different holiday destinations
- Forming questions
- Discussing advantages and disadvantages

Einheit 2 Wo werden wir wohnen? — 136
- Describing types of holiday accommodation
- Using *wer*, *wen* and *wem*
- Recognising negatives

Einheit 3 Mein schrecklicher Urlaub — 138
- Describing problems on holiday
- Revising possessive adjectives
- Practising a holiday role-play

Einheit 4 Wie waren die Schulferien? — 140
- Describing a past holiday
- Using past participles with inseparable prefixes
- Talking about the weather in the past

Einheit 5 Ich möchte um die Welt reisen! — 142
- Describing future and ideal holidays
- Using interrogative and demonstrative adjectives
- Practising the *w* and *v* sounds in German

Grammatik 1 — 144
Grammatik 2 — 146
Lese- und Hörtest — 148
Mündlicher Test — 150
Schreibtest — 152
Wörter — 154

vier

Inhalt

Kapitel 7 *Unsere Welt*
Theme 1: People and lifestyle;
Theme 3: Communication and the world around us

Kulturzone *Wir verbessern die Welt!* — 156
- Learning more about activism in German-speaking countries
- Revising prepositions with the accusative and dative cases

Einheit 1 *Was ist dir wichtig?* — 158
- Discussing issues facing young people today
- Using pronouns in the accusative and dative cases
- Using verbs followed by prepositions

Einheit 2 *Unser armer Planet* — 160
- Discussing how environmental issues are being addressed
- Understanding *wollen* and revising other modal verbs
- Revising compound nouns

Einheit 3 *Jeder kann was tun!* — 162
- Discussing personal responsibilities and actions
- Revising frequency phrases
- Understanding and using verbs in three time frames

Einheit 4 *Wir wollen eine bessere Welt!* — 164
- Discussing international responsibilities and actions
- Developing listening and reading skills
- Using *man*

Einheit 5 *Dialog ist wichtig!* — 166
- Expressing and justifying complex opinions and points of view
- Using phrases of debating in speaking
- Pronouncing *r* sounds correctly

Grammatik 1 — 168
Grammatik 2 — 170
Lese- und Hörtest — 172
Mündlicher Test — 174
Schreibtest — 176
Wörter — 178

Kapitel 8 *Wie sieht die Zukunft aus?*
Theme 1: People and lifestyle

Kulturzone *Ich will helfen* — 180
- Learning about military and civilian service
- Using *möchten* and *wollen*

Einheit 1 *Was wirst du nach deinen Prüfungen machen?* — 182
- Discussing plans for after exams
- Using reflexive verbs
- Revising ways to refer to the future

Einheit 2 *Was ist dein Traumberuf?* — 184
- Discussing what jobs you would like to do in the future
- Using *werden* (to become)
- Forming past participles of *-ieren* verbs

Einheit 3 *Was kannst du gut?* — 186
- Discussing characteristics and skills
- Revising subordinating conjunctions
- Extending your written work

Einheit 4 *Ein Zwischenjahr? Warum nicht?* — 188
- Discussing gap years
- Revising relative clauses
- Asking questions

Einheit 5 *Meine Träume für die Zukunft* — 190
- Discussing hopes for the future
- Dealing with unfamiliar vocabulary
- Consolidating key language and grammar points

Grammatik 1 — 192
Grammatik 2 — 194
Lese- und Hörtest — 196
Mündlicher Test — 198
Schreibtest — 200
Wörter — 202
Grammatik: Wiederholung Kapitel 1–8 — 204

Wiederholung

Kapitel 1 *Zurück zur Schule!* — 210
Kapitel 2 *Endlich mal Freizeit!* — 212
Kapitel 3 *Meine Welt, deine Welt* — 214
Kapitel 4 *Bleib gesund!* — 216
Kapitel 5 *Meine Gegend* — 218
Kapitel 6 *Schöne Ferien!* — 220
Kapitel 7 *Unsere Welt* — 222
Kapitel 8 *Wie sieht die Zukunft aus?* — 224

Speaking support

Speaking test revision: Conversation questions — 226
Speaking test revision: German phonics — 228
Speaking test revision: Role-play skills — 230
Speaking test revision: Photo card task — 232
Verb tables — 234
Derivational morphology — 240

Kapitel 1 — Zurück zur Schule!

Meine Schule, deine Schule
- Understanding the school system in Great Britain and in the German-speaking world
- Using articles and plural nouns

a) Deutschland
Typischer Schultag:	7:30–13:00 Uhr
Ferien:	10–13 Wochen
Hausaufgaben:	2–3 Stunden
Zu Fuß zur Schule:	47%
Mit dem Fahrrad zur Schule:	11%

b) die Schweiz
Typischer Schultag:	8:00–16:00 Uhr
Ferien:	12–14 Wochen
Hausaufgaben:	2–3 Stunden
Zu Fuß zur Schule:	50%
Mit dem Fahrrad zur Schule:	18%

c) Großbritannien
Typischer Schultag:	8:30–15:30 Uhr
Ferien:	13–15 Wochen
Hausaufgaben:	1–2 Stunden
Zu Fuß zur Schule:	42%
Mit dem Fahrrad zur Schule:	2%

d) Österreich
Typischer Schultag:	7:30–13:00 Uhr
Ferien:	14–16 Wochen
Hausaufgaben:	2–3 Stunden
Zu Fuß zur Schule:	40%
Mit dem Fahrrad zur Schule:	20%

e) Austausch in Großbritannien: Die Schule ist anders!

Maximillian von Reichelt

Großbritannien	Deutschland
Die Kinder gehen schon mit vier oder fünf Jahren in die Schule.	Die Kinder gehen mit sechs Jahren in die Schule.
Die Kinder bekommen keine Schultüte. 🙁	Die Kinder bekommen eine Schultüte. 🙂
Fast alle Schüler tragen eine Schuluniform.	Die Schüler tragen meistens keine Schuluniform.
Die Lehrer haben „ihr" Klassenzimmer und die Schüler gehen zu den Lehrern.	Die Schüler haben „ihr" Klassenzimmer und die Lehrer gehen zu den Schülern.
Alle Schüler bekommen Bücher von der Schule. Das finde ich toll! ❤	Die Schüler kaufen einige Bücher selber. Das finde ich in Großbritannien besser.
Die Schüler müssen nie sitzenbleiben.	Die Schüler müssen sitzenbleiben, wenn sie schlechte Noten haben.

die Schultüte — a cone of treats children get on their first day at primary school

der Austausch — exchange

Kulturzone

Kapitel 1

Lesen 1 Read the statistics (a–d) about typical schools in Germany, Switzerland, Great Britain and Austria. Copy and complete the sentences below in English.

1. The school day in Germany begins at …
2. Students in Switzerland have … hours of homework.
3. Students in Great Britain have … weeks' holiday.
4. The country where most students walk to school is …
5. In Great Britain, …% of students cycle to school compared to …% in Austria.
6. The country with the longest school day is … and the countries with the shortest are … and …

Lesen 2 Read the table (e) and write down <u>six</u> key differences between schools in Great Britain and in Germany.

Lesen 3 Look at the flyer. Write the letter of the correct item of clothing (a–f) for each German word.

1. die Hose
2. der Rock
3. die Schuhe
4. die Jacke
5. das Hemd
6. das T-Shirt

Angebote für den Schulbeginn!

a €7,99
b €29,99
c €18,50
d €15,60
e €16,50
f €79,99

| das Angebot (-e) | offer |
| ein paar | a few |

Hören 4 Listen to the conversation. Look at the pictures in exercise 3. Write down a–f. Tick (✓) the items they buy and cross (✗) the ones they don't.

Sprechen 5 Memory game: In pairs, take turns to say what you are going to buy, adding an extra item each time.

- Ich gehe einkaufen und ich kaufe <u>einen Rock</u>.
- Ich gehe einkaufen und ich kaufe <u>einen Rock</u> und …

The word *Umlaut* means 'sound changer'.

Listen and repeat the words.
Then practise reading them out.

R**o**ck (skirt)   R**ö**ck**e** (skirts)
Sch**u**le (school)   Sch**ü**ler (pupils)

G Learn the **plural forms of nouns** as well as the gender. Here are some patterns:

	singular	plural
m	der Rock (¨-e) der Schuh (-e)	die Röck**e** die Schuh**e**
f	die Hose (-n) die Jacke (-n)	die Hose**n** die Jacke**n**
nt	das Hemd (-en) das T-Shirt (-s)	die Hemd**en** die T-Shirt**s**

G

	definite article 'the'		indefinite article 'a'	
	nominative	accusative	nominative	accusative
m	der	den	ein	einen
f	die	die	eine	eine
nt	das	das	ein	ein
pl	die	die	–	–

Nom (subject): **Ein** Rock kostet 25 Euro. **Der** Rock ist teuer!
Acc (direct object): Ich brauche **einen** Rock. Ich kaufe **den** Rock nicht.

Page 18

Schreiben 6 Look at the photo and write <u>five</u> short sentences about it in German.

Example: Es gibt Schuhe. Es gibt eine …

Es gibt	einen Rock / einen Pullover. eine Hose / eine Schultasche. ein Hemd. Hemden/Schuhe.
(Der Rock) ist (Die Schuhe) sind	braun/grau/rot/schwarz/weiß.

sieben **7**

1 Welche Fächer hast du dieses Jahr?

- Talking about your school subjects
- Using the present tense
- Using *weil* to give and justify opinions

Hören 1 Listen to the students talking about their new timetables. Decide if each person is talking about the timetable below (✓) or not (✗). (1–6)

	Montag	Dienstag	Mittwoch	Donnerstag	Freitag
1. Stunde	Mathe	Chemie	Englisch	Deutsch	Physik
2. Stunde	Biologie	Englisch	Mathe	Englisch	Chemie
			Pause		
3. Stunde	Deutsch	Mathe	Geschichte	Kunst	Theater
4. Stunde	Englisch	Kunst	Deutsch	Geschichte	Mathe
5. Stunde	Erdkunde	Informatik	Religion	Musik	Biologie
			Mittagspause		
6. Stunde	Musik	Sport	Physik	Sport	Erdkunde

In der ersten / zweiten / dritten / vierten / fünften / sechsten Stunde habe ich (Mathe).

Naturwissenschaften sciences (**Physik, Biologie, Chemie**)
Informatik IT

Hören 2 Listen again. Write the correct letter of the opinion adjective you hear. (1–6)

- **a** boring
- **b** great
- **c** complicated
- **d** not so good
- **e** easy
- **f** difficult

Be careful with cognates! Listen and repeat the words. Then practise reading them out.

- g *Biologie*
- ch *Chemie*
- e *Englisch*
- sp *Sport*
- th *Mathe, Theater*
- y *Physik*

G Use the **present tense** to talk about what you **do** or **are doing** now.

Ich lerne Deutsch. I **learn** German. / I **am learning** German.

	regular verbs: lernen	verbs with a stem ending in -d or -t: finden
ich (*I*)	lern**e**	find**e**
du (*you*)	lern**st**	find**est**
er/sie/es/man (*he/she/it/one*)	lern**t**	find**et**
wir (*we*)	lern**en**	find**en**
ihr (*you plural*)	lern**t**	find**et**
Sie (*you formal, sg and pl*)	lern**en**	find**en**
sie (*they*)	lern**en**	find**en**

Page 19

Sprechen 3 In pairs, take turns to ask and answer questions about your timetable.

- *Was hast du am Montag in der ersten Stunde?*
- *Am Montag in der ersten Stunde habe ich Englisch.*
- *Wie findest du Geschichte?*
- *Ich finde es schwierig. Was hast du am Freitag nach der Pause?*
- *Am Freitag nach der Pause habe ich …*

Was hast du (am Montag) in der (ersten/zweiten/dritten) Stunde?
Am (Montag) in der (ersten) Stunde habe ich (Englisch).
Wie oft hast du (Mathe)?
Ich habe (Mathe) (einmal/zweimal/dreimal) pro Woche / pro Tag.
Wie viele Stunden hast du (am Nachmittag / nach der Pause)?
Wie findest du (Englisch)?
Ich finde es einfach/kompliziert/langweilig/leicht/schwierig/toll.
Was ist dein Lieblingsfach?
Mein Lieblingsfach ist (Deutsch).

8 *acht*

Kapitel 1

Hören 4 Listen to and read the interview with Sarah. Translate the words in blue into English. Then translate the phrases in **bold** into English.

> ❓ Hallo Sarah! *Welche* Fächer lernst du dieses Jahr?
> Dieses Jahr lerne ich Mathe, Englisch, Deutsch, Sport, Geschichte, Kunst, Theater und Musik.
>
> ❓ *Was ist dein Lieblingsfach?*
> Mein Lieblingsfach ist Englisch.
>
> ❓ *Warum?*
> **Weil es einfach ist**.
>
> ❓ *Wann hast du Englisch?*
> Ich habe Englisch am Dienstag, am Mittwoch und am Freitag.
>
> ❓ *Welches Fach magst du nicht und warum?*
> Ich mag Mathe nicht, **weil ich nicht gut in Mathe bin**.
>
> ❓ *Wie findest du Deutsch?*
> Ich mag Deutsch, **weil es interessant und wichtig ist**.
>
> ❓ *Was machst du in der Pause?*
> In der Pause spiele ich Tennis.

Sprechen 5 In pairs, take turns to ask and answer the questions in the interview in exercise 4.

Ich mag (Englisch), Ich liebe (Deutsch), Ich mag (Mathe) (nicht),	weil	es	interessant wichtig nützlich einfach/leicht praktisch schwer/schwierig kompliziert langweilig	ist.
		ich es		finde.
		ich (nicht)	gut in (Mathe)	bin.
In der Pause		esse ich … / trinke ich … / spiele ich … spreche ich mit meinen Freunden.		

G *weil* sends the <u>verb</u> to the end.

Ich mag Englisch. Ich finde es einfach.
I like English. I find it easy.

*Ich mag Englisch, **weil** ich es einfach <u>finde</u>.*
I like English **because** I <u>find</u> it easy.

Page 19

mit meinen Freunden — with my friends

Schreiben 6 Translate the sentences into German.

- 'I am learning' and 'I learn' are the same in German. → 1 I am learning German, music and history.
- 2 Anna finds maths great.
- What is different about the verb endings of *finden*? → 3 They find English difficult.
- 4 After the lunch break we have PE. → Verb in second place, no comma needed in German.
- 5 I like art because it is interesting.

Schreiben 7 Write a paragraph about your timetable this year and your opinions of different school subjects.

The **verb** is always the **second idea** in a German sentence (not necessarily the second word).
<u>Nach der Mittagspause</u> **haben** wir Sport.
<u>first idea</u>   **second idea**

G

	haben	sein
ich (*I*)	habe	bin
du (*you*)	hast	bist
er/sie/es/man (*he/she/it/one*)	hat	ist
wir (*we*)	haben	sind
ihr (*you plural*)	habt	seid
Sie (*you formal, sg and pl*)	haben	sind
sie (*they*)	haben	sind

Page 19

neun 9

2 Was trägst du in der Schule?

- Talking about school uniforms
- Using adjectives with nouns
- Describing a photo

Lesen 1 Read the speech bubbles. Write the letter of the correct photo (a–d) for each speech bubble.

1 Die Mädchen tragen:
- ein grünes Kleid
- braune Schuhe.

Die Jungen tragen:
- braune Shorts
- ein braunes T-Shirt.

2 Die Schüler und Schülerinnen tragen:
- Jeans
- ein T-Shirt
- Sportschuhe.

Sie haben keine Schuluniform.

3 Sie tragen alle:
- eine dunkelblaue Jacke
- entweder einen grauen Rock oder eine graue Hose
- ein weißes Hemd
- eine rot-weiße Krawatte.

4 Die Jungen tragen:
- eine schwarze Hose
- einen schwarzen Pullover.

Die Mädchen tragen:
- einen schwarzen Rock
- ein weißes Hemd.

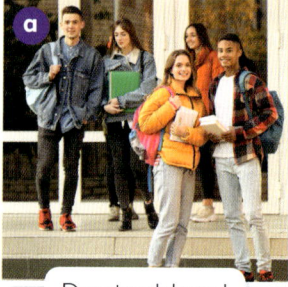

a Deutschland
b Großbritannien 
c Südafrika 
d Japan 

entweder … oder	either … or
der Pullover	jumper
die Krawatte	tie

Hören 2 Listen to some students describing what they wear to school. Select the correct option to complete each sentence.

1 I wear black **trousers / jeans** and a **white / grey** shirt.
2 I normally wear **grey / light blue** jeans and a **yellow / brown** T-shirt.
3 I wear a **blue / black** jacket and a **red / dark red** tie.
4 At school we wear a **grey / green** skirt and a **grey / green** jumper.

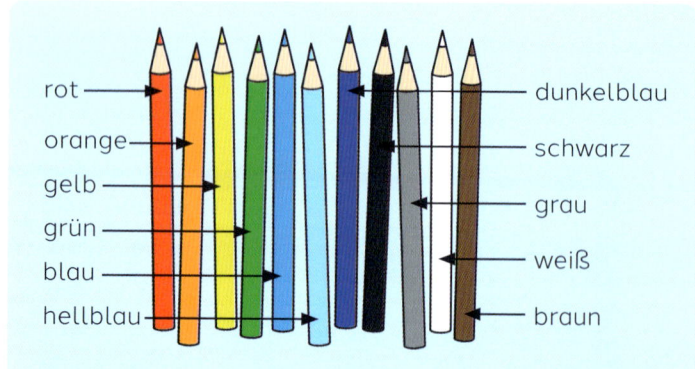

rot — dunkelblau
orange — schwarz
gelb — grau
grün — weiß
blau — braun
hellblau

Two adjectives can be combined in German to form a new adjective:
hell (light) + blau (blue) → hellblau (light blue)
dunkel (dark) + blau (blue) → dunkelblau (dark blue)

Adjectives used before nouns must **agree** with the noun. **G**

Ich trage	ein**en** kein**en**	blau**en**	Rock.
	ein**e** kein**e**	blau**e**	Hose. Jacke.
Wir tragen	ein kein	blau**es**	Hemd. Kleid.
	–	blau**e**	Schuhe.
	kein**e**	blau**en**	Jeans.

kein (not, not a) has the same endings as the indefinite article:
Ich trage **keinen** *schwarz***en** *Pullover.*
Wir tragen **keine** *rot***e** *Krawatte.*
Sie tragen **kein** *weiß***es** *Hemd.*

10 zehn

Schreiben 3

Translate the sentences into German.

1. I wear black trousers and a red jumper.
2. We wear a blue dress and a dark blue jacket.
3. She wears a grey skirt and a white shirt.
4. He wears black shoes and a yellow tie.
5. What do you wear?

Trousers are feminine singular in German.

Tragen changes its vowel sounds in the du and er/sie/es/man forms.

G
Some **irregular verbs** change their **vowel sounds** in the *du* and *er/sie/es/man* forms.

	tragen (to wear)	fahren (to drive, go)
ich	trage	fahre
du	tr**ä**gst	f**ä**hrst
er/sie/es/man	tr**ä**gt	f**ä**hrt

Page 19

Hören 4

Listen to and read the forum and decide which statements about school uniforms are positive (**P**), negative (**N**) or both (**P+N**). Then translate the phrases in **bold** into English. Write down **two** opinions you agree with.

Wie findest du die Schuluniform?

1 Ganz-froh: Ich finde die Schuluniform sehr praktisch.

2 Einmaleins: **Es gibt kein Mobbing** und das finde ich toll.

3 Elfmeter: Aber **eine Schuluniform ist sehr teuer!** Ich finde sie auch langweilig.

4 Mitzi: Ja, das finde ich auch. **Ich mag meine Schuluniform nicht, weil sie so unbequem ist.**

5 Modefan: **Meine Kleidung zeigt meinen Charakter!** Ich mag meine Schuluniform nicht, weil sie meinen Charakter nicht zeigt.

6 Fata Morgana: Ich bin mehr als meine Kleidung! **Meine Kleidung ist nicht meine Identität!** Eine Schuluniform hat sowohl gute Seiten als auch schlechte Seiten!

unbequem	uncomfortable
die Identität	identity
sowohl ... als auch	both ... and

Hören 5

Listen to the description and decide which photo in exercise 1 is being described. Then write down the answers the person gives to the **two** questions below in English.

1. Was trägst du in der Schule?
2. Wie findest du die Schuluniform?

Auf dem Foto gibt es (drei) Jugendliche: (zwei) Jungen und (ein) Mädchen.
Sie sind ungefähr (15) Jahre alt.
Sie tragen (k)eine Schuluniform.
Der Junge trägt ... / Die Jungen tragen ...
Das Mädchen trägt ... / Die Mädchen tragen ...

Sie	sind	vor der Schule.
		in der Schule.
		auf der Straße.
Sie		sprechen miteinander.
	lachen.	
	lächeln.	

Sprechen 6

In pairs, take turns to describe a photo from exercise 1 and answer the **two** questions in exercise 5 for yourself.

3 Sind Schulregeln wirklich nötig?

- Talking about school rules
- Using modal verbs: *müssen, dürfen, sollen*
- Using opinion phrases with *dass*

Hören 1 Listen to and read the school rules. Write the letter of the correct picture (a–f) for each one.

1 Man muss Respekt zeigen.

2 Man muss seine Hausaufgaben machen.

3 Man soll für den Mathetest lernen.

4 Man soll im Gang ruhig sein.

5 Man darf im Unterricht nicht reden.

6 Man darf im Klassenzimmer nicht essen.

Lesen 2 Find the German in exercise 1 for the English phrases below.

1 You must / have to …
2 You should / ought to …
3 You are allowed to …

Hören 3 Listen. Copy and complete the table in English. (1–6)

	rules	opinions
1	not allowed to eat in the classroom	OK

| Man | muss
soll
darf | im Klassenzimmer
im Gang
im Unterricht
in der Kantine
in der Schule | ruhig sein.
(nicht) laufen.
(nicht) essen.
(nicht) trinken.
(nicht) reden.
eine Uniform tragen.
Respekt zeigen.
seine Hausaufgaben nicht vergessen. |

G Modal verbs are irregular and must be used with another verb in the infinitive at the end of the sentence.

müssen: Man **muss** seine Hausaufgaben <u>machen</u>.
You **must** <u>do</u> your homework.

dürfen: Man **darf** Fußball <u>spielen</u>.
You **are allowed to** <u>play</u> football.

Man **darf** im Unterricht **nicht** <u>reden</u>.
You **are not allowed to** <u>talk</u> in class.

sollen: Man **soll** im Gang langsam <u>gehen</u>.
You **should** <u>walk</u> slowly in the corridor.

Use **man** with modal verbs to mean 'you' generally.

	müssen (*must, have to*)	dürfen (*be allowed to*)	sollen (*should, ought to*)
ich	muss	darf	soll
du	musst	darfst	sollst
er/sie/ es/man	muss	darf	soll

The *ich* and *er/sie/es/man* forms of modal verbs are the same.

Page 20

12 zwölf

Kapitel 1

Schreiben 4
Write four sentences about your school rules using *man*.

Example: 1 Man muss eine Schuluniform tragen.
2 Man darf im Klassenzimmer nicht essen.
3 …

man **muss**	you **have to**
man **muss** <u>nicht</u>	you **don't** have to (**not** you must **not**)
man **darf** <u>nicht</u>	you **are not** allowed to / you must **not**

Hören 5
Listen and read. Translate the phrases in **bold** into English.

Lukas
Wir haben einen neuen Direktor und jetzt muss man aufstehen, wenn der Lehrer kommt. **Ich denke, dass es sehr blöd ist.**

Man muss auch im Gang langsam gehen und man darf nicht laufen. **Ich glaube, dass es nötig ist.**

Ayaan
Man darf im Klassenzimmer nicht essen, nur in der Kantine. **Ich glaube, dass diese Regel falsch ist.** Unsere Kantine ist viel zu klein.

Man darf auch das Handy in der Schule nicht benutzen. **Ich finde, dass es unfair ist.**

Malik
Man muss im Klassenzimmer total ruhig sein und man darf nicht sprechen. **Ich denke, dass es richtig ist.**

Wir bekommen aber jeden Tag so viele Hausaufgaben. **Ich finde, dass es zu viel ist.**

Lesen 6
Read the texts again and answer the questions with the correct name.

Who thinks …?
1 it is unfair that students are not allowed to use their mobile phone in school
2 that standing up when a teacher enters is stupid
3 that the school canteen is too small
4 that being quiet in the classroom is the right thing to do
5 that they get too much homework
6 that it's necessary to walk slowly in the corridor

> **G** *dass* also sends the verb to the end, like *weil*.
> Page 19

Sprechen 7
In pairs, take turns to agree or disagree with the school rules in exercise 1 and give your opinion.

● *Man muss ruhig sein. Was denkst du?*
■ *Ich glaube, dass diese Regel richtig ist.*

| Ich finde, Ich denke, Ich glaube, | dass | es diese Regel | sehr ziemlich nicht | (un)fair wichtig nötig richtig falsch blöd | ist. |

dreizehn **13**

4 Schultage: die beste Zeit deines Lebens?

- Talking about special events at school
- Using the perfect and imperfect tenses
- Practising the *w* sound in German

Lesen 1 Look at the photos. Translate the words below into English, using the photos to help you.

a Sporttag
b Klassenfahrt
c Konzert
d Wandertag
e Skiwoche
f Kreativwoche

Hören 2 Listen to and read the sentences. Write the letter of the correct event (a–f) from exercise 1 for each sentence.

1 Ich bin für eine Woche Skifahren gegangen.
2 Ich habe den ganzen Tag Sport gemacht.
3 Ich habe gesungen und Musikinstrumente gespielt.
4 Ich habe die ganze Woche kreative Dinge gemacht.
5 Ich bin an einem Tag 16km zu Fuß gegangen.
6 Ich bin mit der Schule zu einem Freizeitpark gefahren.

In the German-speaking world, 'hiking days' (*Wandertage*) are part of the school curriculum. In Austria and Switzerland, these can also be whole-school ski days and in some areas, schools organise a week of skiing to give every child the opportunity to learn this national sport.

der Freizeitpark   theme park

Lesen 3 Find the German for the phrases below in exercise 2. In what way are sentences 3, 5 and 6 different from the other three sentences?

1 I did sport.
2 I did creative things.
3 I walked 16km.
4 I sang.
5 I went skiing.
6 I went to a theme park.

G The **perfect tense** is used to describe actions in the past. In German, the perfect tense consists of **two** parts: an auxiliary verb (part of *haben* or *sein*) and the **past participle**.

Ich habe Musik **gehört**.
Wir haben Musik **gehört**.
Ich bin 16km zu Fuß **gegangen**.
Wir sind 16km zu Fuß **gegangen**.

The past participle usually starts with **ge-** and can end in -**t** (regular verbs) or -**en** (irregular verbs).

Page 20

Hören 4 Listen to the students talking about special events at school. Which <u>four</u> events from exercise 1 do they mention? Write the letters. (1–4)

Hast du letztes Jahr eine interessante Aktivität in der Schule gemacht?

14 *vierzehn*

Kapitel 1

5 Hören — Listen and write down the missing words you hear.

1 Letztes Jahr ▬ ich eine Klassenfahrt nach Phantasialand gemacht.
2 Wir ▬ mit dem Bus gefahren und ich ▬ im Bus Musik gehört. Das Wetter war schön.
3 Zu Mittag ▬ ich Pizza gegessen. Das war lecker!
4 Um fünf Uhr ▬ ich wieder mit dem Bus zurück zur Schule gefahren und ich ▬ im Bus geschlafen. Der Tag war total toll!

6 Lesen — Find three sentences containing *war* in exercise 5 and translate them into English.

7 Sprechen — In pairs, use the words to make six sentences in the perfect tense. Add an opinion using the imperfect tense. Pay attention to the w sounds.

ich   wir

haben   sind   bin   habe

Fußball   Pommes frites   Postkarten
im Meer   nach Österreich   ins Café

gefahren   gekauft   geschwommen
gespielt   gegangen   gegessen

es war

schön   schlecht   wunderbar   toll

G
Most verbs take **haben** in the perfect tense, but a few take **sein**. These are mostly verbs of movement and changes of state (e.g. to wake up).

Learn these five common verbs that take *sein*:

Ich **bin gegangen**. (gehen)	I went (on foot).
Ich **bin gefahren**. (fahren)	I went (by means of transport).
Ich **bin gekommen**. (kommen)	I came.
Ich **bin geschwommen**. (schwimmen)	I swam.
Ich **bin geblieben**. (bleiben)	I stayed.

Page 20

G
Use the **imperfect tense** to say how something was (a **past** event). Use *war*.
Das Wetter war schön.   The weather **was** lovely.
Der Tag war toll.   The day **was** great.
Das war spannend.   That **was** exciting.

8 Schreiben — Now write down your six sentences in the perfect tense from exercise 7.

9 Sprechen — In pairs, ask and answer questions about an interesting school event.

- *Hast du letztes Jahr eine interessante Aktivität in der Schule gemacht?*
- *Ja, wir haben eine Klassenfahrt gemacht.*
- *Wie war es?*
- *Es war …*

w in German is always pronounced like the English 'v' sound.

Listen and repeat the sentence. Then practise saying it. How quickly can you say it?

*Der **W**andertag **w**ar **w**underbar, **w**eil das **W**etter **w**arm **w**ar.*

fünfzehn 15

5 Austausch geht auch online!

- Describing school life
- Using the present tense with a future time phrase
- Practising the 50-word exam question

1 Listen to and read the video chat between Nala and Alina. Then find the German for the phrases below.

Nala in Leeds

Hallo Alina! Ich heiße Nala und ich bin deine Online-Austauschpartnerin. Hier in Leeds ist es zwölf Uhr und wir haben im Moment Deutsch.

Ja, ich besuche eine ziemlich große Schule. Wir tragen eine blaue Schuluniform.

In der Mittagspause esse ich und ich verbringe Zeit mit meinen Freunden. Und du?

Gestern bin ich um vier Uhr nach Hause gekommen und ich habe meine Hausaufgaben gemacht. Was machst du heute nach der Schule?

Ich lerne Gitarre, aber ich lerne es in der Schule.

Tschüss. Bis später!

Alina in Köln

Hallo Nala! Hier in Köln ist es ein Uhr und wir haben Englisch. Kannst du deine Schule beschreiben?

Wir haben keine Schuluniform. Was machst du in der Mittagspause?

Ich habe keine Mittagspause, weil die Schule am Mittag endet, also esse ich das Mittagessen zu Hause. Morgens haben wir eine kurze Pause und ich esse einen Imbiss. Was hast du gestern nach der Schule gemacht?

Heute nach der Schule spiele ich Cello. Ich lerne Cello in der Musikschule. Und du?

Nala, meine Stunde endet. Tschüss!

die Gitarre guitar
Tschüss bye

1 exchange partner
2 to describe
3 I spend time with my friends.
4 I have no lunch break because school ends at lunchtime.
5 at home
6 snack
7 My lesson is finishing.

2 Read the video chat again. Select the correct option to complete each sentence.
1 The time difference between Leeds and Cologne is **1 hour** / **2 hours**.
2 Nala is in a **German** / **English** lesson.
3 Alina wears **a uniform** / **no uniform**.
4 Alina eats her lunch **at school** / **at home**.
5 Nala came home at **lunchtime** / **4 o'clock** yesterday and then she **met friends** / **did her homework**.
6 Alina learns the cello **at school** / **at a music school**.

sechzehn

Kapitel 1

Sprechen 3
In pairs, take turns to ask and answer the questions.
- *Was machst du normalerweise in der Mittagspause?*
  - In der Mittagspause ... ich normalerweise ...
- *Was hast du gestern in der Mittagspause gemacht?*
  - Gestern in der Mittagspause ... ich ...
- *Was machst du heute nach der Schule?*
  - Heute nach der Schule ... ich ...

> The **verb** is always the second idea in a German sentence. If you start with a <u>time phrase</u>, the verb and the subject change place.
> <u>Gestern</u> **habe** ich Sport gemacht.

> **G** You can use the **present tense** to talk about events in the **future**.
> Heute nach der Schule **spiele** ich Cello.
> After school today I **am playing** cello.
> Page 21

In der Pause/Mittagspause Nach der Schule	esse	ich (normalerweise)	in der Kantine.
	rede		mit meinen Freunden.
	verbringe		Zeit mit Freunden.
	mache		Sport. meine Hausaufgaben.
	gehe		in einen Club.
Gestern in der Pause/Mittagspause	habe	ich	in der Kantine gegessen. mit meinen Freunden geredet. Sport gemacht. meine Hausaufgaben gemacht.
	bin		in einen Club gegangen.

Hören 4
Listen to Oliver and Finn discussing school uniforms, rules and memorable school days. Copy and complete the sentences in English.
1. Oliver likes not having to ... a lot in the morning.
2. Oliver finds it great that he has a ... day next week.
3. Finn always wears ... clothes.
4. Oliver thinks that they don't have ... often enough.
5. Finn's best day last year was a ... day.
6. The weather was ... for swimming.

Schreiben 5
Write approximately 50 words about your school. Include the following points:
- school subjects
- break time
- school uniform
- school rules
- after-school activities.

The 50-word question

For this question on the writing exam paper, you need to cover the five bullet points given and write in German. The word count is a guide only, but try to keep to around 50 words.

For the highest marks, you should:
- cover all five bullet points
- write as accurately as you can
- try to use a variety of vocabulary and grammatical structures, including opinions and reasons.

In der Schule lerne ich ...
Mein Lieblingsfach ist ..., weil ...
Aber ich mag ... nicht, weil ...
In der Pause/Mittagspause ... ich normalerweise ...
In meiner Schule muss man (eine Schuluniform) tragen.
Man darf im Klassenzimmer nicht essen.
Ich finde, dass es (fair/unfair) ist.
Heute nach der Schule (mache ich meine Hausaufgaben).

siebzehn 17

Grammatik 1

Definite articles and plural nouns (Culture, page 7)

1 Listen and write down the definite articles (the) you hear. Then write down the gender of the nouns (m, f, nt).

Example: 1 das Hemd (nt)

1 ___ Hemd ist zu teuer.
2 ___ Hose ist klein.
3 ___ Rock kostet €20.
4 Wo ist ___ Lehrerin?
5 ___ Klassenzimmer ist groß.
6 Wann beginnt ___ Schultag?

2 Write down the plural forms of the nouns from exercise 1.

Example: die Jacke → die Jacken

German also uses these gender-neutral forms:

gender-neutral form	instead of
Lehrer*innen	Lehrer und Lehrerinnen
Schüler*innen	Schüler und Schülerinnen

Nominative and accusative cases (Culture, page 7)

3 Copy and complete the sentences with the correct definite (the) or indefinite article (a) in the accusative case.

1 Ich habe ___ Jacke. (f, a)
2 Wir kaufen ___ Rock. (m, a)
3 Mein Freund hat ___ T-Shirt. (nt, a)
4 Ich kaufe ___ Hemd. (nt, the)
5 Kaufst du ___ Pullover? (m, the)
6 Sie hat ___ Banane gegessen. (f, the)

A 'case' represents the relationship between the subject and the object of a sentence.

In the following sentence, Olivia is the **subject** (who is doing the action of buying) and the skirt is the <u>object</u> (the thing that is being bought).

Olivia kauft <u>einen Rock</u>. **Olivia** buys <u>a skirt</u>.

The **nominative case** is always used for the **subject**.
The **accusative case** is always used for the **direct object**.

	definite article 'the'		indefinite article 'a'	
	nominative	accusative	nominative	accusative
m	der	den	ein	einen
f	die	die	eine	eine
nt	das	das	ein	ein
pl	die	die	–	–

4 Translate the sentences into German. Use the words in the box below to help you. Think carefully about which case to use.

1 I have a T-shirt and a skirt.
2 The skirt is red.
3 We buy the shoes.
4 He buys the jacket.
5 The shirt is white.
6 She finds the uniform great.

T-Shirt (nt)   Rock (m)   Schuhe (pl)
Jacke (f)   Hemd (nt)   Uniform (f)

18 achtzehn

The present tense (Unit 1, page 8–9; Unit 2, page 11)

Schreiben 5 Copy and complete the sentences with the correct form of the verb in brackets.

1 Ich *lerne* gern Deutsch. (*lernen*)
2 Was ___ du in der Pause? (*machen*)
3 Mein Bruder ___ Geschichte. (*lieben*)
4 Wir ___ Mathe toll. (*finden*)
5 Sara ___ ihre Hausaufgaben. (*machen*)
6 ___ du ein Instrument? (*spielen*)

> Go back to page 8 to refresh your memory on regular verbs in the present tense. Remember that:
> - verbs with a stem ending in **-d** or **-t** (e.g. *finden*), add an **-e-** in the *du*, *er/sie/es/man* and *ihr* forms.
> - some irregular verbs (e.g. *tragen*, *fahren*) change their vowel sounds in the *du* and *er/sie/es/man* forms.

Lesen 6 Select the correct verb form to complete each sentence.

Example: 1 *fahre*

1 Ich **fahre** / **fahrt** / **fährst** mit dem Fahrrad zur Schule.
2 Wir **habt** / **haben** / **habe** am Montag Deutsch und Englisch.
3 Meine Freundin **ist** / **bist** / **bin** sehr gut in Mathe.
4 **Trage** / **Trägst** / **Trägt** du gern eine Schuluniform?
5 Was **habe** / **hat** / **hast** du in der dritten Stunde?
6 Ich **ist** / **bin** / **bist** total gegen Schuluniformen.

> **haben** and **sein** are irregular verbs.
>
> | | haben | sein |
> |---|---|---|
> | ich | habe | bin |
> | du | hast | bist |
> | er/sie/es/man | hat | ist |
> | wir | haben | sind |
> | ihr | habt | seid |
> | Sie | haben | sind |
> | sie | haben | sind |

Schreiben 7 Translate the sentences into German.

Example: 1 *Joel lernt Englisch und Geschichte.*

1 Joel learns English and history.
2 We don't wear a school uniform.
3 Arya has art once a week.
4 How do you find maths?
5 My favourite subject is German.
6 He is playing football.

weil and dass (Unit 1, page 9; Unit 3, page 13)

Sprechen 8 In pairs, take turns to link the sentences using *weil*. Say each sentence twice.

Example: 1 *Ich liebe Kunst, weil es einfach ist.*

1 Ich liebe Kunst. Es ist einfach.
2 Ich mag Chemie nicht. Es ist schwierig.
3 Wir finden Englisch schwer. Wir sind nicht gut in Englisch.
4 Ich mag Musik. Ich finde es interessant.
5 Sascha findet Basketball toll. Er ist sportlich.
6 Du isst eine Banane in der Pause. Du hast oft Hunger.

Schreiben 9 Put the words in the correct order to make sentences, starting with the words in **bold**. Then translate the sentences into English.

Example: 1 *Wir glauben, dass … / We believe that …*

1 nicht fair **Wir glauben,** dass ist es
2 finde, diese Regel nötig **Ich** ist dass
3 du, Schuluniformen sind? dass **Findest** bequem
4 dass denke, Klassenfahrt **Ich** war die toll

> Remember that *weil* and *dass* send the verb to the end of the clause.

Grammatik 2

Modal verbs (Unit 3, page 12)

1 **Rewrite the sentences using the correct form of the modal verb in brackets.**

Example: 1 Ich soll für den Mathetest lernen.

1 Ich lerne für den Mathetest. (*sollen*)
2 Wir tragen eine Schuluniform. (*müssen*)
3 Sie benutzt das Handy nicht in der Schule. (*dürfen*)
4 Wir essen nicht im Klassenzimmer. (*dürfen*)
5 Sie zeigen Respekt. (*müssen*)
6 Wir sind ruhig im Gang. (*sollen*)

Remember that **modal verbs** are irregular.

	müssen (must, have to)	dürfen (be allowed to)	sollen (should, ought to)
ich	muss	darf	soll
du	musst	darfst	sollst
er/sie/es/man	muss	darf	soll
wir	müssen	dürfen	sollen
ihr	müsst	dürft	sollt
Sie	müssen	dürfen	sollen
sie	müssen	dürfen	sollen

2 **Translate the sentences into English.**

Example: 1 I have to eat in the canteen.

1 Ich muss in der Kantine essen.
2 Ich darf im Klassenzimmer nicht essen.
3 Ich soll heute meine Hausaufgaben machen.
4 Ich darf meine Hausaufgaben nicht vergessen.
5 Ich soll für den Mathetest lernen.
6 Ich darf mein Handy nach der Schule benutzen.

The perfect tense (Unit 4, pages 14–15)

3 **Copy and complete the table with the past participles from the box.**

infinitive	past participle
machen	gemacht
spielen	1
kaufen	2
gehen	gegangen
essen	3
trinken	4
treffen	5
fahren	6
schlafen	7
schwimmen	8
besuchen	**be**sucht

gespiel**t**   getroff**en**   getrunk**en**
geschlaf**en**   gefahr**en**   gegess**en**
geschwomm**en**   gekauf**t**

Remember:
- past participles of regular verbs end in **-t**
- past participles of irregular verbs end in **-en**
- past participles of verbs starting with **be-** don't add **ge-**

4 **Identify the three verbs from exercise 3 that take *sein* as the auxiliary verb.**

5 **In pairs, take turns to create sentences using the past participles from exercise 3.**

Example: 1 Ich bin in die Stadt gegangen.

1 ich – in die Stadt (*went*)
2 er – ein T-Shirt (*bought*)
3 wir – zu Fuß (*went*)
4 sie (*she*) – Kuchen (*ate*)
5 du – Cola (*drank*)
6 ich – meine Oma (*visited*)
7 wir – Fußball (*played*)
8 sie (*they*) – Freunde (*met*)

Kapitel 1

The imperfect tense (Unit 4, page 15)

Schreiben 6 Rewrite these sentences using the imperfect tense.

Example: 1 *Es war langweilig.*

1 Es ist langweilig.
2 Wir sind müde.
3 Das Wetter ist warm.
4 Wir sind in Deutschland.
5 Ich bin in der 9. Klasse.
6 Sie ist heute in der Schule.
7 Meine Freunde und ich sind in der Kantine.
8 Der Tag ist toll.

> Use the **imperfect tense** to describe how something **was**:
>
> | **sein** (*to be*) |
> |---|
> | ich war |
> | er/sie/es/man war |
> | wir waren |

Using the perfect and imperfect tense (Unit 5, pages 14–15)

Hören 7 Listen and write down the missing perfect and imperfect tense verbs that you hear.

Am Montag **1** waren wir mit der Schule in einem Museum. Das **2** langweilig, aber am Dienstag **3** wir in Chemie ein Experiment **4** und das **5** ziemlich interessant. Am Mittwoch **6** ich nach der Schule mit meinen Freunden in den Park **7** und wir **8** Fußball **9** . Das Wetter **10** gut und danach **11** wir in ein Café **12** und **13** Kuchen **14** und Cola **15** . Es **16** Spaß **17** und es **18** ein toller Tag.

Using the present with a future time frame (Unit 5, page 17)

Schreiben 8 Rewrite the sentences in the correct order, starting with the time phrase.

1 Schule Heute der mache ich Sport nach
2 habe Nach ich Englisch Mittagspause der
3 Pause Mathe haben Nach der wir
4 Heute ich Abend verbringe meinen Freunden Zeit mit

Los geht's!

Schreiben 9 Translate the sentences into German.

- Singular in German!
- Use *dass* and remember to use the correct word order.
- Which tense do you need here?

1 I wear black trousers, a white shirt, a red jumper and black shoes.
2 Music is my favourite subject because it is interesting.
3 I think that maths is very difficult.
4 Yesterday I bought a jacket.
5 I went into town.
6 We played football and it was very cold.

- Remember to make the adjective agree with the noun.
- What happens to the verb after *weil*?
- You need the imperfect tense here.

einundzwanzig **21**

Kapitel 1: Lese- und Hörtest

Reading

Lesen 1

School subjects. Some German students are discussing their school subjects. What do they say? Write the correct name to answer each question. Write **E** for **Elif**, **M** for **Mika** or **L** for **Leonie**.

> **Elif** ▸ Ich habe Englisch dreimal in der Woche, aber das mag ich nicht. Mathe ist schwierig und langweilig.
>
> **Mika** ▸ Ich liebe Mathe, weil es praktisch und interessant ist. Ich finde Kunst toll und das ist mein Lieblingsfach.
>
> **Leonie** ▸ Wissenschaften mag ich nicht, weil sie nicht interessant sind. Englisch ist einfach und der Lehrer ist nett.

Always read the title and the instructions, so that you know the context of the reading passage and who the people are.

What do you think you should do first? Read the text or read the questions? Discuss this with your partner and decide which works best for you and why.

Don't expect the questions to follow the order of the texts in this task. Bear in mind too that each name may not necessarily appear twice as an answer.

In this task, you have to match up the question with the right person. Read the texts carefully, watch out for negatives and make sure you know the meaning of adjectives.

1 Who loves maths?
2 Who dislikes sciences?
3 Who thinks art is great?
4 Who has English three times a week?
5 Who thinks maths is difficult?
6 Who thinks English is easy?

Lesen 2

My school uniform. Read Matteo's blog about uniform at his exchange school.

> In der Schule trage ich eine dunkelblaue Jacke, ein weißes Hemd und eine graue Hose. Wir haben auch einen schwarzen Pullover und schwarze Schuhe. Die Mädchen tragen eine blaue Jacke und weiße Socken. Die Jungen müssen schwarze Socken tragen, aber das finde ich nicht schön, weil ich sie langweilig finde. In der **Turnhalle** muss man immer Laufschuhe tragen.

1 Matteo wears grey …
   A shoes.   **B** trousers.   **C** socks.

2 Girls in his school wear …
   A a shirt.   **B** a skirt.   **C** a jacket.

3 Matteo doesn't like his …
   A jacket.   **B** socks.   **C** sportswear.

4 Which lesson would you have in a **Turnhalle**? Write the correct letter, **A**, **B** or **C**.
   A PE   **B** maths   **C** science

*In question 4, you have to work out the meaning of a word that you might not have met before (**Turnhalle**). Read the last sentence of the blog carefully and use the context to help you.*

22 zweiundzwanzig

Lesen 3
Translate these sentences into English.

1. Ich lerne oft Mathe.
2. Die Schüler müssen eine Uniform tragen.
3. In der Pause spielen wir mit Freunden.
4. Ich mag Englisch, aber ich finde Erdkunde sehr schwierig.
5. Letztes Jahr bin ich mit meiner Schule nach Österreich gefahren.

> Check that you have translated every word, including intensifiers and qualifiers such as *sehr* or *ziemlich*, or time expressions such as *nie* or *oft*, which can be easily missed.
>
> Don't be afraid to change the word order in English to make your translation sound more natural.

Listening

Hören 4
Opinions about school. A German student is talking about various aspects of school life. What opinions does he have? Write **P** for a **positive** opinion, **N** for a **negative** opinion or **P+N** for a **positive and negative** opinion.

1 uniform 2 subjects 3 rules 4 sport

> Listen carefully for verbs of like or dislike, as well as positive and negative opinion words and adjectives. Words such as *aber* (but) may indicate a change of opinion.

Hören 5
Listen to Eva giving her opinion about school rules. Answer the questions in English.

1. Which rule does she mention?
2. Why does she agree with this rule?

Dictation

Hören 6
You will hear <u>four</u> short sentences. Write down exactly what you hear in German.

> Think carefully about how these sounds are pronounced when you write down what you hear. Remember that cognates are often not pronounced the same as in English.
> e, u, ü, o, ö, y
> g, ch, th, sp, w

> You will hear each sentence three times. Try to transcribe (write down) as much as you can on the first listening. Use the second listening to make sure that you have written **every** word. Use the final listening to check the sounds and spellings.

dreiundzwanzig 23

Kapitel 1 Mündlicher Test

Role-play

1 Look at the role-play task and prepare what you are going to say.

> You can describe any aspect of your school. It could be the size, buildings, type, number of teachers and/or students.

> You are talking to your Austrian friend.
> 1 Say **one** thing about your school.
> 2 Say **one** thing you normally do at breaktime.
> 3 Give **one** opinion about your school uniform.
> 4 Say **one** rule there is at your school.
> 5 ? Ask your friend a question about a school subject.

> To score full marks, you must include a verb in your response to each numbered point.

> Remember that modal verbs send the second verb to the end.

> You could ask about their favourite subject, an opinion of a subject or how often they have a subject. Remember to use a question word (*was, wie*, etc.) or invert the subject and the verb (*Magst du …?*).

2 Practise what you have prepared. Then, using your notes, listen and respond to the teacher.

3 Listen to Ethan's answers. Make a note of:
  a how he answers the questions for points 1–4
  b what question he asks for point 5.

Reading aloud

4 Look at this task. With a partner, read the sentences aloud, paying attention to the underlined letters.

> Ich lerne M<u>a</u>the und <u>E</u>nglisch.
>
> Die Sch<u>ü</u>ler finden die Hausaufgaben sch<u>w</u>ierig und sehr lang<u>w</u>eilig.
>
> <u>W</u>ir m<u>ü</u>ssen graue R<u>ö</u>cke und S<u>o</u>cken tragen.
>
> Eine typische St<u>u</u>nde dauert f<u>ü</u>nfzig Min<u>u</u>ten.
>
> <u>Sp</u>ort ist mein Lieblingsfach, <u>w</u>eil es <u>w</u>underbar ist.

> Be careful with cognates as they are not pronounced exactly the same way in German. Think carefully about how to pronounce the cognates and these sounds:
> o, ö, u, ü
> w

5 Listen and check your pronunciation.

6 Listen to the teacher asking four follow-up questions. Translate each question into English and prepare your own answer for each one. Then listen again and respond to the teacher.

> Try to expand your answers by including descriptions, opinions and reasons. Use connectives (*aber, denn, weil*) and a range of adjectives in your reasons.

vierundzwanzig

Photo card

Hören 7 Listen to Ethan describing the photos and answer the questions.

1. What subject does Ethan say they are doing in the first photo?
2. How does Ethan describe the teacher? (Give **two** details.)
3. What items does Ethan say are on the desk? (Give **two** details.)
4. What does Ethan say about one of the girls?
5. What does Ethan say about the students in the second photo? (Give **three** details.)
6. What does he say about the teacher?

You will be asked to talk about the content of these photos. You must say at least one thing about each photo.

After you have spoken about the content of the photos, you will be asked questions related to any of the topics within the theme of **People and lifestyle**.

Your responses should be as **full and detailed** as possible.

Sprechen 8 Prepare your own description of the photos. Then, with a partner, take turns describing them.

Auf dem ersten Foto gibt es …

Hören 9 Listen to the teacher's first follow-up question, *Wie findest du deine Schule?* and Ethan's response. Write the letters (a–e) in the order in which Ethan mentions these topics.

a school rules
b eating facilities
c opinion of school
d what the school is like
e classrooms

You could use the following phrases:
Vorne gibt es … At the front, there is/are …
Im Hintergrund gibt es … In the background there is …
in der Mitte in the middle
auf der rechten Seite on the right-hand side
auf der linken Seite on the left-hand side
You don't need to describe all the people you can see. You could pick one person and use singular verbs such as *er/sie hat/ist/trägt* …

Hören 10 Listen to Ethan answering the question, *Was hast du gestern in der Schule gemacht?* Write down the missing word for each gap.

Gestern hatte ich viele Fächer. Die **1** Stunde war Musik und wir haben **2** . Das war toll, weil Musik mein **3** ist. Dann **4** wir Mathe und Deutsch. Die letzte **5** war Sport und wir haben Basketball **6** .

Sprechen 11 Listen to two more follow-up questions and prepare your answers. Then respond to the recording.

Sprechen 12 Prepare your own answers to as many of the Module 1 questions on page 226 as you can. Then practise with a partner.

Think about how you can add extra detail to make your German more interesting. Aim to use the different structures and vocabulary you have learned in this module:
- modal verbs: *Ich muss …, Man soll …*
- connectives: remember that **dass** and **weil** send the verb to the end of the sentence: *Ich denke, **dass** es sehr wichtig ist.*
- the perfect tense: *Ich bin ins Klassenzimmer gegangen und ich habe meine Hausaufgaben gemacht.*
- adjectives used in different ways: *Meine Jacke ist rot. Ich habe eine rote Jacke.*
- two verbs in one sentence: *Ich darf mein Handy nicht im Unterricht benutzen.*
- plurals: *Schuhe, Bücher*, etc.

fünfundzwanzig 25

Kapitel 1 Schreibtest

Describing a photo

Schreiben 1 Look at this writing exam task and correct the mistakes in Emily's response.

1. Es gibt zwei Personen auf dem Foto.
2. Man sieht auch einen Lehrer.
3. Sie trägt eine Jacke.
4. Die Schüler sind in der Stadt.
5. Die Schüler sprechen.

You see this photo on Instagram.

What is in the photo?
Write **five** sentences in **German**.

Schreiben 2 Prepare your own answer to the task.

Make sure you use a verb in each sentence and describe only what you see in the photo.
- Try to use *ich sehe* (I see) or *man sieht* (you see) and other verbs, rather than repeating *es gibt* (there is/are) in every sentence.
- Remember to use plural verbs if talking about more than one person.

Grammar task

Schreiben 3 Using your knowledge of grammar, select the correct option to complete each sentence.

Look at the verb ending to help you work out the subject pronoun.

1. Ich **finden** / **finde** / **findest** Mathe schwierig.
2. **Ich** / **Er** / **Wir** lernen heute Geschichte.
3. Wir haben ein **großen** / **große** / **großes** Klassenzimmer.
4. **Der** / **Die** / **Das** Schule beginnt um 9 Uhr.
5. Gestern habe ich in der Pause Musik **gehört** / **höre** / **hören**.

Remember that time expressions give you a clue about tense.

Try to learn nouns with their gender. There are some patterns: for example, singular nouns ending in -**e** are often feminine.

Translation

Schreiben 4 Translate the following sentences into German.

Remember that a modal verb sends the other verb to the end.

1. My favourite subject is sport.
2. I sometimes play football at breaktime.
3. We have to be quiet in the classroom.
4. My school has a big canteen.
5. On Monday I did my homework.

Think about adjective endings.

Which tense do you need here?

26 *sechsundzwanzig*

50-word writing task

5 Look at this writing exam task and then, for each bullet point:

1. think about the vocabulary and structures you have learned, which you could use in your answers. For example:
   - **nouns** and **verbs** to write about school subjects
   - **verbs** and **adjectives** to describe your school day and homework
   - language for **narrating a story** about what you do with friends and at breaktime.
2. write down three or four ideas you could write about.
3. write down which verbs you will need to use in your answer.

> Some young German visitors are coming to your school.
>
> Write a short description of your school.
>
> Write approximately **50** words in **German**.
>
> You must write something about each bullet point.
>
> Mention:
> - school subjects
> - your school day
> - homework
> - school friends
> - lunchtime.

6 Read Emily's answer to the exam task. Answer the questions in the coloured boxes (1–5).

1. Emily uses a **variety of nouns**. What does this word mean? Find two other examples of nouns.

2. Which connective could you use here to form an **extended sentence**? Find two other connectives Emily uses.

> Mein Lieblingsfach ist Erdkunde, weil ich das sehr einfach finde.
>
> Mein Schultag beginnt um acht Uhr und ich habe sechs Stunden.
>
> Ich muss viele Hausaufgaben machen und ich finde, dass das sehr langweilig ist.
>
> Meine Freundin heißt Lena und wir sprechen in der Pause.
>
> Ich esse in der Mittagspause. Manchmal spiele ich auch Basketball.

3. This is an example of **complex language**. What does it mean? Find two more examples of complex language.

4. Which other **person of the verb** could Emily have used here? Find two other examples where she could add variety by using different persons of the verb.

5. How could Emily **avoid repetition** here?

7 Read Emily's answer again and answer these questions in English.

1. Why does Emily like geography?
2. What does Emily find very boring?
3. What does Emily do with Lena? (Give **two** details.)
4. What does Emily sometimes do at lunchtime?

8 Prepare your own answer to the task.

- Think about how you can develop your answer for each bullet point.
- Look back at your notes from exercises 5 and 6.
- Look at the 'Challenge checklist' and consider how you can show off your German!
- Write a **brief** plan and organise your answer into paragraphs.
- Write your answer and then check carefully for accuracy.

Challenge checklist

🥨
- ✓ ich + conjugated verb
- ✓ und as a connective
- ✓ A verb and a simple adjective (*es ist gut*)

🥨🥨
- ✓ Different persons of the verb (*man, wir*)
- ✓ More varied opinions and verbs (*mein Lieblingsfach ist, ich finde*)
- ✓ Qualifiers (*ziemlich, total*)
- ✓ Time expressions (*manchmal, immer, jede Woche*)

🥨🥨🥨
- ✓ Complex language (subject–verb inversion, modal verbs + infinitive)
- ✓ Adjectival agreement (*ich trage einen grauen Rock*)
- ✓ More varied conjunctions (*weil, dass* + verb to the end)

siebenundzwanzig

Kapitel 1 Wörter

Key:
bold = this word will appear in higher exams only
* = this word is not on the vocabulary list but you may use it in your own sentences

Meine Schule, deine Schule (pages 6–7):

Das Schulleben	School life
der **Austausch**	exchange
das Buch	book
die Ferien	holidays
die Hausaufgaben	homework
das Klassenzimmer	classroom
der Lehrer	teacher
die Schule	school
der Schüler	pupil
der Schultag	school day
zu Fuß	on foot
mit dem Fahrrad	by bike
sitzenbleiben	to repeat a school year

Wie ist dein Stundenplan dieses Jahr? (pages 8–9):

Schulfächer	School subjects
Was hast du (am Montag) in der (ersten/zweiten/dritten) Stunde?	What do you have (on Monday) in the (first/second/third) lesson?
Am (Montag) in der (ersten) Stunde habe ich …	On (Monday) my (first) lesson is …
Biologie	biology
Chemie	chemistry
Deutsch	German
*Englisch	English
Erdkunde	geography
Französisch	French
Geschichte	history
*Informatik	computing
Kunst	art
Mathe	maths
Musik	music
Physik	physics
Religion	religious education
*Spanisch	Spanish
Sport	sport
(Natur)wissenschaften	(natural) sciences

Tage	Days
Montag	Monday
Dienstag	Tuesday
Mittwoch	Wednesday
Donnerstag	Thursday
Freitag	Friday

Wie oft hast du (Mathe)? / How often do you have (maths)?
Ich habe (Mathe) (einmal/zweimal/dreimal) pro Woche / pro Tag. / I have (maths) (once/twice/three times) a week / a day.

Wie viele Stunden hast du (am Nachmittag / nach der Pause)? / How many lessons do you have (in the afternoon / after break)?
Was ist dein Lieblingsfach? / What is your favourite subject?
Mein Lieblingsfach ist (Deutsch). / My favourite subject is (German).
Wann hast du (Englisch)? / When do you have (English)?

Fragen	Questions
Wann …?	When …?
Was …?	What …?
Wie …?	How …?
Wie viel(e) …?	How much / How many …?
Wie oft …?	How often …?
Warum …?	Why …?
Welcher/Welche/Welches …?	Which …?

Welches Fach magst du (nicht) und warum? / Which subject do you (not) like and why?
Ich mag … (nicht), weil es … ist. / I (don't) like … because it is …
  einfach / easy
  interessant / interesting
  kompliziert / complicated
  langweilig / boring
  leicht / easy
  nützlich / useful
  praktisch / practical
  schwer / difficult/hard/tough
  schwierig / difficult/hard/tough
  wichtig / important

In der Pause … / At break …
  spreche ich mit meinen Freunden/Freundinnen. / I talk to my friends.
  esse ich … / I eat …
  trinke ich … / I drink …
  spiele ich … / I play …

Was trägst du in der Schule? (pages 10–11):

Schuluniform	School uniform
Ich trage …	I wear …
einen *Pullover	a sweater
einen Rock	a skirt
eine Hose	a pair of trousers
eine Jacke	a jacket
(eine) *Jeans	(a pair of) jeans
eine *Krawatte	a tie
ein Hemd	a shirt
ein Kleid	a dress
ein T-Shirt	a T-shirt
Schuhe	shoes
*Shorts	shorts
Sportschuhe	trainers

Farben	Colours
blau	blue
braun	brown
dunkelblau	dark blue
gelb	yellow
grau	grey
grün	green
hellblau	light blue
rot	red
schwarz	black
weiß	white

achtundzwanzig

Wie findest du die Schuluniform?	What do you think of school uniform?
Ich finde (die Schuluniform) ...	I find (school uniform) ...
(sehr) praktisch	(very) practical
langweilig	boring
teuer	expensive
unbequem	uncomfortable
Was gibt es auf dem Foto?	What is there in the photo?
Auf dem Foto gibt es (drei) Jugendliche: (zwei) Jungen und (ein) Mädchen.	On the photo there are (three) young people: (two) boys and (one) girl.
Sie sind ungefähr (15) Jahre alt.	They are about (15) years old.
Der Junge trägt ... / Die Jungen tragen ...	The boy is wearing ... / The boys are wearing ...
Das Mädchen trägt ... / Die Mädchen tragen ...	The girl is wearing... / The girls are wearing ...
Die Schüler und Schülerinnen tragen ...	The students/pupils are wearing ...
(k)eine Schuluniform.	(no) school uniform.
Sie sind ...	They are ...
vor der Schule.	in front of the school.
in der Schule.	at school.
auf der Straße.	on the street.
Sie ...	They ...
sprechen miteinander.	are talking to each other.
lachen.	are laughing.
lächeln.	are smiling.

Sind Schulregeln wirklich nötig? (pages 12–13):

Schulregeln und Meinungen	School rules and opinions
Man muss ...	You have to / must ...
Man soll ...	You should / ought to ...
Man darf ...	You are allowed to ...
Man darf ... nicht ...	You must not / are not allowed to ...
im Klassenzimmer	in the classroom
im Gang	in the corridor
im Unterricht	during lessons
in der Kantine	in the canteen, cafeteria
in der Schule	at school
ruhig sein	be quiet
laufen	run
eine Uniform tragen	wear a uniform
*Respekt zeigen	show respect
seine Hausaufgaben vergessen	forget your homework
Ich denke, ...	I think ...
Ich glaube, ...	I believe ...
Ich finde, ...	I find ...
dass diese Regel ... ist.	that this rule is ...
blöd	stupid, dumb
*(un)fair	(un)fair
falsch	wrong
nötig	necessary
richtig	right
wichtig	important

Schultage: die beste Zeit deines Lebens? (pages 14–15):

Verben	Verbs
Ich habe / Wir haben ...	I/We ...
gegessen	ate
gespielt	played
gemacht	made/did
gehört	heard/listened (to)
gekauft	bought
geschlafen	slept
Ich bin / Wir sind ...	I/We ...
gegangen	went (on foot)
gefahren	drove/travelled
gekommen	came
geschwommen	swam
geblieben	stayed
Es war ...	It was ...
interessant	interesting
lecker	tasty
schlecht	bad
schön	beautiful
spannend	exciting
wunderbar	wonderful
Ich war / Wir waren müde.	I was / We were tired.

Austausch geht auch online! (pages 16–17):

Der Schultag	The school day
Was machst du normalerweise in der (Mittags)pause?	What do you normally do in your (lunch) break?
In der Pause/Mittagspause ...	In my break / lunch break, I ...
esse ich (normalerweise) in der Kantine.	(normally) eat in the canteen.
rede ich mit meinen Freunden.	talk to my friends.
verbringe ich Zeit mit Freunden.	spend time with friends.
mache ich Sport / meine Hausaufgaben.	do sports / my homework.
gehe ich in einen Club.	go to a club.
Was machst du heute nach der Schule?	What are you doing today after school?
Heute nach der Schule (mache ich meine Hausaufgaben).	After school today (I'm doing my homework).
Was hast du gestern nach der Schule gemacht?	What did you do yesterday after school?
Gestern nach der Schule habe ich ...	Yesterday after school I ...
mit meinen Freunden geredet.	talked to my friends.
Sport gemacht.	did sport.
Ich bin in einen Club gegangen.	I went to a club.
In der Schule lerne ich ...	At school I'm learning ...
Mein Lieblingsfach ist ..., weil ...	My favourite subject is ... because ...
Aber ich mag ... nicht, weil ...	But I don't like ... because ...
Wir haben jeden Tag ... Stunden und ... Pausen.	Every day we have ... lessons and ... breaks.
In meiner Schule muss man (eine Schuluniform) tragen.	At my school you have to wear (a school uniform).

Kapitel 2

Endlich mal Freizeit!

Kennst du diese Musiker?
- Learning about German-speaking musicians
- Giving opinions

Ein musikalisches Abenteuer mit deutschsprachigen Stars!

Magst du lieber Die Prinzen oder Wise Guys? Hörst du lieber elektronische Musik oder Rap? Ist dein(e) Lieblingsmusiker*in Conchita oder Beethoven?

der Musiker (-)	musician
deutschsprachig	German-speaking

Herbert Grönemeyer
- Stil: Popmusik
- Beliebtes Lied: „Der Weg"
- Am 12. April 1956 geboren
- In Göttingen, Deutschland, geboren

Herbert Grönemeyer ist ein deutscher Sänger und er schreibt auch Musik. Er singt über Familie, Liebe und sein Leben als Kind in Deutschland. Seine Lieder sind schön, aber oft ruhig und traurig.

Wolfgang Amadeus Mozart
- Stil: klassische Musik
- Beliebtes Lied: „Eine kleine Nachtmusik"
- Am 27. Januar 1756 geboren
- In Salzburg, Österreich, geboren

Mozart war ein berühmter Musiker und ist für seine wunderbare klassische Musik in der ganzen Welt bekannt. Er hat über 600 Musikstücke geschrieben! Seine Musik ist normalerweise schnell und laut, aber einige Lieder sind wirklich entspannend.

Namika
- Stil: Rap
- Beliebtes Lied: „Lieblingsmensch"
- Am 23. August 1991 geboren
- In Frankfurt, Deutschland, geboren

Sängerin und Rapperin Namika ist sehr bekannt. Ihre Rap-Musik ist manchmal schnell, manchmal auch langsam, aber immer modern. Namikas Familie ist in den 70er Jahren von Marokko nach Deutschland gekommen und das hört man an ihrer Musik.

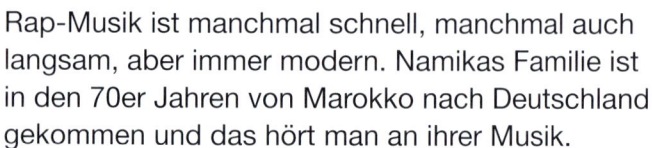

Die Ärzte
- Stil: Punkrock und Pop
- Musiker: Farin Urlaub, Bela B und Rodrigo González
- Beliebtes Lied: „Hurra"
- Aus Berlin, Deutschland

Die Ärzte sind eine sehr berühmte deutsche Band. Sie haben viele Fans in Deutschland, aber die Band ist auch international bekannt. Ihre Musik ist besonders spannend und kann auch ziemlich laut sein!

Kulturzone — Kapitel 2

Hören 1 Listen to and read the article. Copy and complete the sentences. Use words from the box. There are more words than gaps.

1. Herbert Grönemeyer's songs are often … and sad.
2. Mozart's music is normally … and loud.
3. Die Ärzte's music is particularly …
4. Namika's rap songs are always …

> exciting modern traditional calm fast well-known

Schreiben 2 Translate the text into English.

> Meine Lieblingssängerin ist Helene Fischer.
> Sie singt Popmusik auf Deutsch und auf Englisch.
> Sie ist auch Tänzerin und sie ist besonders beliebt.
> Ihre Musik ist manchmal schnell und laut, aber nicht langweilig.

Sprechen 3 Read out the text in exercise 2. Pay attention to the *ie*, *ei* and *i* sounds.

> **ie** is pronounced like the English letter 'e':
> L**ie**blings bel**ie**bt
>
> **ei** is pronounced like the English letter 'i':
> m**ei**ne langw**ei**lig
>
> **i** on its own is a long 'ee' sound before a single consonant:
> Mus**i**k Nam**i**ka
>
> **i** is a short 'i' sound before two or more consonants, like in the English word 'bit':
> **i**st s**i**ngt
>
> Listen and repeat the words.

Hören 4 Listen to two friends discussing their music preferences. Write down **one** description given for each type of music below.

1. classical music
2. Wise Guys' music
3. rap music
4. Cro's music

Sprechen 5 In pairs, take turns to ask and answer the questions below.

- *Wie findest du klassische Musik?*
- *Ich liebe klassische Musik.*
- *Warum?*
- *Denn sie ist wirklich spannend.*
- *Was ist deine Lieblingsmusik?*
- *Meine Lieblingsmusik ist Popmusik, denn sie ist ganz laut.*

> Remember to add **intensifiers and qualifiers** to your opinions to make them more varied.
> **wirklich** (really)   Popmusik ist **wirklich** modern.
> **sehr** (very)   Die Musik von Mozart ist **sehr** interessant.
> **zu** (too)   Ich finde Rockmusik **zu** laut.
> **ganz** (quite)   Tanzmusik ist **ganz** spannend.
>
> You can use **denn** (because) to add reasons to your opinions. Unlike *weil*, *denn* does not send the verb to the end of the phrase.
> Ich mag Popmusik, **denn** sie ist **wirklich** modern.

> To say 'I **don't** like …', use:
> *ich mag (Metal) nicht.*
> *Nicht* comes after the type of music.

Wie findest du (Rockmusik)?
Magst du die Musik von (Helene Fischer)?
Was ist deine Lieblingsmusik?

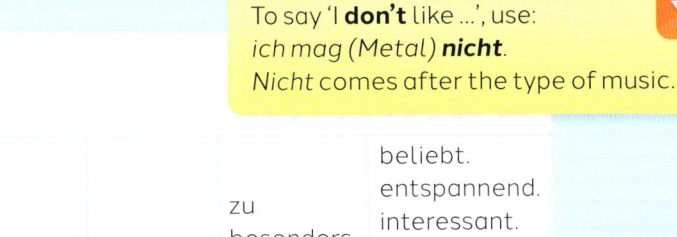

| Ich | liebe / mag | die Musik von (Mozart), klassische Musik (*f*), Metal (*m*), Popmusik (*f*), Rap (*m*), Rock (*m*), Tanzmusik (*f*), | denn | er/sie ist | zu besonders sehr wirklich ganz ziemlich nicht | beliebt. entspannend. interessant. langweilig. laut. lustig. modern. ruhig. schnell. spannend. |

Meine Lieblingsmusik ist

einunddreißig 31

1 Was machst du gern in deiner Freizeit?

- Talking about your free time
- Expressing preferences
- Using frequency phrases with correct word order

Hören 1 Listen and read. Answer the questions with the correct name.

Freizeitfieber!
Was machst du gern in deiner Freizeit?
Wie oft machst du das?

Lea: Ich bin jeden Tag ziemlich aktiv: <u>ich spiele gern Basketball</u>, aber <u>ich gehe lieber schwimmen</u>. Ich gehe auch gern ins Kino.

Matteo: Wir machen in der Schule Sport, aber <u>ich spiele nicht gern Basketball</u>. Meine Eltern gehen gern wandern, aber ich interessiere mich lieber für Kunst.

Clara: <u>Ich höre sehr gern Musik</u>, aber ich lese auch gern Bücher. Meine beste Freundin liest nicht gern, denn sie macht lieber Fotos.

Leon: Meine Freunde und ich singen sehr gern und <u>wir kochen auch gern in einem Schulclub</u>. Ich spiele lieber am Computer und manchmal sehe ich auch gern Filme.

1 Who doesn't like playing basketball?
2 Who likes reading books?
3 Who prefers playing on the computer?
4 Who likes going to the cinema?
5 Who likes cooking with friends?
6 Who prefers art to hiking?

G To say how much we like doing something, we add *(nicht) gern* or *lieber* after the verb.

✗ *Ich spiele **nicht gern** Tennis.*
I **don't like** playing tennis.

♥ *Ich gehe **(sehr) gern** in die Stadt.*
I **(really) like** going into town.

♥♥ *Ich spiele **lieber** am Computer.*
I **prefer** playing on the computer.

Page 42

G Remember, we use the **present tense** to say what we do regularly or are doing.

regular verbs: spielen (to play)	verbs with change to their vowel sounds in the *du* and *er/sie/es/man* forms: sehen (to see, watch)
ich spiel**e**	ich seh**e**
du spiel**st**	du s**ie**h**st**
er/sie/es/man spiel**t**	er/sie/es/man s**ie**h**t**
wir spiel**en**	wir seh**en**
ihr spiel**t**	ihr seh**t**
Sie spiel**en**	Sie seh**en**
sie spiel**en**	sie seh**en**

Page 42

Lesen 2 Translate the <u>underlined</u> phrases into English.

Hören 3 Listen. Copy and complete the table in English. (1–3)

	activity they don't like	activity they like	activity they prefer
1			

Listen carefully for small words like *nicht*, *gern* and *lieber*. The speakers in exercise 3 don't always give information in the same order as the table.

Schreiben 4 Write sentences to say what you don't like, (really) like or prefer doing. Use the emojis to help you.

Example: 1 *Ich spiele **gern** Basketball.*

1  2  3  4  5  6

32 zweiunddreißig

Kapitel 2

Schreiben 5 Translate the text into English.

> Ich spiele jeden Tag Basketball, aber ich spiele nie Tennis. Am Wochenende gehe ich schwimmen und ich gehe oft wandern. Ich gehe gern schwimmen, aber ich gehe lieber wandern. Manchmal spiele ich mit meiner Freundin Fußball und ich fahre ab und zu Fahrrad.

> The **a** sound in German is often a long 'aah' sound when it is followed by a single consonant (e.g. **A**bend). It is usually a short 'ah' sound when it is followed by two or more consonants (e.g. m**a**nchmal) or when it is a one-syllable word.
>
> Listen and repeat this tongue-twister.
> *Wir t**a**nzen m**a**nchm**a**l **a**m N**a**chmitt**a**g.*

Sprechen 6 In pairs, take turns to ask and answer the questions about free time using the pictures for ideas. Remember to use frequency expressions and pay attention to the **a** sounds.

- Was machst du gern am Wochenende?
- Ich wandere gern und ich mache oft Fotos.
- Was machst du nicht gern?
- Ich fahre nicht gern Fahrrad.

a often

b sometimes

c at the weekend

G

The **verb** is always the second idea in a German sentence.

first idea	second idea (verb)	rest of sentence
Ich	bin	jeden Tag ziemlich aktiv.
Ich	spiele	manchmal Basketball.
Ich	gehe	ab und zu wandern.

If the sentence starts with a **frequency expression**, the **verb** remains in the second position.

first idea	second idea (verb)	rest of sentence
Jeden Tag	bin	ich ziemlich aktiv.
Manchmal	spiele	ich Basketball.
Ab und zu	gehe	ich wandern.

Page 43

Was machst du gern in deiner Freizeit?

Ich	spiele		am Computer.
	gehe		wandern.
			in die Stadt.
			einkaufen.
		nicht gern	schwimmen.
		(sehr) gern	ins Kino.
	fahre	lieber	Fahrrad.
	besuche		Freunde.
		(fast) nie	Fotos.
	mache	ab und zu	Sport.
	höre	manchmal	Musik.
		am Wochenende	
	sehe	(sehr) oft	fern.
		jeden Tag / täglich	Filme.
	lese		Bücher.
	koche		
	tanze		in einem Schulclub.
	singe		

Hören 7 Listen to the teenagers discussing their free time. Copy and complete the table in English. (1–4)

	activity	how often?	opinion
1			

Schreiben 8 Write your own post about your free time. Use the key language box to help you.

dreiunddreißig 33

2 Was machst du online?

- Discussing how you spend time online
- Using separable verbs in the present tense
- Practising the *sch*, *sp*, *st* sounds at the start of words

Hören 1
Listen and read. Write the correct letters to match the pictures (a–i) to each person.

Welche Technologie benutzt du?

Leonie:
- Ich habe einen Computer. Ich **lade** oft Musik **herunter**.
- Ich habe ein Handy. Ich **bringe** es überall **mit**!
- Ich habe keinen Laptop.

Bruno:
- Ich habe ein Handy. Ich **rufe** jeden Tag meine Freunde **an**. Ich schicke Nachrichten.
- Ich habe einen Fernseher. Ich **sehe** jeden Abend sehr gern **fern**.
- Ich habe keine Spielkonsole.

Aaliyah:
- Ich habe einen Laptop. Ich **lade** viele Fotos **hoch**. Ich benutze soziale Medien.
- Ich habe ein Tablet. Ich **sehe** mir normalerweise Filme **an**.
- Ich habe kein Handy.

| der Fernseher | television |
| die Spielkonsole | games console |

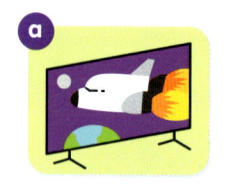

Lesen 2
Find the corresponding sentences in exercise 1 for the infinitives below.

Example: 1 *Ich sehe jeden Abend sehr gern fern.*

1 fernsehen (to watch TV)
2 ansehen (to watch)
3 herunterladen (to download)
4 hochladen (to upload)
5 mitbringen (to bring along)
6 anrufen (to call, to phone)

> **G** Separable verbs contain a **separable prefix**. In the present tense, this prefix 'snaps off' and goes to the end of the sentence.
>
> **herunterladen** (to download)
> Ich **lade** oft Musik **herunter**.
>
> **anrufen** (to call, to phone)
> Ich **rufe** Freunde **an**.
>
> **fernsehen** (to watch TV)
> Ich **sehe** jeden Abend **fern**.
>
> Page 43

Hören 3
Listen to the journalist's introduction. Write down the words you hear to complete the text.

Hallo! Ich __1__ einen __2__ über Technologie. Ich __3__ mit einer __4__ von __5__ und Schülerinnen aus Hamburg.

Hören 4
Listen to the journalist interviewing people. Copy and complete the first two columns of the table in English. (1–3)

	devices at home	activities they do	how often?
1	mobile phone …	uses social media …	

34 *vierunddreißig*

Hören 5 Listen again. How often do the people do the activities they mention? Complete the final column of the table in exercise 4.

Lesen 6 Read the article and make a list of things that Heike does (a) by herself, and (b) with her friends. Then read again and write down how often she does each activity.

> Ich mag die Technologie und nehme mein Handy immer mit. Und was mache ich online? Also, ich lade jeden Tag Musik herunter. Meine beste Freundin Silke hört auch gern Musik, und wir machen das immer im Schulbus zusammen.
>
> Mein Bruder hat zu Hause eine Spielkonsole und spielt natürlich jeden Abend seine Lieblingsspiele, aber ich lese lieber Bücher. Ich habe auch ein Tablet und streame oft Serien.
>
> Und was mache ich mit meinen Freunden? Ich rufe meine Freunde an und spreche am Wochenende auch mit Freunden. Leider muss ich in der Woche meine Hausaufgaben machen und habe keine Zeit für soziale Medien.

Sprechen 7 In pairs, take turns to ask and answer the questions below. Pay attention to the **sch**, **sp** and **st** sounds.

- Welche Technologie benutzt du zu Hause?
- Ich benutze …
- Was machst du online? Und wie oft?
- Ich streame jeden Tag Musik.

> German words with **sch**, **sp** or **st** at the start usually sound like 'sh', 'shp' and 'sht'. Some words borrowed from English don't follow this pattern, but some do.
>
> Listen and repeat the words.
>
> **sch**reiben   **Sp**ielkonsole   **St**udent   **St**ars   **st**reamen

Schreiben 8 Write answers in German to the questions below about your life online.

1. **Welche Technologie benutzt du?**
   Ich benutze einen Laptop …

2. **Was machst du online? Und wie oft?**
   Ich spreche jeden Tag mit Freunden. Ich … auch …

Welche Technologie benutzt du?		
Ich benutze / Wir benutzen		einen Computer/Laptop. eine Spielkonsole. ein Handy.
Was machst du online? Und wie oft?		
Ich sehe mir		Filme/Videos an.
Ich lade	normalerweise	Musik hoch. Apps herunter.
Ich rufe	oft	meine Freunde an.
Ich benutze	jeden Tag	soziale Medien.
Ich spreche	jeden Abend jede Woche immer	mit Freunden.
Ich schreibe/lese/schicke		Nachrichten/E-Mails.
Ich streame		Filme/Musik/Seifenopern.

Kapitel 2

fünfunddreißig 35

3 Das Leben als Star

- Discussing the pros and cons of celebrity culture
- Asking questions
- Practising the role-play section of the exam

Lesen 1 Read the information cards. Copy and complete the table in English.

Name: Jamal Musiala
Beruf: Fußballprofi
Leistung / Erfolg: Er hat mit 17 für Bayern München gespielt.
Vorteile: Er kann sein Hobby als Beruf machen. Es macht Spaß.
Nachteile: Es gibt Mobbing von Fans, wenn man schlecht spielt.

Name: Angelique Kerber
Beruf: Tennisspielerin
Leistung / Erfolg: Sie hat viele internationale Spiele gewonnen.
Vorteile: Sie kann um die Welt reisen und neue Leute kennenlernen.
Nachteile: Sie muss immer fit sein und viel Training machen.

der Profi — professional

	profession	successes/achievements	advantages	disadvantages
1				

Sprechen 2 Prepare your answers to the role-play below, then practise the dialogue with a partner.

You are talking to your Austrian friend.
Your teacher will play the part of your friend and will speak first.

- *Wer ist deine Lieblingspersönlichkeit?*
1 **Say which celebrity you like. (Ich mag …)**
- *Warum ist er/sie berühmt?*
2 **Say what this person does. Give one detail. (Er/Sie ist …)**
- *Was kann er/sie gut machen?*
3 **Say one thing this person is good at. (Er/Sie kann …)**
- *Sag mir einen Vorteil von seinem/ihrem Leben.*
4 **Give one advantage of their life. (Er/Sie kann …)**
- *Interessant!*
5 **? Ask your friend a question about celebrities. (Wer/Warum …?)**

	ist	Fußballprofi. Tennisspieler(in). Musiker(in). Sänger(in).	
Er Sie	kann	sehr gut extrem gut	Fußball spielen. singen.
	hat	viele Spiele gewonnen. für … gespielt. viel Musik gemacht.	
Ein Vorteil ist,		er/sie kann um die Welt reisen. er/sie hat viel Geld. er/sie kann sein/ihr Hobby als Beruf machen.	
Ein Nachteil ist,		er/sie muss immer fit sein. er/sie muss immer gut aussehen. er/sie hat kein Privatleben.	

sechsunddreißig

Lesen 3 Match the German and English verbs.

aufstehen   sich ansehen   machen   sagen   zeigen   reisen   treffen   lieben   schlafen

to say   to do/make   to sleep   to travel   to get up   to look at   to meet   to show   to love

Lesen 4 Read the interview. Answer the questions in English.

Mein Leben als Influencerin!

Was macht diese berühmte deutsche Influencerin den ganzen Tag?

Hallo Annika! Wie geht's?
Gut, danke!

Möchtest du deinen Alltag beschreiben?
Ich stehe um sieben Uhr auf und sehe mir sofort mein Handy an. Super! Ich habe über Nacht zweitausend neue Followers bekommen! Dann mache ich ein Video über mein Frühstück!

Was machst du nach dem Frühstück?
Ich gehe in die Stadt und sehe mir neue Kleidung an. Ich mache ein Video und sage meine Meinung über die Kleidung.

Was musst du auch oft machen?
Ich muss immer meinen Followern neue Kleidung zeigen. Ich reise auch oft, aber diese Woche bin ich zu Hause und ich möchte viel schlafen!

Willst du immer Influencerin sein?
Im Moment gefällt mir mein Job sehr. Ich treffe immer neue Leute, habe viel moderne Kleidung und kann oft reisen – ich liebe mein Leben!

1 What is the first thing Annika does when she wakes up?
2 What is her first video of the day about?
3 What does she have to do in her clothes videos?
4 Why is this week more relaxing than usual?
5 Why does she feel her life is so good? (Give **three** details.)

Lesen 5 Translate the interview questions in **bold** into English.

G To form a yes/no question, start with the verb. The infinitive goes to the end of the question.
Möchtest du berühmt sein? **Would you like** to be famous?
Willst du einkaufen gehen? **Do you want** to go shopping?

To ask other types of questions, you can use a question word (e.g. wann, wo, wie, warum) and swap the verb and subject round:
Was machst du nach dem Frühstück?
What do you do after breakfast?

Page 43

Sprechen 6 In pairs, read the interview aloud.

Hören 7 Listen to the conversation between Erik and Yusuf. Copy and complete the sentences.
1 Erik is …
2 He went … in Berlin.
3 He found the music festival … because he was …
4 He doesn't like … because he …

Be careful with **o** and **ö** – they are different sounds in German.

Listen and repeat the words.
Mode   Moment
Woche   oft
können   möchte

Schreiben 8 Write a description (50 words) of a celebrity from exercise 1, or someone else you know of. Mention:
- who the person is and what they are famous for
- what they can do well
- what they have done/achieved
- an advantage of being famous
- a disadvantage of being famous.

siebenunddreißig 37

4 Wie war der Film?

- Expressing preferences about films and TV shows
- Using the imperfect and perfect tenses together
- Practising the *eu* sound in German

Lesen 1
Read the descriptions of some TV shows. Write the letter of the best show (a–f) for each person in the sentences below.

< Gestern   Heute   Morgen >
< 14:00   15:00   16:00 >

a Emil und die Detektive
Emil und seine Freunde sind in Berlin unterwegs. Ein toller Actionfilm für die ganze Familie!

b Sportschau
Sport aus Deutschland, Europa und der Welt.

c Türkisch für Anfänger
Eine beliebte, lustige Geschichte über eine deutsch-türkische Familie.

d Gute Zeiten, schlechte Zeiten
Eine dramatische Seifenoper über Freunde und Familien in Berlin.

e Nosferatu: Phantom der Nacht
Ein klassischer, deutscher Horrorfilm. Natürlich mit Vampiren …

f Conchita: Unstoppable
Eine interessante Sendung über die weltberühmte Sängerin Conchita und ihr Leben.

1 Ich liebe witzige Komödien.
2 Ich sehe gern Actionfilme.
3 Ich sehe sehr gern Horrorfilme.
4 Ich interessiere mich für die Stars.
5 Ich bin Fußballfan – ich sehe also lieber Sendungen über Sport.
6 Ich interessiere mich sehr für Familiengeschichten.

Lesen 2
Sort the words below into two categories: 'qualifiers/intensifiers' or 'adjectives'.
Then translate them into English.

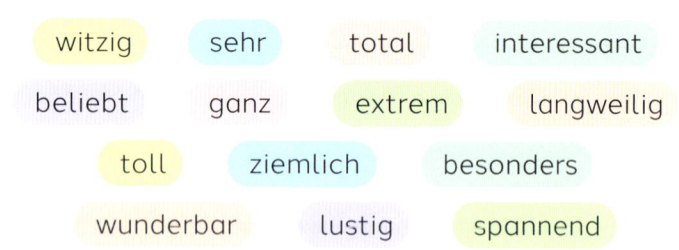

witzig   sehr   total   interessant
beliebt   ganz   extrem   langweilig
toll   ziemlich   besonders
wunderbar   lustig   spannend

> **Adjectives**, such as *interessant* (interesting), are describing words and are great for giving your opinion.
>
> Qualifiers and intensifiers, such as *ganz* (quite) and *sehr* (very), modify the adjective, so go just before it.
>
> Ich finde Actionfilme *sehr* **interessant**.
> I find action films very **interesting**.

Hören 3
Listen and select the correct option to complete each statement. (1–3)

1 Alina finds **comedies** / **sports shows** very **boring** / **bad**.
2 She likes **action films** / **documentary films** because they are **totally** / **quite** interesting.
3 She finds game shows **particularly exciting** / **really great**.

achtunddreißig

Kapitel 2

Sprechen 4 In pairs, take turns to ask and answer questions about your favourite types of films and TV shows. Try to include qualifiers and intensifiers.

- Wie findest du Sportsendungen?
- Ich finde Sportsendungen ganz langweilig. Und du?
- Ich finde Sportsendungen sehr interessant.
- Wie findest du Horrorfilme?
- Ich finde Horrorfilme …

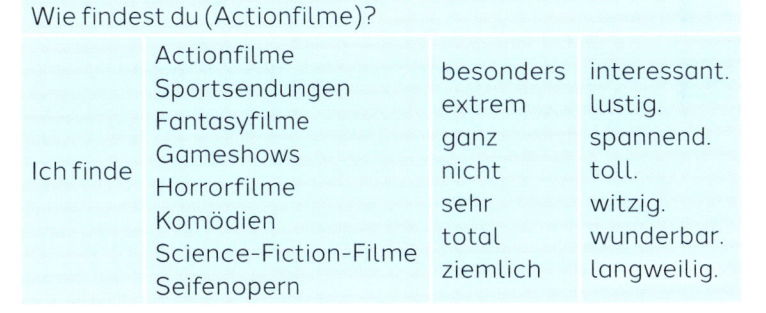

Wie findest du (Actionfilme)?			
Ich finde	Actionfilme Sportsendungen Fantasyfilme Gameshows Horrorfilme Komödien Science-Fiction-Filme Seifenopern	besonders extrem ganz nicht sehr total ziemlich	interessant. lustig. spannend. toll. witzig. wunderbar. langweilig.

Hören 5 Listen to and read Lola's blog. Answer the questions in English.

Ich bin gestern Abend mit meinen Eltern ins Kino gegangen. Wir haben den neuen Actionfilm *Aktion-Katzen* gesehen.

Normalerweise liebe ich Actionfilme, aber dieser Film war langweilig – ich habe ihn so lang und kompliziert gefunden! Die Schauspieler waren auch ganz schlecht.

Nach dem Film haben wir im Restaurant gegessen und das war wunderbar, weil das Essen lecker war.

Heute Abend sehe ich mir eine Komödie an.

der Schauspieler (-) actor

1. Who did Lola go to the cinema with?
2. What sort of film did they see?
3. Give two reasons why Lola disliked the film.
4. What did Lola do after the film?
5. How did she find that and why?
6. What sort of film is Lola going to watch this evening?

Hören 6 Listen and fill in the gaps in the dialogue. Pay attention to the *eu* sounds.

- Welche Filme siehst du gern?
- Ich sehe sehr gern **1**, weil sie wirklich spannend sind.
- Wie findest du Sportsendungen?
- Ich mag Sportsendungen nicht, denn ich finde sie ziemlich **2**.
- Was hast du letztes Wochenende gemacht?
- Ich bin letztes Wochenende mit meiner **3** ins Kino gegangen. Wir haben eine **4** gesehen. Ich habe den Film **5** witzig gefunden, aber die Kinokarten waren **6**!
- Was machst du **7** Abend?
- Heute Abend sehe ich eine **8** Seifenoper mit meiner Familie zu Hause.

The **eu** sound in German is pronounced 'oy' as in 'b**oy**'. Listen and repeat these words.
n**eu**   Fr**eu**ndin   h**eu**te

Schreiben 7 Write approximately 90 words about films and TV shows. Include the following points:

- what types of TV shows or films you like and why
- some information about a film you have seen recently
- what you are going to watch this evening.

Wie war (der Film / die Show)?
Der Film war …
Die Schauspieler(innen) waren …
Ich habe / Wir haben (den Film) … gefunden.
Was machst du heute Abend?
Heute Abend sehe ich …

You can use the **present tense** with a future time phrase to talk about what you are going to do.
Heute Abend **sehe** ich mir eine Komödie **an**.

The **perfect tense** is used to talk about events in the past:
Ich **habe** *den Film toll* **gefunden**.

Sein and **haben** are often used in the **imperfect tense**:
ich war I was   *ich hatte* I had

Page 44

neununddreißig 39

5 Hast du Pläne?

- Using the future tense to describe plans for the weekend
- Using the 'time – manner – place' rule
- Practising the ä sound

Hören 1 Listen to and read Samira's diary entries.

Was wirst du machen?

Freitag
- Ich werde mit Johanna und Laura ausgehen.
- Wir werden in der Stadtmitte einkaufen gehen.
- Ich werde Kinokarten kaufen.
- Das wird wunderbar sein!

Samstag
- Ich werde Basketball spielen.
- Mutti und ich werden Tennis spielen.
- Ich werde um 21:00 Uhr nach Hause gehen und schlafen!
- Das wird toll sein!

Sonntag
- Ich werde keine Hausaufgaben machen.
- Ich werde mein Handy benutzen.
- Mein Onkel und ich werden schwimmen gehen.
- Das wird entspannend sein!

Sprechen 2 In pairs, take turns to say an activity from exercise 1 and guess the day of the week.
- Was wirst du am Wochenende machen?
- Ich werde Sport machen.
- Am Sonntag?
- Nein! Ich werde auch schlafen.
- Aha, das ist am Samstag!

Lesen 3 Translate the diary entry for Saturday (*Samstag*) into English.

> **G** To form the **future tense** in German, use the correct form of **werden** and put the infinitive at the end of the clause.
>
> | ich werde | wir werden |
> | --- | --- |
> | du wirst | ihr werdet |
> | er/sie/es/man wird | Sie werden |
> | | sie werden |
>
> Ich **werde** am Wochenende keine Hausaufgaben **machen**.
> I **will** not **do** any homework at the weekend.
>
> Nächstes Wochenende **wird** wunderbar **sein**!
> Next weekend **will be** wonderful!
>
> Page 45

Was wirst du am Wochenende machen?				
Ich werde Er/Sie wird Wir werden	später heute Nachmittag heute Abend morgen nächsten (Samstag) am Wochenende	allein mit meinem Freund mit meiner Freundin mit meiner Familie	am Strand im Park in der Stadt(mitte) im Kino in Stuttgart zu Hause	(Rockmusik) hören. (Fußball) spielen. (einkaufen) gehen. (Bücher) lesen. (mein Handy) benutzen. (Videos) streamen. (einen Film) sehen. fernsehen.

40 vierzig

Kapitel 2

Hören 4 Listen to Kian talking about his plans for this weekend. Copy and complete the table in English. (1–3)

	when?	with whom?	where?	activity
1				

Sprechen 5 In pairs, take turns to talk about your future plans using the notes below.

Example: 1 *Ich werde um 16:00 Uhr allein zu Hause Hausaufgaben machen.*

	time	manner (with whom)	place	activity
1	um 16:00 Uhr	allein	(house)	(writing)
2	nächsten Samstag	mit meiner Freundin	(town)	(basketball)
3	später	mit meiner Familie	(cinema)	(watching film)
4	am Wochenende	mit meinem Onkel	Hamburg	(shopping)

The **ä** sound in German can be a short sound like the English 'e' in 'g**e**t' or a longer sound like the 'ay' in 's**ay**'.
Listen and repeat the words and decide if they have a short or long **ä** sound.
n**ä**chstes   Aktivit**ä**t   sp**ä**ter

G The correct **word order** for elements in a German sentence is:

time (when) – **manner** (how) – **place** (where).

*Ich werde **morgen allein zu Hause** ein Buch lesen.*
*Wir werden **nächsten Sonntag mit Freunden im Park** Fußball spielen.*

Page 45

Lesen 6 Read the text about Max's weekend plans. Is each statement below true or false?

Ich werde am Samstagmorgen mit meinen Freunden im Sportzentrum Basketball spielen. Am Samstagnachmittag werde ich mit meinem Bruder ins Kino gehen. Wir werden einen Fantasyfilm sehen. Meine Eltern werden am Sonntag wandern gehen, aber ich werde allein zu Hause Bücher lesen. Am Sonntagabend werde ich mit meiner Familie im Restaurant essen. Das wird toll sein!

1 Max will play basketball on Saturday afternoon.
2 Max will go to the cinema with his friend.
3 Max will watch a fantasy film.
4 Max will go hiking with his parents on Sunday.
5 On Sunday evening, Max will eat at a restaurant with his family.

Schreiben 7 Write <u>four</u> sentences about your plans for next weekend. Try to include 'time', 'manner' and 'place' elements in each sentence.

einundvierzig 41

Grammatik 1

Regular verbs in the present tense (Unit 1, page 32)

Lesen 1 Select the correct present tense form of the verb in the sentences below.

Example: 1 Ich **spiele** sehr gern Basketball.

1 Ich **spiele / spielst / spielt** sehr gern Basketball.
2 Wir **mache / macht / machen** viele Fotos.
3 Meine Freundin **mache / macht / machen** nicht gern Hausaufgaben.
4 Und du, Tobias? **Spiele / Spielst / Spielt** du gern Tennis?
5 Meine Eltern **gehen / gehst / geht** oft einkaufen.
6 **Geht / Gehen / Gehe** ihr morgen wandern?

Irregular verbs in the present tense (Unit 1, page 32)

Hören 2 Listen. Copy and complete the sentences with the correct form of the irregular verbs. (1–4)

1 Ich **sehe** mir sehr gern Filme an, aber meine Freundin ___ lieber fern.
2 ___ du jeden Tag Bücher? Peter ___ fast nie!
3 Meine Schwester ___ nach Österreich, aber mein Vater und ich ___ in die Schweiz.
4 Meine Mutter und mein Vater ___ oft Fastfood, aber Jonas ___ immer sehr gesund.

> Some verbs, such as **sehen** (to see), **lesen** (to read), **fahren** (to go, to travel) and **essen** (to eat) are **irregular**.
>
> The endings are the same as for regular verbs, but there are changes to the stem in the **du** and the **er/sie/es/man** forms.

	sehen	lesen	fahren	essen
ich	sehe	lese	fahre	esse
du	siehst	liest	fährst	isst
er/sie/es/man	sieht	liest	fährt	isst
wir	sehen	lesen	fahren	essen
ihr	seht	lest	fahrt	esst
Sie	sehen	lesen	fahren	essen
sie	sehen	lesen	fahren	essen

Using gern and lieber (Unit 1, page 32)

Schreiben 3 Rewrite the sentences using *nicht gern* (✖), *gern* (♥) or *lieber* (♥♥).

Example: 1 Ich fahre **lieber** Fahrrad.

1 Ich fahre Fahrrad. ♥♥
2 Ich spiele Tennis. ✖
3 Ich höre Musik. ♥
4 Ich gehe ins Kino. ♥♥
5 Ich mache Sport. ✖

> Remember to put adverbs such as (*sehr*) *gern* and *lieber* **after** the verb when expressing an opinion.
>
> ✖ Meine Freunde und ich gehen **nicht gern** in die Stadt.
> ♥ Ich sehe **gern** Filme.
> ♥♥ Meine Schwester sieht **lieber** Sportsendungen.

zweiundvierzig

Using frequency phrases with correct word order (Unit 1, page 33)

Schreiben 4 Rewrite the sentences starting with the **bold** words.

Example: 1 **Später** spiele ich Basketball.

1 Ich spiele **später** Basketball.
2 Mein Stiefvater sieht **heute** einen Film.
3 Wir hören **ab und zu** Rockmusik.
4 Ich möchte **jeden Tag** Sport machen.
5 Ich war **letzte Woche** sehr aktiv.
6 Ich gehe **am Wochenende** schwimmen.

> Remember that the conjugated verb is always the second idea in a German sentence.

Sprechen 5 Read out the sentences from exercise 4.

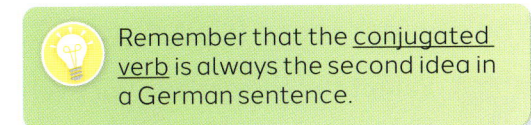

Separable verbs in the present tense (Unit 2, page 34)

Schreiben 6 Copy and complete the sentences with the correct form of the separable verb in brackets. Then translate them into English.

Example: 1 Ich **mache** das Licht **aus**. – I turn the light off.

1 Ich ___ das Licht ___ . (*ausmachen*)
2 Ich ___ meine Freunde ___ . (*anrufen*)
3 Ich ___ mir Filme ___ . (*ansehen*)
4 Ich ___ jeden Abend ___ . (*fernsehen*)
5 Ich ___ mein Handy ___ . (*mitnehmen*)
6 Ich ___ Musik ___ . (*herunterladen*)

Asking questions (Unit 3, page 36)

Schreiben 7 Copy and complete the table with the questions and statements.

question	statement
Willst du berühmt sein?	Ich will berühmt sein.
	Ich will ein Privatleben haben.
Musst du immer um die Welt reisen?	
	Ich muss immer fit sein.
Kannst du neue Leute treffen?	
	Ich kann sehr gut singen.

Grammatik 2

The perfect tense (Unit 4, page 39)

1 Select the correct auxiliary verb to complete each perfect tense sentence.
Example: 1 Ich **habe** Basketball gespielt.

1 Ich **habe** / **bin** Basketball gespielt.
2 Ich **habe** / **bin** gestern ins Kino gegangen.
3 Ich **habe** / **bin** Rockmusik gehört.
4 Ich **habe** / **bin** den Film gesehen.
5 Ich **habe** / **bin** in die Stadt gefahren.
6 Ich **habe** / **bin** das Konzert toll gefunden.
7 Ich **habe** / **bin** im Restaurant gegessen.
8 Ich **habe** / **bin** mein Handy benutzt.

> Remember that most verbs take **haben** in the perfect tense. Those that take **sein** usually involve movement or a change of state, such as *gehen* (to go) and *aufstehen* (to get up).

2 Copy and complete the sentences with the correct past participle of the verb in brackets. Then listen to check your answers.

1 Ich habe eine Sportsendung *gesehen*. (*sehen*)
2 Ich habe den Film witzig ___. (*finden*)
3 Jan hat Musik ___. (*hören*)
4 Wir haben Fußball ___. (*spielen*)
5 Ich bin in die Stadt ___. (*fahren*)
6 Lisa ist ins Kino ___. (*gehen*)
7 Wie viele Kinokarten hast du ___? (*kaufen*)
8 Sie haben viel Sport ___. (*machen*)

> Remember that the past participle usually starts with **ge-** and can end in **-t** (regular verbs) or **-en** (irregular verbs). Don't add **ge-** if the verb starts with **be-** or **ver-**.

The imperfect tense (Unit 4, page 39)

3 Translate the sentences into English.
1 Ich hatte ein Hobby.
2 Wir waren sehr bekannt.
3 Er hatte ein neues Handy.
4 Ich war sehr aktiv.
5 Wir hatten keinen Computer.
6 Der Film war ganz interessant.

> Some verbs are used more commonly in the **imperfect tense**:
> *ich/es* **war** (I/it was)
> *ich/es* **hatte** (I/it had)
>
> | | haben | sein |
> |---|---|---|
> | ich | hatte | war |
> | er/sie/es/man | hatte | war |
> | wir | hatten | waren |

4 Copy and complete the sentences to match the English translations.

1 ___ ein Handy.
   I had a mobile phone.
2 ___ besonders beliebt.
   Mozart was particularly popular.
3 ___ einen Laptop.
   She had a laptop.
4 ___ nicht sehr spannend.
   The film was not very exciting.
5 ___ Kinokarten.
   We had cinema tickets.
6 ___ ziemlich langweilig.
   It was quite boring.

44 vierundvierzig

The future tense (Unit 5, page 40)

Schreiben 5 Put the words in the correct order to make sentences. Start with the word in **bold** and end with the <u>infinitive</u>.

1. werden   Musik   **Wir**   hören
2. Freund   **Mein**   einkaufen   <u>gehen</u>   wird
3. <u>kaufen</u>   die   nächsten   **Ich**   Samstag   Karten   werde
4. ich   werden   Schwester   <u>herunterladen</u>   und   **Meine**   Apps

> 💡 Remember that to form the **future tense** in German, you use the correct form of **werden** and put the <u>infinitive</u> at the end of the clause.

Word order: time – manner – place (Unit 5, page 41)

Lesen 6 Decide if the phrases in the box are 'time', 'manner' or 'place' phrases. Copy and complete the table.

time	manner	place
heute Abend		

mit meiner Familie — in Österreich
heute Abend — zu Hause
mit meiner Freundin — später
nächstes Wochenende — allein
am Strand — morgen
mit meinem Bruder — ins Kino

Schreiben 7 Translate the sentences into German. Use the table from exercise 6 to help you.

1. *I will listen to music at home with my brother this evening.*
   Ich werde heute Abend … Musik hören.
2. *I will go shopping next weekend in Austria with my friend.*
   Ich werde _____ einkaufen gehen.
3. *I will go to the cinema with my family later.*
   Ich werde _____ gehen.
4. *I will read books alone on the beach tomorrow.*
   Ich werde _____ Bücher lesen.

Los geht's!

Lesen 8 Read the text below and find an example of each of the <u>eight</u> grammar features.

Ich liebe neue Technologie. Ich lade Musik herunter und ich spreche sehr gern mit meinem Freund. Ich gehe auch ab und zu ins Kino. Willst du dir später einen Film ansehen? Ich bin gestern mit meiner Schwester ins Kino gegangen und der Film war wunderbar! Morgen werden wir einen Actionfilm sehen!

1. Separable verbs (e.g. **fern**sehen)
2. Opinions using *gern* or *lieber*
3. Frequency expressions (e.g. *oft*)
4. Questions
5. Time – manner – place
6. Perfect tense
7. Imperfect tense
8. Future tense

Sprechen 9 Read out the text in exercise 8.

fünfundvierzig **45**

Kapitel 2 — Lese- und Hörtest

Reading

Lesen 1

Hobbies. Some Austrian teenagers are discussing their hobbies. What do they say? Write the correct name to answer each question. Write **A** for **Anja**, **D** for **David** or **T** for **Thea**.

Anja

Ich habe gestern meinen Lieblingsschauspieler in seinem neuen Film gesehen. Der Film war sehr spannend.

David

Ich gehe nicht gern ins Kino, aber ich sehe gern Videos. Ich mag Sport und Kochen. Ich koche und dann mache ich Fotos für meinen Blog.

Thea

Ich mache nicht gern Sport, aber ich gehe gern ins Kino. Nächste Woche gehe ich mit meinem Bruder ins Kino. Wir werden zuerst einkaufen gehen. Das macht immer Spaß.

1. Who likes shopping?
2. Who saw a film recently?
3. Who doesn't like the cinema?
4. Who likes sport?
5. Who has made plans with a family member?
6. Who likes cooking?

Lesen 2

Free-time activities. Mila writes a blog about her free time. What does she say about her hobbies? Write **P** for something she did **in the past**, **N** for something she is doing **now** and **F** for something she will do **in the future**.

Ich bin sehr aktiv und habe viele Interessen. Ich spiele gern Basketball und das mache ich einmal pro Woche nach der Schule. Im Sommer werde ich Tennis spielen. Manchmal gehe ich mit meiner Freundin in die Stadt. Letzte Woche sind wir ins Kino gegangen und wir haben einen wunderbaren Fantasyfilm gesehen. Am Donnerstag möchte ich im Restaurant essen, weil meine Freundin Geburtstag hat.

1. basketball
2. tennis
3. going into town
4. cinema
5. visiting a restaurant

> Look carefully at the verbs to help you work out which time frame is being used. Time expressions will also give you a clue.

Kapitel 2

Lesen 3
Hobbies. Translate these sentences into English.

1 Ich sehe jeden Abend fern.
2 Mein Lieblingssänger hat viele Fans.
3 Am Wochenende hören wir Musik und wir machen Fotos.
4 Ich finde Seifenopern sehr langweilig, aber Komödien sind lustig.
5 Letzten Samstag habe ich im Park Fußball mit meinem Freund gespielt.

Your English word order will be different, but make sure you don't miss out any words.

Read every sentence carefully. It is easy to miss out key words.

Think carefully about the tense used here.

Listening

Hören 4
Technology. You hear Sophia and Dario talking about using technology. Which **two** activities does each person use their technology for? Write the **two** correct letters for each person.

A	Sends texts to friends
B	Phones friends
C	Uses social media
D	Downloads music
E	Streams soap operas
F	Watches TV

Read the context and question carefully. In this task you are listening for details of how they use technology.

Make sure you know how many pieces of information you need to listen out for.

Listen carefully to help you discount the distractors (incorrect answer options that are similar to correct answers). Options A and B both mention friends, but in what context are friends mentioned on the recording?

Before you start listening, look at the answer options and anticipate the vocabulary you might hear.

Hören 5
My weekend. Katrin is talking about her weekend activities. Listen to the recording and write **A, B or C** to complete each sentence.

1 Katrin usually goes ...
   A to a friend's house.
   B swimming.
   C shopping.

2 Katrin ...
   A likes going to the cinema.
   B doesn't like watching films.
   C thinks cinema tickets are expensive.

You may hear words in the recording that relate to the incorrect answer options. For example, you will hear all the options mentioned for question 1, but Katrin did two of the activities last week and only one is a regular activity. Listen carefully to discount the incorrect options.

Dictation

Hören 6
You will hear **four** short sentences. Write down exactly what you hear in German.

Think carefully about how these sounds are pronounced when writing down what you hear:
a, ä, o, ö
ei, ie, i, eu
sp, st, sch

siebenundvierzig 47

Kapitel 2 Mündlicher Test

Role-play

1 Look at the role-play card and prepare what you are going to say.

> Remember that your responses to points 1–5 must all contain verbs.

> Keep your answers short and simple: you need to give one detail each time.

> Remember to keep the verb as the second idea in your sentence if you put a time phrase first.

You are talking to your Swiss friend.
1. Say **one** thing you do in your free time.
2. Say how often you listen to music. (Give **one** detail.)
3. Say what you like doing with your family. (Give **one** detail.)
4. Say what you wear at the weekend. (Give **one** detail.)
5. ? Ask your friend a question about films.

> You could ask about their favourite film or their opinion of a certain genre of film.

2 Practise what you have prepared. Then, using your notes, listen and respond to the teacher.

3 Listen to Leah's response. Make a note of:
a how she answers the questions for points 1–4
b what question she asks for point 5.

Reading aloud

4 Look at this task. With a partner, read the sentences aloud, paying attention to the underlined letters.

> Ich streame täglich Filme.
>
> Meine Schwester hört gern klassische Musik, aber das mag ich nicht.
>
> Ihre Freunde spielen lieber am Computer.
>
> Ich liebe Sportsendungen, weil sie spannend sind.
>
> Wir möchten heute Abend ins Kino gehen.

> Think carefully about how to pronounce these sounds. Remember that cognates are often not pronounced the same as in English.
> a, ä, o, ö
> ei, ie, i, eu
> sp, st, sch

5 Listen and check your pronunciation.

6 Listen to the teacher asking four follow-up questions. Translate each question into English and prepare your own answer to each one. Then listen again and respond to the teacher.

48 *achtundvierzig*

Kapitel 2

Photo card

Hören 7 Listen to Leah's descriptions of the two photos and answer the questions.

1. What does Leah think the man in the first photo does for a living?
2. Give **two** other details she mentions about him.
3. What does Leah think the girl in the second photo is doing?
4. What does she say about her appearance? (Give **two** details.)

You will be asked to talk about the content of these photos. You must say at least one thing about each photo.

After you have spoken about the content of the photos, you will be asked questions related to any of the topics within the theme of **Popular culture**.

Your responses should be as **full and detailed** as possible.

Sprechen 8 Prepare your own description of the photos. Then, with a partner, take turns describing them.

> Auf dem ersten Foto gibt es …

Hören 9 Listen to the teacher's first follow-up question, *Wie findest du Musik?* Listen to Leah's response and answer the questions.

1. What is Leah very good at?
2. What does she do at the weekend?
3. Why does she like rap music? (Give **two** details.)
4. Which type of music does she **not** like, and why?

Hören 10 Listen to Leah answering the question, *Welchen Sport treibst du gern?* Write down the missing word for each gap.

> Ich bin jeden Tag ziemlich **1** : im Sommer spiele ich **2** Tennis, aber ich gehe **3** schwimmen. Ich spiele Basketball mit meinen **4** , weil das sehr **5** ist. Fußball spiele ich aber **6** gern.

Notice how Leah develops her answer and shows off her language skills by using:
- *aber* and *weil* plus an opinion and the correct word order
- *gern* and *lieber*
- qualifiers/intensifiers (*ziemlich, sehr*)
- time phrases (*jeden Tag, im Sommer*)
- inversion after a time phrase
- a negative.

Sprechen 11 Listen to two more follow-up questions and prepare your answers. Then respond to the recording. Make your answers as full as possible, including opinions and reasons.

Try to use language structures from the module to develop more detailed responses, such as those in Leah's response in exercise 10.

Sprechen 12 Prepare your own answers to as many of the Module 2 questions on page 226 as you can. Then practise with a partner.

neunundvierzig 49

Kapitel 2 Schreibtest

Describing a photo

Schreiben 1 Look at this writing exam task. Copy and complete Alfie's responses, adding a suitable verb into each gap.

1 Es ___ vier Männer.
2 Sie ___ Basketball.
3 Die Männer ___ T-Shirts.
4 Sie ___ in einem Sportzentrum.
5 Sie ___ kurze Haare.

Schreiben 2 Prepare your own answer to the task.

*Don't worry if you see something in the photo which you don't know in German. Focus on what you **do** know.*

You see this photo on Instagram.

What is in the photo?

Write **five** sentences in **German**.

Translation

Schreiben 3 Read the English sentences and Alfie's translations. Correct the <u>two</u> mistakes in each translation.

1 I don't have a laptop.
2 Every week, my friend goes into town.
3 I would like to watch a soap opera.
4 I never download music.
5 I watched a comedy on my mobile phone.

1 Ich habe ein Handy.
2 Jeden Tag geht meine Freundin in die Schule.
3 Ich möchte einen Film hören.
4 Ich lade oft Musik hoch.
5 Ich habe einen Krimi auf meinem Laptop gesehen.

Schreiben 4 Translate these sentences into German.

Remember: Time – Manner – Place.

Modal verbs send the second verb to the end, in the infinitive form.

1 I have a mobile phone.
2 At the weekend, my friend goes to the cinema.
3 I would like to play basketball.
4 I often listen to music.
5 I played tennis in the park.

You need two parts to form the perfect tense: the auxiliary verb and a past participle.

90-word writing task

Schreiben 5 Look at this writing exam task and then, for each bullet point:

1 think about vocabulary and structures to use:
  • **nouns**, **verbs** and **adjectives** to write about free-time activities
  • language for **describing** a film you have seen
  • how to explain what you **will do** and **why**.
2 write down three or four ideas for what you could write about.
3 identify which tense(s) you could use in your answer.

You are writing to your German friend about your free time.

Write approximately **90** words in **German**.

You must write something about each bullet point.

Describe:
• what you like doing in your free time
• a film you saw last weekend
• your plans for next weekend.

50 *fünfzig*

Kapitel 2

Lesen 6 Read Alfie's response to the exam task. Answer the questions in the coloured boxes (1–5).

1 This is an example of **complex language**. What does it mean? Find three more examples of complex language in the text.

2 Alfie uses a **variety of time phrases**. What do these words mean? Find two more examples.

3 Which **tense** is this? What other examples can you find? Does Alfie use any other tenses?

Ich benutze jeden Abend mein Handy. Ich finde das immer spannend. Ich sehe mir Videos an und schicke manchmal Nachrichten. Ich höre auch gern Musik und ich lade sie oft herunter. Ich mag Popmusik, aber ich mag klassische Musik nicht. Sie ist zu langweilig.

Am Freitag bin ich mit meiner Freundin ins Kino gegangen. Wir haben eine Komödie gesehen, aber ich habe den Film blöd gefunden. Ich mag lieber Actionfilme, weil ich sie spannend finde.

Ich werde nächstes Wochenende mit meinen Eltern im Sportzentrum schwimmen gehen. Das wird viel Spaß machen!

4 How could Alfie **avoid repetition** by using a synonym here?

5 Which connective could you use here to form an **extended sentence**? What other connectives does Alfie use?

Lesen 7 Read Alfie's answer again and answer the questions.

1 How often does Alfie send messages?
2 Why does Alfie **not** like classical music?
3 What did Alfie think of the film?
4 Who will Alfie go swimming with?

Schreiben 8 Prepare your own response to the task.

- Think about how you can develop your answer for each bullet point.
- Look back at your notes from exercises 5 and 6.
- Look at the 'Challenge checklist' and consider how you can show off your German!
- Write a **brief** plan and organise your answer into paragraphs.
- Write your answer and then check carefully for accuracy.

Checking your work is important.
- Make sure you have answered all three bullet points.
- Check your verbs: do they match the time frames in the bullet points?
- Check your word order: think about inversion and sending verbs to the end of a clause.
- Check your spelling.

Challenge checklist

🥨	✓ ich + conjugated verb in the present (*ich spiele Fußball*)
	✓ A verb and a simple adjective (*es ist gut*)
🥨🥨	✓ Different persons of the verb (*meine Freunde, sie*)
	✓ More varied opinions and verbs (*ich denke, ich glaube*)
	✓ A wider range of interesting vocabulary (*allein, Spaß machen*)
	✓ Separable verbs (*ich sehe gern fern*)
🥨🥨🥨	✓ Frequency words (*oft, nie*)
	✓ Qualifiers and intensifiers (*ziemlich, besonders*)
	✓ More varied conjunctions (*weil, dass*)
	✓ Past and future tenses (*ich habe Tennis gespielt, ich werde Tennis spielen*)

einundfünfzig 51

Kapitel 2 Wörter

Key:
bold = this word will appear in higher exams only
* = this word is not on the vocabulary list but you may use it in your own sentences

Kennst du diese *Musiker? (pages 30–31):

Musik	Music
Wie findest du (Rockmusik)?	What do you think of (rock music)?
Magst du die Musik von (Helene Fischer)?	Do you like (Helene Fischer's) music?
Was ist deine Lieblingsmusik?	What is your favourite music?
Ich liebe / mag … (nicht) / hasse …	I love / (don't) like / hate …
Rock	rock
die Musik von (Mozart)	the music of (Mozart)
klassische Musik	classical music
*Popmusik	pop music
Tanzmusik	dance music
denn er/sie/es ist …	because it is …
besonders	particularly
ganz	quite
nicht	not
sehr	very
wirklich	really
ziemlich	rather
zu	too
beliebt	popular
entspannend	relaxing
interessant	interesting
komisch	funny, strange
langsam	slow
langweilig	boring
laut	loud
lustig	funny
modern	modern
schnell	fast, quick
spannend	exciting

Was machst du gern in deiner Freizeit? (pages 32–33):

Freizeitaktivitäten	Free time activities
Was machst du gern in deiner Freizeit?	What do you like to do / doing in your free time?
Mein *Lieblingshobby ist …	My favourite hobby is …
Ich interessiere mich (sehr/nicht) für …	I'm (very/not) interested in …
Einkaufen	shopping
Fahrradfahren	cycling
Fernsehen	TV
*Gaming	gaming
Lesen	reading
Sport	sport
Ich spiele am Computer.	I play on the computer.
Ich gehe …	I go …
einkaufen.	shopping.
ins Kino.	to the cinema.
in die Stadt.	to town.
schwimmen.	swimming.
wandern.	hiking.
Ich besuche (Freunde).	I visit (friends).
Ich tanze/koche/singe.	I dance/cook/sing.
Ich fahre Fahrrad.	I cycle.
Ich mache Fotos.	I take photos.
Ich mache Sport.	I do sport.
Ich lese Bücher.	I read books.
Ich höre Musik.	I listen to music.
Ich sehe fern/Filme.	I watch TV/films.
ab und zu	now and again
am Wochenende	at the weekend
jeden Tag / täglich	every day
manchmal	sometimes
(fast) nie	(almost) never
(sehr) oft	(very) often

Was machst du online? (pages 34–35):

Technologie	Technology
Welche Technologie benutzt du zu Hause?	What technology do you use at home?
Ich habe … / Wir haben …	I have … / We have …
Ich benutze … / Wir benutzen …	I use … / We use …
einen Computer	a computer
einen *Fernseher	a TV
einen Laptop	a laptop
eine *Spielkonsole	a games console
ein Handy	a mobile phone
ein *Smartphone	a smart phone
ein *Tablet	a tablet
Was machst du online?	What do you do online?
Ich sehe mir (Filme/Videos) an.	I watch (films/videos).
Ich sehe fern.	I watch TV.
Ich lade (Apps) herunter.	I download (apps).
Ich lade (Fotos/Musik) hoch.	I upload (photos/music).
Ich rufe (meine Freunde) an.	I call/phone (my friends).
Ich benutze soziale Medien.	I use social media.
Ich spreche (mit Freunden).	I speak (with friends).
Ich schreibe/lese/schicke … Nachrichten/E-Mails.	I write/read/send … messages/emails.
Ich streame (Musik/Filme/Seifenopern).	I stream (music / films / soap operas).
Und wie oft?	And how often?
immer	always
jeden Abend	every evening
jeden Tag	every day
jede Woche	every week
nie	never
normalerweise	normally
oft	often

zweiundfünfzig

Das Leben als Star (pages 36–37):

Wer ist deine Lieblingspersönlichkeit?	Who is your favourite personality?
Warum ist er/sie berühmt?	Why is he/she famous?
Er/Sie ist *Fußballprofi/ Tennisspieler(in).	He/She is a footballer / tennis player.
Er/Sie ist *Musiker(in)/ Sänger(in).	He/She is a musician/singer.
Was kann er/sie gut machen?	What can he/she do well?
Er/Sie kann sehr gut Fußball spielen.	He/She can play football really well.
Er/Sie kann extrem gut singen.	He/She can sing extremely well.
Was hat er/sie gemacht?	What has he/she done?
Er/Sie hat viele Spiele gewonnen.	He/She has won lots of matches.
Er/Sie hat für … gespielt.	He/She has played for …
Er/Sie hat viel Musik gemacht.	He/She has made a lot of music.
Ein Vorteil ist, …	One advantage is (that) …
er/sie kann um die Welt reisen.	he/she can travel around the world.
er/sie hat viel Geld.	he/she has a lot of money.
er/sie kann sein/ihr *Hobby als Beruf machen.	he/she can do his/her hobby as a job.
Ein Nachteil ist, …	One disadvantage is (that) …
er/sie muss immer *fit sein.	he/she always has to be fit.
er/sie muss immer gut aussehen.	he/she always has to look good.
er/sie hat kein Privatleben.	he/she doesn't have any private life.
Möchtest du berühmt sein?	Would you like to be famous?

Wie war der Film? (pages 38–39):

Film und Fernsehen	Film and TV
Der Film war …	The film was …
Die Schauspieler(innen) waren …	The actors/actresses were …
Ich habe / Wir haben den Film … gefunden.	I/We found the film …
Wie findest du …?	How do you find …?
Ich finde …	I find …
*Actionfilme	action films
*Fantasyfilme	fantasy films
*Gameshows	game shows
*Horrorfilme	horror films
Komödien	comedies
*Science-Fiction-Filme	science fiction films
Seifenopern	soap operas
Sportsendungen	sport programmes
besonders	particularly
extrem	extremely
total	totally
kompliziert	complicated
lang	long
lustig	funny
schwach	weak
toll	great, amazing
traurig	sad
witzig	funny, witty

Hast du Pläne? (pages 40–41):

Das Wochenende	The weekend
Was wirst du am Wochenende machen?	What will you do at the weekend?
Ich werde …	I will …
später	later
heute Nachmittag	this afternoon
heute Abend	this evening
heute Nacht	tonight
morgen	tomorrow
nächsten (Samstag)	next (Saturday)
am Wochenende	at the weekend
allein	alone
mit meinem Freund / meiner Freundin	with my friend
mit meiner Familie	with my family
am Strand	at the beach
im Park	in the park
in der Stadt(mitte)	in the town (centre)
im Kino	in the cinema
in (Stuttgart)	in (Stuttgart)
zu Hause	at home
(Bücher) lesen.	read (books).
(mein Handy) benutzen.	use (my mobile phone).
(im Restaurant) essen.	eat (in a restaurant).
(Videos) streamen.	stream (videos).
Das wird … sein.	It/That will be …
entspannend	relaxing
toll	great, terrific
wunderbar	wonderful

Kapitel 1–2 Grammatik: Wiederholung

Present tense

Schreiben 1 Copy and complete the sentences with the correct form of the verbs in brackets.
1 Ich ___ (*spielen*) gern Basketball, aber mein Lieblingssport ___ (*sein*) Tennis.
2 Martin ___ (*gehen*) ins Theater und ___ (*fahren*) um 22:00 Uhr nach Hause.
3 Ich ___ (*essen*) gern in der Pause, aber meine Schwester ___ (*essen*) lieber nichts.
4 Mila ___ (*kaufen*) gern Schuhe. Heute ___ (*tragen*) sie neue Sportschuhe.
5 ___ (*haben*) du in der ersten Stunde Biologie? ___ (*finden*) du Biologie interessant?
6 Ich ___ oft Musik ___ (*herunterladen*), aber wir ___ (*benutzen*) keine Handys im Unterricht.
7 Mein Bruder ___ (*haben*) heute keine Hausaufgaben, also ___ er den ganzen Abend ___ (*fernsehen*).
8 Wann ___ (*beginnen*) der Film? Ich ___ dich später ___ (*anrufen*).

> Sentences 6–8 include a separable verb.

Word order in subordinate clauses

Schreiben 2 Rewrite each pair of sentences as one sentence linked with *weil*.
1 Ich spiele gern Fußball. Es ist toll.
2 Tim macht die Hausaufgaben nicht. Sie sind schwierig.
3 Ich lerne gern Mathe. Der Lehrer ist super.
4 Wir kaufen Kinokarten. Der neue Film ist im Kino.
5 Ich gehe am Mittwoch gern in die Schule. Ich habe Sport.
6 Elif fährt um 18:00 Uhr in die Stadt. Das Konzert ist um 19:00 Uhr.
7 Wir essen Pizza. Wir haben Hunger.
8 Ich liebe diese Sängerin. Sie ist sehr berühmt.

> Remember that *weil* sends the verb to the end of the clause.

Perfect and imperfect tenses

Schreiben 3 Rewrite your linked sentences from exercise 2 in the past. Use the perfect tense for the main clause and the imperfect tense for the subordinate clause.
Example: 1 *Ich habe gern Fußball gespielt, weil ...*

> Go back to pages 14 and 15 to refresh your memory on how to form the perfect and imperfect tenses.

Modal verbs

Lesen 4 Read the notice. Are these statements true or false?
1 There are only female students at this school.
2 Students are not allowed to eat in the classrooms.
3 Students are allowed to play on the computers during break.
4 Students should bring water bottles into school.
5 Students mustn't buy drinks.
6 You have to pay for water.

> **Informationen für alle Schüler*innen**
> Man darf im Klassenzimmer nicht essen.
> Man kann in der Pause in den Computerraum gehen, aber man darf keine Computerspiele spielen.
> Schüler*innen sollen eine Wasserflasche in die Schule mitnehmen.
> Man muss keine Getränke kaufen. Wasser kostet nichts.

54 vierundfünfzig

Grammatik: Wiederholung — Kapitel 1–2

Articles and adjectives

Lesen 5 Decide whether you need the nominative or accusative and select the correct article and adjective to agree with each noun.

1 Ich habe **ein / einen lustigen / lustiger** Film gesehen.
2 Der Basketballprofi ist **ein / einen berühmten / berühmter** Star.
3 Die Fans lieben **der / den junge / jungen** Schauspieler.
4 Am Samstag gibt es **keinen / keine neues / neue** Sendung im Fernsehen.
5 Hast du **den / das spannende / spannendes** Fußballspiel gesehen?
6 **Den / Der interessanten / interessante** Horrorfilm ist nicht für Kinder.
7 Ich kaufe **eine / einen rotes / rote** Jacke.
8 In der Stadt ist **ein / eines großes / großen** Theater.

> Think carefully about the gender of each noun.
> Masculine: *Film, Star, Schauspieler*
> Feminine: *Jacke, Sendung*
> Neuter: *Spiel, Theater*

Future tense

Schreiben 6 Rewrite these sentences in the future tense.

1 Ich gehe nach Hause.
2 Wir lernen Geschichte.
3 Die Schüler spielen Tischtennis.
4 Ich lese Bücher.
5 Du kaufst neue Kleidung.
6 Mia ruft mich an.
7 Meine Freundin hat kein Handy.
8 Der Film ist lustig.

Word order: verb as second idea

Schreiben 7 Use your answers from exercise 6 to answer these questions. Change the word order to begin each answer with the time phrase in **bold** in the question.

Example: 1 *Morgen werde ich …*

1 Was wirst du **morgen** machen?
2 Was werdet ihr **nächstes Jahr** lernen?
3 Was werden die Schüler **nächsten Freitag** machen?
4 Was wirst du **am Wochenende** machen?
5 Was werde ich **am Samstag** machen?
6 Was wird Mia **später** machen?
7 Was wird deine Freundin **nächste Woche** nicht haben?
8 Wie wird der Film **heute Abend** sein?

Word order: time – manner – place

Gestern   bin ich   allein   zur Schule   gegangen.

Schreiben 8 Rewrite the model sentence, substituting one element in German each time.

1 Copy the model sentence, changing the time to 'on Friday'.
2 Copy sentence 1, changing the manner to 'with my friend'.
3 Copy sentence 2, changing the place to 'to the cinema'.
4 Translate the sentence: 'On Friday I will go to the cinema with my friend' by changing the tense to the future tense in sentence 3.

Kapitel 3 — Meine Welt, deine Welt

Feste in der deutschsprachigen Welt
- Describing festivals and cultural events
- Giving opinions and justifications

Wir feiern!

Im Winter gibt es …

1 Nikolaustag
Im Dezember feiert man den Nikolaustag in jeder Stadt. Weißt du, an welchem Tag?

2 Eisfasching
Wenn das Wetter kalt ist, gibt es Eisfasching in Berlin. Machst du mit?

3 Rosenmontag
In Eupen feiert man Rosenmontag. Eupen ist eine Kleinstadt in Belgien. Hier spricht man Deutsch.

Im Frühling gibt es …

4 „Buskers" Straßenkunstfest
Vaduz ist die Hauptstadt von Liechtenstein, ein kleines Land zwischen der Schweiz und Österreich. Willst du mitmachen?

Im Sommer gibt es …

5 „Kärnten läuft"
Komm mit deinen Sportschuhen und mach mit! „Kärnten läuft" ist für alle Sportfans.

Im Herbst gibt es …

6 Oktoberfest
Dieses Fest in München ist sehr bekannt. Tanzt du gern?

---

a Möchtest du im eiskalten Wasser schwimmen gehen? Im Winter kommen Schwimmer aus Deutschland und aus dem Ausland zum Orankesee. Das Fest dauert einen Tag. Willst du das nächstes Jahr machen?

b Das ist ein Lauffest am Wörthersee in Österreich. Es dauert drei Tage und es gibt Events für sportliche Erwachsene, Kinder und Familien. Nimm deine Sportschuhe mit!

c Das ist ein großes Bierfest in der Hauptstadt von Bayern. Es dauert zwei Wochen und man trägt oft traditionelle Kleidung. Hier isst, trinkt und lacht man viel!

d Das ist der beste Tag in der Karnevalswoche. In dieser deutschsprachigen Stadt feiert man Karneval mit schönen Festwagen. Es gibt viele Musiker. Man kann auch leckeres Essen kaufen.

e Im Dezember feiert man dieses Fest in der deutschsprachigen Welt. Am Morgen finden die Kinder kleine Geschenke in ihren Schuhen!

f Zwei Tage lang gibt es ein wunderbares Fest. Man kann Künstler sehen: Tanz, Musik, Humor, Akrobaten und Tricks. Alles passiert auf der Straße. Hier gibt es auch leckeres Essen und Getränke.

der Fasching	another word for **Karneval** (carnival)
der Festwagen	(carnival) float

Kulturzone Kapitel 3

Lesen 1 Look at the photos and captions (1–6) and read the descriptions of the festivals (a–f). Write the letter of the correct festival for each photo.

Hören 2 Listen and write down in English exactly when each festival takes place. (1–6)

Listen carefully for dates:
- 'on' a date is *am…*
- ordinal numbers up to 19th (**19.**) end in **-ten**; above that, they end in **-sten**:
*am **elften** März*, *am **zwanzigsten** Juli*

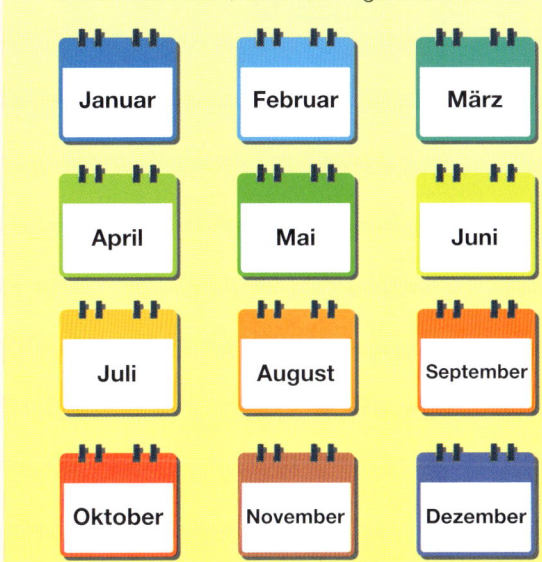

Januar | Februar | März
April | Mai | Juni
Juli | August | September
Oktober | November | Dezember

Lesen 3 Find the German for the phrases below in the descriptions.

1 from abroad
2 the festival lasts for one day
3 bring your trainers
4 you often wear
5 you laugh a lot
6 people celebrate
7 in the German-speaking world
8 you can see artists

Lesen 4 Read the descriptions again and answer the questions.

1 Name <u>three</u> festivals at which you can get something to eat.
2 During which festival do children receive presents?
3 Which <u>two</u> festivals are for sporty people?
4 Which festival lasts two weeks?

Hören 5 Listen (1–5) and write the letter of the festival (a–e) that suits each person best.

a Thüringer Bachwochen
b Blumenfest Röthenbach 
c Granfondo Radsportfest Vaduz 
d Bad Dürkheimer Wurstmarkt 
e Weihnachtsmarkt in Luxemburg 

Hören 6 Listen and check your answers. (1–5)

die Blume (-n) flower

Sprechen 7 In pairs, discuss the festivals in the photos above.

- *Wie findest du den Weihnachtsmarkt in Luxemburg?*
- *Ich finde den Markt schön, weil er interessant ist. Wie findest du das Radsportfest?*
- *Ich finde …*

Ich finde	den Markt das Fest	interessant, toll, schön, bunt, wunderbar, langweilig, teuer, schlecht, laut,	weil	das Spaß macht. das mein Lieblingshobby ist. das (nicht) interessant ist. ich Sport (nicht) mag. ich die Natur (nicht) mag. er/es schön/toll ist. er/es teuer/laut ist. es (zu) viele Leute gibt. das Essen lecker ist.
Meiner Meinung nach ist	der Markt das Fest			

siebenundfünfzig **57**

1 Wie ist deine Familie?

- Describing family members
- Using possessive adjectives
- Using relative pronouns

Hören 1
Listen and read. Write the correct letter to match each description to a family portrait (a–d).

Eleanor
Ich habe einen Bruder und eine Schwester.
Mein Bruder heißt Max. Er hat blaue Augen und ist ziemlich groß.
Meine Schwester Sofie ist ganz klein und hat lange, schwarze Haare.
Wir haben ein braunes Pferd.

Akin
In meiner Familie gibt es meine Eltern und meine drei Brüder.
Meine Brüder heißen Kaya, Ilyas und Devin.
Ilyas ist mittelgroß und ist 10 Jahre alt.
Wir haben eine schwarze Katze. Sie heißt Sascha.

Alex
In meiner Familie gibt es meinen Onkel, meine Tante, meine Cousine, meinen Cousin und meine Väter. Ich bin Einzelkind.
Meine Väter Jonas und Felix haben viele Fische.
Mein Cousin heißt Milan und meine Cousine heißt Helena.
Milan und Helena haben blonde Haare.

Sandra
Ich habe zwei Schwestern.
Mein Stiefvater ist groß und er hat kurze, blonde Haare.
Meine Mutter ist groß und sie hat lange, schwarze Haare.
Wir haben einen Hund. Er heißt Frank und ist sehr lustig.

Lesen 2
Read the texts again and answer the questions in English.

Who …?
1 has a brother called Max
2 has a brother of medium height
3 has cousins with blond hair
4 has a funny dog
5 has fish
6 has a stepdad with blond hair
7 has a black cat
8 has a small sister

Possessive adjectives follow the same pattern as the indefinite article *ein*.
Only the masculine form changes in the accusative.

	nominative (subject)	accusative (object)
masc	mein Fisch	meinen Fisch
fem	meine Oma	meine Oma
neut	mein Pferd	mein Pferd
pl	meine Eltern	meine Eltern

(subject) **Mein** Fisch heißt Otto. **My** fish is called Otto.
Ich finde (object) **meinen** Fisch süß. I find **my** fish sweet.

Page 68

Schreiben 3
Translate the sentences into German.
1 My sister has long, black hair.
2 My brother has brown eyes.
3 My cousin (f) has short, red hair.
4 My dads are very funny.

Hören 4
Listen to Jens, Maria and Mohammed talking about their families.
Select the correct word to complete each statement. (1–6)

1 There are **three / four** people in Jens' family.
2 Jens has no **pets / siblings**.
3 Maria has a **big / small** family.
4 Maria has four **half-sisters / brothers**.
5 Mohammed has two **brothers / mothers**.
6 Mohammed **has black hair / is very tall**.

achtundfünfzig

Kapitel 3

5 In pairs, take turns to read out the sentences. Pay attention to the **u**, **ü** and **y** sounds. Then listen and check.

1 Es gibt keine t**y**pische Familie in Deutschland.
2 Jede Familie ist anders **u**nd das finde ich g**u**t.
3 In meiner Familie z**u**m Beispiel gibt es meine zwei Halbbr**ü**der.
4 In meiner Familie gibt es meinen Stiefvater **u**nd meine M**u**tter.
5 Meine M**u**tter hat gr**ü**ne Haare.
6 Meine beiden M**ü**tter sind sehr l**u**stig.

> The **u** sound can be long or short.
> **ü** and **y** sound similar.
> Listen and repeat the words.
> **u** — Meinung, Mutter, lustig, Bruder, gut
> **ü** and **y** — süß, Brüder, grün, Mütter, typisch

6 Read the text and match the key phrases in **bold** to the English translations.

> Ich wohne mit meinen Eltern und meinen drei Schwestern zusammen. Mein Vater, **der Jens heißt**, ist 43 Jahre alt. Er hat kurze, braune Haare und blaue Augen. Meine Mutter, **die Julia heißt**, ist 41 Jahre alt. Sie hat lange, graue Haare und grüne Augen. Meine Schwester Johanna, **die lange, blonde Haare hat**, ist sehr lustig und freundlich. Meine Schwester Julieta, **die dreizehn Jahre alt ist**, ist immer böse und nie freundlich! Meine kleine Schwester, **die sehr glücklich ist**, heißt Janina. Mein Pferd, **das sehr süß ist**, heißt Kanye.

1 who is 13 years old
2 who is called …
3 who is very sweet
4 who is very happy
5 who has long, blond hair

7 Listen and write down the words you hear to complete the sentences.

1 Mein ___, ___ Sven ___, ist sehr ___.
2 ___ Eltern, ___ ziemlich ___ ___, ___ Julia und Jens.
3 Ich habe ___ ___, ___ schwarz und ___.
4 ___, ___ braune Haare ___, ___.

Relative pronouns (who, which) refer back to someone or something. They send the <u>verb</u> to the end of the clause.

masc	Mein Vater, **der** …	My dad, who …
fem	Meine Mutter, **die** …	My mum, who …
neut	Mein Pferd, **das** …	My horse, which …
pl	Meine Eltern, **die** …	My parents, who …

Page 68

8 Write a description of a famous or fictional family, imagining you are part of this family.

Beschreib deine Familie!
In meiner Familie gibt es meinen (Bruder) / meine (Schwester) / meine (Eltern).

Mein (Bruder), Meine (Schwester),	der … heißt, die … heißt,	hat		lange/kurze braune/rote/blonde/schwarze	Haare.
				blaue/braune/grüne/graue	Augen.
		ist			groß. klein.
Mein (Pferd), Meine (Eltern), Er/Sie/Es ist … Sie sind …	das … heißt, die … heißen,	ist sind	ab und zu manchmal oft immer nie	nicht ziemlich sehr total	lustig. glücklich. sportlich. freundlich. lieb. böse.

neunundfünfzig 59

2 Deine Beziehungen

- Saying how you get on with people and why
- Using pronouns and possessive adjectives in the dative
- Using qualifiers and intensifiers

Schreiben 1 Sort the German adjectives below into two groups: positive or negative. Can you justify your choices?

aktiv böse ehrlich faul freundlich
geduldig gemein glücklich höflich
komisch kreativ laut lustig negativ
nett positiv ruhig sportlich

Intensifiers (*sehr, wirklich*) make an adjective stronger.
Qualifiers (*ziemlich, ganz*) make an adjective less strong.

Hören 2 Listen to and read the online magazine posts about family relationships. Write down the <u>eight</u> missing qualifiers and intensifiers you hear and translate them into English.

Das Familienleben

Hallo Leute!
Die Frage der Woche: Wie verstehst du dich **mit deiner Stieffamilie**? Ohan, Anna, Markus und Beniko haben uns geschrieben.

Ich verstehe mich [1] gut **mit meiner Stiefschwester**. Sie ist ein [2] sportliches Mädchen und wir spielen gern Tennis zusammen. Ich verstehe mich sehr gut **mit ihr**, denn sie ist immer lustig und nie gemein.
— Ohan 

Ich verstehe mich nicht so gut **mit meinem Stiefvater**, denn er ist oft [3] negativ. Ich verstehe mich nicht so gut **mit ihm**, aber er ist [4] geduldig. Er ist nicht so freundlich und ist ab und zu nicht [5] nett, aber er ist nie böse.
— Anna

Ich verstehe mich gar nicht gut **mit meinen Stiefschwestern**. Sie sind nicht nett und nie glücklich, und wir haben nicht dieselben Interessen. Sie gehen mir [6] auf die Nerven.
— Markus

Ich verstehe mich sehr gut **mit meinem Halbbruder**. Ich verstehe mich **mit ihm**, denn er ist [7] positiv und nett. Er kann manchmal [8] laut sein, aber das ist ganz normal, finde ich.
— Beniko

Lesen 3 Read the magazine posts again. Copy and complete the table for Ohan, Anna, Markus and Beniko.

family member(s)	gets on well? Y/N	qualities	other details
Ohan's stepsister			

G Some prepositions, like *mit* (with), are always followed by **dative** pronouns or possessive adjectives.
Ich verstehe mich gut / nicht gut …

mit mein**em** Vater	mit **ihm**
mit mein**er** Schwester	mit **ihr**
mit mein**em** Kind	mit **ihm**
mit mein**en** Eltern	

Page 69

60 sechzig

Kapitel 3

Hören 4 Listen and select the correct option to complete each sentence. (1–6)
1 Elke gets on well with her **parents** / **grandparents**.
2 Axel's sister is too **quiet** / **loud**.
3 Charlotte's grandfather is very **mean** / **nice**.
4 Chivan's stepfather is **patient** / **angry**.
5 Gabi **does** / **doesn't** get on well with her parents.
6 Elias gets on better with his **aunt** / **uncle**.

Sprechen 5 Look at the picture and imagine you are Luna. In pairs, take turns to ask and answer questions.
- *Verstehst du dich gut mit deinem Bruder, Theo?*
- *Ja, ich verstehe mich gut mit meinem Bruder / mit ihm.*
- *Warum?*
- *Er ist total freundlich.*

Bruder: Theo
Vater: Kurt
Ich: Luna
Großvater: Martin
Großmutter: Christel
Mutter: Frida

Hören 6 Listen to Lena talking about her friend Mikel. Answer the questions in English, giving as much detail as you can. (1–3)
1 How does Lena describe her friend?
2 Why does Lena get on well with him?
3 What are Lena and Mikel going to do this evening?

Verstehst du dich gut mit …	**deinem** (Vater/Stiefvater/Opa/Onkel/Bruder)? **deiner** (Mutter/Stiefmutter/Oma/Tante/Schwester)? **deinen** (Eltern/Großeltern)?			
Ja, ich verstehe mich gut mit … Nein, ich verstehe mich nicht gut mit …	**meinem** (Vater) / **ihm**, **meiner** (Mutter) / **ihr**, **meinen** (Eltern),	denn	er/sie ist	ganz (gar) nicht sehr	böse. freundlich. geduldig.
			sie sind	so total wirklich ziemlich zu	gemein. glücklich. laut. lustig. nett.
			er/sie geht mir sie gehen mir	immer nie	auf die Nerven.

Schreiben 7 Write approximately 50 words in German about your friend(s). Include the following points:
- their name and age
- their appearance
- their personality
- why you get on well
- what you like doing together.

Mein Freund heißt (Max). Er ist (fünfzehn) Jahre alt. Er ist (groß) und hat (kurze Haare).
Meine Freundin heißt (Lea). Sie ist (vierzehn) Jahre alt. Sie ist (klein) und hat (blaue Augen).
Er/Sie ist sehr positiv und gar nicht böse.
Ich verstehe mich gut mit ihm/ihr. Er/Sie ist (total freundlich).
Wir fahren gern Fahrrad / spielen gern Fußball / gehen gern ins Kino.

einundsechzig 61

3 Wer ist dir wichtig?

- Discussing people who inspire you
- Using two time frames together: past and present
- Word order with *da* and *weil*

Lesen 1 Read what Simon and Aisha say about people who are important to them and answer the questions below.

Simon

Meine Oma ist Lehrerin und ist total hilfsbereit. Sie ist mir sehr wichtig, da sie immer Zeit für mich hat und sie mich akzeptiert. In ihrer Arbeit hat sie junge Leute immer unterstützt, weil sie das Beste für sie will.

Aisha

Ich brauche andere Leute als Inspiration nicht. Ich habe Stars immer total langweilig gefunden, da sie mich einfach nicht interessieren. Die Persönlichkeiten, die immer in den sozialen Medien posten, haben nichts zu sagen. Ihre Welt ist nicht echt und sie sind nicht wichtig für mich!

Who …?
1 supports people
2 has nothing to say
3 is very helpful
4 feels accepted
5 is not interested in celebrities
6 lives in an artificial world

Hören 2 Listen to Rainer and Sibylle talking about what they think of celebrities. Write down the words you hear to complete the text.

Rainer: Ich habe berühmte Persönlichkeiten oder Stars immer sehr nützlich **1**. Sie **2** mir, man kann erfolgreich **3**, wenn man hart **4**. Zum Beispiel ist Roger Federer so gut, weil er so viel Training **5**.

Sibylle: Ich finde Stars nicht wichtig, da meine Familie viel wichtiger für mich **6**. Mein Opa hat mir jeden Tag **7**, dass berühmt sein gar nicht wichtig ist. Er **8** immer Zeit für mich **9** und er **10** mich und meine Meinungen.

> **G** Use the **present** and past tenses alongside each other to add interest and complexity to your German.
> Er *hat* immer Zeit für mich *gehabt* und er **akzeptiert** mich.
> Page 70

Sprechen 3 In pairs, take turns to read out Rainer and Sybille's texts.

Schreiben 4 Translate the sentences into German, using the texts in exercises 1 and 2 to help you.
1 He accepts me.
2 Famous people don't interest me.
3 My family is much more important to me.
4 She always has time for me.
5 I have always found stars important.
6 She has supported young people.

62 zweiundsechzig

Kapitel 3

Lesen 5 Read the text about the model Claudia Schiffer. Answer the questions in English.

Claudia Schiffer ist im Jahr 1970 in Deutschland geboren. Als sie 17 Jahre alt war, hat man sie in einer Disko in Düsseldorf gesehen und dann ist sie Modell geworden.

Sie war extrem erfolgreich und hat überall auf der ganzen Welt gearbeitet.

Sie ist auch Schauspielerin und Geschäftsfrau. In ihrer Freizeit liebt sie Kunst und sie hat viele Bilder zu Hause.

Sie ist natürlich sehr berühmt und reich, aber sie arbeitet viel mit Organisationen, die gegen Armut arbeiten.

die Armut — poverty

1 Where was Claudia Schiffer discovered?
2 Where has she worked?
3 What <u>two</u> other jobs does she have?
4 What is her hobby?
5 Name <u>two</u> adjectives used to describe her.
6 Who does she work with?

Mein Opa Meine Mutter Meine Familie Meine Freundin Anna	ist mir (nicht) wichtig,	da weil	er sie	(nie) Zeit für mich hat. mich (nicht) akzeptiert. mich (nicht) unterstützt. mich (nicht) versteht. so viel macht. so hart arbeitet.
Berühmte Persönlichkeiten Stars Bekannte Leute	sind mir (nicht) wichtig,	da weil		sie erfolgreich sind. sie mir Inspiration geben. sie hart arbeiten. sie anderen Menschen helfen. sie nicht in der echten Welt leben. ich sie nicht brauche.
Ich finde ihn/sie	geduldig. interessant. kreativ. langweilig.			

Sprechen 6 In pairs, ask and answer questions about someone who is important to you. Use the key language box to help you.

- *Wer ist dir wichtig?*
- *... ist mir wichtig.*
- *Warum?*
- *Weil/Da er/sie ...*

- *Was macht er/sie?*
- *Er/Sie ...*
- *Was hat er/sie gemacht?*
- *Er/Sie hat ...*

Schreiben 7 Translate the sentences into German.
1 My sister Lena is totally important to me.
2 She understands me and she is very patient.
3 Famous people are not important to me because they don't live in the real world.
4 My mum is very important to me because she always supports me.

G Remember that **da** and **weil** send the <u>verb</u> to the end of the sentence or clause.
*Stars sind mir wichtig, **weil** sie mir Inspiration <u>geben</u>.*
*Berühmte Persönlichkeiten sind mir nicht wichtig, **da** ich sie nicht <u>brauche</u>.*

If you want to use the reasons in the key language box without *da* or *weil*, the **verb** needs to be the second idea in the sentence:
*Berühmte Leute sind mir wichtig, **da** sie erfolgreich <u>sind</u>.*
Berühmte Leute <u>sind</u> erfolgreich.

Page 69

dreiundsechzig

4 Wir haben gefeiert!

- Describing a family celebration in the past
- Practising word order
- Using time phrases

Hören 1 Listen to and read the online forum about celebrations. Write down what each person did and where they did it in English.

Walda: Nach den Prüfungen habe ich mit Freundinnen in einem Freizeitpark gefeiert.

Uwe: Am Samstag haben wir eine Party mit Freunden im Garten gemacht, weil mein Bruder einen neuen Job hat.

August: An meinem letzten Geburtstag habe ich mit meiner ganzen Familie im Restaurant gefeiert.

Lise: Am 31. Dezember sind meine Geschwister und ich in die Stadt gegangen. Wir haben dort Silvester gefeiert.

Samira: Letzten Monat hat meine Tante am Strand geheiratet. Wir haben eine Party organisiert.

Milan: Am Samstag bin ich mit meiner Familie und meinem besten Freund ins Kino gegangen. Wir haben den Anfang der Schulferien gefeiert.

Sprechen 2 In pairs, take turns to select a person from exercise 1 and guess who your partner is.
- *Ich habe am Strand gefeiert.*
- *Du bist Samira?*
- *Ja, richtig!*

G Remember the word order rule: **time** (when) – **manner** (how) – **place** (where).

*Ich bin **gestern** **mit dem Bus** **zum Fest** gefahren.*
***Im Juli** haben wir meinen Geburtstag **mit Freunden** **im Restaurant** gefeiert.*

Page 70

Hören 3 Listen to some young people talking about celebrations. Copy and complete the table in English. (1–5)

	when?	with whom?	where?
1			

⭐ Listen carefully for **time phrases**.
- *gestern* — yesterday
- *am Samstag* — on Saturday
- *nach (den Prüfungen)* — after (exams)
- *letzten Monat* — last month
- *dieses Jahr* — this year

Lesen 4 Read Torsten's blog about *Karneval*. Write down the missing phrases from the box. Then listen and check your answers.

Letztes Jahr bin ich **1** **2** **3** zum Karneval in Düsseldorf gegangen. Der Karneval war in der Stadtmitte. **4** **5** haben wir tolle Musik gehört. **6** **7** gab es eine große Party. Die Menschen haben **8** gesungen. **9** **10** haben viele Leute **11** **12** getragen. Das war toll.
Der Karneval hat mir wirklich gut gefallen. Ich habe den ganzen Tag getanzt und wir haben dort viel Spaß gehabt.

G Remember that *geben* can be used as an **impersonal verb** with es.

Present tense:
es gibt there is/are

Imperfect tense:
es gab there was/were

lustige Kleidung   Am Morgen   mit meinen Eltern
Am Abend   laut   Am Nachmittag

64 vierundsechzig

Kapitel 3

Hören 5
Listen and write down the missing words and phrases you hear to complete the sentences.

1. Am Montag ▭ wir zusammen im Restaurant ▭.
2. Letztes Jahr ▭ Elke zum Karneval ▭.
3. Gestern ▭ wir mit der Bahn zum Musikfest ▭.
4. Am Abend ▭ die Stimmung wirklich spannend.

> **Time phrases** can give you a clue about the <u>tense</u> of a sentence:
>
> **Gestern** <u>haben</u> wir <u>gefeiert</u>.   **Yesterday** we <u>celebrated</u>.
>
> Remember that the <u>verb</u> still stays in second position.

| *die Stimmung* | atmosphere |

Sprechen 6
In pairs, take turns to ask and answer the questions about a celebration.

- *Wie hast du gefeiert?*
- *<u>Letzte Woche</u> bin ich … gegangen.*
- *Wann war das?*
- *Das war <u>am Montag</u>.*
- *Was hast du gemacht?*
- *Ich habe <u>gesungen</u>.*
- *Was hast du gegessen und getrunken?*
- *Ich habe … gegessen und … getrunken.*
- *Wie war es?*
- *Das war <u>toll</u>.*

Wer feiert was?

1	Ein Jude / eine Jüdin		a Weihnachten
2	Ein(e) Sikh		b Diwali
3	Ein Christ / eine Christin	feiert	c Eid al-Fitr
4	Ein Muslim / eine Muslimin		d Chanukka
5	Ein(e) Hindu		e Hola Mohalla

Schreiben 7
Write approximately 90 words in German about a celebration in the past. Include the following points:

- when it was and who you were with
- what you did or saw
- what you thought of it.

Gestern Am Wochenende Letzte Woche Letzten Monat Letztes Jahr In den Ferien Im Winter/Sommer Nach den Prüfungen	habe ich haben wir	meinen Geburtstag Karneval Silvester Diwali Vesakh Chanukka Eid al-Fitr Weihnachten/Ostern	gefeiert.
	hat mein Bruder/Onkel/Cousin hat meine Schwester/Tante/Cousine		geheiratet.

Ich habe Wir haben	mit Freunden mit meiner Familie zu Hause in der Stadt in einem Restaurant	gefeiert. eine Party gemacht. (viel) gelacht/gesungen. (viel) gegessen/getrunken. (viel) Spaß gehabt. (viel) getanzt.
	nette Leute	kennengelernt.
Ich bin Wir sind	(zu Fuß) ins Kino (mit dem Bus) zum Fest (mit dem Zug) zur Party	gegangen. gefahren.
Es war	toll/lustig/spannend/langweilig/schlecht.	

fünfundsechzig **65**

5 Partyzeit!

- Discussing a party
- Using two time frames: past and future
- Using *in* + accusative or dative

Hören 1 Listen to and read the statements about birthdays. Match each activity to a picture (a–h). Then read the statements again and decide whether the activity is happening in the past (P) or the future (F).

1. Letzten Sommer habe ich eine Party für meine Tante organisiert.
2. Das Wetter war ziemlich schön und wir sind den ganzen Abend im Garten geblieben.
3. Wir haben viel gesungen und getanzt.
4. An meinem nächsten Geburtstag werde ich mit vier Freunden ins Kino gehen.
5. Danach werden wir in einem Restaurant essen.
6. Wir werden auch einen Kuchen essen.
7. Dann werde ich nach Hause fahren.
8. Zu Hause werde ich Musik hören.

Sprechen 2 Read out the sentences in exercise 1. Pay attention to the *v*, *w* and *z* sounds.

In German, the letters **v**, **w** and **z** are pronounced differently from English.

Listen and repeat the words.
- **v** like English 'f'   **v**iel
- **w** like English 'v'   **w**ir
- **z** like English 'ts'   **z**u

Hören 3 Listen to some people talking about celebrations. Copy and complete the table in English. (1–6)

	past or future?	type of celebration
1		

Schreiben 4 Translate the sentences into German.

1. Last week, we saw a comedy at the cinema.
2. That was fun.
3. After that we went home.
4. Next summer, I will organise a party for my friends.
5. We will eat a big cake.
6. We will sing, dance and laugh.

The **verb** is always the **second idea** in a German sentence (not necessarily the second word).
An meinem Geburtstag **werde** *ich feiern.*
   first idea   **second idea**

To add interest and complexity to your German, use the **past** and **future tenses** in your work.

Past	Future
Ich **habe** eine Party **organisiert**.	Ich **werde** eine Party **organisieren**.
Wir **haben gesungen**, **getanzt** und **gelacht**.	Wir **werden singen**, **tanzen** und **lachen**.
Wir **haben** Kuchen **gegessen**.	Wir **werden** Kuchen **essen**.
Das **hat** viel Spaß **gemacht**.	Das **wird** viel Spaß **machen**.
Ich **bin** in die Stadt **gegangen**.	Ich **werde** in die Stadt **gehen**.
Wir **sind** ins Kino **gegangen**.	Wir **werden** ins Kino **gehen**.
Es **gab** viele Menschen dort.	Es **wird** viele Menschen dort **geben**.
Es **war** toll.	Es **wird** toll **sein**.

Page 71

66 sechsundsechzig

Kapitel 3

Lesen 5 Read Julian's post on an online forum and translate the coloured phrases into English.

Im Juli haben wir nach den Prüfungen eine Party **in der Schule** gehabt. Die Party war **in der Sporthalle** und das war wirklich wunderbar. Wir haben viel Spaß gehabt. Es gab Spiele, Musik und Sport. **Im Klassenzimmer** haben wir die Wände dekoriert. Danach sind wir **in den Park** gegangen und haben ein Picknick gegessen. Das war ein wunderbarer Tag und ich werde das nie vergessen.

In den Sommerferien werden wir **ins Kino** oder **ins Sportzentrum** gehen. Ich glaube, **im Sportzentrum** wird es besser sein, denn Sport macht Spaß. Ich möchte auch **in die Stadtmitte** gehen, denn ich möchte kleine Geschenke für meine Freunde kaufen. Das wird toll sein!

dekorieren to decorate

Lesen 6 Read the text again and answer the questions in English.
1. What type of party did Julian attend?
2. Where did the party take place?
3. What was there to do?
4. What does Julian say about the day?
5. Where does he want to go in the summer?
6. What would Julian also like to do?

G

Some prepositions such as *in* can be followed by either the accusative or the dative case, depending on whether movement is involved.

		masc	fem	neut	pl
accusative case (indicating movement)	ich gehe	in **den** Park	in **die** Stadt	in **das** Kino	in **die** Gärten
dative case (indicating position)	ich bin	in **dem** Park	in **der** Stadt	in **dem** Kino	in **den** Gärten

in dem is often abbreviated to *im*.
in das is often abbreviated to *ins*.

Page 71

Sprechen 7 In pairs, take turns to ask and answer the questions about celebrations in the past and future.
- *Was hast du an Silvester gemacht?*
- *Ich bin in die Stadt gefahren und ich habe getanzt und gesungen.*
- *Was wirst du an deinem Geburtstag machen?*
- *Ich werde mit meinen Freunden im Restaurant essen.*

Ich bin	am (Diwali-/Vesakh-)Fest	zum Fest	gegangen.
Ich habe	am Karneval	mit meiner Familie	gefeiert.
	an Chanukka/Eid al-Fitr	viel	getanzt/gesungen.
	zu Weihnachten	im Restaurant	essen/trinken.
Ich werde	an meinem Geburtstag	ins Kino	gehen.
	im Sommer/Winter	eine Party	organisieren.

siebenundsechzig

Grammatik 1

Possessive adjectives (Unit 1, page 58)

1 Write down the correct possessive adjective (*mein*, *meine* or *meinen*) to complete the sentences.

1 Hallo, ich bin Michaela und **meine** Familie ist ganz klein. (nominative)
2 ___ Onkel Klaus wohnt in Wien und ich sehe ihn nicht sehr oft. (nominative)
3 Aber ich sehe ___ Onkel Max wenigstens dreimal im Jahr, weil er in Bern wohnt. (accusative)
4 ___ Tanten wohnen in Vaduz. (nominative)
5 ___ Bruder ist ___ bester Freund. (nominative)
6 Aber ___ ältere Schwester ist sehr oft faul. (nominative)
7 Tiere habe ich auch. Ich mag ___ Pferd, Hund und ___ Fische. (accusative)

	masc	fem	neut	pl
nominative (subject)	mein	meine	mein	meine
accusative (object)	mein**en**	meine	mein	meine

nom: *Mein Bruder ist sportlich.*
acc: *Ich treffe meinen Bruder.*

These possessive adjectives also follow the same pattern:
dein (your – familiar, sg), **sein** (his), **ihr** (her), **unser** (our), **eu(e)r** (your – familiar, pl), **Ihr** (your – formal), **ihr** (their)

💡 Remember that the endings must agree with the noun that follows.

2 Copy and complete the sentences with the correct possessive adjectives.

1 **Sein** (*his*) Vater (*m*) ist ziemlich jung.
2 ___ (*her*) Pferd (*nt*) ist süß.
3 Ich finde ___ (*their*) Pferd (*nt*) noch süßer.
4 ___ (*my*) Geburtstag (*m*) war einfach toll.
5 ___ (*her*) Eltern (*pl*) sind sportlich.
6 Ich finde ___ (*our*) Eltern (*pl*) sehr freundlich.
7 Ich treffe ___ (*your, familiar, sg*) Freunde (*pl*) oft im Park.
8 ___ (*your, familiar, sg*) Freund (*m*) spielt gern Fußball.

Relative pronouns (Unit 1, page 59)

3 Select the correct relative pronoun to complete each sentence. Then translate the sentences into English.

1 Mein Onkel, **der / die / das** Bruno heißt, schwimmt nicht gern.
2 Seine Schwester, **der / die / das** gern Musik hört, heißt Layla.
3 Meine Freundin, **der / die / das** 14 ist, ist sehr nett.
4 Sie hat Freunde, **der / die / das** sehr sportlich sind.
5 Diese Party, **der / die / das** in Köln ist, ist sehr groß.
6 Ihr (*your*) Bruder, **der / die / das** Bernd heißt, ist sehr ernst.

	masc	fem	neut	pl
nom	der	die	das	die
acc	den	die	das	die

Relative pronouns must be used in the same case as the noun to which they refer.

Subject (nom): *Dein Vater, **der** Jan heißt, ist sehr freundlich.* (here, **der** – referring back to **dein Vater** – is the subject of the relative clause)

Object (acc): *Dein Vater, **den** ich gut kenne, ist sehr freundlich.* (here, **ich** is the subject and **den** is the object of the relative clause)

4 Read out these sentences. Then decide whether each relative pronoun is in the nominative (**N**) or accusative (**A**) case.

1 Es gibt viele Leute, <u>die</u> auf der Straße tanzen.
2 Das Geschenk, <u>das</u> du mir gibst, ist toll.
3 Der Karneval, <u>den</u> wir besuchen, ist in Mainz.
4 Wir sprechen nicht mit Menschen, <u>die</u> wir nicht kennen.
5 Mein Pferd, <u>das</u> ich liebe, ist weiß.
6 Die Party, <u>die</u> im Park war, war toll.

68 achtundsechzig

Pronouns and possessive adjectives in the dative case (Unit 2, page 60)

5 Copy and complete the sentences with the correct form of *meinem, meiner* or *meinen*.

1 Letztes Jahr bin ich mit ▨meinen▨ Eltern (pl) nach Österreich gefahren.
2 Ich gehe immer mit ▨▨ Schwester (f) ins Kino.
3 Ich gehe gern mit ▨▨ Pferd (nt) wandern.
4 Ich verstehe mich gut mit ▨▨ Bruder (m).
5 Ich gehe oft mit ▨▨ Freundinnen (pl) aus.
6 Ich verstehe mich gut mit ▨▨ Mutter (f), mit ▨▨ Vater (m) und auch mit ▨▨ Großeltern (pl).

	masc	fem	neut	pl
nominative (subject)	mein	meine	mein	meine
dative (indirect object)	mein**em**	mein**er**	mein**em**	mein**en**

6 Listen. Copy and complete the sentences with the correct family member and dative pronoun. (1–6)

1 Meine ▨Stiefschwester▨ ist so freundlich! Ich verstehe mich gut mit ▨ihr▨.
2 Meine ▨▨ ist immer sehr lieb. Ich verstehe mich sehr gut mit ▨▨.
3 Meine ▨▨ ist aber zu ernst. Ich verstehe mich nicht so gut mit ▨▨.
4 Mein ▨▨ ist auch lustig. Ich verstehe mich ziemlich gut mit ▨▨.
5 Mein ▨▨ ist so laut. Ich verstehe mich nicht so gut mit ▨▨.
6 Du bist mein bester ▨▨! Ich verstehe mich wirklich gut mit ▨▨!

nominative	accusative	dative
ich	mich	**mir**
du	dich	**dir**
er	ihn	**ihm**
sie	sie	**ihr**
es	es	**ihm**

Remember that **mit** is followed by the dative.
Sie geht mit **mir**. She goes with me.
Wir sprechen mit **ihm**. We speak with him.

ihm   Bruder
ihr   ~~Stiefschwester~~
ihr   Mutter
dir   Cousin
~~ihr~~   Freund
ihm   Oma

da and *weil* (Unit 3, page 63)

7 Put the words in the correct order to make sentences.

1 Stars interessieren mich nicht,   sind   langweilig   sie   weil
2 Berühmte Leute sind mir nützlich,   eine Inspiration   da   sind   sie
3 Meine Oma ist mir wichtig,   immer   für mich   sie   hat   Zeit   weil
4 Mein Bruder ist erfolgreich,   arbeitet   weil   jeden Tag   er   hart

💡 Remember that *da* and *weil* send the verb to the end.

neunundsechzig **69**

Grammatik 2

Using two time frames: past and present (Unit 3, page 62)

1 Sort the sentences into the correct time frames (past or present). Copy and complete the table. Then read out the sentences.

1. Früher hatte er schwarze Haare.
2. Er hat viel Sport gemacht.
3. Ich habe ein Kleid getragen.
4. Jetzt hat er grüne Haare.
5. Berühmte Leute sind mir eine Inspiration.
6. Er macht keinen Sport.
7. Ich trage eine rote Hose.
8. Es gab nicht viele Stars.

past	present
1, …	

2 Listen and write down the verbs you hear to complete each sentence.

1. Bekannte Leute *sind* mir eine Inspiration.
2. Meine Oma ___ mich und meine Meinungen.
3. Letztes Wochenende ___ ich meinen Geburtstag ___.
4. Letzten Samstag ___ ich eine Party ___.
5. Gestern ___ meine Schwester sehr müde.
6. Am Wochenende ___ ich in die Stadt ___.

> 💡 Look at any time phrases to help you anticipate which tense you are likely to hear.

3 Copy and complete the sentences with the correct tense of the verb in brackets.

1. Heute *feiern* wir meinen Geburtstag. (*feiern*)
2. Heute ___ mir berühmte Stars sehr wichtig. (*sein*)
3. Früher ___ meine Schwester eine Brille ___. (*tragen*)
4. Normalerweise ___ ich nicht gern auf Partys. (*gehen*)
5. Als Kind ___ Julia viele Geschenke ___. (*bekommen*)
6. Letzte Woche ___ wir auf eine Party ___. (*gehen*)

> 💡 Remember that in the perfect tense:
> - verbs involving movement or a change of state take **sein**:
>   Ich **bin** auf eine Party gegangen.
> - not all **past participles** are regular:
>   gehen → Ich bin **gegangen**.
>   tragen → Ich habe **getragen**.
>   bekommen → Ich habe **bekommen**.

Word order: time – manner – place (Unit 4, page 64)

4 Put the words in the correct order to make sentences, starting with the words in bold.

1. war   sehr   aktiv   Max   **Als** Kind   zu Hause
2. gut   verstehe   mich   **Ich**   mit meiner Schwester   normalerweise
3. **Ich**   mit meiner Familie   im Restaurant   feiere
4. bin   zur Party   gefahren   **Ich**   mit dem Bus
5. **Wir**   im Garten   im Sommer   gefeiert   haben   zusammen
6. zum Karneval   jedes Jahr   **Ich**   mit meinem Freund   gehe

Kapitel 3

Using two time frames: past and future (Unit 5, page 66)

Schreiben 5 Copy and complete the sentences with the correct verbs in the perfect, imperfect and future tenses.
1 Letzte Woche `hatte` er braune Haare, aber nächste Woche `wird` er grüne Haare `haben`. (haben)
2 Früher haben wir das nicht ___, aber nächstes Jahr werden wir das ___. (feiern)
3 Gestern sind wir zur Party ___, aber morgen ___ wir ins Kino gehen. (gehen)
4 Letztes Jahr haben wir im Restaurant ___, aber nächstes Jahr werden wir zu Hause ___. (essen)
5 Gestern ___ ich Musik ___, aber morgen ___ ich Computerspiele ___. (hören, spielen)
6 Gestern ___ es eine Party im Garten, aber morgen ___ wir zu Hause ___. (geben, bleiben)

Sprechen 6 In pairs, take turns to read out the questions in the perfect tense and fill in the gaps to change them to the future tense.
1 Was hast du an Silvester gemacht? — Was `wirst` du an Silvester `machen`?
2 Wie hast du deinen letzten Geburtstag gefeiert? — Wie ___ du deinen nächsten Geburtstag ___?
3 Was für Geschenke hast du bekommen? — Was für Geschenke ___ du ___?
4 Was hast du letztes Jahr im Kino gesehen? — Was ___ du dieses Jahr im Kino ___?
5 Was hast du auf der Party gegessen und getrunken? — Was ___ du auf der Party ___ und ___?
6 Wohin bist du am Wochenende mit deiner Familie gegangen? — Wohin ___ du am Wochenende mit deiner Familie ___?

in + accusative or dative (Unit 5, page 67)

Hören 7 Listen. Copy and complete the sentences with *in* + the article in the accusative or dative case.
1 Ich fahre `in die` Stadt (f).
2 Ich kaufe Geschenke ___ Stadtmitte (f).
3 Ich möchte ___ Café (nt) gehen.
4 Sie ist ___ Museum (nt).
5 Er hat das ___ Internet (nt) gekauft.
6 Ich spiele ___ Park (m) Fußball.
7 Ich treffe sie ___ Restaurant (nt).
8 Ich gehe ___ Kino (nt).

	masc	fem	neut	pl
accusative	in den	in die	in das	in die
dative	in dem	in der	in dem	in den

in + das → ins
in + dem → im

Remember to use the accusative when there is movement involved and the dative when there is no movement.

Hören 8 Listen and write down the sentences you hear. (1–4)

Los geht's!

Schreiben 9 Translate the sentences into German.
1 I get on very well with my brother, who is very friendly.
2 I go to the cinema with my friend every weekend.
3 Last week we went to the park, but tomorrow we will go into town.
4 Before, my mother was very angry, but now she is always funny.

> Remember *mit* is followed by the dative.
> Think about word order here.
> Make sure you use the right tense with each time phrase.

einundsiebzig 71

Kapitel 3 Lese- und Hörtest

Reading

Lesen 1 *Family.* Some German students are discussing their families. What do they say? For each person, write **P** for a **positive** opinion, **N** for a **negative** opinion or **P + N** for a **positive and negative** opinion.

Samira
Ich habe einen Stiefbruder, der elf Jahre alt ist. Er ist meistens nett und lieb, aber er geht mir manchmal auf die Nerven.

Murat
Ich verstehe mich gar nicht gut mit meiner Schwester. Sie ist wirklich zu laut und ist immer böse.

Katja
Meine Mütter verstehen mich und unterstützen mich immer.

Jakob
Mein Opa ist mir sehr wichtig, weil er immer Zeit für mich hat. Ich verstehe mich sehr gut mit ihm.

Lesen 2 *A festival.* You read Lili's blog about a festival she went to.

Lili
Gestern sind meine ganze Familie und ich zu einem Fest in Köln gegangen. Das Fest war am Marktplatz im Stadtzentrum und dort gab es so viele Leute! Ich habe lustige Kleidung getragen, und alle haben gesungen und viel getanzt. Am Abend gab es auch eine große Party.

Das Fest war bunt und spannend und hat viel Spaß gemacht. Es gab viel zu essen und ich habe traditionelle **Kekse** gekauft, die sehr lecker waren.

1 Answer the following questions **in English**.
 (i) Where was the festival? (Give **two** details.)
 (ii) What did Lili do at the festival? (Give **two** details.)
2 Read the final sentence again. What would you do with **Kekse**?
 A watch them **B** wear them **C** eat them

> Use the context of the text and the surrounding language to help you work out what the unknown word might mean.

72 *zweiundsiebzig*

Lesen 3

Translate these sentences into English.

Pay attention to subjects of the verbs, to help you translate accurately.

Make sure you translate all the 'little' words that can easily be overlooked.

Look carefully at verbs to help you identify the correct tense.

1 Seine Schwester heißt Nadia.
2 Ihr Stiefvater, der Thomas heißt, ist sehr sportlich.
3 Meine Freunde und meine Familie sind mir wichtig.
4 Ich gehe jedes Wochenende mit meinem Halbbruder ins Kino.
5 Letztes Wochenende haben wir Weihnachten gefeiert.

Think about grammatical constructions you have learned, to help you with meaning.

Make your translations sound natural in English – don't be afraid to change the word order if necessary.

Listening

Hören 4

Best friends. Kirstin is talking about her best friend, Lara. What does she say? Listen to the recording and write **A**, **B** or **C** to complete each sentence.

1 Lara …
   A is an only child.   B has a sister.   C has a brother.
2 Lara has …
   A green eyes.   B blue eyes.   C long, blonde hair.
3 Lara is …
   A angry.   B patient.   C happy.
4 Kirstin and Lara …
   A go shopping together.   B do sport together.   C like watching films.

Remember that in this type of task, any of the answer options could be mentioned in the recording. Listen carefully for words like negatives which can change the meaning of a sentence.

Dictation

Hören 5

You will hear four short sentences. Write down exactly what you hear in German.

There will be some words in the dictation task that are not on the vocabulary list, but don't panic: use your knowledge of sound–spelling links to help you transcribe these words accurately.

Think carefully about how these sounds are pronounced, when writing down what you hear:
v, w, z
u, ü, y

Kapitel 3 — Mündlicher Test

Role-play

1 Look at the role-play card and prepare what you are going to say.

> You are talking about friends and relationships with a German friend.
> 1. Say what sort of person you are. (Give **one** detail.)
> 2. Say how often you see your friends.
> 3. Say **one** activity you like doing with your best friend.
> 4. Say **one** thing about your best friend.
> 5. ? Ask your friend a question about their birthday.

Remember that your answer needs to include a verb. A time phrase on its own is not enough to score full marks for this question.

Keep your answers short and simple: you only need to give one detail each time.

Use a verb + *gern*.

You could ask the date or ask how they celebrate.

2 Practise what you have prepared. Then, using your notes, listen and respond to the teacher.

3 Listen to Alex's answers. Make a note of:
   a how he answers the questions for points 1–4
   b what question he asks for point 5.

Reading aloud

4 Look at this task. With a partner, read the sentences aloud, paying attention to the underlined letters.

> Ich liebe Feiertage.
>
> Wir essen zu viel Kuchen.
>
> Wir singen, tanzen und spielen zusammen.
>
> Meine Familie ist sehr lustig und eine Party für Freunde macht uns ganz glücklich.
>
> Ich bekomme wunderbare Geschenke zu meinem Geburtstag.

Think carefully about how to pronounce these sounds:
v, w, z
u, ü

5 Listen and check your pronunciation.

6 Listen to the teacher asking four follow-up questions. Translate each question into English and prepare your own answer to each one. Then listen again and respond to the teacher.

74 *vierundsiebzig*

Photo card

7 Listen to Alex describing the photos and put the nouns (a–h) in the order in which they are mentioned.

- **a** cake
- **b** dresses
- **c** girl
- **d** brother
- **e** hair
- **f** grandmother
- **g** party
- **h** birthday

> You will be asked to talk about the content of these photos. You must say at least one thing about each photo.
>
> After you have spoken about the content of the photos, you will be asked questions related to any of the topics within the theme of **Popular culture**.
>
> Your responses should be as **full and detailed** as possible.

8 Prepare your own description of the photos. Then, with a partner, take turns describing them.

Auf dem ersten Foto gibt es …

9 Listen to the teacher's first follow-up question, *Wie möchtest du nach den Prüfungen feiern?* and Alex's response. Write down the six missing infinitives to complete the text.

> Ich möchte zuerst mit meiner Familie **1** . Wir werden eine kleine Party im Garten **2** und meine Großeltern werden auch **3** . Am Abend werde ich mit meinen Freunden in der Schule feiern. Wir werden Musik **4** und viel **5** . Das wird wunderbar **6** .

10 The teacher then asks Alex, *Wie feierst du normalerweise deinen Geburtstag?* Listen to his response and answer the questions.

1. What is the date of his birthday?
2. What is the weather often like?
3. Who does he go into town with?
4. What does he like buying?

11 Listen to two more follow-up questions and prepare your answers. Then respond to the recording. Make your answers as full as possible, including opinions and reasons.

> Listen carefully to the questions and make sure you answer in the correct tense. Which tense does each question use in exercises 9 and 10?

12 Prepare your own answers to as many of the Module 3 questions on page 226 as you can. Then practise with a partner.

fünfundsiebzig **75**

Kapitel 3 Schreibtest

Describing a photo

Schreiben 1 Look at this writing exam task. Unjumble the verbs in **bold** to complete Jenna's responses.

1 Es **sti** eine Hochzeit.
2 Es **bitg** eine Frau und einen Mann.
3 Die Frau **ägtrt** ein Kleid.
4 Sie **cehllän**.
5 Sie **nisd** im Garten.

Schreiben 2 Prepare your own answer to the task.

> Use language that you know best. You could say where the people are and what they are doing, what they are wearing and what they look like. Don't forget to write full sentences, each containing a verb.

You see this photo on Instagram.

What is in the photo?

Write **five** sentences in **German**.

Translation

Lesen 3 Read the English sentences and reorder the words in Jenna's German translations.

1 I have a brother who is tall.
2 My brothers go to the cinema every week.
3 I would like to celebrate my birthday at home.
4 She is a football player, and she is very successful.
5 Yesterday I went to the party by bus.

1 einen Bruder, ist Ich groß der habe.
2 Brüder gehen Meine ins Kino jede Woche.
3 feiern zu Hause möchte meinen Geburtstag Ich.
4 sehr ist Sie Fußballspielerin und erfolgreich ist sie.
5 dem mit gefahren ich zur Gestern Feier Bus bin.

Schreiben 4 Translate these sentences into German.

> A relative pronoun must agree with the person or thing it refers to.

> Remember that the verb must be in second position after a time phrase at the start of a sentence.

1 I have a sister who is 11 years old.
2 At the weekend my grandmother cooks.
3 I would like to see the Christmas market.
4 He is a tennis player and he is very well known.
5 Last week I bought a present for my stepmother.

> Modal verbs send the second verb to the end, in the infinitive form.

> Which tense do you need here?

90-word writing task

Schreiben 5 Look at this writing exam task and then for each bullet point:
1. think about vocabulary and structures to use:
   - **nouns**, **verbs** and **adjectives** to write about festivals and the **name** of a festival you might choose
   - language for **narrating a story** about how you celebrated
   - how to explain what you **will do** and **why**.
2. write down three or four ideas for what you could write about.
3. identify which tense(s) you could use in your answer.
4. make a list of verbs, connectives, intensifiers and sequencing words you would like to use.

> You are writing to your friend about celebrations.
>
> Write approximately **90** words in **German**.
>
> You must write something about each bullet point.
>
> Describe:
> - your favourite celebration or festival
> - what you did to celebrate a birthday recently
> - how you will celebrate the end of your exams.

Lesen 6 Read Jenna's response to the exam task. Answer the questions in the coloured boxes (1–5).

1 Jenna uses a **variety of nouns**. What do these words mean?

2 Which connective could you use here to form an **extended sentence**?

> Ich feiere gern meinen Geburtstag. Ich liebe viele Geschenke. Ich glaube, dass sie toll sind.
>
> Partys machen mir keinen Spaß, weil sie zu langweilig sind. Es gibt immer viele Menschen. Das mag ich gar nicht.
>
> Meine Freundin, die Petra heißt, ist sehr nett und sie ist sehr sportlich. Zu ihrem Geburtstag sind wir schwimmen gegangen. Dann gab es ein Fußballspiel im Park, aber wir haben nicht gewonnen!
>
> Nach den Prüfungen werden wir Fahrrad fahren und dann gibt es eine Party im Park – das wird toll sein.

3 This is an example of **complex language**. What does it mean? Find two more examples of complex language in the text.

4 Which **tense** is this? When is it used?

5 To **avoid repetition**, which synonyms or alternative words could Jenna use?

Schreiben 7 Prepare your own response to the task.
- Think about how you can develop your answer for each bullet point.
- Look back at your notes from exercises 5 and 6.
- Use the 'Challenge checklist' and consider how you can show off your German!
- Write a **brief** plan and organise your answer into paragraphs.
- Write your answer and then check your work carefully.

Challenge checklist

🥨	✓ *ich* + conjugated verb in the present ✓ A verb and a simple adjective (*es ist gut*)
🥨🥨	✓ different persons of the verb (*meine Eltern, mein Bruder*) ✓ More varied opinions and verbs (*ich denke, ich glaube*) ✓ A wider range of interesting vocabulary (*zu, manchmal, böse*) ✓ More varied conjunctions (*weil, dass*)
🥨🥨🥨	✓ Relative pronouns (*meine Freundin, die Petra heißt*) ✓ Dative possessives (*mit meiner Familie, mit meinem Freund*) ✓ Past and future tenses (*wir haben gefeiert, ich werde zum Fest gehen*)

siebenundsiebzig 77

Kapitel 3 Wörter

Key:
bold = this word will appear in higher exams only
* = this word is not on the vocabulary list but you may use it in your own sentences

Feste in der deutschsprachigen Welt (pages 56–57):

Feste	Festivals/celebrations
Ich finde …	I find/think …
den (Weihnachts)markt	the (Christmas) market
Meiner Meinung nach ist …	In my opinion … is
(der) **Karneval**	carnival
(der) Markt	market
(das) Fest	festival, celebration
der Weihnachtsmarkt	the Christmas market
das *Radsportfest	the cycling festival
das *Blumenfest	the flower festival
interessant, …	interesting
langweilig, …	boring
laut, …	loud
schlecht, …	bad
schön, …	beautiful

teuer, …	expensive
toll, …	great, amazing
weil …	because …
das Spaß macht.	it's fun.
das mein Lieblingshobby ist.	it's my favourite hobby.
das (nicht) interessant ist.	it's (not) interesting.
ich … (nicht) mag.	I (don't) like …
es (zu) viele Leute gibt.	there are (too) many people.
das Essen lecker ist.	the food is delicious.
weil er/es … ist.	because it is …
laut	loud/noisy.
schön	lovely/beautiful.
teuer	expensive.
toll	great/amazing.

Wie ist deine Familie? (pages 58–59):

Familie	Family
Beschreib deine Familie!	Describe your family!
In meiner Familie gibt es …	In my family, there are my …
meinen (Halb)bruder.	my (half-)brother.
meinen Onkel.	my uncle.
meinen Opa.	my grandpa.
meinen Hund.	my dog.
meine (Stief)schwester.	my (step-)sister.
meine Tante.	my aunt.
meine Oma.	my grandma.
meine Katze.	my cat.
meine Eltern/Geschwister.	my parents/siblings.
Ich bin Einzelkind.	I am an only child.
Mein/Meine …, der/die/das … heißt,	My …, who is called …,
hat … Haare/Augen.	has … hair/eyes.
blaue	blue
*blonde	blond(e)
braune	brown
graue	grey
grüne	green
kurze	short

lange	long
rote	red
schwarze	black
ist …	is …
groß	big/tall
klein	small
ab und zu	now and again
immer	always
manchmal	sometimes
nie	never
oft	often
sehr	very
total	completely
ziemlich	rather
böse	angry
freundlich	friendly
glücklich	happy
lieb	kind
lustig	funny
sportlich	sporty

Deine Beziehungen (pages 60–61):

Beziehungen	Relationships
Verstehst du dich gut mit … ?	Do you get on well with …?
deinem (Vater)	your (father)
deiner (Tante)	your (aunt)
deinen (Großeltern)	your (grandparents)
Ja, ich verstehe mich gut mit …	Yes, I get on well with …
meinem (Onkel) / ihm, denn er ist …	my (uncle) / him, because he is …
meiner (Stiefmutter) / ihr, denn sie ist …	my (stepmother) / her, because she is …
meinen (Eltern), denn sie sind …	my (parents), because they are …
aktiv	active
böse	angry
ehrlich	honest
faul	lazy

freundlich	friendly
geduldig	patient
gemein	mean
glücklich	happy
höflich	polite
komisch	funny, strange
kreativ	creative
laut	loud
lustig	funny
negativ	negative
nett	nice
positiv	positive
ruhig	quiet
sportlich	sporty
Er/Sie geht / Sie gehen mir auf die Nerven.	He/She gets / They get on my nerves.

achtundsiebzig

Kapitel 3

Wer ist dir wichtig? (pages 62–63):

Wer ist dir wichtig?	Who is important to you?
Mein/Meine ... ist mir (nicht) wichtig, da/weil ...	My ... is (not) important to me because ...
er/sie (nie) Zeit für mich hat.	he/she (never) has time for me.
er/sie mich akzeptiert.	he/she accepts me.
er/sie mich unterstützt.	he/she supports me.
er/sie mich versteht.	he/she understands me.
er/sie so viel gemacht hat.	he/she has done so much.
Berühmte Persönlichkeiten ...	Famous personalities ...
Stars ...	Stars ...
Bekannte Leute ...	Well-known people ...
sind mir (nicht) wichtig, da/weil ...	are (not) important to me because ...
sie erfolgreich sind.	they are successful.
sie mir *Inspiration geben.	they give me inspiration.
sie hart arbeiten.	they work hard.
sie anderen Menschen helfen.	they help other people.
sie nicht in der echten Welt leben.	they don't live in the real world.
ich sie nicht brauche.	I don't need them.
Ich finde ihn/sie ...	I find him/her ...
geduldig	patient
interessant	interesting
kreativ	creative
langweilig	boring
nützlich	useful

Wir haben gefeiert! (pages 64–65):

Feste	Festivals/celebrations
Wie hast du gefeiert?	How did you celebrate?
Wann war das?	When was that?
Was hast du gemacht?	What did you do?
Was hast du gegessen und getrunken?	What did you eat and drink?
Wie war es?	How was it?
Gestern	Yesterday
Am Wochenende	At the weekend
Letzte Woche	Last week
Letztes Jahr	Last year
In den Ferien	In the holidays
Im Winter/Sommer	In winter/summer
Nach den Prüfungen	After the exams
habe ich ... / haben wir ... gefeiert.	I/we celebrated ...
meinen Geburtstag	my birthday
*Chanukka	Hanukkah
*Diwali	Diwali
*Eid al-Fitr	Eid al-Fitr
*Hola Mohalla	Hola Mohalla
Karneval	Carnival
Ostern	Easter
Silvester	New Year's Eve
*Vesakh	Vesakh
Weihnachten	Christmas
der Christ / die Christin	Christian
der/die Hindu	Hindu
der Jude / die Jüdin	Jew
der Muslim / die Muslimin	Muslim
der/die *Sikh	Sikh
Ich habe ... / Wir haben ...	I/We ...
mit Freunden / mit meiner Familie / im Restaurant ...	with friends / with my family / in a restaurant.
eine Party gemacht	had a party
gefeiert	celebrated
(viel) gelacht	laughed (a lot)
gesungen	sang
getanzt	danced
(viel) gegessen	ate (a lot)
getrunken	drank
nette Leute kennengelernt	got to know nice/kind people
(viel) Spaß gehabt	had (lots of) fun
Ich bin ... / Wir sind ... gefahren/gegangen.	I/We went ...
mit dem Bus / mit dem Zug / zu Fuß	by bus / by train / on foot.
ins Kino	to the cinema.
zum Fest / zur Party	to the festival/party.

Partyzeit! (pages 66–67):

Partys	Parties
der Geburtstag	birthday
der Kuchen	cake
der Sommer	summer
die Musik	music
die Party	party
das Fest	festival
das Kino	cinema
die Ferien	holidays
das Silvester	New Year's Eve
das Weihnachten	Christmas
essen	eat
feiern	celebrate
lachen	laugh
organisieren	organise
planen	plan
singen	sing
Spaß haben	have fun
tanzen	dance
danach	afterwards
letzt...	last
nächst...	next
Was hast du (an Silvester) gemacht?	What did you do (on New Year's Eve)?
Ich habe ...	I ...
gefeiert	celebrated
getanzt	danced
gesungen	sang
Ich bin ... gegangen.	I went ...
Was wirst du (an deinem Geburtstag) machen?	What will you do (on your birthday)?
Ich werde ...	I will ...
essen	eat
trinken	drink
gehen	go
organisieren	organise

neunundsiebzig 79

Kapitel 4 Bleib gesund!

Ich liebe Sport
- Learning about favourite sports in the German-speaking world
- Using comparative adjectives and adverbs

A Weißt du was?

Fahrradfahren

Schwimmen

Wandern

Skifahren

1. In der Schweiz macht man gern Sport: Wandern (56,9%), Fahrradfahren (42%), Schwimmen (38,6%) und Skifahren (34,9%).

2. In Österreich fahren 38% der Österreicher oft Fahrrad, und in Deutschland gibt es fast so viele Fahrräder wie Menschen!

3. Schwimmen im Freibad ist in Österreich beliebter als Schwimmen im Hallenbad: es gibt über 300 Freibäder.

4. In der Schweiz machen 59% der Jugendlichen (15 bis 24 Jahre alt) mehr als drei Stunden pro Woche Sport.

5. Deutschland ist eine sehr große Ski-Nation – 38% der Deutschen machen gerne Wintersport.

6. Die Schweiz hat 38 Berge, die höher als 4 000m sind.

das Freibad (¨er)	outdoor swimming pool
das Hallenbad (¨er)	indoor swimming pool

B

1 Aïsha

Welchen Sport machst du oft?

Ich gehe gern laufen und ich spiele einmal pro Woche Tennis.

Was ist dein Lieblingssport?

<u>Mein Lieblingssport ist Fußball, aber im Winter gehe ich lieber Ski fahren.</u> Ich finde Skifahren spannender als Tennis.

2 Mia

Welchen Sport machst du oft?

Ich mache jede Woche Fitnesstraining und ich spiele auch gern Basketball.

Und welchen Sport machst du nicht so gern?

Ich gehe nicht gern wandern, weil es meistens langweilig ist. <u>Ich finde Schwimmen viel interessanter als Wandern!</u>

3 Leon

Welchen Sport machst du oft?

Ich mache normalerweise viel Sport. Ich spiele zweimal pro Woche Fußball und am Wochenende fahre ich oft mit meiner Familie Fahrrad.

Was war deine beste Leistung?

Ich bin letztes Jahr 65km mit dem Fahrrad gefahren! <u>Es war toll und ich möchte das öfter machen.</u> Ich finde Fahrradfahren besser als Fußball.

80 achtzig

Kulturzone — Kapitel 4

Lesen 1 Read the article (A). Copy and complete the sentences.
1. The most popular sport in Switzerland is …
2. In Germany, there are almost as many … as people.
3. In Austria, there are over 300 …
4. In Switzerland, most … do more than three hours of sport per week.
5. 38% of Germans like to do …
6. 38 mountains in Switzerland are … than 4,000 metres.

Hören 2 Listen to and read the interviews with Aïsha, Mia and Leon (B). Translate the underlined sentences into English.

Lesen 3 Find six comparative adjectives in texts A and B on page 80.
Example: beliebter

Hören 4 Listen and write down the sentences you hear. (1–4)

Schreiben 5 Translate the sentences into German.
1. Germany is bigger than Austria.
2. I find swimming more interesting than hiking.
3. The mountains in Switzerland are higher than in Germany.
4. Football is more popular in Germany than in Switzerland.
5. Switzerland is smaller than Germany.
6. I find football more boring than tennis.

> ⭐ To translate 'more …' into German, add **-er** to the adjective.
>
> Remember that some comparatives are irregular. Think about whether these adjectives also add an umlaut in the comparative:
> interessant   klein   beliebt
> langweilig   hoch   groß

Sprechen 6 In pairs, take turns to ask and answer the following questions. Pay attention to the **schw** sound.
- Welchen Sport machst du oft?
- Was ist dein Lieblingssport?
- Welchen Sport machst du nicht so gern?
- Welchen Sport findest du besser: Fahrradfahren oder Tennis?

Schreiben 7 Write down your answers to exercise 6, adding more information where possible.

G The **comparative** is used to **compare** two things: just add **-er** to the adjective and use **als** to mean 'than'.

| klein small | klein**er** small**er** |
| beliebt popular | beliebt**er** **more** popular |

*Die Schweiz ist klein**er als** Österreich.*
Switzerland is smaller **than** Austria.

Fußball ist beliebter als Handball.
Football is more popular **than** handball.

The comparative is sometimes translated as 'more …' in English, but this is never the case in German.

Some adjectives are **irregular**:
gut – **besser**   good – **better**
hoch – **höher**   high – **higher**

One-syllable adjectives often add an umlaut:
groß – **größer**   tall/big – **taller/bigger**
nah – **näher**   near – **nearer**
oft – **öfter**   often – **more often**

Page 92

Ski is pronounced like the English 'she'.
Skifahren can also be spelled **Schi**fahren.
The letter combination **schw** is pronounced like 'shv'.
Listen and repeat the sentence.
*Die **Schw**eizer gehen gern **schw**immen, aber sie fahren lieber **Ski**.*

Remember that **sp** and **st** sound like 'shp' and 'sht'.

---

	spiele		Fußball. Tennis. Basketball.
Ich	mache	oft ab und zu nie	Fitnesstraining. Sport.
	fahre		Fahrrad. Ski.
	gehe		laufen. schwimmen. wandern.

Mein Lieblingssport ist …, aber ich … auch gern …
Ich … nicht gern …, weil …
Ich finde … besser als …

einundachtzig 81

1 Willst du fit und gesund sein?

- Talking about healthy lifestyles
- Revising modal verbs
- Practising a role-play about health and fitness

Hören 1 Listen to and read the blog posts. Then answer the questions below.

Sophia

Meine Gesundheit ist sehr wichtig für mich. **Ich will später Profi-Fußballspielerin werden** und deshalb **soll ich immer gesund essen**: wenig Zucker, aber viel Obst und Gemüse. Ich gehe jeden Tag ins Fitness-Studio, denn **ich will in Form sein**, und ich trinke keinen Alkohol.

Florian

Gesund leben ist schwer für mich. Ich trinke nicht gern Wasser und ich esse regelmäßig Fastfood. Meine Freunde treiben viel Sport, denn **sie wollen fit bleiben**. Ich bin aber oft müde und habe keine Energie. Ich habe immer das Gefühl, dass mein Körper so schwach ist.

Marlene

Einige Freunde trinken viel Alkohol (Wein, Bier und so weiter) und rauchen E-Zigaretten. Sie denken, dass es Spaß macht, wenn sie betrunken sind, aber das finde ich blöd. Manchmal nehmen sie auch Drogen, aber **das will ich nie machen**, weil ich es gefährlich und ungesund finde.

die E-Zigarette — vape

1. Why does Sophia eat healthily?
2. What does Sophia **not** do?
3. Why is it difficult for Florian to live healthily? (Give two reasons.)
4. What do Florian's friends do?
5. What do Marlene's friends sometimes do?
6. What does Marlene think of that? (Give two details.)

Lesen 2 Translate the phrases in **bold** in exercise 1 into English.

> **G** Remember that **modal verbs** are usually used with another verb in the infinitive form at the end of the sentence.
>
> Ich **will** fit bleiben.   I **want** to keep fit.
> Sie **sollen** gesund essen.   They **should** eat healthily.
>
> Page 92

Schreiben 3 Translate these sentences into German.

Remember to use *gern* after the verb.

Use *nie* after the modal verb.

1. We do lots of sport every day.
2. I like to eat fast-food.
3. My sister never wants to take drugs.
4. I should not drink alcohol because it is unhealthy.

Modal verbs need another verb at the end of the clause, in the infinitive form.

weil sends the verb to the end of the clause.

Kapitel 4

Hören 4 Listen to Aisha and Fred talking about what is healthy or unhealthy about their lifestyle. Copy and complete the table in English with <u>two</u> details for each box.

	healthy	unhealthy
Aisha		
Fred		

G *mögen* (to like) is a modal verb, but it is not always used with an infinitive. It is most commonly used with a noun.

	mögen
ich	mag
du	magst
er/sie/es/man	mag
wir	mögen
ihr	mögt
Sie	mögen
sie	mögen

Ich mag Wasser. I like water.

Remember, to say you like doing something, use *gern* after the verb.

Ich trinke gern Wasser.
I like drinking water.

Page 93

Lesen 5 Read Detlev's blog post and select the <u>three</u> correct statements.

Ich trinke mindestens zwei Liter Wasser pro Tag. Ich mag Obst und ich esse auch viel Gemüse mit Hähnchen. Ich glaube auch, wir sollen keinen Alkohol trinken, weil das sehr schlecht für die Gesundheit ist.

Ich habe einige Freunde, die ab und zu auf Partys rauchen und das finde ich ungesund. Ich muss aber sagen, dass ich nicht genug schlafe und abends viel zu lange am Computer spiele.
Detlev

1 Detlev drinks plenty of water.
2 He doesn't like fruit.
3 He drinks alcohol.
4 His friends sometimes smoke at parties.
5 He gets plenty of sleep.
6 He spends too much time playing on the computer.

Hören 6 Listen to the role-play and write down in English the answers you hear.

You are talking to your Austrian friend. You should address your friend as *du*.
- *Wie bleibst du gesund?*
- Say how you stay healthy.
- *Wie bleibst du fit?*
- Say **one** activity you do to keep fit.
- *Was machst du, das ungesund ist?*
- Say something you do which is unhealthy.
- *Wie findest du Fastfood?*
- Give **one** opinion about fast food.
- *Ich auch!*
- Ask a question about smoking.
- *Ich finde Rauchen blöd.*

Wie bleibst du gesund?
Wie bleibst du fit?
Was machst du, das ungesund ist?

Ich	esse		Obst und Gemüse. Fastfood.
	trinke	viel jeden Tag (sehr) oft jede Woche regelmäßig immer nie (nicht) genug	Wasser. Alkohol.
	gehe		schwimmen. laufen. ins Fitness-Studio.
	treibe		Sport.
	spiele		Tennis. Fußball. Basketball.

Wie findest du Fastfood/Rauchen?

| Ich finde | Rauchen | sehr ziemlich total nicht | blöd. gefährlich. lecker. ungesund. |
| | Fastfood | | |

Sprechen 7 Prepare your own answers using the key language box and practise with a partner.

dreiundachtzig 83

2 Es geht mir nicht gut

- Talking about accidents and illnesses
- Using modal verbs in the imperfect tense
- Using *vor*

Hören 1 Listen to the problems and write the letters (a–k) for the parts of the body mentioned. (1–8)

There are several ways of forming plural nouns in German:

singular	plural
der Kopf	die K**ö**pf**e**
der Fuß	die F**ü**ß**e**
die Hand	die H**ä**nd**e**
das Bein	die Bein**e**
der Arm	die Arm**e**
das Auge	die Auge**n**
das Ohr	die Ohr**en**

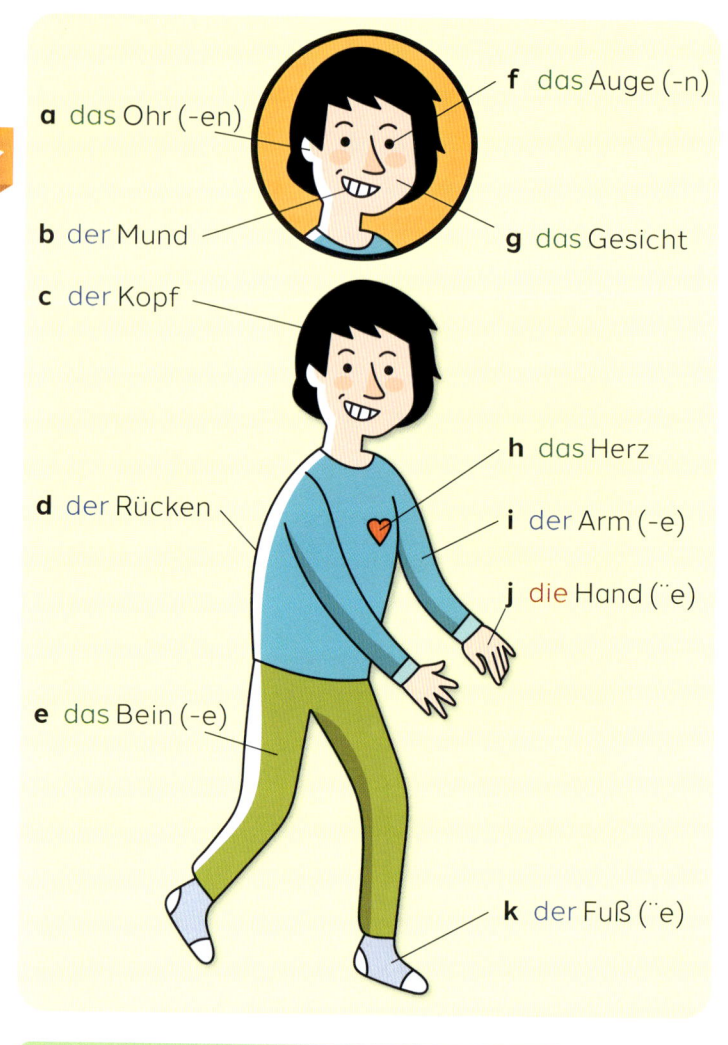

a das Ohr (-en)
b der Mund
c der Kopf
d der Rücken
e das Bein (-e)
f das Auge (-n)
g das Gesicht
h das Herz
i der Arm (-e)
j die Hand (¨e)
k der Fuß (¨e)

Schreiben 2 Select <u>six</u> body parts from exercise 1 and write sentences describing what's wrong.

Sprechen 3 In pairs, create dialogues. Take turns to read out a question, point to a part of the body and respond.

- *Wie geht es dir?*
- *Ich habe <u>Kopfschmerzen</u>.*

Wie geht es dir?	Es geht mir nicht gut. Es geht mir schlecht.
Was ist los?	Ich habe (Kopf)schmerzen. Ich habe mir (den Arm) verletzt. Ich habe mir (das Bein) gebrochen.

Use **vor** to mean 'ago' in German. The <u>time phrase</u> which follows needs to be in the dative case.

masc: Ich habe **vor** <u>ein**em** Monat</u> Tennis gespielt.
fem: Ich bin **vor** <u>ein**er** Woche</u> gefallen.
neut: Ich bin **vor** <u>ein**em** Jahr</u> Fahrrad gefahren.
pl: Ich bin **vor** <u>zwei Woch**en**</u> wandern gegangen.

Page 93

Lesen 4 Read the forum posts and find the German for the time phrases below.

a) Vor einem Monat habe ich Fußball gespielt und habe mir den Fuß verletzt. <u>Ich musste drei Tage zu Hause bleiben.</u>

b) Ich war vor einer Woche im Fitness-Studio und habe mir einen Muskel im Arm verletzt. <u>Ich wollte heute Basketball spielen, aber das konnte ich nicht.</u>

c) Gestern bin ich schwimmen gegangen und jetzt habe ich Ohrenschmerzen. <u>Ich konnte heute Morgen nichts hören</u>!

d) Vor einem Jahr war ich in Österreich und ich habe Wintersport gemacht. <u>Ich durfte nicht Ski fahren</u>, weil ich Rückenschmerzen hatte.

e) Wir sind vor drei Wochen auf eine Party gegangen und die Musik war zu laut. Danach hatte ich Kopfschmerzen und <u>ich musste viel schlafen</u>.

f) Ich bin vor zwei Wochen Fahrrad gefahren. Ich bin gefallen und habe mir das Bein verletzt.

1 two weeks ago
2 one month ago
3 one week ago
4 three weeks ago
5 yesterday
6 one year ago

84 *vierundachtzig*

5 Translate the underlined sentences in exercise 4 into English.

6 Translate the sentences into German.
1. Three weeks ago, I played basketball.
2. A week ago, I did sport.
3. I had to stay at home.
4. A month ago, I couldn't drink anything.

Kapitel 4

G

Modal verbs in the **imperfect tense** have these endings.

können (can, be able to)	**dürfen** (may, be allowed to)	**müssen** (must, have to)	**wollen** (want to)
ich konn**te**	ich durf**te**	ich muss**te**	ich woll**te**
du konn**test**	du durf**test**	du muss**test**	du woll**test**
er/sie/es/man konn**te**	er/sie/es/man durf**te**	er/sie/es/man muss**te**	er/sie/es/man woll**te**

Ich konnte (nicht) schlafen. — I was (not) able to / could (not) sleep.
Du durftest (nicht) Fußball spielen. — You were (not) allowed to play football.
Er musste zu Hause bleiben. — He had to stay at home.
Sie musste nicht zu Hause bleiben. — She didn't have to stay at home.
Ich wollte schwimmen gehen. — I wanted to go swimming.

Page 94

---

7 Listen (1–4). Copy and complete the table in English.

	invitation to ...	problem	when did it happen
1			

The German letter **s** at the beginning of a word or before a vowel is pronounced like the English 'z'. Listen and repeat the words.

Ge**s**icht   zu Hau**s**e   **s**ehr   **s**ind   **S**ie

8 Look at the role-play card and write your own responses using the key language box.

You are talking to your German friend.
You should address your friend as *du*.
- *Hallo! Wie geht's?*
- ■ Say you are ill/unwell.
- *Was ist los?*
- ■ Say what's wrong.
- *Wie ist das passiert?*
- ■ Say how it happened.
- *Wann ist das passiert?*
- ■ Say when it happened.
- *Das tut mir leid.*
- ■ Ask how your friend is.
- *Es geht mir gut, danke!*

Wie geht's dir?	Mir geht's gut. Mir geht es nicht gut. Ich bin krank.
Was ist los?	Ich habe …schmerzen. Ich habe mir … gebrochen/verletzt.
Wie ist das passiert?	Das ist im Fitness-Studio passiert. Ich bin schwimmen gegangen. Ich bin auf ein lautes Konzert gegangen. Ich habe zu viel am Computer gespielt.
Wann ist das passiert?	Gestern. Am Wochenende. Vor zwei Wochen / einem Monat.

9 In pairs, take turns to practise the role-play, giving your own answers.

fünfundachtzig 85

3 Was möchte ich verbessern?

- Talking about good and bad habits
- Revising present, past and future tenses
- Pronouncing umlauts

Lesen 1 Read the problems (1–5) and match them to the correct photos (a–e). Then translate the verbs in **bold**.

1 Ich **verbringe** zu viel Zeit auf meinem Handy.
2 Ich **bin** nicht aktiv und gar nicht fit.
3 Ich **esse** ungesund.
4 Ich **schlafe** nicht genug.
5 Ich **sehe** zu viel **fern**.

Lesen 2 Match the problems from exercise 1 to the solutions below.

a Ich werde mehr Sport machen.
b Ich werde mehr Obst und Gemüse essen.
c Ich werde mir weniger lange Filme ansehen.
d Ich werde mein Handy weniger benutzen.
e Ich werde früher ins Bett gehen.

> **G** Remember that the **future tense** is formed using a part of **werden** + the infinitive.
>
> Ich **werde** mehr Obst essen.
> **Wirst** du weniger fernsehen?
> Er **wird** viel Wasser trinken.
> Wir **werden** mehr Sport machen.
>
> Page 94

Hören 3 Listen. Copy and complete the table. (1–4)

	problem	solution
1		

Sprechen 4 In pairs, take turns to ask and answer the questions below.

- Was ist das Problem?
- Ich mache nicht genug Sport.
- Was wirst du machen?
- Ich werde mehr Sport machen.

Was ist das Problem?			
Ich	esse / trinke / mache	zu viel / nicht genug	Fastfood/Obst/Gemüse. Kaffee/Wasser. Sport.
Was wirst du machen?			
Ich	werde	mehr / weniger	Fastfood/Obst/Gemüse essen. Kaffee/Wasser trinken. Sport machen.

86 sechsundachtzig

Kapitel 4

Hören 5 Listen to and read Frieda's diary entry describing her problems and the solutions she has found. Answer the questions in English.

1 What was the problem on Monday night?
2 What did Frieda order on Tuesday?
3 How did Frieda eat on Wednesday?
4 What did Frieda do on Thursday afternoon?
5 What effect did this have on Frieda on Thursday night?
6 How does Frieda describe herself in the final sentence?

er/sie fand es … he/she found it …

Liebes Tagebuch!

Letzte Woche war ganz schwierig für mich – ich hatte viele Probleme. Ich habe Montagnacht nicht genug geschlafen. Ich habe zu spät ferngesehen. Am Dienstag sind wir ins Restaurant gegangen und ich habe nicht gesund gegessen – ich habe viele Pommes bestellt.

Jetzt ist mein Leben aber total anders! Ich habe am Mittwoch mein Handy weniger benutzt und ich habe gesünder gegessen (und kein Fastfood bestellt!). Am Donnerstag bin ich am Nachmittag mit meinem Bruder wandern gegangen. Wir sind 10km gegangen – mein Bruder fand es schwierig. Danach bin ich früher ins Bett gegangen und ich habe Donnerstagnacht besser geschlafen. Ich bin jetzt auch viel fitter!

Frieda

G Remember that the **perfect tense** is formed with **haben** or **sein** and the past participle.

Ich habe Musik gehört.
Ich bin gewandert.

You will need to learn irregular past participles:
essen (to eat)   *Ich habe Pommes gegessen.*
trinken (to drink)   *Sie hat mehr Wasser getrunken.*
verbringen (to spend time) *Er hat weniger Zeit auf dem Handy verbracht.*
besuchen (to visit)   *Wir haben den Arzt besucht.*

How many examples of past participles can you find in the text?

Page 95

Hören 6 Listen to and read the sentences. Write down if they are in the past (Pa), present (Pr) or future (F) tense. Then translate the sentences into English.

1 Ich werde nächsten Samstag Zeit mit Freunden verbringen.
2 Ich gehe nicht zu spät ins Bett.
3 Ich habe früher viele Bücher gelesen.
4 Ich esse öfter Obst und Gemüse.
5 Ich werde dieses Jahr mein Leben verändern.
6 Ich bin jeden Abend joggen gegangen.

present	past	future
Ich **mache** nicht viel Sport.	Ich **habe** nicht viel Sport **gemacht**.	Ich **werde** mehr Sport **machen**.
Ich **benutze** mein Handy zu viel.	Ich **habe** mein Handy zu viel **benutzt**.	Ich **werde** mein Handy weniger **benutzen**.
Ich **verbringe** zu viel Zeit auf dem Handy.	Ich **habe** zu viel Zeit auf dem Handy **verbracht**.	Ich **werde** weniger Zeit auf dem Handy **verbringen**.
Ich **esse** ungesund.	Ich **habe** ungesund **gegessen**.	Ich **werde** gesünder **essen**.
Ich **schlafe** nicht genug.	Ich **habe** nicht genug **geschlafen**.	Ich **werde** mehr **schlafen**.
Ich **gehe** zu spät ins Bett.	Ich **bin** zu spät ins Bett **gegangen**.	Ich **werde** früher ins Bett **gehen**.
Ich **bin** nicht aktiv.	Ich **bin** nicht aktiv **gewesen**.	Ich **werde** aktiver **sein**.

Sprechen 7 Read out the sentences in exercise 6, paying attention to the sounds with umlauts. Then translate them into English.

Remember that an umlaut acts as a 'sound changer'. In German, only **a**, **o** and **u** can have an umlaut. Listen and repeat the words.

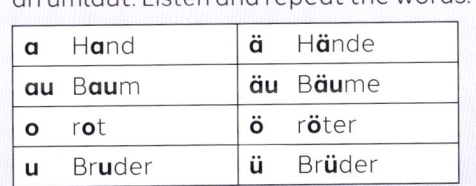

a	Hand	ä	Hände
au	Baum	äu	Bäume
o	rot	ö	röter
u	Bruder	ü	Brüder

Schreiben 8 Write two paragraphs describing:
• a problem you had in the past and how it is better now
• a problem you have now and how it will be better in the future.

siebenundachtzig **87**

4 Gute Tage, schlechte Tage

- Talking about wellbeing
- Using *wenn*
- Pronouncing *-ig* at the end of words

Lesen 1 Read the sentences and decide if they are positive (P) or negative (N). Then translate the sentences into English.

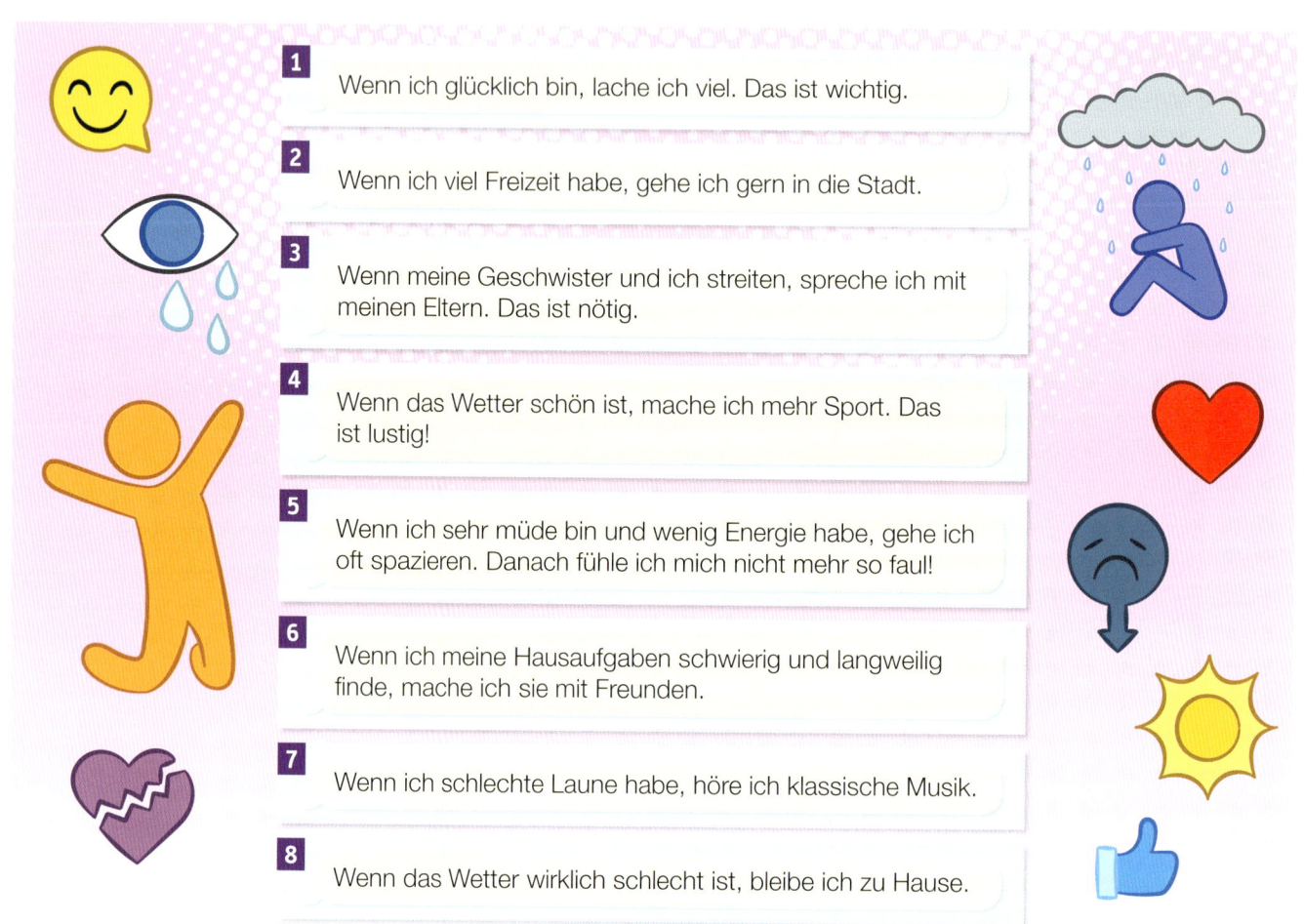

1. Wenn ich glücklich bin, lache ich viel. Das ist wichtig.
2. Wenn ich viel Freizeit habe, gehe ich gern in die Stadt.
3. Wenn meine Geschwister und ich streiten, spreche ich mit meinen Eltern. Das ist nötig.
4. Wenn das Wetter schön ist, mache ich mehr Sport. Das ist lustig!
5. Wenn ich sehr müde bin und wenig Energie habe, gehe ich oft spazieren. Danach fühle ich mich nicht mehr so faul!
6. Wenn ich meine Hausaufgaben schwierig und langweilig finde, mache ich sie mit Freunden.
7. Wenn ich schlechte Laune habe, höre ich klassische Musik.
8. Wenn das Wetter wirklich schlecht ist, bleibe ich zu Hause.

Sprechen 2 Read out the sentences in exercise 1. Pay attention to the *-ig* sounds. Then listen and check.

> **G** The conjunction **wenn** can mean 'when', 'whenever' or 'if', and is used to express what you do in certain situations. Note the **verb-comma-verb** structure:
>
> **Wenn** ich nicht glücklich **bin**, **spreche** ich mit Freunden.
> **When** I **am** not happy, I **speak** to friends.
>
> Page 95

Hören 3 Listen. Copy and complete the table in English. (1–6)

	problem	advice	
		when ...	I ...
1	exam tomorrow	I am in a bad mood	listen to music

The letter combination **-ig** at the end of a word is pronounced like the German word **ich** (meaning 'I').

Listen and repeat the words.
langweil**ig**   wicht**ig**   schwier**ig**
wen**ig**   zwanz**ig**   bill**ig**

88 *achtundachtzig*

Lesen 4 Read the forum posts, then answer the questions below with the correct name.

Was macht dich glücklich?

Matteo Wenn ich draußen in der Natur bin, bin ich sehr froh. Ich mag die frische Luft, die Pflanzen und die Bäume. Ich gehe entweder mit meinem Hund oder allein spazieren und das kann wirklich ruhig sein.

Johanna Manchmal gibt es Streit in meiner Familie, denn meine Eltern sind ziemlich streng, aber wenn ich mit Freunden zusammen bin, kann ich alles vergessen. Also, wenn ich traurig bin, rufe ich sie an und wir gehen zusammen in die Stadt. Wir haben viel Spaß miteinander und das macht mich glücklich.

Yusuf Nach einer schwierigen Woche in der Schule habe ich oft wenig Energie. Ich treibe gern Sport, aber das kann ich einfach nicht. Also gehe ich ins Kino und ich sehe mir einen lustigen Film an. Wenn ich lache, geht es mir besser.

Alina Wenn ich schlechte Laune habe, schlafe ich nicht so gut und wenn ich nicht gut schlafe, bin ich oft traurig. Früher habe ich oft einen Film auf meinem Handy im Bett gesehen, aber das blaue Licht kann ein Problem sein. Wenn ich abends ein Buch lese, schlafe ich besser. Dann bin ich morgens viel glücklicher.

Who ...?
1 feels better when they are laughing
2 has had a problem with sleep
3 is happy when they are outside
4 finds watching a film helps them
5 calls their friends when they are sad
6 finds going on a walk peaceful

Schreiben 5 Translate the following sentences into German using the key language box.
1 When I have little energy, I talk to friends.
2 When the weather is very bad, I go to bed earlier.
3 When I am in a bad mood, I do sport.
4 When I have too much homework, I talk to my teacher.
5 When I am not very happy, I go for a walk.
6 When I have an exam, I revise with friends.

Wenn	ich	nicht sehr glücklich / ganz traurig	bin,	spreche ich mit meinem Lehrer / meiner Lehrerin.
		schlechte Laune / nicht genug Freizeit / zu viele Hausaufgaben / wenig Energie / eine Prüfung	habe,	rede ich mit Freunden. / lerne ich mit Freunden. / mache ich Sport. / gehe ich spazieren. / gehe ich früher ins Bett.
	das Wetter	gut/schlecht	ist,	

Sprechen 6 In pairs, take turns to ask and answer the questions below.
- *Was machst du, wenn du müde bist?*
- *Wenn ich müde bin, ...*
- *Was machst du, wenn du viel Freizeit hast?*
- *Wenn ich viel Freizeit habe, ...*
- *Was machst du, wenn du schlechte Laune hast?*
- *Wenn ich schlechte Laune habe, ...*
- *Was machst du, wenn das Wetter schön ist?*
- *Wenn das Wetter schön ist, ...*

Remember that these sentences need to follow the **verb–comma–verb** rule.

Kapitel 4

neunundachtzig 89

5 Das finde ich wichtig!

- Talking about what is important to you
- Understanding questions in different tenses
- Writing about lifestyle and wellbeing

Lesen 1 Read the questions. Write down whether they are in the past (Pa), present (Pr) or future (F) tense.

1 Bist du normalerweise glücklich?
2 Wirst du heute Sport machen?
3 Hast du letzte Woche gesund gegessen?
4 Hattest du gestern schlechte Laune?
5 Welchen Sport hast du letztes Wochenende gemacht?
6 Was machst du, wenn du traurig bist?
7 Was wirst du in der Zukunft für deine Gesundheit machen?
8 Was ist für dich wichtig im Leben?

Noah

Lesen 2 Read the statements. Match the answers to the questions from exercise 1.

a Nein, ich werde keine Zeit haben.
b Meine Hobbys und meine Familie sind für mich besonders wichtig.
c Nein, ich habe letzten Freitag Pizza und Pommes gegessen.
d Ja! Ich bin fast nie traurig und ich weine selten.
e Ja! Ich hatte eine Prüfung in der Schule und sie war schwierig.
f In der Zukunft werde ich mehr Sport machen.
g Letzten Samstag habe ich Basketball gespielt.
h Wenn ich traurig bin, simse ich meinem besten Freund.

Hören 3 Listen to the interview with Noah and check your answers to exercise 2. Write down <u>one</u> additional detail he gives in response to each question in English. (1–8)

Lesen 4 Select <u>six</u> ideas from the four boxes. Copy and complete the pyramid, putting the ideas in order of importance to you, with the most important at the top of the pyramid.

Gesundheit
- oft Sport machen
- gesundes Essen
- genug schlafen
- sich bewegen

Freizeit
- Sport
- Spaß
- Spiel

Andere Leute
- Familie
- Freunde
- andere Leute akzeptieren
- einen Partner finden

Karriere
- Geld
- Erfolg
- anderen Menschen helfen
- eine gute Arbeit
- mit anderen Menschen zusammenarbeiten

Hören 5 Listen to the teenagers discussing what is important to them. Copy and complete the table in English. (1–4)

	important	not important
1		

90 neunzig

Kapitel 4

Sprechen 6 In pairs, take turns to say what is important and not important to you. Use the key language box below to help you.

- *Was ist dir wichtig?*
- *Meine Freunde sind mir sehr wichtig.*
- *Und was ist dir nicht wichtig?*
- *Die Schule ist mir nicht wichtig!*

Für mich Mir	ist	Erfolg eine gute Arbeit/Karriere meine Familie Sport Musik die Schule das Geld meine Gesundheit	sehr ziemlich total extrem auch nicht genauso	wichtig.
	sind	meine Freunde/Freundinnen meine Hobbys		
Anderen Menschen helfen Mit anderen Menschen zusammenarbeiten Genug schlafen Gute Laune haben Glücklich sein	ist	für mich mir		

Lesen 7 Read what Samira says is important to her in life. Answer the questions in English.

1 What does Samira do when she's not happy?
2 How often does she do sport?
3 What did she do last week for her health?
4 Why does she want to be a teacher?
5 What is <u>not</u> important to her?

Lesen 8 Read the blog again and find the German for the phrases below.

1 I would just like to be happy.
2 My health is also important to me.
3 I also sleep for eight hours every night.
4 In the future, I will find a good job.

Schreiben 9 Write approximately 90 words about lifestyle and wellbeing. You must write something about each bullet point:

- what is important to you in life, with reasons
- activities you have done recently to stay happy and healthy
- what you will do in the future to improve your wellbeing.

Was ist für dich wichtig im Leben?

Für mich sind meine Familie und meine Freunde sehr wichtig. Wenn ich nicht glücklich bin oder schlechte Laune habe, spreche ich mit meinen Eltern.

Wie wichtig ist dir deine Gesundheit?
Meine Gesundheit ist mir auch wichtig. Ich esse nicht oft Fastfood und ich mache zwei Stunden pro Woche Sport. Ich schlafe auch jede Nacht acht Stunden.

Samira

Was hast du letzte Woche für deine Gesundheit gemacht?
Ich habe Basketball gespielt und ich bin laufen gegangen. Ich habe auch viel Obst und Gemüse gegessen.

Was wirst du in der Zukunft machen?
In der Zukunft werde ich eine gute Arbeit finden. Ich möchte Lehrerin werden, denn ich will anderen Menschen helfen. Geld ist mir nicht wichtig – ich möchte nur glücklich sein.

Think carefully about the tenses you need to use to write about each bullet point. For the third bullet point, you can use the future tense or the present tense with a future time phrase. Try to include opinions and reasons to extend your writing.

einundneunzig 91

Grammatik 1

Comparatives (Culture, page 81)

Lesen 1 Read the comparative sentences and translate the underlined words into English.
1 Ich finde Tennis <u>interessanter als</u> Wandern.
2 Fahrradfahren ist <u>beliebter als</u> Laufen.
3 Der Snowdon ist <u>schöner als</u> der Ben Nevis.
4 Fahrradfahren ist in Deutschland <u>wichtiger als</u> Skifahren.
5 Ich mache <u>öfter als</u> meine Schwester Sport.
6 Tennis ist <u>einfacher als</u> Basketball.

Hören 2 Listen and write down the comparative adjectives you hear.
1 Fußball ist *interessanter* als Wandern.
2 Fahrradfahren ist ___ als Spazierengehen.
3 Mein Bruder findet Schwimmen ___ als Basketball.
4 Ich finde Tennis ___ als Fußball.
5 Findest du Sport ___ als Lesen?
6 Dieses Eis ist ___ als der Kuchen!

Schreiben 3 Copy and complete the table with the correct forms of the irregular adjectives.

1 kalt (*cold*)	kälter (*colder*)
2 (*warm*)	wärmer (*warmer*)
jung (*young*)	**3** (*younger*)
4 (*old*)	älter (*older*)
gut (*good*)	**5** (*better*)
6 (*short*)	kürzer (*shorter*)
lang (*long*)	**7** (*longer*)
8 (*high*)	höher (*higher*)
stark (*strong*)	**9** (*stronger*)
10 (*weak*)	schwächer (*weaker*)
groß (*big/tall*)	**11** (*bigger/taller*)

> These adjectives also add an umlaut:
> lang – l**ä**nger   long – longer
> hoch – h**ö**her   high – higher
> oft – **ö**fter   often – more often
>
> To say something is the **same as** something else, use **(genau)so … wie**:
> *Fahrradfahren ist **(genau)so** beliebt **wie** Wandern.*
> *Cycling is **(just) as** popular **as** hiking.*
>
> German **adjectives** can be used as **adverbs** without changing their form.
>
> *Er spricht **gut** Deutsch.*   He speaks German **well**.
> *Sie läuft **schneller**.*   She runs **more quickly**.

Revising modal verbs (Unit 1, page 82)

Schreiben 4 Put the words in the correct order to make sentences.
Example: 1 *Er soll nicht rauchen.*
1 soll rauchen Er nicht
2 Wasser soll mehr trinken Ich
3 essen Obst muss mehr Ich
4 Tag treiben jeden Wir Sport wollen
5 dürfen Sie keinen trinken Partys Alkohol auf
6 du spielen Willst Fußball heute?

> Remember that modal verbs usually need a second verb in the infinitive form at the end of the sentence.

Using *mögen* (Unit 1, page 83)

5 Copy and complete the sentences with the correct part of *mögen*.

1 Ich ___ Obst nicht.
2 ___ ihr Wasser?
3 Toni und Yusuf ___ Käse.
4 Wir ___ Pommes nicht.
5 Charlotte ___ Eis.
6 Mohammed, ___ du Brot?

	mögen
ich	mag
du	magst
er/sie/es/man	mag
wir	mögen
ihr	mögt
Sie	mögen
sie	mögen

Vor (ago) (Unit 2, page 84)

6 Copy and complete the sentences by translating the time phrase into German.

Example: 1 Ich habe **vor zwei Wochen** Fußball gespielt.

1 Ich habe (*two weeks ago*) Fußball gespielt.
2 (*Three weeks ago*) bin ich ins Café gegangen.
3 Ich habe (*one year ago*) viele Probleme gehabt.
4 (*One week ago*) habe ich nicht genug Wasser getrunken.
5 Ich bin (*five weeks ago*) nach Schottland gefahren.
6 (*One month ago*) bin ich ins Fitness-Studio gegangen.

> Remember that **vor** takes the dative case in German.
>
> vor ein**em** Monat — one month ago
> vor ein**er** Woche — one week ago
> vor ein**em** Jahr — one year ago
> vor zwei Wochen — two weeks ago

7 Translate the diary entry into English.

> Vor einem Jahr war ich nicht **s**o fit wie meine Freunde. Ich bin vor **s**echs Wochen ins Fitness-Studio gegangen und jetzt gehe ich jeden **S**amstag. Vor einem Monat bin ich zu Fuß zur Schule gegangen und ich fahre jetzt nie mit dem Auto zur Schule. Ich bin vor einer Woche **schw**immen gegangen und jetzt bin ich viel fitter!

8 Read out the diary entry in exercise 7.

9 Translate the sentences into German.

1 Six weeks ago, I played tennis.
2 I played basketball three weeks ago.
3 One year ago, I played more sport.
4 I went to the supermarket a week ago.
5 Two weeks ago, I was healthier.
6 I watched a film one month ago.

> Remember that the letter combination **schw** is pronounced like 'shv'.
>
> The German letter **s** at the beginning of a word or before a vowel is pronounced like the English 'z'.

> Remember, the verb is always the **second idea** in a sentence.

Grammatik 2

Modal verbs in the imperfect tense (Unit 2, page 85)

Lesen 1 Translate the sentences into English.
1. Ich durfte schwimmen gehen.
2. Du musstest meine Musik nicht mögen.
3. Du durftest kein Fastfood essen.
4. Ich konnte zwei Wochen lang nicht gehen.
5. Er musste ins Krankenhaus gehen.
6. Sie durfte nichts trinken.

Sprechen 2 Read out the message. Then listen and check your pronunciation.

> Ich wollte am Wochenende ins Kino gehen, aber ich konnte nicht, denn ich musste für eine Prüfung lernen. Ich musste auch mein Zimmer sauber machen, aber das wollte ich nicht, und deshalb durfte ich auch nicht fernsehen.

> All modal verbs follow the same pattern of endings in the imperfect tense:
>
> | **können** (can, be able to) | **dürfen** (may, be allowed to) | **müssen** (must, have to) | **wollen** (want to) |
> |---|---|---|---|
> | ich konn**te** | ich durf**te** | ich muss**te** | ich woll**te** |
> | du konn**test** | du durf**test** | du muss**test** | du woll**test** |
> | er/sie/es/man konn**te** | er/sie/es/man durf**te** | er/sie/es/man muss**te** | er/sie/es/man woll**te** |
>
> Note that there is no umlaut on modal verbs in the imperfect tense.

Schreiben 3 Translate the sentences into German.
1. I couldn't eat.
2. She had to go to hospital.
3. I was allowed to see my friend.
4. He wanted to play tennis.
5. I had to stay in bed.
6. She wasn't allowed to watch TV.

Revising the future tense (Unit 3, page 86)

Schreiben 4 Rewrite the sentences in the future tense.

Example: 1 Ich **werde** jeden Tag sehr gesund <u>essen</u>.

1. Ich <u>esse</u> jeden Tag sehr gesund.
2. Wir <u>gehen</u> am Wochenende schwimmen.
3. Julia <u>trinkt</u> mehr Wasser.
4. Später <u>mache</u> ich mehr Fitnesstraining.
5. Nächste Woche <u>geht</u> mein Vater zum Arzt.
6. Am Sonntag <u>sehen</u> wir fern.

> Remember that the future tense is formed using a part of **werden** + the <u>infinitive</u> at the end of the sentence.
>
> | | **werden** |
> |---|---|
> | ich | werde |
> | du | wirst |
> | er/sie/es/man | wird |
> | wir | werden |
> | ihr | werdet |
> | Sie | werden |
> | sie | werden |
>
> Ich **werde** in der Zukunft wenig Fleisch <u>essen</u>.
> Am Freitag **werde** ich ins Fitness-Studio <u>gehen</u>.

94 vierundneunzig

Revising the past tense (Unit 3, page 87)

Lesen 5 Translate the sentences into English.
1. Ich habe letzte Woche viel Sport gemacht.
2. Karin ist letzten Sommer zehn Kilometer gelaufen.
3. Wir haben jeden Tag viel Obst und Gemüse gegessen.
4. Vor einem Monat bin ich zum Krankenhaus gefahren.
5. Gestern hat mein Bruder nicht genug Wasser getrunken.
6. Letztes Wochenende sind meine Freunde und ich schwimmen gegangen.

Lesen 6 Copy and complete the sentences with the correct irregular past participle.
1. Mein Bruder hat den Arzt ___. (*besuchen*)
2. Wir haben Pizza ___ und Cola ___. (*essen, trinken*)
3. Ich habe acht Stunden ___. (*schlafen*)
4. Wo hast du das ___? (*lesen*)
5. Meine Eltern haben gestern einen Film ___. (*sehen*)
6. Ich habe weniger Zeit auf dem Handy ___. (*verbringen*)

wenn + present tense (Unit 4, page 88)

Sprechen 7 In pairs, take it in turns to read out a sentence for your partner to then translate into English.

1. Wenn ich oft ins Fitness-Studio gehe, bin ich glücklicher.
2. Wenn ich früher ins Bett gehe, schlafe ich viel besser.
3. Wenn ich nicht müde bin, gehe ich laufen.
4. Wenn ich traurig bin, spreche ich mit meinen Eltern.

Schreiben 8 Translate the sentences into German.
1. When the weather is bad, I go to the cinema.
2. When I am tired, I go to bed.
3. When I have a problem, I speak to my parents.
4. When I am quite sad, I go for a walk.
5. When I am not very happy, I talk to friends.
6. When I have enough free time, I do sport.

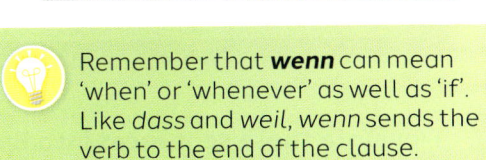

> Remember that **wenn** can mean 'when' or 'whenever' as well as 'if'. Like *dass* and *weil*, *wenn* sends the verb to the end of the clause.
>
> Go back to page 88 to refresh your memory on the **verb-comma-verb** rule with *wenn*. Then test a partner.

Los geht's!

Hören 9 Listen and write down the words or sentences you hear. Then write down if the sentences are in the past (Pa), present (Pr) or future (F) tense.
1. ___ ist ___ als Basketball.
2. Ich habe ___ einer Woche ___ gehabt.
3. Ich ___ gestern ins ___ gehen.
4.
5.
6.

Kapitel 4 Lese- und Hörtest

Reading

Lesen 1

My priorities. Some Austrian students are discussing their priorities in life. Who says what? Write **Y** for Yuki, **F** for Finn or **K** for Kim.

Yuki Meine Karriere ist mir sehr wichtig. Ich liebe meine Familie und meine Freunde, aber Erfolg ist genauso wichtig. Für mich ist Sport nicht wichtig.

Finn Geld ist mir gar nicht wichtig. Glücklich sein ist viel wichtiger für mich. Ich muss jeden Tag meine Freunde treffen und ich spreche oft mit meiner Familie.

Kim Für mich ist die Gesundheit sehr wichtig. Ich bewege mich jeden Tag, weil ich das gesund finde. Ich finde die Schule langweilig und nicht wirklich wichtig.

1 Who doesn't enjoy school?
2 Who has a lot of contact with friends and family?
3 Who finds success important?
4 Who likes to be active?
5 Who prioritises happiness over money?
6 Who thinks a career is important?

Lesen 2

Healthy living. You read Kai's lifestyle blog. Write **P** for something he did **in the past**, **N** for something he does **now** or **F** for something he will do **in the future**.

Für mich ist gesund leben manchmal schwer. Mein Freund geht gern ins Fitness-Studio und früher habe ich das auch oft gemacht, aber wenn ich jetzt Freizeit habe, spiele ich lieber am Computer.

Ich esse oft Fastfood und das finde ich ungesund, also werde ich gesünder essen. Das werde ich aber schwer finden, denn ich liebe Wurst und Pommes!

Meine Mutter glaubt, man soll acht Stunden schlafen. Ich weiß, dass ich nicht genug schlafe, weil ich oft müde bin und wenig Energie habe.

1 Going to the gym
2 Using technology
3 Eating healthily
4 Not getting enough sleep

Lesen 3

Translate these sentences into English.

Remember that German word order does not mirror English word order. Think about where you would naturally place time expressions in English sentences.

1 Ich rauche nie Zigaretten.
2 Laufen ist schwieriger als Fußball.
3 Ich finde Obst gesund, aber ich esse nicht oft Gemüse.
4 Wenn wir Freizeit haben, spielen wir Basketball.
5 Vor einer Woche bin ich ins Fitness-Studio gegangen.

Think about how to translate comparatives.

Break compound nouns (words made of more than one noun) into parts to work out the meaning.

Can you remember what *vor* means? Where will the English equivalent go in your translation?

sechsundneunzig

Hören 4

Sport. Sascha is talking about her sporting activities. What does she say? Listen to the recording and write **A**, **B** or **C** to complete each sentence.

1 (i) Sascha goes hiking …
   A regularly.
   B at the weekend.
   C often.

 (ii) Sascha likes cycling …
   A during the week.
   B at the weekend.
   C now and again.

2 (i) In summer, Sascha prefers …
   A swimming.
   B cycling.
   C playing tennis.

 (ii) In winter, Sascha is not keen on …
   A playing tennis.
   B swimming indoors.
   C swimming outdoors.

 (iii) Sascha is not interested in …
   A football.
   B running.
   C swimming.

> Listen carefully for which frequency and time phrases are used with each sporting activity. Listen also for negatives or other phrases that change the meaning of a sentence, to help you rule out any distractors (incorrect answer options which are also mentioned in the recording).

Hören 5

A problem. You hear Leon talking about a problem he had last week and what he is doing about it. What does he say? Listen to the recording and answer the questions in **English**. You do not need to write in full sentences.

1 What happened last week at school?
2 What is Leon doing differently this week?
3 What will Leon do next week?

Dictation

Hören 6

You will hear <u>four</u> short sentences.
Write down exactly what you hear in German.

> Remember that there will always be some words that are not on the vocabulary list. Use your knowledge of sound–spelling links to help you spell the words correctly.

> Make sure the words you write down work together grammatically and remember that all nouns in German need a capital letter.

> Think carefully about how these sounds are pronounced when writing down what you hear:
> a, ä
> au, äu
> o, ö
> u, ü
> s, schw
> -ig

> Some words in these sentences contain umlauts, so make sure you can distinguish between a pure vowel sound, such as a as in *Hand*, and the sound of a vowel with an umlaut, such as ä as in *Hände*. Practise pronouncing vowel sounds in pairs: *Mutter* and *Mütter*, *Vater* and *Väter*, *schon* ('already') and *schön* ('nice'), *Haus* and *Häuser*.

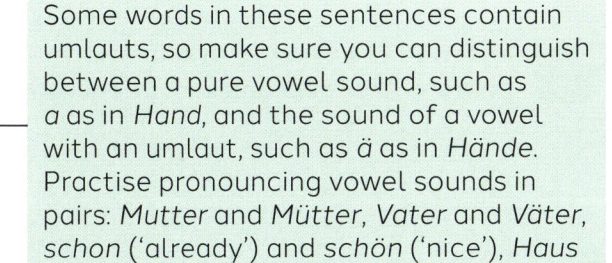

siebenundneunzig **97**

Kapitel 4 Mündlicher Test

Role-play

1 Look at the role-play card and prepare what you are going to say.

You can use a frequency phrase such as 'every day' or 'sometimes', or say 'once/twice ... per week' using -mal.

You are talking to your Austrian friend about health and lifestyle.
1 Give **one** detail about how you feel today.
2 Say how often you do sport.
3 Say what you like to drink. (Give **one** detail.)
4 Give **one** opinion about smoking.
5 ? Ask your friend a question about food.

You could make a general comment about feeling well or ill, or you could say what is wrong with you, for example 'I have a headache'.

You could use *gern* (with a verb) or *ich mag* (plus a noun).

You could start with a question word like *wann* or *wie oft*, or you could use inversion (verb and then subject pronoun) to create a question with 'Do you ...?'

2 Practise what you have prepared. Then, using your notes, listen and respond to the teacher.

3 Listen to Toni's answers and make a note of:
a how she answers the questions for points 1–4
b what question she asks for point 5.

To achieve full marks, you must use complete sentences, each containing a correct verb.

Reading aloud

4 Look at this task. With a partner, read the sentences aloud, paying attention to the underlined sounds.

Wir gehen fr**ü**her ins Bett.
Ich gehe t**ä**glich **schw**immen.
Meine **Schw**ester ist glücklich, wenn **s**ie l**äu**ft.
Mein Br**u**der f**ä**hrt n**o**rm**a**lerwei**s**e im **S**ommer in die **Schw**ei**z**.
M**a**n **s**ollte **ö**fter Gem**ü**se **u**nd **au**ch **O**bst essen – d**a**s ist wicht**ig**.

Think carefully how to pronounce these sounds:
a, ä
au, äu
o, ö
u, ü
s, ski, schw
-ig

5 Listen and check your pronunciation.

6 Listen to the teacher asking four follow-up questions. Translate each question into English and prepare your own answer for each one. Then listen again and respond to the teacher.

achtundneunzig

Kapitel 4

Photo card

You will be asked to talk about the content of these photos. You must say at least one thing about each photo.

After you have spoken about the content of the photos, you will be asked questions related to any of the topics within the theme of **People and lifestyle**.

Your responses should be as **full and detailed** as possible.

Hören 7 Listen to Toni describing the photos and answer the questions.
1. Who does Toni think is in the first photo?
2. What does she say they are doing, and where?
3. What does she say about the weather?
4. What does she say about the people in the second photo? (Give **three** details.)

> You will find that most people who appear in photos are teenagers, so these words will be useful:
>
> ein/zwei **Mädchen** — a girl / two girls
> ein **Junge** / zwei **Jungen** — a boy / two boys
> ein **Schüler** / eine **Schülerin** — a male/female pupil
> drei **Schüler** — three pupils
> drei **Schülerinnen** — three (female) pupils
> vier **Jugendliche** — four teenagers

Sprechen 8 Prepare your own description of the photos. Then, with a partner, take turns describing them.

> Auf dem ersten Foto gibt es …

Hören 9 Listen to the teacher's first follow-up question, *Welchen Sport hast du letzte Woche gemacht?*, and Toni's response. Write down the <u>four</u> missing past participles you hear.

> Letzte Woche war ich sehr aktiv und ich habe jeden Tag Sport **1**. Meine Familie und ich sind am Montag schwimmen **2** und ich bin dreimal mit meinem Bruder **3**. Ich habe auch Fußball in der Schule **4**.

Hören 10 The teacher then asks Toni, *Was wirst du in der Zukunft für deine Gesundheit machen?* What does Toni say? Make notes in English under these four headings:

a meat
b bedtime
c mobile phone
d sport

> For the follow-up questions, you will be expected to develop your ideas; give and justify your opinions, answer using past, present and future time frames and demonstrate the full range of your ability to speak German. Try to include:
> - modal verbs + infinitive (*ich soll/muss/kann mehr Sport machen*)
> - comparatives (*ich schwimme lieber, es ist gesünder, ich muss öfter …*)
> - intensifiers (*das ist viel besser, mir ist Sport ziemlich wichtig, ich finde das besonders gut*)
> - a range of conjunctions (*weil, dass, wenn*, which send the verb to the end, and *denn*, which has no effect on word order)
> - different ways of expressing opinions (*ich finde, ich glaube, ich denke, meiner Meinung nach*)
> - time phrases (*gestern, vor einer Woche, meistens*)
> - a range of adjectives to vary your vocabulary (*spannend, toll, wunderbar, entspannend*).

Sprechen 11 Listen to two more follow-up questions and prepare your answers. Then respond to the recording.

Sprechen 12 Prepare your own answers to as many of the Module 4 questions on page 226 as you can. Then practise with a partner.

neunundneunzig 99

Kapitel 4 Schreibtest

50-word writing task

Schreiben 1 **Look at this writing exam task and then, for each bullet point:**
1 think about the vocabulary and structures you have learned which you could use in your answer. For example:
- **nouns** and **adjectives** to write about food and drink
- **verbs of opinion** and **adjectives** to give reasons.
2 write down one idea for what you could write about in each bullet point.
3 write down which verbs you will need to use in your answer.

> You are writing a review for an online forum. Write a short description of your lifestyle.
>
> Write approximately **50** words in **German**.
>
> You must write something about each bullet point.
>
> Mention:
> - fast-food
> - drinks
> - smoking
> - exercise
> - sleep.

Lesen 2 **Read Theo's response to the exam task and answer the questions in English.**

> Ich esse oft Fastfood, denn mein Lieblingsessen ist Pommes – Pommes sind lecker! Aber ich trinke Wasser und das finde ich gesund. Ich rauche nie, weil Rauchen ungesund und blöd ist. Ich mache gern Sport und spiele zweimal pro Woche Fußball. Ich schlafe nicht genug, also werde ich acht Stunden pro Nacht schlafen.

1 What is Theo's favourite food?
2 What does he think of smoking? (Give **two** details.)
3 How often does he play football?
4 What is he going to do?

Schreiben 3 **Prepare your own answer to the task.**

Grammar task

Schreiben 4 **Using your knowledge of grammar, select the correct option to complete each sentence.**

> When you are working out a subject pronoun, look at the verb. If the verb is plural (*haben, sind, gehen*), the pronoun also needs to be plural (*wir, ihr, sie*).

1 Meine Schwester **bin** / **ist** / **sind** sehr gesund.
2 **Ich** / **Er** / **Wir** machen oft Fitnesstraining.
3 Ich habe einen **leckeren** / **leckere** / **leckeres** Kuchen gegessen.
4 **Der** / **Das** / **Die** Pommes sind ungesund.
5 Gestern Abend habe ich nicht genug **schlafe** / **geschlafen** / **schlafen**.

> Look at the verb to help you make your choice.

> Which tense is used here? The verb *habe* is used as an auxiliary verb and the phrase *Gestern Abend* gives you another clue.

100 hundert

90-word writing task

5 Look at this writing exam task and then, for each bullet point:

1. think about vocabulary and structures to use:
   - **nouns**, **verbs** and **adjectives** to write about healthy lifestyles
   - language for **narrating a story** about what you did
   - how to explain what your **plans** are and **why**
   - connectives and intensifiers you would like to use.
2. write down some ideas for what you could write about.
3. identify which tense(s) you could use in your answer.

> You are writing to your Swiss friend about healthy lifestyles.
>
> Write approximately **90** words in **German**.
>
> You must write something about each bullet point.
>
> Describe:
> - what you like to eat and drink
> - what exercise you did last week
> - what you will do to be healthy in the future.

6 Read Theo's response to the exam task. Answer the questions in the coloured boxes (1–5).

1 This is an example of **complex language**. What does it mean? Find two more examples of complex language in the text.

2 Theo uses several **frequency words**. What does this word mean? Find two more examples of frequency words or phrases.

Meine Gesundheit ist mir sehr wichtig. Ich darf keinen Alkohol trinken und ich trinke normalerweise Wasser. Ich liebe Obst und esse immer gern Gemüse, aber ich soll weniger Fleisch essen. Ich esse das dreimal pro Tag. Ich finde Fleisch sehr lecker.

Letztes Wochenende habe ich Sport gemacht. Ich bin mit meinem Bruder spazieren gegangen. Wir haben auch Fußball im Sportzentrum gespielt. Ich finde Fußball spannend.

In der Zukunft möchte ich Basketball lernen und wenn ich mehr Zeit habe, werde ich öfter mit meinem Bruder spazieren gehen.

3 Which connective could you use here to form an **extended sentence**? What other connectives does Theo use?

4 How could Theo **avoid repetition** here?

5 What **tense** is this? What other examples can you find? Which other tenses does Theo use?

7 Prepare your own answer to the task.
- Think about how you can develop your answer for each bullet point.
- Look back at your notes from exercises 5 and 6.
- Look at the 'Challenge checklist' and consider how you can show off your German!
- Write a brief plan and organise your answer into paragraphs.
- Write your answer and then carefully check it for accuracy.

Challenge checklist

- ✓ Connectives (*und, aber*)
- ✓ Some extended sentences
- ✓ An opinion (*Ich finde das gesund.*)

- ✓ Intensifiers and qualifiers
- ✓ Different persons of the verb
- ✓ A wider range of vocabulary
- ✓ A variety of time frames

- ✓ More complex connectives (*weil, da, dass, wenn*)
- ✓ Modal verbs in the imperfect tense (*ich musste, sollte, wollte*)
- ✓ Varied time phrases
- ✓ Comparatives (*einfacher, besser*)

hunderteins

Kapitel 4 Wörter

Key:
bold = this word will appear in higher exams only
* = this word is not on the vocabulary list but you may use it in your own sentences

Ich liebe Sport (pages 80–81):

Gesundheit und Fitness	Health and fitness
Ich ...	I ...
spiele ... (Fußball/Tennis/Basketball).	play (football/tennis/basketball) ...
mache ... (Fitnesstraining/Sport).	do (fitness training/sport) ...
fahre ... (Fahrrad/*Ski).	(ride a bike/ski) ...
gehe ... (laufen/schwimmen/wandern).	go (running/swimming/hiking) ...
ab und zu	now and again
nie	never
oft	often
Mein Lieblingssport ist ..., aber ich ... auch gern ...	My favourite sport is ..., but I also like ...
Ich ... nicht gern ..., weil ...	I don't like ..., because ...
Ich finde ... besser als ...	I find ... better than ...
das *Freibad	outdoor swimming pool
das *Hallenbad	indoor swimming pool
groß	tall/big
gut	good
hoch	high
klein	small
nah	near
besser	better
größer	bigger/taller
höher	higher
kleiner	smaller/shorter
näher	nearer

Willst du fit und gesund sein? (pages 82–83):

Gesundes Leben	Healthy living
Wie bleibst du gesund?	How do you stay healthy?
Wie bleibst du *fit?	How do you keep fit?
Was machst du, das (un)gesund ist?	What do you do that is (un)healthy?
Ich ...	I ...
gehe ... (schwimmen / laufen / ins Fitness-Studio).	go (swimming / running / to the gym)
treibe ... Sport.	do sport.
spiele ... (Tennis/Fußball/Basketball).	play (tennis/football/basketball).
esse ... (Obst und Gemüse / Fastfood).	eat (fruit and vegetables / fast food).
trinke ... (Wasser).	drink (water).
viel/wenig	a lot of / a little
(nicht) genug	(not) enough
jeden Tag	every day
(sehr) oft	(very) often
jede Woche	every week
regelmäßig	regularly
immer	always
Ich trinke (keinen Alcohol).	I don't drink any alcohol.
Ich trinke nie (Bier/Wein).	I never drink (beer/wine).
Wie findest du (Fastfood/Rauchen)?	What do you think of (fast food / smoking)?
Ich finde Fastfood/Rauchen ...	I find fast food / smoking ...
sehr	very
ziemlich	quite
total	totally
nicht	not
blöd	stupid
gefährlich	dangerous
lecker	tasty
ungesund	unhealthy
der Körper	body

Es geht mir nicht gut! (pages 84–85):

Unfälle und **Krankheiten**	Accidents and illnesses
der Arm	arm
der Fuß	foot
der Kopf	head
der Mund	mouth
der Rücken	back
die Hand	hand
das Auge	eye
das Bein	leg
das Gesicht	face
das Herz	heart
das Ohr	ear
Wie geht es / geht's dir?	How are you?
Mir geht's gut.	I'm well.
Es geht mir nicht gut. / Mir geht es nicht gut.	I'm not well.
Es geht mir schlecht.	I'm feeling bad.
Was ist los?	What is the matter?
Ich habe (Kopf)schmerzen.	I have (a) (head)ache.
Ich habe mir (den Arm) verletzt.	I have injured/hurt my (arm).
Ich habe mir (das Bein) gebrochen.	I have broken my (leg).
Wie ist das passiert?	How did it happen?
Das ist im Fitness-Studio passiert.	It happened in the gym.
Ich bin schwimmen gegangen.	I went swimming.
Ich bin auf ein lautes Konzert gegangen.	I went to a loud concert.
Ich habe zu viel am Computer gespielt.	I played on the computer too much.
Wann ist das passiert?	When did it happen?
Gestern.	Yesterday.
Am Wochenende.	At the weekend.
Vor einer Woche.	A week ago.
Vor einem Monat.	A month ago.
Vor einem Jahr.	A year ago.
Vor zwei Wochen.	Two weeks ago.

Was möchte ich verbessern? (pages 86–87):

Probleme und **Lösungen**	*Problems and solutions*
Ich habe nicht viel Sport gemacht.	*I have not done / did not do much sport.*
Ich habe mein Handy zu viel benutzt.	*I (have) used my phone too much.*
Ich habe ungesund gegessen.	*I have eaten / ate unhealthily.*
Ich habe nicht genug geschlafen.	*I have not slept / didn't sleep enough.*
Ich bin zu spät ins Bett gegangen.	*I have gone / went to bed too late.*
Ich bin nicht aktiv gewesen.	*I have not been active.*
benutzen	*to use*
essen	*eat*
fernsehen	*watch television*
gehen	*go, walk*
schlafen	*sleep*
schwimmen	*swim*
verändern	*to change*
verbessern	*to improve*
verbringen	*spend (time)*
werden	*become*
die Woche	*week*
die Zeit	*time*
das Bett	*bed*
das Gemüse	*vegetable*
das Handy	*mobile phone*
das Obst	*fruit*
das Problem	*problem*
das *Tagebuch	*diary*
Ich (esse/trinke/mache) (zu viel / nicht genug) …	*I (eat/drink/do) (too much/not enough) …*
Was wirst du machen?	*What will you do?*
Ich werde …	*I will …*
mehr/weniger …	*more/less …*
Fastfood/Obst/Gemüse essen.	*eat … fast food / fruit / vegetables.*
Kaffee/Wasser trinken.	*drink … coffee/water.*
Sport machen.	*do … sport.*

Gute Tage, schlechte Tage (pages 88–89):

Das *Wohlbefinden	*Wellbeing*
Wenn ich … bin, …	*When I am …, …*
nicht sehr glücklich	*not very happy*
ganz traurig	*quite sad*
Wenn ich schlechte Laune habe, …	*When I'm in a bad mood …*
Wenn ich … habe, …	*When I have …*
nicht genug Freizeit	*not enough free time*
zu viele Hausaufgaben	*too much homework*
wenig Energie	*little energy*
eine Prüfung	*an exam*
Wenn das Wetter gut/schlecht ist, …	*When the weather is good/bad …*
spreche ich mit meinem Lehrer / meiner Lehrerin.	*I talk to my teacher.*
rede ich mit Freunden.	*I talk to my friends.*
lerne ich mit Freunden.	*I study with friends.*
mache ich Sport.	*I do sport.*
gehe ich spazieren.	*I go for a walk.*
gehe ich früher ins Bett.	*I go to bed earlier.*

Das finde ich wichtig! (pages 90–91):

Was ist dir wichtig?	*What is important to you?*
Für mich ist/sind … sehr wichtig.	*For me … is/are very important.*
der Erfolg	*success*
die Gesundheit	*health*
die Freizeit	*free time*
die Karriere	*career*
Anderen Menschen helfen	*Helping other people*
Mit anderen Menschen zusammenarbeiten	*Working with other people*
Genug schlafen	*Sleeping enough*
Gute Laune haben	*Being in a good mood*
Glücklich sein	*Being happy*
… ist für mich … wichtig.	*… is … important to me.*
ziemlich	*quite*
total	*totally*
extrem	*extremely*
genauso	*just as*

Kapitel 5 — Meine Gegend

Wo spricht man Deutsch?
- Learning key facts about German-speaking countries
- Revising the comparative

A

Belgien
- Hauptstadt: Brüssel
- Nationalfeiertag: 21. Juli
- Größe: 30 528km^2
- Berg: die Botrange (694m)
- Fluss: die Maas

Deutschland
- Hauptstadt: Berlin
- Nationalfeiertag: 3. Oktober
- Größe: 358 000km^2
- Berg: die Zugspitze (2 962m)
- Fluss: der Main

Österreich
- Hauptstadt: Wien
- Nationalfeiertag: 26. Oktober
- Größe: 83 871km^2
- Berg: der Großglockner (3 798m)
- Fluss: die Enns

Namibia
- Hauptstadt: Windhoek
- Nationalfeiertag: 21. März
- Größe: 824 292km^2
- Berg: der Brandberg (2 573m)
- Fluss: der Fischfluss

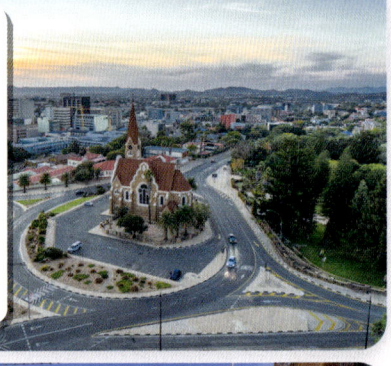

Luxemburg
- Hauptstadt: Stadt Luxemburg
- Nationalfeiertag: 23. Juni
- Größe: 2 586km^2
- Berg: der Kneiff (560m)
- Fluss: die Sauer

Die Schweiz
- Hauptstadt: Bern
- Nationalfeiertag: 1. August
- Größe: 41 285km^2
- Berg: die Dufourspitze (4 634m)
- Fluss: die Aare

der Quadratkilometer (km^2) square kilometre

B

Vaduz, Liechtenstein

Weißt du was?

Deutsch ist die einzige offizielle Sprache in Deutschland, Österreich und Liechtenstein.

In der Schweiz, Luxemburg und Belgien ist Deutsch eine offizielle Sprache. In Luxemburg spricht man auch Luxemburgisch und Französisch. In Belgien spricht man auch Niederländisch und Französisch. In der Schweiz spricht man auch Französisch, Italienisch und Rätoromanisch.

Deutsch ist eine regionale offizielle Sprache in Südtirol in Italien. Man spricht Deutsch auch in Namibia und Südafrika (Afrika), Paraguay und Brasilien (Südamerika).

hundertvier

Kulturzone — Kapitel 5

Lesen 1 — Read the information cards (A). Is each statement below true or false?
1. Der Nationalfeiertag von Belgien ist im Juli.
2. Die Dufourspitze in der Schweiz ist höher als der Großglockner in Österreich.
3. Luxemburg ist kleiner als Deutschland.
4. Der Fluss in Namibia heißt der Main.
5. Die Schweiz ist größer als Luxemburg.
6. Bern ist die Hauptstadt von Österreich.

Hören 2 — Listen to a description of South Tyrol. Copy and complete the final information card.

Südtirol (Italien)
- Hauptstadt:
- Nationalfeiertage: ___ und ___
- Größe:
- Berg:
- Fluss:

Practise saying these higher numbers:
500 – *fünfhundert*
980 – *neunhundertachtzig*
2 000 – *zweitausend*
3 780 – *dreitausendsiebenhundertachtzig*
4 364 – *viertausenddreihundertvierundsechzig*
2.606,02 – *zweitausendsechshundertsechs Komma null zwei*

German uses small spaces or a full stop to separate thousands and a comma as a decimal point – the opposite of the format used in English!

Lesen 3 — Read the article (B). Copy and complete the table in English with the names of the countries where German is (the):

only official language	one of the official languages	regional official language

G — Remember that we use the **comparative** to compare people, places and things. To form the comparative add **-er** to the end of the adjective.
Das Land ist klein. The country is small.
Das Land ist kleiner als Deutschland. The country is smaller than Germany.

Some adjectives add umlauts to the vowel in the comparative.
groß – größer
lang – länger
hoch – höher (Note: the c is omitted)

Page 116

Sprechen 4 — In pairs, take turns to give **three** details about one of the countries in text A and guess which it is.

Welches Land ist das?
- Der Nationalfeiertag ist am …
- Die Größe ist …
- Der Berg heißt … und ist … Meter hoch.
- Der Fluss heißt …
- Das Land ist größer/kleiner als …

Schreiben 5 — Fill in the gaps to translate the sentences into German.
1. The river in Austria is longer than the river in Luxembourg.
   Der Fluss in Österreich ist ___ als der Fluss in Luxemburg.
2. The mountain in Switzerland is higher than the mountain in Belgium.
   Der Berg in der Schweiz ist ___ als der Berg in Belgien.
3. Germany is bigger than Luxembourg.
   Deutschland ist ___ ___ Luxemburg.
4. Liechtenstein is smaller than Austria.
   Liechtenstein ist ___ als ___.

Schreiben 6 — Use the information on the cards to write a short description of one of the German-speaking countries.

Die Hauptstadt von Belgien heißt Brüssel.
Der Nationalfeiertag ist am 21. Juli.
Die Größe ist 30 528 Quadratkilometer.
Der Berg heißt die Botrange und ist 694 Meter hoch.
Der Fluss heißt die Maas.

hundertfünf 105

1 Wo wohnst du?
- Describing where you live
- Using prepositions followed by the dative
- Using a variety of adjectives with intensifiers and qualifiers

Hören 1
Listen and read. (1–4) Write the correct letters for where the people live and the facilities they have (a–l).

1 Ich wohne mit meiner Mutter in einer Kleinstadt. Sie ist im Westen von Österreich. Es gibt hier kulturelle Aktivitäten. Man kann zum Beispiel ins Theater gehen.

2 Ich wohne bei meinen Großeltern in einem Dorf. Das ist im Norden von der Schweiz. Es gibt hier keine Moschee, aber es gibt eine kleine Kirche.

3 Ich wohne auf dem Land. Mein Haus ist im Osten von der Schweiz. Es gibt keinen Flughafen, aber es gibt eine Moschee in der Nähe.

4 Ich wohne mit meinem Vater in München. München ist eine Großstadt im Süden von Deutschland. Es gibt einen großen Flughafen.

a in einer Kleinstadt
b in einem Dorf
c in einer Großstadt
d auf dem Land

die Großstadt — city

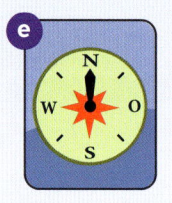

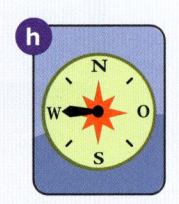

Lesen 2
Translate the underlined sentences in exercise 1 into English.

Hören 3
Listen to Arda talking about where he lives and answer the questions in English.
1 Where does Arda live?
2 Where is it situated?
3 What is his region like?
4 What is there where he lives?
5 What is there not where he lives?
6 How does he go to school?

Es gibt (there is / there are) is followed by the accusative.
Masc: Es gibt *einen* Flughafen.   There is **an** airport.
Fem: Es gibt *keine* Universität.   There is **no** university.
Neut: Es gibt *kein* Kino.   There is **no** cinema.
Check the gender of the noun you are using and remember to use the correct form of the indefinite article.

Sprechen 4
Select an option for each highlighted box and write down your choices in secret. Ask your partner the questions. Your partner has to answer, guessing which options you selected. If your partner goes wrong, start again.

- Wo wohnst du?
- Ich wohne **in einem Dorf / in der Stadtmitte / am Stadtrand**.
- Wo ist das?
- Das ist im **Norden / Süden / Osten / Westen** von Großbritannien.
- Wie ist deine Region?
- **Meine Gegend / Mein Ort / Meine Umgebung** ist sehr **schmutzig / ruhig / sicher**.
- Was gibt es dort?
- Es gibt **ein Stadion / viele Geschäfte**, aber **keinen Tempel / keine Synagoge / keine Moschee**.

der Stadtrand — outskirts (of town)

106 hundertsechs

5 Listen to and read the descriptions. Copy and complete the table below in English.

Hier wohne ich!

1 Ich wohne bei meinen Großeltern in der Stadtmitte von Vaduz. Sie wohnen seit einem Jahr hier, aber sie kommen aus der Schweiz. Vaduz ist die Hauptstadt von Liechtenstein. Die Stadt ist sehr ruhig und nicht sehr interessant, finde ich. Die Gegend ist sicher, grün und ziemlich sauber. Es gibt viele Pflanzen und Bäume und **der Blick von meinem Zimmer aus ist wirklich schön**. Es gibt auch einen neuen Supermarkt. Es gibt keinen Bahnhof und keinen Flughafen in meiner Gegend, aber **ich fahre jeden Tag mit dem Bus zur Schule, außer Freitag, wenn ich zu Fuß gehe**.
— Bente

2 Meine Eltern, meine Geschwister und ich wohnen in Windhoek. Das ist die Hauptstadt von Namibia. Unser Haus ist groß und extrem modern. Ich wohne gern hier. Das Stadtzentrum ist besonders laut, weil es viele Autos und Busse gibt. Die Stadt ist nie langweilig und die Leute sind total freundlich! Es gibt kein großes Stadion, aber es gibt ein neues Einkaufszentrum in der Stadt. **Heute nach der Schule werde ich dort einkaufen gehen**.
— Mika

	what there is	what there isn't
1		

6 Find the <u>six</u> qualifiers and intensifiers in the text and translate them into English.

7 Translate the phrases in **bold** in the text into English.

8 Write approximately 50 words describing where you live. Include the following points:
- where you live
- what it is like
- what the people are like
- what there is and isn't in your area
- what you can do there.

Ich wohne in …
Meine Region/Gegend ist …
Die Leute sind …
Es gibt …
Man kann …

G Some **prepositions** in German are always followed by the **dative**:

außer	except	**nach**	after, to, according to
aus	from, out of	**seit**	since, for
bei	at, near, by	**von**	from, by, of, about
gegenüber	opposite	**zu**	to
mit	with, by means of		

Er geht **aus dem** Zimmer.   He is going out of the room.

Es gibt einen Park in der Nähe **von** mein**em** Haus.
There is a park near my house.

Seit is used with the <u>present tense</u> in German to indicate something that started in the past and is still ongoing.

Ich <u>wohne</u> **seit** einem Monat hier.
I have been living here **for** one month.

Remember:
- zu + dem → zum
  zu + der → zur
  von + dem → vom
- *in* can take the accusative or the dative, depending on whether it indicates movement or position.

Page 116

Remember to use qualifiers and intensifiers in front of adjectives to add detail to your descriptions.

Die Gegend ist **ziemlich** sauber.   The area is **quite** clean.

hundertsieben

2 Wie fährst du?

- Discussing transport in your local area
- Using prepositions with the accusative
- Using correct word order with *weil* and *obwohl*

Lesen 1 Match the pictures (a–g) to the phrases (1–7) below.

Ich fahre ...
1 mit dem (Elektro)auto.
2 mit dem Bus.
3 mit dem Zug / der Bahn.
4 mit dem Fahrrad.
5 mit dem Schiff.

Ich fliege ...
6 mit dem Flugzeug.

Ich gehe ...
7 zu Fuß.

Wie fährst du?

das Elektroauto electric car

Hören 2 Listen. Copy and complete the table. (1–8)

	when?	how? (transport)	where?
1			

G
- Remember: Time – Manner – Place
  Im Winter fahre ich *mit dem Auto* *in die Stadt*.
  Time   Manner   Place

- If you are giving reasons, remember that **weil** sends the verb to the end of the sentence.
  Ich gehe zu Fuß in die Stadt. Ich wohne in der Nähe.
  Ich gehe zu Fuß in die Stadt, **weil** ich in der Nähe wohne.

- To express more complex reasons, you can use **obwohl** (although). Just like *weil*, *obwohl* sends the verb to the end of the sentence.
  Ich fliege mit dem Flugzeug, **obwohl** das teuer ist.
  I travel by plane, **although** that is expensive.

Page 117

Hören 3 Listen and write down the words you hear to complete the sentences. Be careful with the *s* sound.

1 Ich fahre ___ ___ zur Schule, weil es nicht weit ist.
2 Wir ___ ___ in die Stadt, weil es schnell ist.
3 Ich ___ ___ nach Hause, weil es nicht zu teuer ist.
4 ___ ___ ___ nach Hause, weil das praktisch ist.

Das Jungfraujoch in der Schweiz ist 3 454 Meter hoch und es gibt dort einen Bahnhof.
Die Jungfraubahn fährt 365 Tage im Jahr. Die Fahrt ist echt toll und das Gebiet sieht von oben sehr schön aus.

s, *ss/ß*, *st*, *sp* and *sch* are pronounced differently. Listen and repeat the words.

s like 'z'	**S**ee	**S**onntag
ss/ß like 's'	be**ss**er	zu Fu**ß**
st like 'sht'	**St**adt	**St**rand
sp like 'shp'	**sp**ielen	**sp**rechen
sch like 'sh'	**Sch**ule	**Sch**iff

108 *hundertacht*

4 Sprechen
In pairs, ask and answer the questions about using transport where you live.

- Wie fährst du zur Schule?
- Wie fährst du in die Stadt?
- Wie fährst du nach Hause? Warum?

Ich fahre Wir fahren	manchmal oft normalerweise immer jeden Tag in den Ferien	mit dem Auto mit dem Bus mit dem Fahrrad mit dem Fahrzeug mit dem Schiff mit dem Zug mit der Bahn	nach Frankreich, ins Stadtzentrum, nach Hause, zum Bahnhof, zum Flughafen, zur Schule,	weil obwohl	das bequem ist. das billig ist. das praktisch ist. das schnell ist. das teuer ist. das langsam ist. ich in der Nähe wohne. ich weit weg wohne.
Ich fliege Wir fliegen		mit dem Flugzeug	in die USA, nach Griechenland,		

5 Lesen
Read the text about Karla's visit to the Swiss Steam Park. Then translate the sentences in bold into English.

Besuchen Sie den Schweizer Dampfpark!

Letzten Sommer habe ich den Schweizer Dampfpark besucht, weil meine Brüder Züge interessant finden. Das interessiert mich aber nicht und **ich war gegen die Idee! Wir sind ohne das Auto dorthin gefahren**. Wir sind mit dem Schiff nach Saint-Gingolph gefahren, obwohl das langsam war. Dann sind wir mit dem Fahrrad zum Park gefahren, weil er nicht weit weg war. Die Eintrittskarten waren nicht teuer – **wir haben CHF45 für die Karten bezahlt**.

Wir sind mit einem kleinen Dampfzug durch den Park gefahren und dann haben wir ein Picknick gemacht. **Der Besuch war toll, weil die Landschaft um den Park sehr grün und schön war.** Obwohl die Fahrt mit dem Dampfzug nicht sehr spannend war, hat der Tag mir gut gefallen und **wir sind bis 18 Uhr dort geblieben!**

der Dampf	steam
der Eintritt	entrance
CHF (Schweizer Franken)	Swiss francs

6 Schreiben
Translate the sentences into German.
1. I am travelling without my friends.
2. She is driving through the town centre.
3. I stayed there until 8 p.m.
4. He has CHF50 for the tickets.
5. We often go for a walk around the lake.
6. I am against the rules.

G These **prepositions** are always followed by the **accusative**:

bis	until
durch	through
für	for
gegen	against
ohne	without
um	around, about

Ich kaufe Karten **für meinen** Bruder.
Ich kaufe Karten **für meine** Schwester.
Ich kaufe Karten **für mein** Kind.
Ich kaufe Karten **für meine** Eltern.

Page 117

Kapitel 5

hundertneun

3 Wo gehst du gern einkaufen?

- Discussing shopping habits
- Using compound nouns
- Using plurals of nouns

Lesen 1 Read the brochure about shopping in Bern. Find <u>one</u> example of each type of shop in the brochure and write the name below.

Die Stadt Bern hat viele schöne Geschäfte und <u>die Einkaufsstraßen sind 6km lang!</u>

Brauchen Sie Kleidung und Schuhe?

Im Kleidungsgeschäft „Peter Hahn" kann man schöne T-Shirts kaufen.

Im großen Geschäft „Loeb" verkauft man Schuhe.

Möchten Sie Geschenke kaufen?

Im Geschäft „Feines" gibt es <u>bunte Poster, Karten und Papier</u>.

Im Geschäft „Bucherer" kann man Uhren aus der Schweiz kaufen.

Haben Sie Hunger?

Im Geschäft „Sterchi" kann man 15 handgemachte Brotsorten finden.

Im Käsegeschäft „Chäsbueb" gibt es 250 Käsesorten.

1 a clothes shop
2 a stationery shop
3 a clock shop
4 a bread shop
5 a cheese shop
6 a shoe shop

> Use *man* with modal verbs to mean 'you' generally.
>
> Remember that **modal verbs** like *können* must be used with another verb in the <u>infinitive</u> at the end of the sentence.
>
> Man **kann** Uhren <u>kaufen</u>.   You **can** <u>buy</u> clocks.

Lesen 2 Translate the <u>four underlined</u> phrases in the brochure into English.

Hören 3 Listen to the advert for a shopping centre and answer the questions in English.

1 At what time does the centre open on a Saturday?
2 How many shops are there?
3 Name <u>three</u> modes of public transport you can use to get to the centre.
4 Where can you find peace and quiet?
5 What is there for young people?
6 What is there for children?

> **G**
> German often combines two or more words to form new **compound nouns**. The two words could be two nouns:
> *Käse + Geschäft → Käsegeschäft*
>
> Sometimes extra letters may be added to make pronunciation easier:
> *das Schokolade**n**geschäft   das Kleidung**s**geschäft*
>
> The gender of the compound noun is always determined by the gender of the **final** noun.
>
> Page 118

Schreiben 4 Translate the sentences into German.

1 The shopping streets are 4km long.
2 There are three shoe shops.
3 You can find cards and paper in the supermarket.
4 There are 50 types of cheese in the cheese shop.

> **G**
> Remember that there are lots of ways to form **plurals of nouns**, but there are patterns you can follow:
>
> | | singular | plural |
> |---|---|---|
> | (-e) | Geschäft | Geschäft**e** |
> | (¨e) | Supermarkt | Sup**ä**rmkt**e** |
> | (-n) | Straße | Straße**n** |
> | (-en) | Uhr | Uhr**en** |
> | (-) | Zimmer | Zimmer |
> | (-er) | Kind | Kind**er** |
> | (¨er) | Krankenhaus | Krank**ä**nh**ä**us**er** |
> | (-s) | T-Shirt | T-Shirt**s** |
>
> Note: the plural of *Museum* is *Museen*.
>
> Page 118

110 hundertzehn

Lesen 5 Read the information about why people shop online. Write the correct letter to match each sentence (1–8) to a reason (a–h).

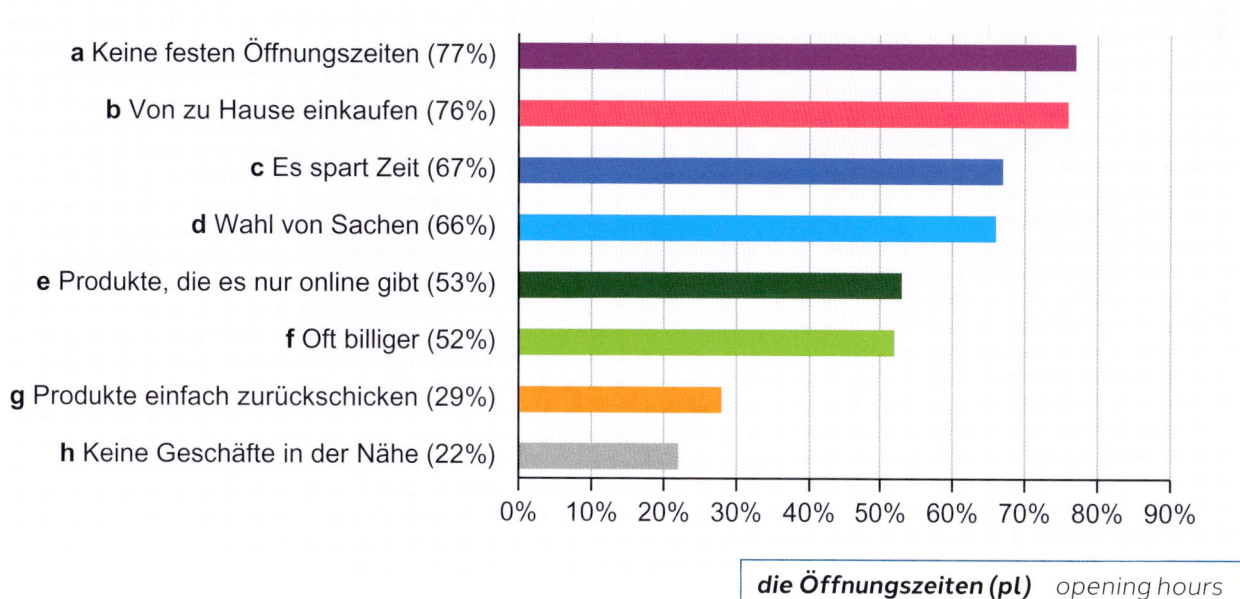

Warum shoppst du online?

- **a** Keine festen Öffnungszeiten (77%)
- **b** Von zu Hause einkaufen (76%)
- **c** Es spart Zeit (67%)
- **d** Wahl von Sachen (66%)
- **e** Produkte, die es nur online gibt (53%)
- **f** Oft billiger (52%)
- **g** Produkte einfach zurückschicken (29%)
- **h** Keine Geschäfte in der Nähe (22%)

die Öffnungszeiten (pl) opening hours

1 Wenn etwas nicht passt, kann ich es zurückschicken.
2 Das ist praktischer, weil das Online-Geschäft immer offen ist.
3 Ich kann nichts in meinem Dorf kaufen.
4 Es gibt so viele Produkte.
5 Es kostet nicht so viel.
6 Das ist schneller.
7 Die Produkte kommen zu mir zu Hause.
8 Man kann nicht alles im Geschäft finden.

Sprechen 6 In pairs, take turns to ask and answer the questions.
- Was für Geschäfte gibt es in deiner Stadt / in deinem Dorf?
- Wo gehst du gern einkaufen und warum?
- Kaufst du lieber im Geschäft oder online ein und warum?

In meinem Dorf In meiner Stadt	gibt es	keine/viele Geschäfte. einige Secondhandgeschäfte. viele Cafés. einen großen Supermarkt. ein großes Einkaufszentrum.
Ich kaufe (nicht) gern	im Einkaufszentrum online	ein, …
…, weil das	einfach/einfacher billig/billiger praktisch/praktischer	ist.
Man kann	Zeit	sparen.
	schöne Sachen	finden.
Man kann Produkte	einfach sofort	zurückschicken.
	von zu Hause	einkaufen.
Man bekommt	bessere	Informationen. Preise.

hundertelf **111**

4 Mein idealer Wohnort

- Describing an ideal place to live
- Using a range of tenses
- Using *ich möchte*

Hören 1 Listen to and read the forum posts. Answer the questions below in English.

Franka: Als ich klein war, habe ich in Berlin gewohnt. Wir haben in einer modernen Wohnung gewohnt. Jetzt wohne ich in einem alten Haus in einem kleinen Dorf und es gefällt mir sehr. Das Dorf ist besonders sauber und schön.

Thomas: Als ich jünger war, haben wir in einem großen Haus an der Küste gewohnt. Heute wohne ich in einer modernen Wohnung in einer Großstadt. Ich wohne gern hier, weil es viele Aktivitäten für junge Leute gibt.

Steffi: Früher haben wir in einem sehr alten Haus in einem Dorf gewohnt. Das hat mir gut gefallen. Heute wohne ich in einem modernen Haus in einem großen Dorf. Das ist ideal für mich und es gibt viele Pflanzen und Bäume.

Peter: Als kleines Kind habe ich in einer kleinen Wohnung in einer Kleinstadt gewohnt. Es gab nur vier Zimmer und wir hatten keinen Garten. Jetzt wohne ich in einer großen Wohnung in Bern, der Hauptstadt von der Schweiz. Die Leute sind so freundlich.

Who …?
1. lives in a capital city
2. lived in a modern flat when they were younger
3. lived in a very old house when they were younger
4. lives in a small village
5. likes having lots of activities
6. lives somewhere ideal for them

Lesen 2 Find the German for the phrases below in exercise 1.
1. When I was a small child, I lived in a small flat.
2. We lived in a large house.
3. Today I live in a modern house.
4. Now I live in Bern, the capital of Switzerland.
5. The village is especially clean and beautiful.
6. There are lots of activities for young people.

> **G** The **perfect tense** is used in spoken German and more informal writing.
> *Ich habe in Berlin gewohnt.* I lived in Berlin.
>
> The **imperfect tense** is used more in written narrative accounts, stories and reviews. Some verbs are used more commonly in the imperfect than the perfect tense:
> *ich war* I was   *ich hatte* I had
> *es gab* there was/were

Sprechen 3 In pairs, imagine you are one of the people in exercise 1. Ask and answer the questions below.

- *Wo hast du früher gewohnt?*
- *Als ich jünger war, habe ich in einem großen Haus an der Küste gewohnt.*
- *Wie hat es dir gefallen?*
- *Es hat mir nicht gefallen, weil es ziemlich langweilig war.*
- *Wo wohnst du jetzt?*
- *Heute wohne ich in einer modernen Wohnung in einer Großstadt.*
- *Wie gefällt es dir?*
- *Es gefällt mir sehr, weil es viele Aktivitäten für junge Leute gibt.*

The German **w** is pronounced like the English 'v'.
Listen and repeat the words.
wohnt   **w**ar   Sch**w**eiz
Wohnung   **W**ohnort   **w**enig

112 *hundertzwölf*

Kapitel 5

Hören 4 Listen to Yasmin answering the quiz questions below and write down the letter she gives for each answer.

Sprechen 5 In pairs, ask and answer the questions from the quiz.

Wie ist dein idealer Wohnort?

1 Wo möchtest du leben?
- A Ich möchte in einem Dorf in Amerika leben.
- B Ich möchte in einer Kleinstadt in Europa leben.
- C Ich möchte in einer Hauptstadt in Asien leben.

2 Möchtest du lieber in einer Wohnung oder in einem Haus wohnen?
- A Ich möchte lieber in einem großen Haus wohnen.
- B Ich möchte lieber in einem kleinen Haus wohnen.
- C Ich möchte lieber in einer modernen Wohnung wohnen.

3 Was möchtest du in deinem idealen Wohnort haben?
- A Ich möchte viele Bäume und Pflanzen haben.
- B Ich möchte ein Kino haben.
- C Ich möchte einen Bahnhof haben.

4 Was möchtest du dort machen?
- A Ich möchte spazieren gehen.
- B Ich möchte mit Freunden ins Café gehen.
- C Ich möchte einkaufen gehen.

du solltest you should

Hast du mehr As, Bs oder Cs?
As Du liebst die Natur und die frische Luft. Du solltest auf dem Land wohnen.
Bs Du liebst die Natur, aber du magst auch die Stadt. Du solltest in einer Kleinstadt wohnen.
Cs Du liebst das Leben in der Großstadt. Du solltest im Stadtzentrum wohnen.

Hören 6 Listen to Anna describing how she would improve her town and where she would like to live in the future. Is each statement below true or false?

1. Anna dislikes living in her town.
2. There are not many activities for young people.
3. Anna would like a new gym and a new park.
4. Anna's town does enough to protect the environment.
5. In the future, Anna wants to live in Switzerland.
6. Anna would like to live beside a lake.

Schreiben 7 Imagine you are a famous person. Write approximately 90 words about your area. Include the following points:
- where you lived when you were younger
- where you live now and what it is like
- your opinion of where you live
- where you would like to live.

Als ich klein war, Als ich jünger war, Mit (drei) Jahren	habe ich	in der Schweiz in Deutschland in Italien in England/Schottland/ Wales/Großbritannien	gewohnt.
Heute wohne ich Jetzt wohnen wir		in einer Kleinstadt. in einer Großstadt. in einem Dorf.	
Es ist Sie ist Die Leute sind	genauso nicht so besonders	ideal. sauber/schmutzig. schön. freundlich/unfreundlich.	
In der Zukunft möchte ich	hier in den USA im Ausland an der Küste	leben.	

G Remember that the **conditional** is used to say what you **would like**. It is used with an infinitive at the end of the phrase.

Ich möchte in einem großen Haus wohnen.
I **would like** to live in a big house.

Page 118

hundertdreizehn **113**

5 Bei mir zu Hause

- Describing your home
- Using prepositions with the accusative and the dative
- Working out the meaning of compound nouns

Hören 1 Listen to Jonas describing his house. Write the correct letter to match each activity (a–g) to the correct room.

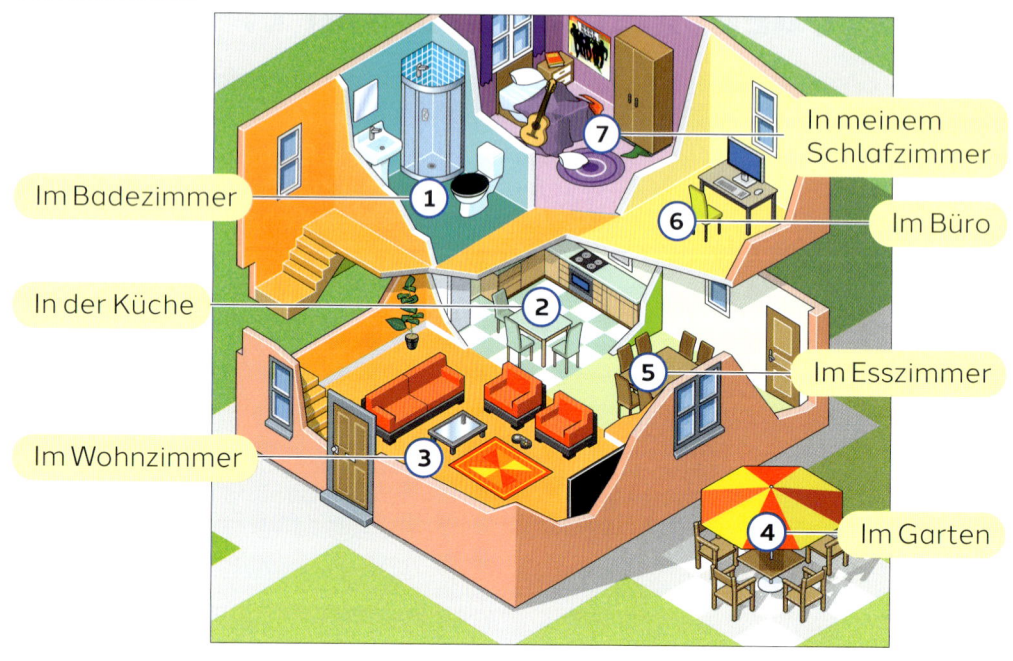

Im Badezimmer
In der Küche
Im Wohnzimmer
In meinem Schlafzimmer
Im Büro
Im Esszimmer
Im Garten

a mache ich meine Hausaufgaben.
b sehe ich fern und ich spiele auf dem Computer.
c höre ich Musik und ich lese.
d frühstücke ich.
e essen wir im Sommer.
f arbeitet meine Mutter.
g dusche ich.

duschen to shower

Lesen 2 Work out the meanings of the following compound nouns.

1 das Arbeitszimmer
2 das Gästezimmer
3 das Gartenhaus
4 die Haustür
5 das Spielzimmer

German often combines two or more words to form new compound nouns. The two words could be:
- two nouns
  Musik (music) + Zimmer (room) →
  das Musikzimmer (music room)
- a verb stem and a noun
  schlafen (to sleep) + Zimmer (room) →
  das Schlafzimmer (bedroom)
- an adjective and a noun
  klein (small) + Stadt (town) → die Kleinstadt (small town)

The gender of the compound noun is always determined by the gender of the **final** noun.
die Stadt → **die Klein**stadt
das Zimmer → **das Schlaf**zimmer

Sprechen 3 In pairs, ask each other what you do in each room at home.

- *Was machst du in der Küche?*
- *In der Küche …*
- *Was machst du im Wohnzimmer?*
- *Im Wohnzimmer …*

Im Badezimmer	dusche ich.
Im Büro / Im Arbeitszimmer	arbeite ich. mache ich meine Hausaufgaben.
Im Esszimmer	esse ich (zu Mittag / zu Abend).
Im Schlafzimmer	schlafe ich. höre ich Musik.
Im Garten	lese ich.
Im Wohnzimmer	sehe ich fern. spiele ich auf dem Computer.
In der Küche	koche ich.
In der Garage	gibt es das Auto.

- Remember that the **verb** must be the second idea if you put the room first:
  In der Küche **esse** ich.
- Pay attention to the word order when using separable verbs:
  fernsehen → Im Wohnzimmer **sehe** ich **fern**.
- When using separable verbs after a subordinating conjunction (*weil, wenn, obwohl*), the verb comes back together again:
  Ich mag mein Zimmer. Ich sehe dort fern.
  Ich mag mein Zimmer, **weil** ich dort **fernsehe**.

114 hundertvierzehn

Kapitel 5

4 Martina is moving into a new flat in Bern. Listen to and read where her furniture goes. Then read the texts aloud in pairs.

Meine neue Wohnung! Wie schön!

Was machen wir mit dem **Bett**?

Das Bett kommt **ins** Schlafzimmer.

Was sollen wir mit dieser schönen **Jacke** machen?

Die Jacke hängen wir **an die** Haustür.

Und der **Tisch**?

Der Tisch kommt **in die** Küche.

Was machen wir mit der **Waschmaschine**?

Die Waschmaschine stellen wir **ins** Badezimmer.

Was soll ich mit der **Pflanze** machen?

Die kannst du **auf den** Tisch stellen.

5 Write down sentences to describe the position of the five underlined objects in exercise 4.

Example: Das Bett ist im Schlafzimmer.

1 das Bett
2 die Jacke
3 der Tisch
4 die Waschmaschine
5 die Pflanze

G Remember that some **prepositions** are followed by the **accusative** when there is movement towards an object, or by the **dative** when there is no movement:

an, auf, in, unter, über, hinter, vor, zwischen, neben

*Wir hängen die Jacke **an die** Tür.*
We are hanging the jacket on the door.
*Die Jacke hängt **an der** Tür.*
The jacket is hanging on the door.

Use the correct definite articles:

	masc	fem	neut	pl
accusative	den	die	das	die
dative	dem	der	dem	den

Page 119

6 Listen and write down the words you hear to complete the sentences. Then decide if each sentence is in the accusative or dative case.

1 Das Bett ist ___ ___ Tür.
2 Ich stelle den Stuhl ___ ___ Tisch.
3 Die Pflanze stellen wir ___ ___ Fenster.
4 Mein Zimmer ist ___ ___ Küche und ___ Badezimmer.
5 Es gibt viel Platz ___ Keller.

7 Translate the sentences into German.

1 My jacket is hanging on the door.
2 I'm hanging my jacket on the door.
3 We're putting the plant behind the table.
4 The plant is behind the table.
5 Are you putting the photo above the bed?
6 The photo is above the bed.

hundertfünfzehn

Grammatik 1

The comparative (Culture, page 105)

1 **Write out the adjectives below in the comparative form.**

Example: 1 *größer*

1 groß
2 klein
3 hoch
4 spät
5 früh
6 lang

> Remember that some adjectives add an umlaut in the comparative.

2 **Copy and complete the sentences with the comparative adjective in brackets.**

1 Das Matterhorn ist höher als der Eiger. (*higher*)
2 Die Donau ist ___ als der Rhein. (*longer*)
3 München ist ___ als Bern. (*bigger*)
4 Bern ist ___ als München. (*smaller*)
5 Juni ist ___ als Februar. (*later*)
6 Januar ist ___ als Dezember. (*earlier*)

Prepositions followed by the dative (Unit 1, page 107)

3 **Copy and complete the sentences with the correct definite article in the dative case. Then listen and check your answers.**

1 Unsere Wohnung ist in der Nähe von der Synagoge (*f*).
2 Um sieben Uhr gehe ich aus ___ Haus (*nt*).
3 Ich fahre mit ___ Bus (*m*) zur Schule.
4 Wir fahren mit ___ Auto (*nt*).
5 Nach ___ Schule (*f*) mache ich Sport.
6 Die Kinder verbringen das Wochenende bei ___ Großeltern (*pl*).

4 **In pairs, read out the dialogue, adding the correct articles and possessive adjectives.**

- Mit wem fährst du zur Schule?
- Ich fahre mit … Bruder (*m*).
- Wo verbringst du das Wochenende?
- Ich verbringe das Wochenende in … Stadt (*f*).
- Wohin gehst du am Sonntag?
- Am Sonntag gehe ich mit … Freunden (*pl*) einkaufen.

> Remember that these prepositions always take the **dative**:
>
> außer — except
> aus — from, out of
> bei — at, near, by
> gegenüber — opposite
> mit — with, by means of
> nach — after, to, according to
> seit — since, for
> von — from, by, of, about
> zu — to
>
> Use the correct **dative** articles:
>
> | masc | fem | neut | pl |
> |---|---|---|---|
> | definite article: the ||||
> | dem | der | dem | den |
> | indefinite article: a, an, negatives and possessive adjectives ||||
> | einem | einer | einem | – |
> | keinem | keiner | keinem | keinen |
> | meinem | meiner | meinem | meinen |

116 hundertsechzehn

Kapitel 5

Word order with subordinating conjunctions (*weil, wenn, obwohl*) (Unit 2, page 108)

Lesen 5 Read out the sentences. Then translate them into English.
1. Wenn es regnet, gehe ich zum Stadion.
2. Wenn es schneit, gehe ich Ski fahren.
3. Wenn ich Geld habe, gehe ich in die Stadt.
4. Wenn ich kein Geld habe, bleibe ich zu Hause.
5. Wenn das Wetter schön ist, fahre ich mit dem Fahrrad.
6. Wenn das Wetter schlecht ist, fahre ich mit dem Bus.

> *Wenn* (if, when) and *obwohl* (although) send the verb to the end, just like *weil*.

Lesen 6 Put the subordinate clauses into the correct order.
1. Ich fahre mit dem Bus,   das / ist / schnell / weil
2. Ich fahre mit dem Auto,   bequem / ist / es / weil
3. Ich fahre mit dem Schiff,   es / nicht / obwohl / ist / bequem
4. Ich fahre mit dem Fahrrad,   gesund / ist / es / weil
5. Ich fahre mit dem Zug,   praktisch / weil / ist / es
6. Ich fliege mit dem Flugzeug,   umweltfreundlich / ist / obwohl / es / nicht

Prepositions followed by the accusative (Unit 2, page 109)

Lesen 7 Copy and complete the sentences with the correct definite article (*den, die, das*) in the accusative.

> Peter will nicht in die Schule gehen.
> - Er fährt mit dem Fahrrad durch **1** Stadt.
> - Er kauft im Supermarkt einen Kuchen für **2** Mittagspause.
> - Danach ist er um **3** Park gefahren.
> - Leider kommt er ohne **4** Kuchen in der Schule an. Er hat ihn im Supermarkt vergessen!

Sprechen 8 Listen and check your answers to exercise 7. Then read out the sentences.

> Remember that these prepositions always take the **accusative**:
> **bis** until
> **durch** through
> **für** for
> **gegen** against
> **ohne** without
> **um** around, about

Use the correct **accusative** articles:

masc	fem	neut	pl
definite article: the			
d**en**	die	das	die
indefinite article: a, an, negatives and possessive adjectives			
ein**en**	ein**e**	ein	–
kein**en**	kein**e**	kein	kein**e**
mein**en**	mein**e**	mein	mein**e**

hundertsiebzehn 117

Grammatik 2

Compound nouns and plural forms of nouns (Unit 3, page 110)

Schreiben 1 Translate the words into German.
1. clothes shop
2. shoe shop
3. bread shop
4. gift shop
5. cheese shop

Schreiben 2 Translate the sentences into German using the correct plural form of the noun.
1. In my town there are lots of streets.
2. There are two hotels.
3. There are lots of clocks.
4. There are fifteen shops.
5. There are lots of houses.
6. There are three markets.

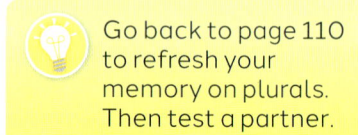

> Go back to page 110 to refresh your memory on plurals. Then test a partner.

The conditional of *mögen* (Unit 4, page 113)

Lesen 3 Put the words into the correct order to make sentences.

1 möchte	große	haben	Wohnung	Ich	eine		
2 Ich	kleines	Haus	modernes	ein	möchte	haben	
3 Wohnzimmer	möchte	neues	Ich	haben	ein		
4 Computer	kaufen	möchte	einen	Sie			
5 fahren	Am	Wochenende	ich	in	Stadt	die	möchte
6 fahren	In	wir	Sommerferien	ins	den	Ausland	möchten

> The verb *mögen* means 'to like'. The conditional form of this verb is **möchten**, which means 'would like'. It is used with an <u>infinitive</u> at the end of the phrase.
>
> Ich **möchte** in Berlin <u>wohnen</u>.   I **would like** <u>to live</u> in Berlin.
>
> | | |
> |---|---|
> | ich möchte | wir möchten |
> | du möchtest | ihr möchtet |
> | er/sie/es/man möchte | Sie möchten |
> | | sie möchten |

Schreiben 4 Put the sentences into the conditional, using the correct conditional form of *mögen*.

Example: 1 *Ich wohne in Europa.* → *Ich möchte in Europa wohnen.*

1. Ich wohne in Europa.
2. Ich wohne auf dem Land.
3. Ich wohne in einem modernen Haus.
4. Ich habe ein großes Wohnzimmer.
5. Wir haben eine kleine Küche.
6. Sie hat einen Computer.
7. Wir wohnen an der Küste.

Kapitel 5

Prepositions with the accusative and the dative (Unit 5, page 115)

Lesen 5 **Translate the instructions into English.**

Example: 1 *The table goes under the window.*

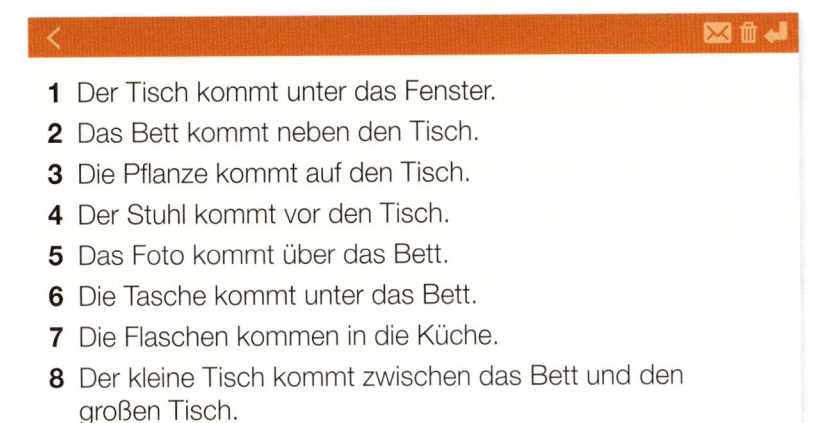

1 Der Tisch kommt unter das Fenster.
2 Das Bett kommt neben den Tisch.
3 Die Pflanze kommt auf den Tisch.
4 Der Stuhl kommt vor den Tisch.
5 Das Foto kommt über das Bett.
6 Die Tasche kommt unter das Bett.
7 Die Flaschen kommen in die Küche.
8 Der kleine Tisch kommt zwischen das Bett und den großen Tisch.

> Remember that some prepositions are followed by the **accusative** when there is movement towards an object, or by the **dative** when there is no movement:
>
> | | |
> |---|---|
> | **an** | on (a vertical surface) |
> | **auf** | on (a horizontal surface) |
> | **hinter** | behind |
> | **in** | in |
> | **neben** | next to |
> | **über** | over, above |
> | **unter** | under |
> | **vor** | in front of |
> | **zwischen** | between |
>
> Go back to page 115 to refresh your memory on using prepositions with the accusative and dative. Then test a partner.

Sprechen 6 **Draw a plan of a house and tell a partner in which room to put the following items. Your partner has to draw the items in the correct room.**

Example: Das Bett kommt neben den Tisch.

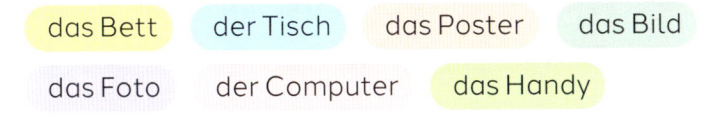

das Bett   der Tisch   das Poster   das Bild
das Foto   der Computer   das Handy

Schreiben 7 **Write a description of the bedroom plan you drew in exercise 6, using as many different prepositions + dative forms as possible.**

Example: Das Bett ist unter dem Fenster.

Schreiben 8 **Translate the sentences into German.**
1 The living room is next to the kitchen.
2 The table goes in the dining room.
3 The garden is behind the house.
4 The bathroom is between the office and the bedroom.
5 I'm putting the table into the cellar.
6 The plant goes on top of the table.

Los geht's!

Schreiben 9 **Copy and complete the text with the correct words from the box.**

– **1** Wo gehst du normalerweise einkaufen, Leon?

– Ich gehe gern ins Einkaufszentrum in **2** Stadtmitte (f), **3** es dort viele Geschäfte gibt. Ich muss heute ein Geburtstagsgeschenk für **4** Stiefvater (m) kaufen. Nach **5** Schule (f) fahre ich mit **6** Bus (m) in **7** Stadt (f). Das ist **8** als mit dem Fahrrad, finde ich.

der	weil
die	meinen
dem	der
~~wo~~	schneller

hundertneunzehn 119

Kapitel 5 — Lese- und Hörtest

Reading

Lesen 1

My town. You read Jana's blog about where she lives. Write **A**, **B** or **C** to complete each sentence.

> Ich wohne in einer Kleinstadt auf dem Land. Sie liegt im Norden von der Schweiz. Die Region ist besonders schön und sehr ruhig. Im Stadtzentrum gibt es einige Geschäfte, einen Supermarkt und eine Kirche. Leider gibt es kein Kino, aber wir haben ein neues Stadion.
>
> Meine Wohnung liegt nicht weit von einem kleinen Park weg. Für die jungen Leute kann es manchmal langweilig sein, aber hier sind die Menschen immer ziemlich freundlich.

1. Jana lives …
   - A in a big city.
   - B in the countryside.
   - C in the south of Switzerland.

   Read the detail of the options carefully. The incorrect statements will often be very similar to what is said in the text, but not quite the same.

2. The town centre **doesn't** have …
   - A any shops.
   - B a cinema.
   - C a stadium.

   All of these answer options are mentioned, so check the text carefully for negatives to identify the correct answer.

3. Jana lives …
   - A not far from her friends.
   - B near a big park.
   - C not far from a park.

4. Jana thinks that the town is …
   - A sometimes boring.
   - B quite unfriendly.
   - C always boring.

   Qualifiers and intensifiers can change the meaning: make sure you know what they all mean.

Lesen 2

Transport. You read these forum posts. What do these people think about different modes of transport? Write **P** for a **positive** opinion, **N** for a **negative** opinion, or **P + N** for a **positive and negative** opinion.

Jonas: Ich fahre oft mit dem Bus in die Stadt, da ich finde, dass es ziemlich billig und praktisch ist. Aber die Reise ist immer zu langsam. Später möchte ich mein eigenes Auto haben.

Samira: Ich wohne in einem Dorf. Jeden Tag fahre ich gern mit meinem Fahrrad zur Schule, weil ich das gesund finde. Ich treffe meine Freundin und wir fahren zusammen. Das macht immer Spaß.

Arda: Ich fahre normalerweise mit dem Zug ins Stadtzentrum, aber leider gibt es oft zu viele Menschen im Zug und das finde ich unbequem. Meiner Meinung nach ist der Zug auch zu teuer.

Lesen 3 Translate these sentences into English.

Don't mirror German word order – make your English translations sound natural.

Make sure you translate every word. It's easy to miss words like *viele*.

1 Ich gehe oft in die Stadt.
2 Es gibt viele Aktivitäten für junge Leute.
3 Wenn es regnet, fährt er mit dem Bus.
4 Ich finde den Zug teuer, aber ich fahre nie mit dem Auto.
5 In den Sommerferien sind wir in die Schweiz geflogen.

Think about the best way to translate *mit* when you are talking about transport.

Pay attention to the tense here.

Listening

Hören 4 *My home.* Katharina is talking about her home. What does she say her home has? Listen to the recording and write the letters of the <u>four</u> correct answers.

A	office
B	living room
C	trees
D	playroom
E	plants
F	kitchen

Hören 5 *Shopping.* You hear Felix talking about shopping in his town. What does he say? Listen to the recording and write A, B or C for each question.

1 Felix normally travels to the shopping centre …
   A by car.   B by train.   C on foot.

2 There used to be more … in the town centre.
   A people   B traffic   C shops

3 He will buy a new …
   A shirt.   B jacket.   C pair of trousers.

4 Buying online will be … than buying in a shop.
   A cheaper   B quicker   C easier

Dictation

Hören 6 You will hear <u>four</u> short sentences. Write down exactly what you hear in German.

Think carefully about how these sounds are pronounced when writing down what you hear:
s, ss and *ß*
sp, st and *sch*
w

In the dictation task, there will always be some words that are not on the vocabulary list. You may not have come across them before, so listen carefully and think about the sounds you hear when you transcribe (write down) these words.

hunderteinundzwanzig

Kapitel 5 Mündlicher Test

Role-play

Sprechen 1 Look at the role-play card and prepare what you are going to say.

> Work with the vocabulary you know. You could use words like 'in a town / a flat / the north'.

You are talking to your Austrian friend about where you live.

1 Say where you live. (Give **one** detail.)
2 Say how you travel to school. (Give **one** detail.)
3 Give **one** opinion about your local area.
4 Say **one** activity you do in your local area.
5 ? Ask your friend a question about a place in town.

> Think about how you would say '**by** bus/train' or '**on** foot'.

> You don't have to give a detailed answer to this. 'I find it ...' or 'It is ...' + adjective is enough.

> You could mention the cinema, shopping or a sport. Make sure you use a correct verb.

> You could use a question word here (*wo, was, wie,* etc.) or you could use subject–verb inversion: 'Is there ...?', 'Can you ...?'

Sprechen 2 Practise what you have prepared. Then, using your notes, listen and respond to the teacher.

Hören 3 Listen to Sam's answers. Make a note of:
  a how he answers the questions for points 1–4
  b what question he asks for point 5.

Reading aloud

Sprechen 4 Look at this task. With a partner, read the sentences aloud, paying attention to the underlined letters.

> Ich finde Einkaufen <u>s</u>pannend.
> Jedes <u>W</u>ochenende gehe ich ins <u>St</u>adtzentrum.
> Hier findet man eine <u>s</u>ehr große Einkauf<u>ss</u>traße.
> Es gibt viele <u>sch</u>öne Ge<u>sch</u>äfte, aber <u>s</u>ie <u>s</u>ind <u>w</u>irklich teuer.
> Oft kaufen <u>w</u>ir <u>S</u>chuhe, <u>Sp</u>ort<u>s</u>achen oder Ge<u>sch</u>enke.

> Think carefully about how to pronounce these sounds:
> *s, ss* and *ß*
> *sp, st* and *sch*
> *w*

Hören 5 Listen and check your pronunciation.

Sprechen 6 Listen to the teacher asking four follow-up questions. Translate each question into English and prepare your own answer to each one. Then listen again and respond to the teacher.

Photo card

You will be asked to talk about the content of these photos. You must say at least one thing about each photo.

After you have spoken about the content of the photos, you will be asked questions related to any of the topics within the theme of **Communication and the world around us**.

Your responses should be as **full and detailed** as possible.

7 Listen to Sam describing the photos and answer the questions.
1 Where does Sam think the people in the first photo are going?
2 Which **three** people does he mention?
3 Where does he say the people in the second photo are?
4 What does he think the man does for a job?

8 Prepare your own description of both photos. Then, with a partner, take turns describing them.

> Auf dem ersten Foto gibt es …

9 Listen to the teacher's first follow-up question, *Was hast du letzte Woche gekauft?*, and Sam's response. Then answer the questions.
1 Where did Sam and his friend go last weekend?
2 Why does Sam think it is great there?
3 What did Sam buy?
4 What was the problem with the shirt?

10 Listen to Sam answering the question, *Was wirst du nächste Woche in deiner Stadt machen?* Write down the <u>six</u> missing words in German.

Am Montag werden wir zum **1** fahren, weil meine Tante kommt. Sie wird eine Woche bei uns **2** . Am Dienstag werden wir ins Kino **3** . Am Samstag werden wir ins **4** gehen und dann essen wir in einem Restaurant. Am Sonntag **5** ich mit meinem Hund im Park **6** .

11 Listen to two more follow-up questions and prepare your answers. Then respond to the recording.

12 Prepare your own answers to as many of the Module 5 questions on page 227 as you can. Then practise with a partner.

- Always mirror the tense of the question you are being asked. To help your answers sound more natural, build up a collection of time phrases, such as *normalerweise* (present), *gestern* (past), *später* (future) and *heute* (any time frame).
- Try to expand your answers if you can. You heard Sam give details and opinions in his responses to the first two follow-up questions (exercises 9 and 10).

hundertdreiundzwanzig

Kapitel 5 Schreibtest

Describing a photo

Schreiben 1 Look at this writing exam task. Copy and complete Lisa's responses with an appropriate verb.

1 Es ___ drei junge Frauen auf dem Foto.
2 Die Frauen ___ viele Taschen.
3 Sie ___ im Stadtzentrum.
4 Eine Frau ___ ein Foto mit einem Handy.
5 Sie ___ und sehen glücklich aus.

Schreiben 2 Prepare your own answer to the task.

> In this task, you must refer directly to what you can see in the picture. Don't give your opinion about it, and make sure all your sentences include a verb.

You see this photo on Instagram.

What is in the photo?
Write **five** sentences in **German**.

Translation

Schreiben 3 Read the English sentences and Lisa's translations. Correct the <u>eight</u> mistakes in the translations.

1 I love my town.	1 Ich liebe meine Gegend.
2 There are lots of shops.	2 Es gibt viele Häuser.
3 Unfortunately, there is no cinema.	3 Leider haben wir ein Kino.
4 When I was younger, we lived in a village.	4 Als ich älter war, haben wir in einem Haus gewohnt.
5 I prefer living in the countryside.	5 Ich lebe nicht gern an der Küste.

Schreiben 4 Translate these sentences into German.

1 I like my area.
2 There are lots of shops and a small cinema.
3 We don't have a station in my town.
4 When I was ten we lived in a flat.
5 My brother prefers living in a house.

> Check your word order and spelling, and remember that nouns have capital letters in German.

90-word writing task

Schreiben 5 Look at this writing exam task and then, for each bullet point:

1 think about the vocabulary and structures you have learned which you could use in your answer. For example:
  • **nouns** and **adjectives** to write about the facilities where you live
  • language for **narrating a story** about a visit to town
  • how to explain what your **plans** are and **why**
  • connectives and intensifiers you would like to use.
2 write down three or four ideas for what you could write about.
3 identify which tense(s) you could use in your answer.

You are writing to your Austrian friend about your local area.

Write approximately **90** words in **German**.

You must write something about each bullet point.

Describe:
• where you live
• what you did in town last week
• where you will live in the future.

124 *hundertvierundzwanzig*

Kapitel 5

Lesen 6 Read Lisa's answer to the exam task. Answer the questions in the coloured boxes (1–5).

1 This is an example of **complex language**. What does it mean? Find <u>three</u> more examples of complex language in the text.

2 Which synonyms or alternatives could Lisa use here to **avoid repetition**?

3 Which form of the **verb** is this? When is it used? Which other tenses does Lisa use?

Es gibt viele Geschäfte im Stadtzentrum. Wir haben einen Supermarkt, Kleidungsgeschäfte und Schuhgeschäfte. Hier kann man auch Bücher, Geburtstagskarten und Käsekuchen kaufen. Die Stadt ist sehr grün und ziemlich sauber. Leider gibt es kein Kino und das Sportzentrum ist ziemlich klein. Ich finde die Stadt langweilig. Sie ist sehr ruhig.

Letzte Woche habe ich Tennis im Park gespielt, weil das mein Lieblingssport ist. Ich habe auch das Schloss besucht. Das ist sehr historisch.

In der Zukunft werde ich in einer Großstadt leben. Ich möchte lieber in einem modernen Haus leben.

4 Lisa uses a variety of **compound nouns**. What do these words mean? Find <u>two</u> more examples.

5 Which connective could you use here to form an **extended sentence**? Which other connectives does Lisa use?

Lesen 7 Read Lisa's answer again. Copy and complete the sentences in English.

1 There are lots of ___ where Lisa lives.
2 Lisa's town is very ___ and quite ___.
3 Lisa thinks it's boring living here because it's very ___.
4 Last week, Lisa visited the ___.
5 Lisa would like to live in a ___.

Schreiben 8 Prepare your own answer to the task.
- Think about how you can develop your answer for each bullet point.
- Look back at your notes from exercises 5 and 6.
- Use the 'Challenge checklist' to help you show off your German!
- Write a **brief** plan and organise your answer into paragraphs.
- Write your answer and then carefully check for accuracy.

Think carefully about word order:
- Make sure that all conjugated verbs are the second idea in the sentence and that past participles and infinitives come last.
- If you are using a subordinating conjunction such as *dass*, *weil*, *da* or *obwohl*, make sure you put the verb at the end of the clause.
- Remember TMP (Time – Manner – Place).

Challenge checklist

✓ Connectives (*und*, *aber*)
✓ Some extended sentences (*Ich fahre mit dem Bus in die Stadt.*)
✓ An opinion (*Ich finde die Hose schön.*)

✓ Intensifiers and qualifiers (*besonders*, *ganz*)
✓ Different persons of the verb (*meine Stadt ist*, *die Geschäfte sind*)
✓ Past, present and future time frames
✓ Compound nouns (*das Stadtzentrum*, *das Kleidungsgeschäft*)
✓ Comparatives (*länger*, *größer*, *höher als ...*)

✓ More complex connectives (*weil*, *dass*, *da*)
✓ Inversion (*leider gibt es*, *in der Zukunft werde ich*, *hier kann man*)
✓ Conditional of *mögen* + infinitive (*Ich möchte an der Küste leben.*)
✓ Accusative prepositions (*für meinen Bruder*, *durch den Park*)
✓ Use of plural nouns (*die Häuser*, *die Straßen*, *die Autos sind*)
✓ Imperfect tense (*früher gab es*, *die Stadt war*, *ich hatte*)

hundertfünfundzwanzig 125

Kapitel 5 Wörter

Key:
bold = this word will appear in higher exams only
* = this word is not on the vocabulary list but you may use it in your own sentences

Wo spricht man Deutsch? (p104–105):

Die *deutschsprachigen Länder	German-speaking countries	der Berg	mountain
Deutschland	Germany	der Fluss	river
*Belgien	Belgium	der Nationalfeiertag	national day
*Liechtenstein	Liechtenstein	die Größe	size
*Luxemburg	Luxembourg	die Hauptstadt	capital city
*Namibia	Namibia	die Region	region
Österreich	Austria	die Sprache	language
die Schweiz	Switzerland	das Land	country, land, state
*Südtirol	South Tyrol	hoch	high
		lang	long
		klein	small
		groß	big/tall

Wo wohnst du? (pages 106–107):

Wo ich wohne	Where I live	Es gibt …	There is …
Ich wohne …	I live …	(k)einen Bahnhof.	no station / a station.
in einem Dorf.	in a village.	(k)einen Flughafen.	no airport / an airport.
in einer Kleinstadt.	in a small town.	(k)einen Supermarkt.	no supermarket / a supermarket.
in einer *Großstadt.	in a city.	(k)eine Kirche.	no church / a church.
in der Stadtmitte.	in the town/city centre.	(k)eine Moschee.	no mosque / a mosque.
am Stadt**rand**.	on the outskirts.	(k)eine Schule.	no school / a school.
auf dem Land.	in the countryside.	(k)eine Synagoge.	no synagogue / a synagogue.
Das ist …	That is …	(k)einen Tempel.	no temple / a temple.
im Norden von …	in the north of …	(k)eine Universität.	no university / a university.
im Osten von …	in the east of …	(k)ein Kino.	no cinema / a cinema.
im Süden von …	in the south of …	(k)ein Schloss.	no castle / a castle.
im Westen von …	in the west of …	(k)ein Stadion.	no stadium / a stadium.
Der Ort ist …	The place/location/town is …	(k)ein Theater.	no theatre / a theatre.
Die Gegend ist …	The region, area is …	viele Geschäfte.	a lot of shops.
Die Region ist …	The region is …	aus	out, out of, from
Die Umgebung ist …	The surroundings are …	außer	except, apart from
		bei	at (the house of), with
alt/neu.	old/new.	mit	with
sauber/schmutzig.	clean/dirty.	nach	to, towards, after, according to
ruhig/laut.	quiet/noisy.	von	from, of
sicher.	safe.	zu	to

Wie fährst du? (pages 108–109):

Das Verkehrsmittel	Means of transport	weil …	because …
Ich fahre / Wir fahren …, …	I/We go …, …	ich in der Nähe wohne.	I live nearby.
mit dem Auto …	by car	ich weit weg wohne.	I live far away.
mit dem Bus …	by bus	es bequem ist.	it is comfortable.
mit dem **Elektroauto** …	by electric car	es billig ist.	it is cheap.
mit dem Fahrrad …	by bicycle/bike	es praktisch ist.	it is practical.
mit dem Fahrzeug …	by vehicle	es schnell ist.	it is fast.
mit dem Schiff …	by ship	es teuer ist.	it is expensive.
mit dem Zug …	by train	es langsam ist.	it is slow.
mit der Bahn …	by rail	bis	until, till, up to, by
Ich fliege / Wir fliegen …, …	I/We fly …, …	durch	through
mit dem Flugzeug …	by plane …	für	for
in die USA	to the USA	gegen	against
in die Stadtmitte	to the town/city centre	ohne	without
nach Hause	home	um	at (… o'clock), around
zum Bahnhof	to the station		
zum Flughafen	to the airport		
zur Schule	to school		

126 *hundertsechsundzwanzig*

Kapitel 5

Wo gehst du gern einkaufen? (pages 110–111):

Einkaufen	*Shopping*
der Supermarkt	supermarket
das Einkaufszentrum	shopping centre
das Geschäft	shop
das Käsegeschäft	cheese shop
das Kleidungsgeschäft	clothes shop
das *Schokoladengeschäft	chocolate shop
das *Secondhandgeschäft	second-hand shop

In meinem Dorf / In meiner Stadt gibt es …
   keine/viele Geschäfte.
   einige Secondhandgeschäfte.
   viele Cafés.
   einen großen Supermarkt.
   ein großes Einkaufszentrum.

In my village/town there is/are …
   no/lots of shops.
   some second-hand shops.
   lots of cafés.
   a large supermarket.
   a large sho pping centre.

Ich kaufe (nicht) gern … ein, …
   im Einkaufszentrum
   online

I (don't) like shopping …
   in the shopping centre,
   online,

weil das … ist.
   einfach(er)
   billig(er)
   praktisch(er)

because it is …
   easy (easier).
   cheap(er).
   practical (more practical).

Man kann Zeit sparen.
Man kann schöne Sachen finden.
Man kann Produkte einfach zurückschicken.
Man kann Produkte sofort zurückschicken.
Man kann Produkte von zu Hause einkaufen.
Man bekommt bessere …
   Informationen.
   Preise.

You can save time.
You can find beautiful things.
You can simply/easily return products.
You can return products immediately.
You can buy products from home.
You get better …
   information.
   prices.

Mein idealer *Wohnort (pages 112–113):

Wie ist dein idealer *Wohnort?	*What is your ideal place to live like?*
freundlich	friendly
sauber	clean
schön	beautiful
ideal	ideal
schmutzig	dirty
schön	beautiful
unfreundlich	unfriendly
der Baum	tree
die *Großstadt	city
die **Hauptstadt**	capital city
die Kleinstadt	small town
die Küste	coast
die Wohnung	flat
das Dorf	village
das Fitness-Studio	gym
das Haus	house

Ich möchte in (Österreich) leben.
Ich möchte im Ausland leben.

I would like to live in (Austria).
I would like to live abroad.

Bei mir zu Hause (pages 114–115):

Zimmer zu Hause	Rooms at home
Im Badezimmer *dusche ich.	I shower in the bathroom.
Im Büro / Im *Arbeitszimmer arbeite ich.	I work in the office/study.
Im Esszimmer esse ich (zu Mittag / zu Abend).	I eat (lunch/dinner) in the dining room.
In der *Garage *parken wir das Auto.	We park the car in the garage.
Im Garten lese ich.	I read in the garden.
In der Küche *frühstücke ich. / kochen wir.	I have breakfast / We cook in the kitchen.
Im Schlafzimmer schlafe ich.	I sleep in the bedroom.
Im Wohnzimmer spiele ich auf dem Computer.	I play on the computer in the living room.

an	on, at
auf	on, onto, at, to
in	in, into
hinter	behind
neben	next to, beside
über	about, above, over
unter	under, below, among
vor	in front of, before, ago
zwischen	between

hundertsiebenundzwanzig

Kapitel 1–5 Grammatik: Wiederholung

Possessive adjectives

Schreiben 1 Everyone loves their pet! Copy and complete the sentences with the correct possessive adjective, using the words from the box.

1 Ich liebe *mein* Haustier.
2 Du liebst ___ Haustier.
3 Er liebt ___ Haustier.
4 Sie liebt ___ Haustier.
5 Das Kind liebt ___ Haustier.
6 Wir lieben ___ Haustier.
7 Ihr liebt ___ Haustier.
8 Frau Maier, Sie lieben ___ Haustier.
9 Die Kinder lieben ___ Haustier.

~~mein~~   ihr   unser   dein   Ihr
euer   sein   ihr   sein

Relative pronouns and possessive adjectives

Lesen 2 Select the correct pronoun and possessive adjective to complete each sentence. Then translate the sentences into English.

1 Das Kind, **der** / **die** / **das** Lukas heißt, ist **mein** / **meine** Bruder.
2 Die Frau, **der** / **die** / **das** blonde Haare hat, ist **unser** / **unsere** Mutter.
3 Der Film, **der** / **die** / **das** heute ins Kino kommt, ist **dein** / **deine** Lieblingsfilm.
4 Die Bücher, **der** / **die** / **das** im Klassenzimmer sind, sind **euer** / **eure** Bücher.
5 Die Ärztin, **der** / **die** / **das** im Krankenhaus arbeitet, ist **mein** / **meine** Tante.
6 Das Fest, **der** / **die** / **das** Karneval heißt, ist **unser** / **unsere** Lieblingsfest.
7 Die Schülerin, **der** / **die** / **das** neben Samira sitzt, ist **ihr** / **ihre** Freundin.
8 Der blaue Rock, **der** / **die** / **das** auf dem Stuhl liegt, ist **mein** / **meine** Rock.

Comparatives

älter   einfacher   interessanter   jünger   kleiner   später

Schreiben 3 Choose a word from the box to complete each sentence.

1 Ich finde Mathe schwieriger als Physik. Physik finde ich ___ .
2 Mein Bruder ist älter als meine Schwester. Meine Schwester ist ___ als mein Bruder.
3 Die Kindersendung kommt früher im Fernsehen als der Actionfilm. Die Nachrichten kommen ___ .
4 Deine Schuhe sind größer als meine. Meine Füße sind ___ als deine.
5 Janas Handy ist neuer als Mias Handy. Ihr Handy ist viel ___ .
6 Das Buch ist langweiliger als der Film. Ich finde den Film ___ .

Subordinating conjunctions

obwohl   wenn   weil   dass

Schreiben 4 Select the correct conjunction to fill the gaps.

Ich finde, ___ mein Bruder manchmal schlechte Laune hat. Ich mag ihn, ___ er nicht immer nett zu mir ist. Aber ich liebe ihn, ___ er mein Bruder ist. Er hat meistens schlechte Laune, ___ er zu viele Hausaufgaben hat.

Grammatik: Wiederholung — Kapitel 1–5

Subordinate clauses

Lesen 5 Match up the main clauses with the subordinate clauses.

1 Das Wetter muss schön sein,
2 Wir wohnen in einem Dorf. Ich finde,
3 Tim möchte keine Party haben,
4 Frida darf den Film nicht sehen,
5 Hast du Ohrenschmerzen? Ich glaube,
6 Meine Geschwister sollen länger schlafen,
7 Ich kann nicht gut lernen,
8 Elias isst viel Kuchen,

a wenn es im Unterricht laut ist.
b obwohl er Geburtstag hat.
c wenn ich im Sommer schwimmen gehe.
d obwohl das ungesund ist.
e weil sie zu jung ist.
f dass die Musik zu laut ist.
g weil sie oft müde sind.
h dass es hier zu ruhig ist.

Subordinate clauses with *wenn*

schlecht, mit dem Auto, habe, viel Energie, ist, feiere, zu Fuß, fahre, das Wetter, mit meiner Familie, ich, Silvester, Basketball, schön, spiele, es, gehe

> Remember the '**verb-comma-verb**' rule when you begin the sentence with a subordinate clause.

Schreiben 6 Translate the sentences into German using words and phrases in the word cloud. Begin each sentence with *wenn*. Some words are used more than once.

1 When the weather is nice I go on foot.
2 When the weather is bad I go by car.
3 When I have a lot of energy I play basketball.
4 When it is New Year's Eve I celebrate with my family.

Modal verbs

Lesen 7 Are these sentences in the present, past or conditional? Write the sentence numbers in the table below.

1 Ich konnte nichts essen.
2 Wir mögen unser Haus.
3 Durftest du spät ins Bett gehen?
4 Meine Eltern wollen ein neues Auto kaufen.
5 Ich möchte aktiver sein.
6 Wir müssen gesünder essen.
7 Möchten Sie Karneval in Deutschland feiern?
8 Er musste Deutsch lernen.

Present	Past	Conditional

Lesen 8 Translate the sentences in exercise 7 into English.

hundertneunundzwanzig 129

Kapitel 1–5 Grammatik: Wiederholung

Prepositions

Schreiben 1 Copy the Venn diagram and fill it in with the prepositions from the box according to whether they take the accusative or dative case. If they can take both cases, write them in the middle.

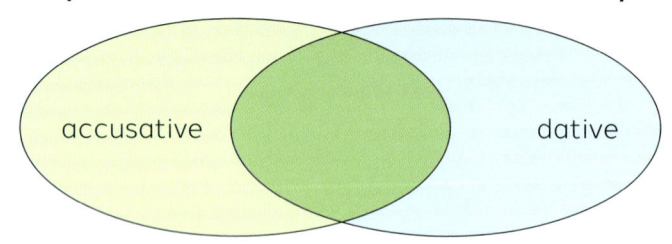

accusative | dative

an auf aus außer bei bis durch
für gegen gegenüber hinter
in mit nach neben ohne seit
über um unter von vor
wider zu zwischen

Lesen 2 Select the correct article or possessive adjective. Think carefully about which case is needed after each preposition.
1 Die Bücher für **der / den / die** Englischstunde liegen auf **der / dem / den** Tisch.
2 Lena fährt mit **der / das / dem** Fahrrad in **die / der / den** Stadt.
3 Wir feiern Weihnachten immer mit **die / den / der** ganzen Familie bei **unserer / unseren / unserem** Tante.
4 Matteo bekommt ein Geschenk von **seinem / seiner / seinen** Onkel **zum / zur / zu den** Geburtstag.
5 Nach **das / der / dem** Essen geht Leon durch **das / dem / den** Zimmer und aus **das / dem / den** Haus.
6 Ich gehe jeden Samstag mit **meinem / meiner / meinen** Freund **im / ins / in den** Kino.

Pronouns in the dative case

Schreiben 3 Write out the correct pronoun to complete each sentence.

ihm   ihr

1 Mein Vater ist nett. Ich verstehe mich gut mit ___.
2 Meine Freundin geht oft einkaufen. Ich gehe gern mit ___ in die Stadt.
3 Mein Onkel wohnt in der Schweiz. Ich habe eine E-Mail von ___ bekommen.
4 Jeden Sommer besuchen wir unsere Oma. Wir verbringen immer eine Woche bei ___.
5 Wir haben ein süßes Pferd. Alle Kinder machen gern Fotos von ___.
6 Mein Halbbruder ist jünger als ich. Ich gehe manchmal mit ___ schwimmen.

Question words

Lesen 4 Match up the questions and answers.

1 Um wie viel Uhr ist das Frühstück?
2 Was willst du essen?
3 Wer isst Pommes?
4 Wohin kommt dieser neue Tisch?
5 Wann beginnt das Spiel?
6 Wo siehst du fern?
7 Wie viele Zimmer hat dein Haus?
8 Wie fühlst du dich?

a Mein Freund.
b Sechs.
c Um 14:00 Uhr.
d Von 8:00 bis 10:00 Uhr.
e Ein Stück Kuchen.
f Im Wohnzimmer.
g Ziemlich müde.
h Ins Wohnzimmer.

Grammatik: Wiederholung — Kapitel 1–5

Compound nouns

Lesen 5 Use the words in the word cloud to form the six pairs of compound nouns listed below. The second word in the first pair will form the first word of the next pair, for example:

a summer holiday: Sommerferien
b holiday house: Ferienhaus

1 a supermarket   b market square
2 a football match   b playing field
3 a hospital   b pet
4 a rock music   b music teacher
5 a large town / city   b town centre
6 a afternoon   b lunch

Word cloud: Essen, groß, Haus, Fußball, Feld, Lehrer, Markt, Kranken, Mittag, Mitte, Musik, nach, Platz, Rock, Spiel, Stadt, super, Tier

One of these compound nouns needs a joining letter. Which one?

Identifying tenses

Lesen 6 Are these time phrases used to show past, present or future tenses? Copy and fill in the table.

morgen · nächste Woche · letztes Wochenende · gestern · jetzt · in der Zukunft · dieses Jahr · früher · heute · nächstes Jahr · später · normalerweise · letzten Dienstag · jeden Tag · als Kind

Past	Present	Future

Past, present and future tenses

Schreiben 7 Copy and complete the sentences with the correct tense (past, present or future) of the verb in brackets.

1 Dieses Jahr ___ ich meinen Geburtstag zu Hause. Letztes Jahr ___ ich mit meiner Familie in einem Restaurant ___ . Nächstes Jahr ___ ich mit meinen Freunden ___ . (*feiern*)

2 Jetzt ___ wir Deutsch. Gestern ___ wir Geschichte ___ . Morgen ___ wir Englisch ___ . (*lernen*)

3 Heute ___ ich ein Käsebrot zu Mittag. Gestern ___ ich Würste ___ . Morgen ___ ich mehr Gemüse ___ . (*essen*)

4 Jetzt ___ meine Mutter Wasser. Gestern ___ sie zum Frühstück Kaffee ___ . Später ___ sie einen Tee ___ . (*trinken*)

5 Jedes Wochenende ___ wir meine Oma. Letztes Wochenende ___ wir auch meine Tante ___ . Nächste Woche ___ wir meinen Opa in Deutschland ___ . (*besuchen*)

6 Jeden Tag ___ ich mit dem Bus zur Schule. Früher ___ ich mit dem Fahrrad ___ . Nächstes Jahr ___ ich mit dem Auto ___ . (*fahren*)

hunderteinunddreißig 131

Kapitel 6 Schöne Ferien!

Im Urlaub und unterwegs
- Learning about German-speaking travel destinations
- Using adjectival endings after the definite article

Haben Sie schon Reiselust?

Wir nehmen Sie auf eine spannende Reise in Deutschland, Österreich und der Schweiz mit. Es gibt dort so viele tolle Orte! Wir zeigen Ihnen die hohen Berge, die schönen Seen, die langen Flüsse, die beliebten Städte und die interessanten Touristenattraktionen. Drei Länder, tausende schöne Orte. Los geht's!

Es gibt in der Nähe von Köln den großen Freizeitpark **Phantasialand**. Hier gibt es spannende Achterbahnen und tolle Attraktionen!

Man kann in Berlin das bekannte und historische **Brandenburger Tor** besuchen. Diese wichtige Attraktion ist ein Symbol von dem Fall der Mauer und von der deutschen Wiedervereinigung.

Die berühmten **Krimmler Wasserfälle** sind im Nationalpark Hohe Tauern. Sie sind besonders hoch – etwa 380 Meter. Man kann hier wunderbare Fotos machen.

Hier im Süden von Deutschland gibt es den alten und ruhigen **Schwarzwald**. Man kann hier leckeres Essen, wie die Schwarzwälder Kirschtorte, finden!

Hier in der Schweiz kann man die lange und traditionelle **Churwalden Pradaschier Rodelbahn** besuchen. Sie ist genau 3 060 Meter lang – und es macht viel Spaß!

die Wiedervereinigung	reunification
die Achterbahn (-en)	roller coaster
die Schwarzwälder Kirschtorte	Black Forest gateau
die Rodelbahn	toboggan run

132 hundertzweiunddreißig

Kulturzone — Kapitel 6

Lesen 1 Read the brochure, then copy and complete the sentences with words from the box below. There are more words than gaps.

1. The Brandenburg Gate is well known and …
2. Phantasialand has … roller coasters.
3. The Black Forest is described as old and …
4. The Krimml Waterfalls are …
5. The Churwalden Pradaschier toboggan run is long and …

important	historic
wonderful	fantastic
traditional	quiet
exciting	famous
tasty	huge

Lesen 2 Read the brochure again and answer the questions in English.

1. What does the Brandenburg Gate symbolise?
2. Where is Phantasialand located?
3. What food can you try in the Black Forest?
4. What activity is possible at the Krimml Waterfalls?
5. How long is the toboggan run at Churwalden Pradaschier?

G The **endings of adjectives** change after the definite article.

	nominative endings	accusative endings
masc	**Der** groß**e** Fluss heißt die Donau.	Man kann **den** groß**en** Fluss besuchen.
fem	**Die** alt**e** Brücke ist kaputt.	Es gibt auch **die** alt**e** Brücke.
neut	**Das** interessant**e** Museum ist im Stadtzentrum.	Hier kann man **das** interessant**e** Museum sehen.
pl	**Die** berühmt**en** Parks sind schön.	Man kann **die** berühmt**en** Parks in der Stadt besuchen.

Page 144

Hören 3 Listen and write down the words you hear to complete the sentences.

1. Hier in Hamburg kann man die ___ und ___ Modelleisenbahn Miniatur Wunderland besuchen.
2. In Stuttgart gibt es das ___ und ___ Mercedes-Benz Museum.
3. Man kann in Österreich und Deutschland die ___ und ___ Donau sehen.

Sprechen 4 In pairs, take turns to read out the text. Pay attention to the *a/ä* and *o/ö* sounds. Then listen and check.

In Süddeutschland kann man das schöne, hohe und historische Schloss Neuschwanstein besuchen.

Obwohl das Schloss sehr groß ist, ist die Burg in Burghausen viel größer. Sie ist aber nicht höher als Neuschwanstein. Schloss Neuschwanstein ist auch sehr alt, aber die Reichsburg in Cochem ist älter.

die Burg fortress

Remember that an umlaut changes the pronunciation of a vowel.
a can be either short (as in *bek**a**nnt*) or long (as in ***A**bend*).
ä sounds like 'e' in 'g**e**t'.
*a*lt → *ä*lter
o can be either short (as in *t**o**ll*) or long (as in *F**o**tos*).
ö sounds like 'ur' in 'ch**ur**n'.
gr*o*ß → gr*ö*ßer
Listen and repeat the words.

Lesen 5 Translate the text in exercise 4 into English.

Schreiben 6 Describe the photo in exercise 4. Write <u>five</u> short sentences in German.

Auf dem Foto gibt es (eine Familie / ein Schloss / viele Bäume).
Man sieht (drei Personen).
Die Leute …
Das Schloss ist …
Das Wetter ist …

hundertdreiunddreißig **133**

1 Wo fahren wir hin?

- Describing different holiday destinations
- Forming questions
- Discussing advantages and disadvantages

Hören 1 Listen to and read the advert for *Ferienpark Müller*. Put the pictures (a–f) in order.

Willkommen im Ferienpark Müller!

Mögen Sie die Küste? Lieben Sie die schönen und spannenden Wälder und Berge in Norddeutschland? Ferienpark Müller ist ideal für Sie, denn wir haben so viele Aktivitäten für Besucher!

Möchten Sie die Kultur kennenlernen? Man kann hier ein traditionelles und auch ein modernes Museum besuchen. Finden Sie Geschichte interessant? Es gibt direkt am Strand ein altes Schloss, das Strandschloss heißt, und ein Besuch hier ist immer sehr beliebt.

Sind Sie aktiv? Hier kann man im Wald Fahrrad fahren oder in der Natur spazieren gehen. Ideal, wenn man Fotos machen will. Möchten Sie eine ruhigere Aktivität machen? Wir haben einen See – und man kann natürlich auch im Meer schwimmen!

Wollen Sie einkaufen gehen? Man kann in der Nähe viele Geschäfte oder den schönen Markt besuchen und Geschenke kaufen. Möchten Sie lieber Ihre Ruhe haben? Hier kann man auch am Strand liegen und vielleicht ein gutes Buch lesen.

Lesen 2 Read the advert again and answer the questions in English.

1. Which <u>two</u> types of museum are advertised?
2. Where exactly is the castle?
3. When is suggested as a good time to take photos?
4. Other than in a lake, where else can you swim?
5. In which <u>two</u> places can you buy presents?
6. Which activity is suggested when lying on the beach?

e is usually short (j*e*tzt) if it's followed by a double consonant (e.g. tt, ck, ch or tz), or if it's at the end of a word.
e is usually long (s*e*hr) if it's followed by any other consonant. However, *e* is short (mach*e*n) if it is the final syllable of a word.
Listen and repeat the tongue twister. Then practise saying it quickly.
*Im Herbst mach**e**n wir gern Feri**e**n an der Küst**e**. Möcht**e**st du m**e**hr l**e**sen? Willst du ein bissch**e**n Ruh**e** hab**e**n?*

Lesen 3 Translate the <u>underlined</u> questions in exercise 1 into English.

Remember the simple way to form **yes/no questions** in German: simply swap around the **subject** and <u>verb</u>. **G**
Sie sind sehr aktiv. → *Sind Sie sehr aktiv?*
Er geht gern wandern. → *Geht er gern wandern?*
Man kann hier schwimmen gehen. → *Kann man hier schwimmen gehen?*

Page 144

134 *hundertvierunddreißig*

Kapitel 6

Sprechen 4 In pairs, take turns to ask and say what people can or can't do at the *Ferienpark Müller*.

- *Kann man im Ferienpark Müller Basketball spielen?*
- *Nein. Man kann im Ferienpark Müller nicht Basketball spielen.*

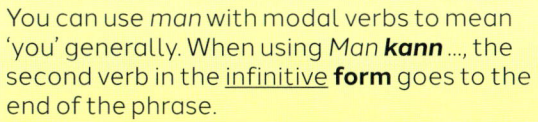

> You can use *man* with modal verbs to mean 'you' generally. When using *Man kann ...*, the second verb in the infinitive form goes to the end of the phrase.
>
> *Man kann die schönen Städte besuchen.*
> You can visit the beautiful towns.
>
> *Man kann Fotos machen.*
> You can take photos.
>
> *Kann man in der Nähe schwimmen gehen?*
> Can you go swimming nearby?

die Ostsee   the Baltic Sea

Hören 5 Listen to a family discussing holiday ideas. Copy and complete the table. (1–3)

	suggestion	advantage	disadvantage
1	the Baltic Sea		

Hören 6 Listen again. Select the correct option to complete each sentence.

1. Mia's best friend went to the Baltic Sea last **summer / month / spring**.
2. Mia's dad suggests **swimming / walking / cycling** in Switzerland.
3. They will travel to Austria by **train / car / coach**.

Schreiben 7 Use the holiday profile cards to describe what you can and can't do in each place. Include how you find that holiday destination and why.

Ort: Zell am See, Österreich

Ort: Sylt, Deutschland

Was denkst du? Wie findest du …?

| Ich finde das
Das ist | gut,
positiv,
schlecht,
negativ, | weil
da

denn | es

das Wetter
das Essen
man kann | besonders
sehr
echt
ganz
ziemlich
(gar) nicht

(nicht) (Tennis) spielen.
(nicht) (schwimmen) gehen. | günstig
ideal
interessant
kalt
langweilig
schön
spannend
wunderbar

gut
schlecht | ist. |

hundertfünfunddreißig **135**

2 Wo werden wir wohnen?

- Describing types of holiday accommodation
- Using *wer*, *wen* and *wem*
- Recognising negatives

Lesen 1 Write the correct letter to match the photos (a–f) to the types of accommodation (1–6).

1 das Ferienhaus
2 das Gästehaus
3 das Hotel
4 der Ferienpark
5 die Ferienwohnung
6 das Hostel

Hören 2 Listen to the adverts for the different types of accommodation. Write the correct letter to match the pictures (a–f) to each advert. (1–6)

Hören 3 Listen to and read the conversation. Translate the questions below into English, then answer the questions.

1 Alina
Was machen wir im Sommer? Ich will nur mit meiner Familie irgendwo sein, wo es warm und sonnig ist. Ich will aber einfach nicht selber kochen.

2 Halim
Ich möchte so gerne draußen sein! Ich will Fahrrad fahren und schwimmen. Wir können jeden Tag 10km wandern und wir werden keine Technologie benutzen. Wir werden so gesund sein!

3 Ben
Nie im Leben! Ich brauche WLAN und muss meinen Computer mitnehmen. Ich will mit meinen Freunden online reden. Ich möchte auch am Strand liegen und nichts machen.

4 Maryam
Ich will mit meinen Freundinnen mit der Bahn wegfahren. Wir wollen ohne unsere Familien tanzen und feiern und wir wollen günstig essen und schlafen. Aber niemand will dasselbe machen! Wie können wir uns entscheiden?

1 Wer will keine Technologie benutzen?
2 Mit wem will Maryam Urlaub machen?
3 Für wen ist viel Bewegung wichtig?
4 Wer will billig essen und schlafen?
5 Für wen ist das Wetter wichtig?
6 Mit wem will Ben sprechen?

> **G** Most interrogatives (question words) don't change their form depending on the case. However, **wer** changes its endings in the accusative and dative.
>
> Nominative: **Wer** will zu Hause bleiben?
> **Who** wants to stay at home?
> Accusative: Für **wen** ist das Wetter wichtig?
> For **whom** is the weather important?
> Dative: Mit **wem** wollen sie fahren?
> With **whom** do they want to travel?
>
> Page 144

Sprechen 4 In groups of 4, read out the conversation in exercise 3. Pay attention to the *ch* sounds.

ch is pronounced like the 'ch' in 'Lo**ch** Ness' when it follows a, o, u or au (e.g. ma**ch**en).
When **ch** follows any other letter, it is a softer sound, like the 'h' in '**H**ugh' (e.g. ni**ch**t).

Listen and repeat the sentence. Then practise saying it quickly.
Ich mö**ch**te nicht sechs Nä**ch**te oder eine Wo**ch**e bleiben; ich brau**ch**e do**ch** a**ch**t Nä**ch**te!

136 *hundertsechsunddreißig*

Kapitel 6

5 Lesen Translate the underlined sentences in exercise 3 into English.

6 Schreiben Translate the questions into German.
1 For whom is technology important?
2 Who wants to be outside?
3 For whom is the food important?
4 With whom does Alina want to go on holiday?

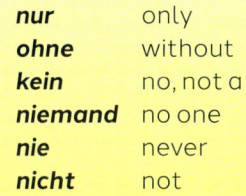

> Watch out for words with a negative meaning:
>
> | | |
> |---|---|
> | **nur** | only |
> | **ohne** | without |
> | **kein** | no, not a |
> | **niemand** | no one |
> | **nie** | never |
> | **nicht** | not |
> | **nichts** | nothing |

7 Sprechen Look at the photos. Prepare a description of them and practise with your partner.

Auf dem ersten/zweiten Foto Auf der linken/rechten Seite Vorne Im Hintergrund	gibt es sehe ich sieht man	einen Ferienpark eine Ferienwohnung ein Hotel/Hostel ein Ferienhaus/Gästehaus	in einer Stadt. auf dem Land. am Meer/See. in den Bergen.
Es gibt Ich sehe Man sieht		einen Mann/Jungen. eine Frau. ein Mädchen. eine Familie.	
Er/Sie trägt Sie tragen		ein Kleid. ein T-Shirt.	
Das Wetter ist		gut/schlecht/sonnig/warm/kalt.	
Die Leute		sehen	glücklich traurig müde	aus.
		lächeln/lachen.	

8 Schreiben Choose an accommodation type from exercise 1. Describe why you would like to stay there and not at the other places. Use the key language box and exercise 3 to help you.

Ich möchte in	einem Ferienpark einem Hotel einem Hostel einem Ferienhaus	wohnen,	weil es	bequem günstig entspannend praktisch	ist.
Ich möchte nie in	einem Gästehaus einer Ferienwohnung			unbequem zu teuer schrecklich unpraktisch	
Ich brauche	WLAN. eine Küche. ein Restaurant.				
Ich möchte	im Stadtzentrum sein. draußen sein. nicht viel Geld ausgeben.				

hundertsiebenunddreißig 137

3 Mein schrecklicher Urlaub

- Describing problems on holiday
- Revising possessive adjectives
- Practising a holiday role-play

Lesen 1 Read the holiday reviews about recent holidays. Write the correct letters to match **two** pictures (a–f) to each review.

Reiserin82 ★☆☆☆☆
Schlechtes Hotel!
Wir waren im Juli im Hotel Schneeglanz und wir werden nie wieder zurückgehen. Wir wollten ein Zimmer mit Blick aufs Meer, aber vor dem Fenster gab es nur Autos. Das Hotel hat auch unsere Taschen verloren und die Tür im Zimmer war kaputt! Ich kann das Hotel nicht empfehlen.

UrlaubLiebhaberin ★★☆☆☆
Praktisch, aber gar nicht ideal!
Zuerst war es im Hotel OK, aber am zweiten Tag gab es eine Party und die Musik war extrem laut. Das Bett war auch sehr unbequem. Das Hotel hat ein anderes Zimmer für mich gefunden und das war viel besser. Das Essen war ganz gut, aber das Hotel war für mich nicht ideal.

Sonne-Fan-Nr1 ★☆☆☆☆
Gar nicht gut!
Das Zimmer im Hotel war klein und kalt, und mein Fenster war schmutzig. Es gab keinen Garten und kein Restaurant. Das WLAN war schlecht und der Stuhl in meinem Zimmer war kaputt. Die Mitarbeiter waren ganz unhöflich und haben nichts gemacht. Es war auch sehr teuer: €180 pro Nacht!

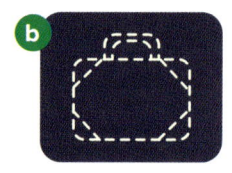

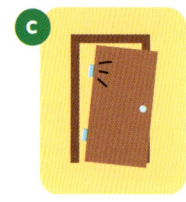

Lesen 2 Copy and complete the sentences with words from the box. There are more words than gaps.

1. Reiserin82 stayed at Hotel Schneeglanz …
2. Hotel Schneeglanz lost Reiserin82's …
3. UrlaubLiebhaberin's bed was …
4. UrlaubLiebhaberin's second room was …
5. Sonne-Fan-Nr1 found his room small and …
6. The chair in Sonne-Fan-Nr1's room was …

broken	bags	worse
in July	uncomfortable	cold
camera	better	yesterday

Sprechen 3 Read out Sonne-Fan-Nr1's review. Then listen and check.

Lesen 4 Translate UrlaubLiebhaberin's review into English.

Hören 5 Listen to some people talking about problems on holiday and write down what went wrong. (1–4)

Ich habe	meinen	Laptop		verloren. vergessen.
	meine	Kamera Tasche		
	mein	Geld Handy Ticket		
	meine	Taschen		
Mein		Stuhl	war	kaputt.
Meine		Tür		
Mein		Bett	war	unbequem.
		Fenster		schmutzig.
		Zimmer		(zu) kalt. (zu) klein
Die		Mitarbeiter	waren	unhöflich. unfreundlich.

138 hundertachtunddreißig

6 Schreiben — Translate the sentences into German.

1. I lost my bag and my bed was very uncomfortable.
2. I forgot my laptop and my window was too small.
3. He lost his money and his chair was broken.
4. She forgot her mobile phone and her room was quite dirty.

G — Remember that **possessive adjectives** (my, his, her, etc.) change in German depending on the case and the gender.

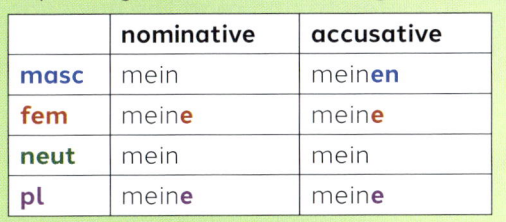

	nominative	accusative
masc	mein	mein**en**
fem	mein**e**	mein**e**
neut	mein	mein
pl	mein**e**	mein**e**

All possessive adjective endings follow the same pattern as the indefinite article.

subject	possessive adjective stem
ich	mein-
du	dein-
er/sie/es	sein-/ihr-/sein-
wir	unser-
ihr	eu(e)r-
Sie	Ihr-
sie	ihr-

Ich habe **meinen** Laptop vergessen.
I have forgotten **my** laptop.
Sie hat **ihre** Tasche verloren.
She has lost **her** bag.
Sein Bett ist unbequem.
His bed is uncomfortable.
Wir haben **unsere** Tickets gekauft.
We have bought **our** tickets.

Page 145

7 Hören — Listen to the conversation and write down the nouns you hear.

- Anna-Lena, wo machst du gern **1** ?
- Normalerweise fahre ich an die **2** und ich wohne in einem kleinen **3** .
- Und was machst du gern in den **4** ?
- Ich liege gern am **5** und ich schwimme jeden Tag im **6** .
- Mit wem verbringst du gern deine Sommerferien?
- Ich verbringe gern die Sommerferien mit meiner **7** . Das macht so viel Spaß.
- Gibt es manchmal **8** im Urlaub?
- Das **9** kann manchmal nicht so gut sein. Und ich finde die **10** immer zu lang. Was für Ferien magst du?
- Ich bleibe lieber zu Hause!

8 Lesen — Read the conversation in exercise 7 again and write the letters of the <u>four</u> aspects that Anna-Lena mentions.

a holiday accommodation
b food
c holiday activities
d the weather
e holiday destination
f transport

9 Sprechen — In pairs, prepare and practise the role-play about holidays.

- Wo machst du gern Urlaub?
- Say where you like to spend your holidays.
- Was machst du normalerweise in den Ferien?
- Name **one** activity you normally do.
- Mit wem verbringst du gern deine Ferien?
- Say who you like to spend your holidays with.
- Gibt es manchmal Probleme im Urlaub?
- Name **one** problem you sometimes have on holiday.
- Ask a question about a holiday.
- Give an appropriate answer.

Remember to use the correct ending on possessive adjectives.

You could use a question word (*Wo …?*, *Was …?*), or invert the subject and verb (*Magst du …?*)

Keep your answers short and only give the information requested.

Remember that each of your answers needs to include a verb.

hundertneununddreißig 139

4 Wie waren die Schulferien?

- Describing a past holiday
- Using past participles with inseparable prefixes
- Talking about the weather in the past

Hören 1 Listen to and read the messages, and select the correct pictures (a–p) from each box below for each person.

> Ich war letzten Monat mit meiner Familie in einer Großstadt in der Schweiz. Wir sind mit dem Zug gefahren und wir haben in einer Ferienwohnung gewohnt. Das Wetter war leider ganz schlecht – es hat fast jeden Tag geregnet.
> **Paula** 15:04

> Ich bin letzte Woche nach Kitzbühel in Österreich geflogen und es hat viel Spaß gemacht. Ich habe in einem Ferienhaus in den Bergen gewohnt. Es hat viel geschneit!
> **Yusef**

> Meine Freunde und ich waren letztes Wochenende an der Küste in Lübeck in Norddeutschland. Wir haben in einem Ferienpark gewohnt und das war ganz spannend. 🙂 Das Wetter war nicht kalt, aber es gab viel Wind.
> **Yannie**

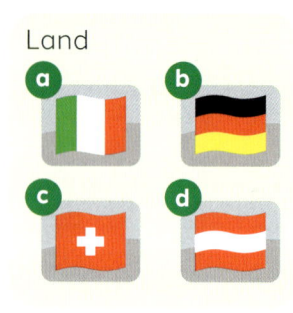

Land: a b c d
Region: e f g h
Wo gewohnt?: i j k l (Hotel)
Wetter: m n o p

Hören 2 Listen to some more people describing their past holidays and select the correct pictures in exercise 1 for each person. (1–2)

G You can describe the weather in the past by:
- using an adjective: *Das Wetter war **schön**. Es war **sonnig**.*
- using a verb: *Es **hat geregnet**. Es **hat geschneit**.*
- using a noun: *Es gab **Wind**. Es gab **Schnee**.*

Page 145

Wo hast du gewohnt?			
Ich habe Er/Sie hat Wir haben	mit der Familie in einem Ferienhaus/Hotel/ Gästehaus/Ferienpark in einer Ferienwohnung	in den Bergen in einer (Groß)stadt auf einer Insel an der Küste in einem Wald	gewohnt.

Was hast du gemacht?		
Ich habe Er/Sie hat Wir haben	Fotos	gemacht.
	Basketball	gespielt.
	das Museum	besucht.
	leckeres Essen	gegessen.
Ich bin Er/Sie ist Wir sind	einkaufen/spazieren/wandern	gegangen.
	im Meer / im See	geschwommen.

Wie war das?				
Das war (nicht)	gut, schlecht,	weil es	besonders echt extrem (gar) nicht wirklich	lecker ideal wunderbar	war.

140 *hundertvierzig*

Kapitel 6

Sprechen 3 Select an option from each **highlighted** box and write down your choices in secret. Ask your partner the questions. Your partner has to answer, guessing which options you selected. If your partner goes wrong, start again!

- Wohin bist du gefahren?
- Ich bin nach **Berlin / Wien / Bern** gefahren.
- Wo hast du gewohnt?
- Ich habe **in einem Hotel / in einer Ferienwohnung** gewohnt. Das war **an der Küste / in den Bergen / in einer Großstadt**.
- Was hast du gemacht?
- Wir haben **leckeres Essen gegessen / Fotos gemacht / das Museum besucht**.
- Wie war das?
- Das war gut, weil es wirklich **spannend / lustig / interessant** war.
- Und wie war das Wetter?
- Das Wetter war **schön / toll / schlecht**.

ß (*Eszett* or *scharfes S*) and **ss** are both pronounced like 'ss' in 'le**ss**'.
s on its own sounds more like the English 'z' in '**z**oo'.
Listen and repeat the words.

sehr	be**s**uchen	**S**onne	**S**ee
Groß**s**tadt	Spa**ß**	hei**ß**
intere**ss**ant	E**ss**en	Wa**ss**er

Hören 4 Listen to and read a description of Emilia's holiday. Put the pictures (a–f) in order by writing the correct letters.

a b c
d e f

Lesen 5 Translate the sentences in **bold** in exercise 4 into English.

Schreiben 6 Translate the following sentences into German.
1 We visited a museum in Berlin.
2 I went to Berlin with my family.
3 First of all, we went shopping.
4 Afterwards, we ordered food in a restaurant.
5 I lost my mobile phone at the station.

Remember **sequencers** help to indicate the order in which events take place.

If a sentence starts with a **sequencer**, the verb will come straight after it.
Am zweiten Tag war das Wetter schön.
On the second day, the weather was lovely.

Schreiben 7 Write your own description of a past holiday (real or imaginary). Include the following points:
- where you went
- which type of accommodation you stayed in
- what the weather was like
- which activities you did.

Hallo!
Normalerweise fahren wir nach Köln, aber dieses Jahr bin ich mit meiner Familie nach Stuttgart gefahren. Das ist eine Großstadt in Süddeutschland. **Wir sind dort vier Tage geblieben.** Am ersten Tag war das Wetter leider schlecht, weil es kalt war – nur 10 Grad!
Zuerst haben wir das Museum besucht. Meine beste Freundin hat mir das Museum beschrieben und es war toll.
Danach sind wir einkaufen gegangen. In Stuttgart kann man gut einkaufen gehen, weil es viele Geschäfte gibt. Ich habe viele Geschenke gekauft! **Leider habe ich mein Handy in der Stadt verloren.**
Wir haben dann in einem schönen Restaurant gegessen und **ich habe leckeres Essen bestellt. Leider habe ich mein Geld vergessen, also hat mein Vater bezahlt!**
Das Wetter war am zweiten Tag sehr heiß und ich habe ein Eis gegessen.
Mein Vater und ich sind spazieren gegangen und das war sehr entspannend. Was für ein schöner Urlaub! Wir kommen bestimmt wieder zurück.
Emilia

G Remember that the perfect tense is formed from a part of *haben* or *sein* + a past participle. The past participle of regular verbs is usually formed by adding **ge-** and replacing the final **-en** with **-t**.
spielen → *gespielt*

Some verbs with **inseparable prefixes** (e.g. **be-** and **ver-**) don't add **ge-** to the start. Some also don't change to **-t** at the end:

besuchen	to visit → **besucht** visited
bestellen	to order → **bestellt** ordered
bezahlen	to pay → **bezahlt** paid
verlieren	to lose → **verloren** lost
vergessen	to forget → **vergessen** forgot

Page 146

hunderteinundvierzig 141

5 Ich möchte um die Welt reisen!

- Describing future and ideal holidays
- Using interrogative and demonstrative adjectives
- Practising the w and v sounds in German

Hören 1 Listen to and read the message thread between Lukas and Jack. Copy and complete the table for Tuesday, Wednesday and Thursday.

	activity
Monday	sleep

G Remember that you can use **werden**, **möchten** and **wollen** to talk about the **future**. The infinitive form of the second verb goes to the end of the phrase.

werden: Ich **werde** das Museum besuchen. → I **will** visit the museum.
möchten: Ich **möchte** in die Stadt gehen. → I **would like** to go into town.
wollen: Was **willst** du kaufen? → What do you **want** to buy?
　　　　　Ich **will** Geschenke kaufen. → I **want** to buy presents.
Note that *ich* **will** means 'I **want to**', not 'I **will**'.

Page 146

Hallo Jack! Du wirst am Montag hier in Heidelberg sein! Ich habe einige Fragen.

Ja! Welche Informationen brauchst du?

Um wie viel Uhr kommst du an?

Um 20 Uhr am Montag. Was werden wir am Montag machen?

Schlafen! 😄 Du wirst sehr müde sein. Welche Aktivität möchtest du am Dienstag machen?

Es gibt in Heidelberg ein Schloss, oder? Werden wir es besuchen?

Ja! Wir wohnen in der Nähe von dem Schloss. Welchen Sport magst du? Willst du vielleicht am Mittwoch Sport machen?

Ja, wunderbar.

Welcher Sport ist besser: Basketball oder Tennis?

Können wir Basketball spielen? Ich will aktiv sein.

Ja, wir können mit vier Freunden und meinem Vater spielen.

Cool!

Welches Essen isst du gern?

Mein Lieblingsessen ist Pizza! 🍕

Toll! Am Donnerstag werden wir im Pizzarestaurant essen. Dieses Restaurant liegt an der Hauptstraße.

Super! Bis bald!

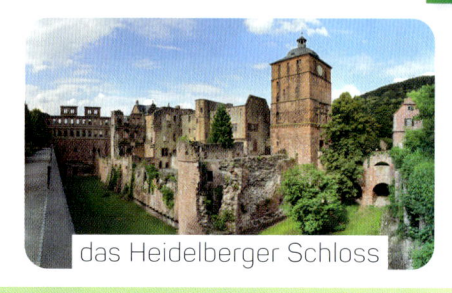

das Heidelberger Schloss

G To say 'which …?' in the nominative case, use the **interrogative adjective welch-** with the correct ending to agree with the noun that follows.

masc	**Welcher** Park ist größer?
fem	**Welche** Pizza ist billiger?
neut	**Welches** Zimmer ist besser?
pl	**Welche** Geschäfte sind größer?

To say 'this …' or 'these …', use the **demonstrative adjective dies-**, which follows the same pattern.

masc	**Dieser** Park ist sehr groß.
fem	**Diese** Pizza ist billig.
neut	**Dieses** Zimmer ist modern.
pl	**Diese** Geschäfte sind im Stadtzentrum.

In the accusative case, only the masculine singular form changes:
Welchen Sport magst du?
Magst du **diesen** Park?

Page 147

Lesen 2 Read the message thread again and answer the questions in English.
1. At what time will Jack arrive?
2. Why does Lukas say Jack will need to sleep?
3. Where does Lukas live in relation to the castle?
4. Why does Jack want to play basketball?
5. Who will they play basketball with?
6. What food does Jack like?

Lesen 3 Translate the five underlined sentences in exercise 1 into English.

Sprechen 4 Read out the sentences in **bold** from the conversation in exercise 1. Pay attention to the w and v sounds.

The German **w** sound is pronounced like the English 'v'.
The German **v** sound is pronounced like the English 'f', except in loanwords such as *Souvenir*.
Listen and repeat the words.
werden　　**v**ier　　**W**inter　　**V**ater
verbringen　**W**ien　　**w**ie **v**iel

142 *hundertzweiundvierzig*

Kapitel 6

5 Listen and write down the words you hear to complete the sentences.
1 ___ Land möchtest du ___?
2 Ich ___ in der ___ nach Deutschland ___.
3 ___ du einkaufen ___?
4 Wir ___ viele ___.

6 In pairs, take turns to ask and answer the questions. Pay attention to the -b, -d and -g sounds.
- Was wirst du in den Ferien machen?
- Ich werde zu Hause bleiben.
- Welche Aktivitäten willst du machen?
- Ich will mit meinem Freund Fußball spielen.
- Wohin möchtest du in Urlaub fahren?
- Ich möchte mit dem Flugzeug nach Griechenland fliegen.
- Was möchtest du dort machen?
- Ich möchte am Strand spazieren gehen.

> The German consonants -b, -d and -g are sometimes unvoiced. This means they have a slightly different sound often when they are at the end of a word.
> -b sounds like a -p: Urlau**b**, Hal**b**bruder
> -d sounds like a -t: Stran**d**, Freun**d**, Lan**d**, Deutschlan**d**
> -g sounds less hard: Zu**g**, we**g**
> Listen and repeat the words.

Was wirst/möchtest/willst in den Ferien machen?
Wohin wirst/möchtest/willst du fahren/reisen?

Ich werde / Wir werden	in den Ferien / in der Zukunft / nächstes Jahr	nach	Frankreich / Griechenland / Spanien / Italien / Berlin	fahren. / reisen.
Ich möchte/will / Wir möchten/wollen		in die	Türkei/Schweiz	
			zu Hause	bleiben.

Was wirst/möchtest/willst du dort machen?

Ich werde / Wir werden	(zehn) Tage in (Köln)	verbringen.
	dieses Schloss/Museum	besuchen.
	im Meer/See	schwimmen.
	einkaufen/spazieren	gehen.
	Fotos	machen.
Ich möchte/will / Wir möchten/wollen	Tennis/Basketball	spielen.
	Geschenke	kaufen.
	in der Sonne	liegen.

7 Listen to the teenagers discussing holidays. Copy and complete the table in English. (1–2)

	things to do in local area	last year's holiday	next year's holiday
1			

8 Write approximately 90 words about holidays. Include the following points:
- where you normally spend your holidays
- what you did in the holidays last year
- what you will do in the next school holidays.

> Think carefully about which tense to use.
> **Present**
> Es **gibt** viele Aktivitäten.
> There are many activities.
> **Perfect**
> Wir **haben** ein Schloss besucht.
> We visited a castle.
> **Imperfect**
> Das Wetter **war** toll.
> The weather was great.
> **Future**
> Ich **werde** nach Deutschland fahren.
> I will travel to Germany.
> **Conditional**
> Ich **möchte** um die Welt reisen.
> I would like to travel around the world.

hundertdreiundvierzig 143

Grammatik 1

Adjectival endings after the definite article (Culture, page 133)

Lesen 1 Select the adjective with the correct ending to complete each sentence.
1. Es gibt den **großen** / **große** Freizeitpark Phantasialand in der Nähe von Köln.
2. Das **schönen** / **schöne** Land Österreich ist mein Lieblingsland.
3. Ich finde die **langen** / **lange** Flüsse in der Schweiz toll.
4. Die **leckeren** / **leckere** Kuchen in Deutschland sind wunderbar.
5. Die **alten** / **alte** Universität in Berlin heißt Humboldt.
6. Ich mag den **grünen** / **grüne** Park Burggarten in Wien.

Schreiben 2 Complete the sentences with the correct form of the adjective in brackets.
1. Die ___ Brücke in Luzern ist mehr als 200m lang. (*historisch*)
2. Wie findest du den ___ Bahnhofmarkt in Zürich? (*beliebt*)
3. Die ___ Parks in München sind ideal für Kinder. (*schön*)
4. Die ___ Schule in Berlin ist eine internationale Schule. (*neu*)
5. Ich finde das ___ Hotel in Salzburg ziemlich billig. (*modern*)
6. Das ___ Museum in Bonn ist sehr bekannt. (*traditionell*)

	nominative endings	accusative endings
masc	der groß**e** Fluss	den groß**en** Fluss
fem	die alt**e** Brücke	die alt**e** Brücke
neut	das neu**e** Museum	das neu**e** Museum
pl	die berühmt**en** Parks	die berühmt**en** Parks

Forming questions (Unit 1, page 134)

Schreiben 3 Rewrite the statements as questions.
Example: 1 Bist du in der Schweiz?
1. Du bist in der Schweiz.
2. Man kann dort einkaufen gehen.
3. Wir gehen am Samstag in die Stadt.
4. Sie möchten in einem Hotel am Meer wohnen.
5. Das Wetter war gut in Österreich.
6. Du wirst in den Sommerferien zu Hause bleiben.

Sprechen 4 In pairs, take turns to ask and answer the questions from exercise 3. Invent your own answers.

Using *wer*, *wen* and *wem* (Unit 2, page 136)

Lesen 5 Select the correct interrogative pronoun to complete each sentence. Then translate the questions into English.
Example: 1 Wer
1. **Wer** / **Wen** / **Wem** findet das Essen lecker?
2. Mit **wer** / **wen** / **wem** fährst du nach München?
3. **Wer** / **Wen** / **Wem** will zu Hause bleiben?
4. Für **wer** / **wen** / **wem** ist Ruhe wichtig?
5. Mit **wer** / **wen** / **wem** wirst du in Berlin wohnen?
6. Für **wer** / **wen** / **wem** ist das Hotel ideal?

> Remember: **wer** (who) changes depending on the case.
> Nominative: *Wer kommt ins Café?* **Who** is coming to the café?
> Accusative: *Für wen kaufen Sie das Geschenk?* For **whom** are you buying the present?
> Dative: *Mit wem schwimmen Sie?* With **whom** are you swimming?

Schreiben 6 Translate the <u>four</u> sentences into German.
1. Who is coming to the cinema?
2. With whom are you travelling to Austria?
3. For whom are you buying the T-shirt?
4. Who wants to go for a walk?

> Look carefully at the meaning of the sentence to help you decide which case you need. Knowing which prepositions take which case will help you.

Kapitel 6

Possessive adjectives in the nominative and accusative cases (Unit 3, page 139)

Schreiben 7 Write the correct possessive adjectives in the nominative case to fill in the gaps. Then fill in the gaps in the accusative table.

nominative	my	your (sg, informal)	his	her
masc	mein	dein	**1** sein	ihr
fem	mein**e**	dein**e**	sein**e**	**2**
neut	mein	**3**	sein	ihr
pl	**4**	dein**e**	sein**e**	ihr**e**

accusative	my	your (sg, informal)	his	her
masc	mein**en**	**5** dein**en**	sein**en**	ihr**en**
fem	mein**e**	dein**e**	**6**	ihr**e**
neut	**7**	dein	sein	ihr
pl	mein**e**	dein**e**	sein**e**	**8**

Schreiben 8 Complete the sentences using the correct possessive adjectives.
1. ___ Vater (m) wohnt in Österreich. (your, sg)
2. ___ Hotel (nt) ist sehr schmutzig. (her)
3. ___ Fotos (pl) waren sehr schön. (his)
4. ___ Jacke (f) ist im Hotel. (my)
5. Ich liebe ___ Ferienhaus (nt)! (his)
6. Ich mag ___ Laptop (m). (her)
7. Ich mag ___ Hund (m). (my)
8. Ich hasse ___ Musik (f). (your, sg)

> 💡 Think carefully about the subject and object of each sentence and remember that only the masculine form changes in the accusative.
> Nominative: *Das ist **mein** Laptop.*
> Accusative: *Ich habe **meinen** Laptop verloren.*

Weather in the past tense (Unit 4, page 140)

Hören 9 Listen and write the words you hear to complete each sentence.
Example: 1 *In Österreich war es **kalt** und es hat **geschneit**!*

1. In Österreich war es ___ und es hat ___ !
2. In Amerika gab es ___ .
3. In Deutschland ___ .
4. In Großbritannien ___ .
5. In der Schweiz ___ und ___ .
6. In der Türkei ___ , aber ___ .

> 💡 To talk about the weather in the past:
> - use the imperfect form **es war** + adjective:
>   **Es war** kalt, aber ganz sonnig.
>   In der ersten Woche **war das Wetter** sehr schön.
> - use verbs in the **perfect tense**:
>   **Es hat** jeden Tag **geschneit**.
>   In der zweiten Woche **hat es geregnet**.
> - use the imperfect form **es gab** + noun:
>   **Es gab** leider viel Schnee.
>   In der ersten Woche **gab es** Wind.

Sprechen 10 In pairs, take turns to ask and say what the weather was like in the past tense.
- *Wie war das Wetter?*
- *Es war … / Es hat … / Es gab …*

hundertfünfundvierzig

Grammatik 2

Past participles with inseparable prefixes (Unit 4, page 141)

Lesen 1 Copy and complete the sentences with the past participles of the verbs in brackets.
1. Ich habe die Küste in Norddeutschland **besucht**. (*besuchen*)
2. Ich habe mein Handy in der Stadt ___. (*verlieren*)
3. Ich habe mein Geld ___. (*vergessen*)
4. Im Restaurant habe ich Wurst mit Pommes ___. (*bestellen*)
5. Ich habe das Zimmer online ___. (*bezahlen*)

Lesen 2 Translate the sentences from exercise 1 into English.

The future tense (Unit 5, page 143)

Hören 3 Listen and write down the words you hear to complete each sentence.

Example: 1 *Wirst …*
1. ___ du nach Österreich ___ ?
2. Wir ___ „Phantasialand" ___ .
3. Wann ___ sie ein Ticket ___ ?
4. Mein Vater ___ das langweilig ___ .
5. Frau Wagner, warum ___ Sie in Deutschland ___ ?
6. Ich ___ jeden Tag ___ gehen.

> Remember: to form the future tense, use the correct form of **werden** and put the infinitive at the end of the clause.
> Ich **werde** nach Spanien fahren.
> I **will** travel to Spain.
>
> | ich | werde |
> | du | wirst |
> | er/sie/es/man | wird |
> | wir | werden |
> | ihr | werdet |
> | Sie | werden |
> | sie | werden |

Sprechen 4 Read out the the following sentences, then translate them into English. Pay attention to the **w** sound.
1. Ich werde nächstes Wochenende in die Schweiz fahren.
2. Wo wirst du am Mittwoch schwimmen gehen?
3. Wir werden durch den Wald wandern.
4. Es wird in Wien wirklich warm sein.

Talking about the future (Unit 5, page 142)

Schreiben 5 Put the words in the correct order to make sentences.

Example: 1 *Ich möchte nach London fahren.*
1. möchte / ich / fahren / nach London
2. einkaufen / werde / ich / in der Stadt
3. ich / verbringen / zehn Tage / will / in der Schweiz
4. werden / Geschenke / wir / kaufen
5. durch Europa / wir / fahren / wollen
6. reisen / möchten / in den Ferien / nach Italien / wir

> Remember: to say what you **would like** or **want** to do, use the correct form of **mögen** or **wollen** and put the infinitive at the end of the clause.
> Ich **möchte** das Museum besuchen.
> I **would like** to visit the museum.
> Wir **wollen** nach Deutschland reisen.
> We **want** to travel to Germany.

Schreiben 6 Translate the sentences into German.
1. I would like to travel to Munich.
2. I want to spend a week in Italy.
3. We want to take photos.
4. We would like to buy a present.

Kapitel 6

Using interrogative and demonstrative adjectives (Unit 5, page 142)

Remember that **welch**... and **dies**... need to agree with the noun that follows, both in gender and in case. These words also change depending on the case they are in.

	nominative	accusative	dative
masc	welch**er** Campingplatz dies**er** Campingplatz	welch**en** Ort dies**en** Ort	welch**em** Bahnhof dies**em** Bahnhof
fem	welch**e** Kirche dies**e** Kirche	welch**e** Region dies**e** Region	welch**er** Stadt dies**er** Stadt
neut	welch**es** Foto dies**es** Foto	welch**es** Auto dies**es** Auto	welch**em** Zimmer dies**em** Zimmer
pl	welch**e** Geschäfte dies**e** Geschäfte	welch**e** Berge dies**e** Berge	welch**en** Personen dies**en** Personen

Hören 7 Listen and write the words for 'which' or 'this'/'these' to complete each sentence.

1 *Welche* Tage (*pl*) sind frei?
2 ___ Kirche (*f*) ist sehr alt.
3 ___ Berg (*m*) ist wirklich groß.
4 ___ Stadt (*f*) werden wir besuchen?
5 ___ Kino (*nt*) ist in der Nähe?
6 Tom, ___ Sport (*m*) magst du?
7 ___ Schloss (*nt*) ist sehr berühmt.
8 ___ Geschäfte (*pl*) sind echt interessant.

Los geht's!

Schreiben 8 Put the words in the correct order to make questions. Then translate them into English.

1 wirst / Land / du / besuchen / Welches / nächstes Jahr / ?
2 möchtest / Mit / du / reisen / wem / ?
3 Wo / du / wohnen / wirst / ?
4 möchtest / du / machen / Was / ?

Sprechen 9 In pairs, take turns to ask and answer the questions in exercise 8 using the pictures to help you.

1
2
3 Hotel
4

hundertsiebenundvierzig **147**

Kapitel 6 Lese- und Hörtest

Reading

Lesen 1

At the hotel. You see some notices in the hotel where you are staying. Which notice matches each **aspect** of a holiday? Write the correct letter, **A, B, C, D or E**.

Only three of the notices will link to an aspect, so read carefully to discount the incorrect options.

A	Das Frühstück im Hotelrestaurant ist von 7 Uhr bis 10:30 Uhr möglich.
B	Wenn Sie mehr als drei Nächte bleiben, bekommen Sie einen günstigeren Preis.
C	Wollen Sie Geschenke kaufen? Unsere Geschäfte haben alles!
D	Die Kulturreise nach Berlin beginnt um 9 Uhr.
E	Kinoabend im Hotel: Samstag um 20 Uhr.

1 Excursions
2 Shopping
3 Meals

You won't find direct translations of these words in the text, so you need to look for language relating to them. For example, for 'Meals', you might see the name of a meal or a food item.

Lesen 2

A holiday park. You read this advert for a holiday park. Write the correct letter, **A, B or C**, to complete each sentence.

Wir haben zwanzig schöne, moderne Ferienhäuser in unserem kleinen Ferienpark. Von jedem Haus kann man den schönen Berg sehen. Man kann in der Sonne liegen, im See schwimmen oder im Wald wandern. Wenn das Wetter kälter ist, kann man das kleine Dorf mit einem berühmten Schloss besuchen oder am Fluss Fahrrad fahren. **Angeln** am Fluss ist auch möglich.

1 The holiday park is …
   A small.   B beautiful.   C modern.
2 From each holiday house you can see the …
   A lake.   B castle.   C mountain.
3 You can go walking …
   A in the woods.   B by the lake.   C in the mountains.
4 You can cycle by the …
   A lake.   B castle.   C river.
5 Read the last sentence again. Where would you be if your hobby were **Angeln**?
   A in a sports centre   B in the air   C by water

- Incorrect answer options are often mentioned in the text, so you need to read very carefully to discount them.
- Read the whole sentence when trying to work out the meaning of a new word; the vocabulary and context in the sentence will help you.

148 *hundertachtundvierzig*

Lesen 3

Translate these sentences into English.

> Remember to translate 'little' words that are sometimes overlooked.

1 Ich liebe die Ferien.
2 Wir verbringen viel Zeit an der Küste.
3 Wir fahren oft ins Ausland, weil das Wetter schöner ist.
4 Wenn es schneit, bleiben wir lieber zu Hause.
5 Letzten Sommer hat es leider viel geregnet.

> How will you translate these comparatives?

> Think carefully about which tense to use in this sentence.

Listening

Hören 4

Past holidays. You hear Arda and Kathi talking about their holidays. Which **two** aspects does each person mention? Write the **two** correct letters (A–F) for each person.

A	friends
B	means of transport
C	holiday accommodation
D	evening activities
E	the weather
F	daytime activities

Hören 5

Issues on holiday. You hear Mia talking about her trip to Berlin. What does she say? Listen to the recording and answer the questions **in English**.

1 What was the problem with Mia's hotel room?
2 What was the issue at the airport?

Hören 6

Opinions of holidays. You hear Jonas talking about holidays. What does he think about these aspects of his holidays? Write **P** for a **positive** opinion, **N** for a **negative** opinion or **P+N** for a **positive and negative** opinion.

1 Nature
2 Holidays in town
3 Hotels

> Listen carefully for opinion words, negatives and the connective *aber*, which can often suggest two opposite opinions.

> Think carefully about how these sounds are pronounced when you write down what you hear:
> long *a*, short *a* and *ä*
> long *e* and short *e*
> long *o*, short *o* and *ö*
> -b, -d, -g
> w and v
> s, ss and ß

Dictation

Hören 7

You will hear **four** short sentences. Write down exactly what you hear **in German**.

hundertneunundvierzig **149**

Kapitel 6

Kapitel 6 Mündlicher Test

Role-play

Sprechen 1 Look at the role-play card and prepare what you are going to say.

> You are talking to your German friend about holidays.
> 1 Say what you like doing in the holidays. (Give **one** detail.)
> 2 Describe the weather in the summer.
> 3 Say **one** activity you do when it rains.
> 4 Give **one** opinion about hotels.
> 5 ? Ask your friend a question about holidays.

This could include activities you do when you stay at home.

This can be any kind of activity, such as swimming or going to the cinema. Work with the vocabulary you know best.

You could ask your friend for an opinion about accommodation or holiday places, or you could ask for information, such as what they like to do in the holidays or where they like to go.

Sprechen 2 Practise what you have prepared. Then, using your notes, listen and respond to the teacher.

Hören 3 Listen to Kim's response and answer the questions in English.
1 What does Kim like doing in the holidays?
2 What is the weather like in the summer?
3 What does Kim do when it rains?
4 What does Kim think of hotels?
5 What question does Kim ask?

Reading aloud

Sprechen 4 Look at this task. With a partner, read the sentences aloud, paying attention to the underlined letters.

> Wir sind in Deutschland.
> Jetzt ist das Wetter wirklich kalt, aber sehr sonnig.
> Mein Halbbruder verbringt zwanzig Nächte in einem großen Hotel auf dem Land.
> Hier kann man viele Aktivitäten machen.
> Mein Vater möchte ein schönes Schloss besuchen.

Think carefully about how to pronounce these sounds:
long a, short a and ä
long e and short e
long o, short o and ö
ch
-b, -d
w and v
s, ss and ß

Hören 5 Listen and check your pronunciation.

Sprechen 6 Listen to the teacher asking **four** follow-up questions. Translate each question into English and prepare your own answers in **German**. Then listen again and respond to the teacher.

Photo card

Hören 7 Listen to Kim describing the photos and answer the questions.

1. Where does Kim think the people are in the first photo?
2. What does she say about the weather?
3. What does she say they are doing?
4. Where does she think the people are in the second photo? (Give **two** details.)
5. What does she say about them? (Give **two** details.)

Sprechen 8 Prepare your own description of both photos. Then, with a partner, take turns describing them.

> Auf dem ersten Foto gibt es …

Hören 9 Listen to the teacher's first follow-up question, *Mit wem bist du in die Ferien gefahren?*, and Kim's response. Write down the letter (A–F) for each of the <u>three</u> correct statements.

A	Kim went on holiday this year.
B	She travelled with her family by car.
C	The journey took twelve hours.
D	Kim's sister played on her games console.
E	Kim read a book.
F	Kim's mother listened to music.

You will be asked to talk about the content of these photos. You must say at least one thing about each photo.

After you have spoken about the content of the photos, you will be asked questions related to any of the topics within the theme of **Communication and the world around us**.

Your responses should be as **full and detailed** as possible.

Hören 10 The teacher then asks Kim, *Wo möchtest du nächstes Jahr Urlaub machen?* Listen and write down the <u>eight</u> missing words to complete Kim's response.

Nächstes Jahr möchte ich ins **1** fahren. Wir werden im Juli mit der **2** nach Wien fahren und zwei **3** in der Hauptstadt **4** . Wir werden ein Museum **5** und in der Stadt **6** gehen. Ich möchte auch **7** fahren und meine Eltern wollen auch **8** gehen.

Sprechen 11 Listen to two more follow-up questions and prepare your answers. Then respond to the recording.

Sprechen 12 Prepare your own answers to as many of the Module 6 questions on page 227 as you can. Then practise with a partner.

> Listen carefully to the question and make sure you answer in the correct tense. Extend your answers and don't forget to include opinions and reasons. Try to use a wide variety of vocabulary and sentence structures from this module and previous modules.

hunderteinundfünfzig 151

Kapitel 6 Schreibtest

Describing a photo

Schreiben 1

Look at this exam writing task. Copy and complete Callum's response with suitable words from the box. There are more words than gaps.

> Strand   reden   Brot   Obst
> zwei   spielen   drei   Fluss

1 Es gibt ▢ Mädchen.
2 Ich sehe auch ▢ Jungen.
3 Sie sind an einem ▢.
4 Sie essen ▢.
5 Sie ▢ und lächeln.

Schreiben 2

Prepare your own answer to the task.

> You see this photo on Instagram.
>
> What is in the photo?
>
> Write **five** sentences in **German**.

- Use phrases such as *es gibt*, *ich sehe* and *man sieht* to describe the content of the photo.
- Make your verbs singular if you are describing one person (*Ein Junge / Ein Mädchen ist/trägt*), and plural for more than one person (*sie sind, sie tragen*).

Grammar task

Schreiben 3

Using your knowledge of grammar, select the correct option to complete each sentence.

> The ending of this irregular verb will help you select the correct pronoun.

> Is *wir* a singular or plural pronoun?

1 Wir **bin / ist / sind** immer glücklich, wenn es sonnig ist.
2 **Ich / Er / Wir** fährt oft ins Ausland.
3 Man kann den **großen / großes / groß** Fluss sehen.
4 **Dieser / Diese / Dieses** Reise ist zu lang.
5 Letzten Sommer habe ich meine Oma **besuche / besucht / besuchen**.

> Use the definite article to help you work out which case this adjective needs to be in.

> Can you remember which gender nouns ending in -e usually are?

> Which tense is this sentence in? Look at the auxiliary verb *haben* and the time phrase *Letzten Sommer*.

90-word writing task

Schreiben 4

Look at this writing exam task and then, for each bullet point:

1 think about the vocabulary and structures you have learned which you could use in your answer. For example:
   - **nouns**, **verbs** and **adjectives** to write about holidays
   - **verbs of opinion** and **adjectives** to give reasons
   - language for **narrating a story** about where you went
   - how to explain **what your plans are**
   - connectives and intensifiers you would like to use.
2 write down three or four ideas for what you could write about.
3 identify which tense(s) you could use in your answer.

> You are writing to your German friend about holidays.
>
> Write approximately **90** words in **German**.
>
> You must write something about each bullet point.
>
> Describe:
> - your opinion of holidays abroad
> - where you went on holiday last year
> - your plans for a holiday in the future.

152   hundertzweiundfünfzig

Kapitel 6

Lesen 5 Read Callum's answer to the exam task. Answer the questions in the coloured boxes (1–5).

1 Callum uses a **variety of infinitives**. What do these words mean? Find <u>two</u> more examples.

2 Which connective could you use here to form an **extended sentence**? Which other connectives does Callum use?

3 Which **tense** is this? Which <u>two</u> other examples can you find? Which other tenses does Callum use?

Ich gehe gern ins Ausland, weil das Wetter schön ist. Ich mag in der Sonne liegen. Man soll neue Orte besuchen. Das macht Spaß. Mein Lieblingsort in Deutschland ist der Schwarzwald. Hier kann man viel machen. Es gibt ein Schloss, einen See und einen großen Wald und dort gehe ich gern wandern.

Letztes Jahr sind wir mit der Bahn nach Deutschland gefahren. Die Reise, die schön, aber lang war, war interessant. Wir sind an einem See geblieben und ich bin Fahrrad gefahren.

Diesen Sommer werden wir auch wieder nach Deutschland fahren. Ich möchte im Meer schwimmen und am Strand wandern.

4 How could Callum **avoid repetition** here?

5 This is an example of **complex language**. What does it mean? Find <u>three</u> more examples of complex language in the text.

Lesen 6 Read Callum's answer again and complete the sentences.

1 Callum likes going abroad because …
2 He likes the Black Forest because …
3 Last year they went on holiday by …
4 This year, Callum would like to …

Schreiben 7 Prepare your own answer to the task.

- Think about how you can develop your answer for each bullet point.
- Look back at your notes from exercises 4 and 5.
- Look at the 'Challenge checklist' and consider how you can show off your German!
- Write a **brief** plan and organise your answer into paragraphs.
- Write your answer and then carefully check it for accuracy.

Challenge checklist

✓ Connectives (*und, aber*)
✓ Some extended sentences (*Wir spielen Tennis im Park.*)
✓ An opinion (*Ich fahre gern nach Deutschland.*)

✓ Weather in the past (*es war sonnig, es hat geregnet*)
✓ Different persons of the verb (*die Reise war, die Ferien waren*)
✓ Past, present and future time frames
✓ Compound nouns (*der Ferienort, die Sommerferien*)
✓ More interesting vocabulary (*Ausland, liegen, Strand*)

✓ Man kann + infinitive (*Man kann im Wald Fahrrad fahren.*)
✓ Möchten + infinitive (*Wir möchten schwimmen gehen.*)
✓ Inversion (*dann möchte ich, im Sommer werde ich*)
✓ Dative prepositions (*im Meer, am Strand, mit dem Zug*)
✓ Use of negatives (*nie, nichts, ohne, kein, niemand*)
✓ Inseparable past participles (*besucht, verloren, vergessen, bezahlt*)
✓ Possessives (*unser Hotel, meine Tasche*)
✓ Adjective endings (*es gibt ein schönes Hotel, einen großen Park, eine alte Brücke, viele Menschen*)

hundertdreiundfünfzig

Kapitel 6 Wörter

Key:
bold = this word will appear in higher exams only
* = this word is not on the vocabulary list but you may use it in your own sentences

Im Urlaub und unterwegs (pages 132–133):

*Reiseziele	Travel destinations
alt	old
bekannt	well-known, famous
beliebt	popular
berühmt	famous
historisch	historic
hoch	high, tall
lang	long
schön	lovely, beautiful
spannend	exciting, thrilling, tense
traditionell	traditional
wunderbar	wonderful
besuchen	visit
zeigen	show
der Berg	mountain
der *Freizeitpark	theme park
der Wald	forest, wood
die *Burg	fortress
das Schloss	castle

Wo fahren wir hin? (pages 134–135):

Vorteile und Nachteile	Advantages and disadvantages
Was denkst du?	What do you think?
Wie findest du …?	How do you find …?
Ich finde das …	I think that (is) …
besonders	particularly
echt	really, genuinely
ganz	quite
(gar) nicht	not (at all)
gut	good
günstig	cheap, good
interessant	interesting
langweilig	boring
negativ	negative
schlecht	bad
schön	lovely, beautiful
spannend	exciting/thrilling, tense
wunderbar	wonderful
weil/da es … ist.	because/since it is …
weil das Wetter / das Essen … ist.	because the weather/food is …
denn man kann (nicht) (Tennis) spielen.	because you can(not) play (tennis).
denn man kann (nicht) (schwimmen) gehen.	because you can(not) go (swimming).

Wo werden wir wohnen? (pages 136–137):

Die *Ferienunterkunft	Holiday accommodation
Auf dem ersten/zweiten Foto gibt es …	In the first/second photo, there is …
Auf der linken/rechten Seite sehe ich …	On the left-hand/right-hand side I see …
Vorne / Im Hintergrund sieht man …	At the front / In the background we/you can see …
einen Ferienpark	a holiday park
eine Ferienwohnung	a holiday apartment
ein Ferienhaus	a holiday house
ein Gästehaus	a guest house
ein Hotel	a hotel
ein *Hostel	a hostel
in einer Stadt.	in a town.
auf dem Land.	in the countryside.
am Meer.	at the seaside / by the sea.
am See.	at/on a lake.
in den Bergen.	in the mountains.
Es gibt …	There is …
Ich sehe …	I (can) see …
Man sieht …	We/You (can) see …
einen Mann / einen Jungen.	a man / a boy.
eine Frau / eine Familie.	a woman / a family.
ein Mädchen.	a girl.
Er/Sie trägt …	He/She is wearing …
Sie tragen …	They are wearing …
ein Kleid.	a dress.
ein T-Shirt.	a T-shirt.
Das Wetter ist …	The weather is …
gut/sonnig/warm.	good/sunny/warm.
schlecht/kalt.	bad/cold.
Die Leute …	The people
sehen glücklich/traurig/müde aus.	look happy/sad/tired.
lächeln.	are smiling.
lachen.	are laughing.
Ich möchte in … wohnen, …	I would like to stay in …, …
Ich möchte nie in … wohnen, …	I would never like to stay in … , …
einem Ferienpark	a holiday park
einer Ferienwohnung	a holiday apartment
einem Ferienhaus	a holiday house
einem Gästehaus	a holiday house
einem Hotel	a hotel
einem *Hostel	a hostel
weil es … ist.	because it is …
(un)bequem	(un)comfortable
günstig / zu teuer	cheap / too expensive
entspannend	relaxing
(un)praktisch	(im)practical
schrecklich	terrible
Ich brauche …	I need …
WLAN.	WiFi.
eine Küche.	a kitchen.
ein Restaurant.	a restaurant.
Ich möchte …	I would like to …
im Stadtzentrum sein.	be in the town/city centre.
draußen sein.	be outside.
nicht viel Geld ausgeben.	not spend much money.

Kapitel 6

Mein schrecklicher Urlaub (pages 138–139):

Was war das Problem?	What was the problem?
Ich habe ... vergessen/verloren.	I forgot/lost ...
meinen Laptop	my key.
meine Kamera	my camera.
meine Tasche	my bag.
mein Geld	my money.
mein Handy	my mobile phone.
mein Ticket	my ticket.
meine Taschen	my bags.
Mein Stuhl war ...	My chair was ...
Meine Tür war ...	My door was ...
Mein Bett war ...	My bed was ...
Mein Fenster war ...	My window was ...
Mein Zimmer war ...	My room was ...
kaputt.	broken.
unbequem.	uncomfortable.
schmutzig.	dirty.
(zu) kalt.	(too) cold.
(zu) klein.	(too) small.
Die Mitarbeiter waren ...	The employees were ...
unhöflich.	impolite.
unfreundlich.	unfriendly.

Wie waren die Schulferien? (pages 140–141):

Schulferien	School holidays
Wo hast du gewohnt?	Where did you stay?
Ich habe / Er hat / Sie hat / Wir haben (in einem Ferienpark) gewohnt.	I/He/She/We stayed (in a holiday park).
in den Bergen	in the mountains
in einer (Groß)stadt	in a (city)/town
auf einer Insel	on an island
an der Küste	on/at the coast
in einem Wald	in a forest
Was hast du gemacht?	What did you do?
Ich habe / Er hat / Sie hat / Wir haben ...	I/He/She/We ...
Fotos gemacht.	took photos.
Basketball gespielt.	played basketball.
das Museum besucht.	visited the museum.
leckeres Essen gegessen.	ate some delicious food.
Ich bin / Er ist / Sie ist / Wir sind ... gegangen.	I/He/She/We went ...
einkaufen	shopping.
spazieren	walking.
wandern	hiking.
im Meer / im See schwimmen	swimming in the sea/lake.
Wie war das?	How was it?
Das war (nicht) gut/schlecht, weil es ... war.	It was (not) good/bad because it was ...
besonders	particularly
echt	real
extrem	extremely
(gar) nicht	not (at all)
wirklich	really
lecker	tasty
ideal	ideal
wunderbar	wonderful
Das Wetter war ...	The weather was ...
heiß.	hot.
kalt.	cold.
schön.	lovely.
sonnig.	sunny.
Es gab viel Wind.	There was a lot of wind.
Es hat geregnet.	It rained.
Es hat geschneit.	It snowed.

Ich möchte um die Welt reisen! (pages 142–143):

Urlaube	Holidays
Was wirst du in den Ferien machen?	What will you do in the holidays?
Wohin wirst/möchtest/willst du (in der Zukunft) fahren/reisen?	Where will you / would you like to / do you want to go to / travel to (in the future)?
Ich werde ...	I will ...
Wir werden ...	We will ...
Ich möchte/will ...	I would like / want to ...
Wir möchten/wollen ...	We would like / want to ...
nach ... fahren/reisen.	go/travel to ...
Deutschland	Germany
Frankreich	France
Griechenland	Greece
Italien	Italy
Spanien	Spain
Berlin	Berlin
in die Schweiz/Türkei fahren/reisen.	go/travel to Switzerland/Turkey.
zu Hause bleiben.	stay at home.
(zehn) Tage in (Köln) verbringen.	spend (ten) days in (Cologne).
dieses Schloss / dieses Museum besuchen.	visit this castle / this museum.
im Meer / im See schwimmen.	swim in the sea/lake.
einkaufen gehen.	go shopping.
spazieren gehen.	go for a walk.
Fotos machen.	take photos.
Geschenke kaufen.	buy presents.
Tennis/Basketball spielen.	play tennis/basketball.
in der Sonne liegen.	lie in the sun.

hundertfünfundfünfzig

Kapitel 7 Unsere Welt

Wir verbessern die Welt!
- Learning more about activism in German-speaking countries
- Revising prepositions with the accusative and dative cases

Mach einen Unterschied

a
Organisation:	FlüWi Österreich
Gründer:	David Zistl, Otto Simon, Michal Sikyta
Gegründet:	2015
Arbeitet **für**:	Menschen, die kein Zimmer oder Bett haben
Initiative:	Zimmer **für** Leute finden, die kein Zuhause in Österreich haben

b
Organisation:	Keine Macht den Drogen (KMDD)
Gründer:	die deutsche Regierung und berühmte Sportler
Gegründet:	**vor** 20 Jahren
Arbeitet **gegen**:	Drogen **unter** Jugendlichen
Initiative:	Freizeitaktivitäten **für** junge Leute

c
Organisation:	#notjustdown
Gründer:	Geschwister Marian und Tabea Mewes
Gegründet:	2017
Informiert:	**über** Down-Syndrom
Initiative:	ein Blog **über** ihre Erfahrungen

der Gründer	founder
gründen	to found, establish
die Macht	power
die Regierung	government
das Zuhause	home

d Ich habe viel Respekt **für** Fatih Akin. Er ist 1973 **in** Hamburg geboren. Seine Eltern sind in den 60er Jahren **aus** der Türkei **nach** Deutschland gekommen. Er macht Filme und hat viele Preise gewonnen. Fatih arbeitet **für** eine bessere Welt **ohne** Angst. Er arbeitet **mit** der Organisation „Soul Kids".

e Ich habe viel Respekt **für** Eneas Pauli. Eneas ist Co-Präsident*in **von** dem „Transgender-Netzwerk" **in** der Schweiz und identifiziert sich als nicht binär. Eneas arbeitet **gegen** Transphobie und Diskriminierung. Eneas möchte sichere Orte **für** Transmenschen im öffentlichen Raum. Eneas glaubt, wir sollen alle Menschen akzeptieren.

die Diskriminierung	discrimination

Was sind deine Pronomen? xier is a gender-neutral pronoun that can be used instead of *er* or *sie*: *Xier geht schwimmen.*

nominative	accusative	dative
xier	xien	xiem

xies is used instead of *sein* or *ihr*: *Das ist xies Buch.*

	masc	fem	neut
nominative	xies	xies**e**	xies
accusative	xies**en**	xies**e**	xies
dative	xies**em**	xies**er**	xies**em**

There are also gender-neutral nouns.
der*die Freund*in	friend
der*die Lehrer*in	teacher
der*die Sänger*in or *die singende Person*	singer
der*die Student*in	student
der*die Studierende	student

The **x** in the gender-neutral pronouns is pronounced 'ks'.

156 *hundertsechsundfünfzig*

Kulturzone

Kapitel 7

Lesen 1
Read fact files a–c. Then read the paragraph below about the organisation *FlüWi Österreich* and translate the text into English.

> Die Idee für die Aktion kommt aus Deutschland und seit 2015 haben mehr als 600 Menschen Zimmer in Österreich gefunden. Die Organisation will Menschen in Kontakt miteinander bringen und sie unterstützen.

Schreiben 2
Now choose **one** of the other two organisations (*KMDD* or *#notjustdown*) and write a similar paragraph to describe it in German.

Lesen 3
Read texts (**d**) and (**e**) and answer the questions with the correct name: Fatih Akin (F) or Eneas Pauli (E)?

1. Who was born in Germany?
2. Whose main work is in film?
3. Who works against transphobia?
4. Who has won lots of prizes?
5. Who wants everyone to be accepted?
6. Who works for a better world?

G — Dual-case prepositions take the <u>accusative when there is movement</u> involved and the <u>dative when there is no movement</u>.

	masc	fem	neut	pl
accusative	d**en** ein**en**	die eine	das ein	die -
dative	d**em** ein**em**	d**er** ein**er**	d**em** ein**em**	

Remember that there are short forms of some prepositions and articles.
in das → ins
in dem → im

Movement: *Ich gehe **ins** Einkaufszentrum.*
No movement: *Ich bin **im** Einkaufszentrum.*

Page 168

Lesen 4
Copy and complete the table with the German prepositions (in **bold** in texts a–e on page 156).

accusative prepositions	dative prepositions	dual case prepositions (accusative or dative)
for – für	with –	in –
against –	to, after –	in front of, ago –
without –	from, of –	about, over –
	out of, from –	among, under –

Hören 5
Listen and write down the words you hear. Then read them out, paying attention to the *-tion* sounds. (1–6)

The *t* in *-tion* is pronounced as 'ts', as in the English word 'ca**ts**', with the tip of the tongue just behind the top teeth, e.g. *Organisa**tion***.

Schreiben 6
Translate the sentences into German.

1. I come from Turkey.
2. She works with the organisation.
3. The organisation is in Switzerland.
4. He works for a better world.
5. She created a blog for young people.
6. He would like a world without fear.

Think carefully about which case to use with each preposition.

Remember that Turkey and Switzerland are used with the definite article in German.

Use *machen*. Which tense do you need here?

You need to use a comparative adjective here. Remember to make it agree with the noun.

Which verb can you use here?

Sprechen 7
In pairs, discuss who you find inspiring and why.

- *Ich habe viel Respekt für …*
- *Warum?*
- *Er/Sie/Xier arbeitet für/gegen ….*

| Er Sie Xier | arbeitet | für | eine bessere Welt. eine Welt ohne Angst. Transmenschen. Menschen, die kein Zuhause haben. Jugendliche. |
| | | gegen | Drogen. Diskriminierung. |

hundertsiebenundfünfzig 157

1 Was ist dir wichtig?

- Discussing issues facing young people today
- Using pronouns in the accusative and dative cases
- Using verbs followed by prepositions

Lesen 1 Read the quiz and decide which <u>three</u> things are the most important to you.

Was ist dir wichtig im Leben?

- meine Freunde
- die Gesundheit
- der Beruf
- die Familie
- die Ausbildung
- das Studium
- die Interessen
- das Geld
- die Freiheit

Hören 2 Listen to some young people explaining what is important to them. (1–8) Write the correct letter(s) to match each person to the issues below (a–h).

- a work
- b friends
- c money
- d education and studies
- e health
- f family
- g interests
- h freedom

Listen out for negative adjectives (**un**wichtig) and phrases with **nicht**, as the speakers sometimes mention what isn't important to them. They also extend their answers using **auch**.
*Das Geld ist mir **auch** wichtig.*

Sprechen 3 In pairs, ask and answer questions about what is most important to you.

- *Was ist dir wichtig im Leben?*
- *Mir ist (die Familie) wichtig. (Die Gesundheit) ist mir auch wichtig.*
- *Ist die Arbeit wichtig für dich?*
- *Für mich ist die Arbeit (nicht / ziemlich / sehr) wichtig.*

G There are two ways to say how important something is to someone.
Für mich ist die Gesundheit wichtig.
Mir ist die Gesundheit wichtig.

Für is followed by the accusative case so we say **für mich**.
Mir means 'to me' and is in the dative case.

	accusative	dative
me	mich	mir
you (singular)	dich	dir
him	ihn	ihm
her	sie	ihr
us	uns	uns
you (plural)	euch	euch
you (formal, sg and pl)	Sie	Ihnen
them	sie	ihnen

Remember that if you are using a plural noun, you need to use **sind** instead of **ist**:
Singular: *Mir **ist** der Beruf wichtig.*
Plural: *Mir **sind** Freunde wichtig.*

Page 168

Hören 4 Listen to three generations of the same family discussing what is most important to them and why. Copy and complete the table in English. (1–3)

	year born	important	not important
1			

Welche Generation ist deine Generation?

1946–1964 geboren	Babyboomer	Als Kinder hatten sie keine Computer.
1965–1979 geboren	Generation X	Als Kinder hatten sie Fernseher und die ersten Computer.
1980–1995 geboren	Millennials (Generation Y)	Als Kinder hatten sie das Internet.
1996–2010 geboren	Generation Z	Als Kinder hatten sie YouTube, die sozialen Medien und moderne Technologie.
nach 2011 geboren	Generation Alpha	

hundertachtundfünfzig

Kapitel 7

5 Listen to and read the texts. Find the German for the phrases below.

Hast du Angst?

Wir haben die Frage „Hast du Angst?" in unserem Forum gestellt und hier sind eure Antworten:

Ja, sicher. Ich habe Angst vor der Zukunft. Geld ist mir nicht sehr wichtig, aber ich hoffe auf genug Geld für alle, weil alles so teuer ist! **Charlotte**

Für mich sind Menschenrechte total wichtig. Ich habe Angst vor Krieg und ich warte auf bessere Zeiten für alle. **Can**

Ich interessiere mich für die Umwelt. Das ist mir sehr wichtig. Ich diskutiere über Umweltprobleme mit meinem Freund. **Robin**

Mir ist das Studium wichtig und deswegen habe ich Angst vor meinen Prüfungen. Ich freue mich auf die Sommerferien! **Yuki**

1 I am waiting for
2 I talk about
3 I am afraid of
4 I am looking forward to
5 I am hoping for
6 I am interested in

6 Read the texts in exercise 5 again and answer the questions below.

1 Who is worried about exams?
2 Who finds human rights really important?
3 Who finds the environment very important?
4 Who is afraid of the future?

7 Listen to Leonie and Mohammed talking and answer the two questions below for each of them.

1 What is important to them?
2 What are their hopes and fears for the future?

G Many verbs in German are followed by **prepositions**. Remember which case each preposition takes and make sure the article that follows agrees with the noun.

diskutieren **über** (+acc)	to talk **about**
sprechen **über** (+acc)	to speak **about**
sich interessieren **für** (+acc)	to be interested **in**
sich freuen **auf** (+acc)	to look forward **to**
hoffen **auf** (+acc)	to hope **for**
warten **auf** (+acc)	to wait **for**
sich kümmern **um** (+acc)	to take care **of** / be concerned **about**
Angst haben **vor** (+dat)	to be afraid **of**

To refer to something you have already mentioned, add **dar-** to the preposition.
Ich interessiere mich **dafür**.
I am interested **in it**.
If the preposition begins with a vowel, add **dar-**.
Ich freue mich **darauf**.
I am looking forward **to it**.

Page 169

8 Write your own post for the forum in exercise 5.

Ich habe Angst vor	der Zukunft. (dem) Mobbing.
Ich diskutiere/ spreche über	die Schule. meine Noten. die Umwelt.
Ich freue mich auf	die Ferien. bessere Zeiten.
Ich hoffe auf	eine bessere Zukunft. gute Noten.
Ich interessiere mich für	mein Studium. die Umwelt. Menschenrechte.

G There are several useful expressions in German which use *haben*:

Angst haben (to be afraid)	Ich habe Angst vor der Zukunft.
Durst haben (to be thirsty)	Ich habe Durst.
Hunger haben (to be hungry)	Ich habe Hunger.
Lust haben (to feel like)	Ich habe keine Lust.
Recht haben (to be right)	Ich habe Recht.

Page 169

hundertneunundfünfzig

2 Unser armer Planet

- Discussing how environmental issues are being addressed
- Understanding *wollen* and revising other modal verbs
- Revising compound nouns

Hören 1 Listen to the environmental concerns. Write the correct letter to match each issue (a–f) to a speaker. Does the person they are speaking to agree with them? (1–6)

Was ist ein großes Umweltproblem in deinem Land?

steigend rising, increasing

a das extreme Wetter
b zu viel Müll
c das schmutzige Trinkwasser
d die steigenden Temperaturen
e weniger Bäume
f Tiere in Gefahr

Sprechen 2 In groups, discuss the environmental problems in exercise 1. Which are important problems in your opinion?

Meiner Meinung nach Mir Für mich	ist (das extreme Wetter)	ein großes Problem. ein wichtiges Problem.
	sind (das extreme Wetter und die steigenden Temperaturen)	große Probleme. wichtige Probleme.

ich stimme (nicht) zu — I (don't) agree
das stimmt (nicht) — that is(n't) correct

- Meiner Meinung nach ist zu viel Müll ein wichtiges Problem. Was denkst du?
- Ich stimme nicht zu. Für mich sind weniger Bäume ein wichtiges Problem.
- Das stimmt nicht! Für mich ist schmutziges Trinkwasser ein wichtiges Problem.

Lesen 3 Read the slogans, then match them to the possible solutions (a–f).

Was können wir machen?

1. Wir wollen frische Luft haben!
2. Wir wollen die steigenden Temperaturen vermeiden!
3. Wir wollen im sauberen Wasser schwimmen!
4. Wir wollen Energie sparen!
5. Wir wollen Tiere in Gefahr retten!
6. Wir wollen mehr recyceln!

a Wir müssen Tiere schützen.
b Wir sollen mehr Windenergie benutzen.
c Wir können Papier sammeln und Glasflaschen kaufen.
d Wir können weniger mit dem Auto fahren.
e Ich glaube, wir sollen weniger Energie benutzen.
f Ich glaube, wir müssen die Flüsse und Seen sauber machen.

G Use *wollen* + infinitive to express what people *want* to do.

ich will	I want
du willst	you want
er/sie/es/man will	he/she/it/one wants
wir wollen	we want
ihr wollt	you (pl) want
Sie wollen	you (formal) want
sie wollen	they want

When using modal verbs, remember that the second verb (**the infinitive**) must go to the end of the sentence.
Wir wollen Tiere in Gefahr **retten**.
We want **to save** animals in danger.
Wir sollen mehr Windenergie **benutzen**.
We should / ought **to use** more wind energy.

Page 170

160 *hundertsechzig*

Kapitel 7

Hören 4 Listen to these young people talking about environmental issues. Copy and complete the table. (1–4)

Was sollen wir machen?

	problem	solution
1		

Schreiben 5 Write a paragraph answering the two questions below.
- What is a big environmental problem where you live?
- What should we do about it?

Meiner Meinung nach ist … ein großes Problem.
… ist auch ein großes Problem.
Sowohl … als auch … sind große Probleme.
Ich glaube, wir sollen …
Wir können auch …

sowohl … als auch …   … as well as …

Lesen 6 Read the texts about the environmental activists. Answer the questions in English.

Sie wollen die Umwelt retten!

Ich finde Luisa Neubauer toll. Sie hat den Schulstreik für den Umweltschutz in Deutschland organisiert. Für sie ist es eine große Sorge, dass wir unsere Erde verschmutzen.

Ich glaube, wir müssen Respekt für die Umwelt zeigen. Wir sollen Energie sparen und Tiere schützen.

Felix

Ich finde Tim Noack toll. Er will uns etwas über die Umweltprobleme in der Unterwasserwelt erzählen. Deswegen hat er eine Webseite, Mantahari Oceancare, gemacht. Die Webseite hat auch ein Online-Geschäft. Als Schwimmer glaubt er, dass zu viel Müll ein wichtiges Problem für die Umwelt ist.

Wir sollen mehr recyceln und weniger wegwerfen, denke ich.

Johanna

der Schulstreik   school strike

1 What did Luisa Neubauer organise?
2 What is a big concern for her?
3 What does Felix think we should do?
4 What does Tim Noack want to tell us about?
5 What does he think is an important problem for the environment?
6 What does Johanna think we should do?

G Remember that **compound nouns** can be formed from
- two nouns:
  Umwelt + Problem → das Umweltproblem
- a verb stem and a noun:
  trinken + Wasser → das Trinkwasser
- an adjective and a noun:
  klein + Stadt → die Kleinstadt

When the first noun ends in a consonant, it is common to add an **s** to link the words:
Verkehr + Mittel → das Verkehr**s**mittel
The gender of a compound noun will always be determined by the gender of the final noun in the word.

Page 170

Lesen 7 Read the texts in exercise 6 again. Find examples of the following and translate them into English.
- Compound nouns
- Modal verbs in the present tense used with an infinitive
- Phrases in the perfect tense

Pay careful attention to the pronunciation of **compound nouns**, making sure you emphasise the first part of the noun and pronounce each individual part clearly.
Listen and repeat the words.
Trinkwasser
Umweltproblem

hunderteinundsechzig **161**

3 Jeder kann was tun!

- Discussing personal responsibilities and actions
- Revising frequency phrases
- Understanding and using verbs in three time frames

Hören 1 Listen to Hanna and Mika completing the survey. Write the letters for the answers Hanna gives.
Example: 1 C

Wie umweltfreundlich bist du?

1 Wie oft kaufst du Plastikflaschen? 
A Ich kaufe sie nie.
B Ich kaufe sie ab und zu.
C Ich kaufe sie täglich.

2 Was recycelst du? 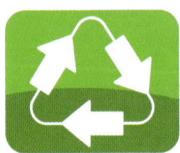
A Ich recycle fast alles.
B Ich recycle Glas und Papier.
C Ich recycle nichts.

3 Sparst du Energie? 
A Ich spare immer Energie.
B Ich spare oft Energie – ich mache das Licht aus.
C Ich spare fast nie Energie.

4 Wie oft gehst du zu Fuß in die Schule? 
A Ich gehe jeden Tag zu Fuß.
B Ich gehe einmal pro Woche zu Fuß.
C Ich gehe nie zu Fuß.

5 Wie oft kaufst du neue Kleidung? 
A Ich kaufe fast nie neue Kleidung.
B Ich kaufe manchmal neue Kleidung.
C Ich kaufe immer neue Kleidung.

6 Sparst du Wasser? 
A Ja, ich spare immer Wasser.
B Ja, ich spare manchmal Wasser.
C Nein, ich spare nie Wasser.

Meistens A	Meistens B	Meistens C
Du bist sehr umweltfreundlich! Du recycelst Müll, du sparst Wasser und Energie und du kaufst nicht so oft neue Kleidung.	Du bist ziemlich umweltfreundlich, aber du sollst mehr machen. Kannst du vielleicht mehr Energie oder Wasser sparen?	Du bist gar nicht umweltfreundlich! Du sollst mehr machen. Du musst weniger Plastikflaschen kaufen und mehr recyceln!

Sprechen 2 In pairs, complete the quiz. Then translate the paragraph from the answer key which corresponds to most of your answers into English.

Schreiben 3 Write a paragraph answering this question.

Was machst du für die Umwelt?

Was machst du für die Umwelt?

Ich kaufe		umweltfreundliche Sachen. neue Kleidung. Glasflaschen.
Ich spare	immer normalerweise jeden Tag (nicht) oft manchmal ab und zu (fast) nie	Energie. Wasser.
Ich recycle		Papier.
Ich sammle		Glas(flaschen).
Ich benutze		weniger Energie.
Ich gehe		zu Fuß.
Ich fahre		mit dem Fahrrad.

162 *hundertzweiundsechzig*

Kapitel 7

Hören 4
Listen to and read the text about how Alex has become more environmentally friendly. What did he do last year? What does he do now? What will he do in future? Write three lists.

Dieses Jahr bin ich viel umweltfreundlicher als letztes Jahr. Ich sammle und recycle jetzt fast alles: Papier, Glas, Kleidung. Letztes Jahr habe ich nur Papier recycelt und ich habe immer neue Kleidung gekauft. Jetzt kaufe ich öfter in Secondhandgeschäften ein. Das ist viel besser für die Umwelt.

Letztes Jahr bin ich zu oft mit dem Auto gefahren – auch kurze Wege! Wenn möglich, fahre ich jetzt mit dem Fahrrad oder ich gehe zu Fuß. Ich habe auch letztes Jahr fast nie Energie gespart. Jetzt benutze ich jeden Tag viel weniger Energie.

Ich muss aber noch mehr machen! In der Zukunft werde ich Glasflaschen in der Schule sammeln und recyceln. Ich werde auch mit einer Gruppe wie den Jungen Grünen arbeiten. Ich möchte mit anderen Menschen an einer gemeinsamen Aktion für die Umwelt teilnehmen.

- Last year: recycled only paper, ...
- Now: recycles almost everything, ...
- In the future: will collect glass bottles, ...

G Understanding and using three time frames in your work will help you to target higher grades.
Present: *Ich **kaufe** umweltfreundliche Sachen.*
Past: *Ich **habe** umweltfreundliche Sachen **gekauft**.*
Future: *Ich **werde** umweltfreundliche Sachen **kaufen**.*

Remember where the prefix goes for separable verbs.
Present: *Ich **kaufe** in Secondhandgeschäften **ein**.*
Past: *Ich **habe** in Secondhandgeschäften **eingekauft**.*
Future: *Ich **werde** in Secondhandgeschäften **einkaufen**.*

Look at the verbs in the key language box in exercise 3 and check that you know the past and future tense forms. Then test a partner.

Page 171

Hören 5
Listen to Franziska, Peter and Lotte discussing what they do to help the environment. Copy and complete the table in English.

	normally	in the last week	in the future
Franziska			

Hören 6
Listen and write down the words you hear, paying attention to the -er sounds. Then translate them into English. (1–6)

-er at the end of a word is 'unstressed' (unsounded):
*Wir sollen die Welt bess**er** schützen.*
*Wir sollen wenig**er** Energie benutzen.*

-er can also be 'stressed' (sounded):
*Wir sollen neu**er**e En**er**gien benutzen.*

Listen and repeat the sentences.

Schreiben 7
Translate the sentences into German.

1 I cycle more often.
2 I save energy from time to time.
3 I often recycled glass.
4 I went on foot to school.
5 I will never buy new clothes.
6 I will shop in second-hand shops.

Remember, the verb must be in second place.

Does this verb take *haben* or *sein*?

How do we form the comparative?

This past participle is irregular.

Think carefully about how to use the infinitive of separable verbs.

Sprechen 8
In pairs, ask and answer the questions below.
- Was machst du normalerweise für die Umwelt?
- Was hast du letzte Woche für die Umwelt gemacht?
- Was wirst du in der Zukunft auch machen?

hundertdreiundsechzig 163

4 Wir wollen eine bessere Welt!

- Discussing international responsibilities and actions
- Developing listening and reading skills
- Using *man*

Lesen 1 Match the sentences to the international organisations (a–f).

Was macht diese internationale Organisation?

Diese Organisation …

1 … reguliert Fußball und internationale Fußballspiele.
2 … arbeitet für bessere Gesundheitssysteme in allen Ländern.
3 … hilft Menschen in Gefahr.
4 … arbeitet für den Naturschutz.
5 … hilft kranken Menschen.
6 … verbessert das Leben für Kinder überall in der Welt.

a ICRC — Internationales Rotes Kreuz

b WWF — Organisation für Natur- und Artenschutz

c FIFA — Weltfußballverband

d WHO — Weltgesundheits-organisation

e MSF — Ärzte ohne Grenzen

f STC — Save the Children

Sprechen 2 In pairs, check your answers. Take turns to read out a sentence from exercise 1 and say which organisation it describes.

- Diese Organisation verbessert das Leben für Kinder überall in der Welt.
- Das ist 'f' – STC!
- Ja, richtig!

Practise reading out the names and abbreviations of the organisations. Think carefully about how to pronounce the letters of the alphabet.

Hören 3 Listen and write down the modal verbs and infinitives you hear. Then translate the sentences into English. (1–4)

1 Man ▭ den Welthunger ▭.
2 Man ▭ kranken Menschen ▭.
3 Man ▭ Menschenrechte ▭.
4 Man ▭ zusammen die Umwelt ▭.

G *Man* can be translated as 'you', 'they', 'people', or occasionally 'one'. Remember when using modal verbs that the second verb in the sentence will be in the **infinitive**.

Man kann (*You can*)
Man will (*You want to*)
Man soll (*You should*)
Man muss (*You must*)
Man darf (*You are allowed to*)

Man kann gemeinsam **arbeiten**.
Man will den Welthunger **beenden**.
Man soll Menschenrechte **schützen**.
Man muss Umweltkatastrophen **vermeiden**.
Man darf in einem anderen Land **wohnen.**

Page 171

164 hundertvierundsechzig

Lesen 4 Read the text about the European Union (EU) and answer the questions in English.

Die Europäische Union (EU) ist eine sehr große Organisation. Es gibt mehr als 448 Millionen Personen, die in der EU leben, und vierundzwanzig offizielle Sprachen.

Als EU-**Bürger** kann man einfach in einem anderen EU-Mitgliedsland wohnen und arbeiten.

Die EU hat ihr eigenes Geld – den Euro. Wenn man etwas in einem EU-Mitgliedsland kauft, kann man normalerweise mit dem Euro zahlen. Das ist ganz praktisch!

Man muss die Umweltgesetze in der EU respektieren und Menschenrechte schützen. Das ist sehr wichtig.

1 How many official languages are there in the EU?
2 What are you allowed to do in other countries in the EU?
3 What is practical in the EU?
4 What must you respect and protect in the EU? (Give two details.)
5 What is a **Bürger**?
   a) a person   b) a country   c) a type of food

das Gesetz (-e) law

Schreiben 5 Translate the sentences into German using *man*.

Which modal verb do you need?

1 People want to protect nature.
2 You can live in another country.
3 You must help people in danger.
4 People should work together.
5 You are allowed to work in Germany.

Remember to put the infinitive at the end of the sentence.

Which case do you need to use here?

Hören 6 Listen to the description of the photo. Write down what you hear and then correct the mistake in each sentence. (1–5)

Sprechen 7 Now describe the picture for yourself. Then answer the questions below.

1 Was machst du normalerweise für die Umwelt?
2 Was soll eine internationale Organisation für Menschen machen?

Auf dem Foto gibt es (vier) Personen.
Sie sind ungefähr (zwanzig) Jahre alt.

Der Mann trägt Die Frau trägt Der Junge trägt Das Mädchen trägt	einen Rock. eine Jacke. eine Hose. ein T-Shirt. ein Hemd. Schuhe.
Sie sind	draußen / zu Hause / in der Schule. am Strand / an der Küste. in der Straße / im Park / in der Stadt.
Das ist vielleicht in	Europa. England / Deutschland / Österreich. der Schweiz / der Türkei.
Im Hintergrund sieht man	das Meer / einen See / einen Fluss. Leute / Häuser / Bäume / Felder / Berge.
Sie sammeln	Papier / Glas.

hundertfünfundsechzig

5 Dialog ist wichtig!

- Expressing and justifying complex opinions and points of view
- Using phrases of debating in speaking
- Pronouncing *r* sounds correctly

Hören 1 Listen to and read the statements. Is each person for or against eating meat?

Vegan essen: bist du dafür oder dagegen?

Layla: Ich esse sehr gern Fleisch und das ist so lecker!

Arda: So wenig veganes Essen auf der Speisekarte? Nein, danke!

Mika: Nur Gemüse essen? Das ist so langweilig!

Kim: Gemüse ist auch lecker und gesünder als Fleisch.

Yannie: Man soll Tiere schützen.

Julian: Die Fleischindustrie ist nicht gut für die Umwelt.

dagegen against it

Hören 2 Listen to and read the conversation. Find the German expressions in **bold** for the opinion phrases below.

Anna: Warum bist du Veganer, Bruno?

Bruno: **Also**, die Umwelt ist mir sehr wichtig. Die Fleischindustrie ist nicht gut für die Umwelt und das finde ich ganz schlecht.

Anna: **Das stimmt** natürlich. **Meiner Meinung nach** ist Fleisch **aber** lecker und **auch** gibt es für Fleischesser viel auf der Karte in Restaurants. Für Veganer gibt es nicht so viel, und **ich glaube**, das ist ein großes Problem.

Bruno: **Ich finde** aber, dass Gemüse leckerer und gesünder als Fleisch ist. **Ich denke** auch, man soll Tiere schützen. Ich will nicht, dass Tiere für mich leiden. Heute muss man kein Fleisch essen, weil es viele andere Möglichkeiten gibt.

Anna: **Du hast Recht**. Vielleicht werde ich das versuchen.

1 I think (Find two expressions.)
2 that's right
3 I believe
4 in my opinion
5 you're right
6 also
7 but/however
8 Well,

Hören 3 Listen to three young people saying why they are vegan and write down the reasons mentioned in English. (1–3)

166 *hundertsechsundsechzig*

Kapitel 7

Sprechen 4 In a group, discuss your opinion of veganism. Are you for or against it? Use as many of the phrases from exercise 2 as possible.

- *Veganer*in sein: bist du dafür oder dagegen?*
- *Ich bin dafür. Ich glaube, das ist gesünder. Was denkst du?*
- *Ich bin dagegen. Meiner Meinung nach …*

Lesen 5 Read the statements for and against wind and solar energy. Copy and complete the table with the numbers of the statements.

1 Sie sind saubere Energiequellen.
2 Sie werden in der Zukunft Geld sparen.
3 Wenn es dunkel ist, funktioniert das nicht.
4 Wenn es keinen Wind gibt, funktioniert das nicht.
5 Sie sind umweltfreundlich.
6 Sie kosten viel Geld.

für Sonnen- und Windenergie	gegen Sonnen- und Windenergie

Sprechen 6 In pairs, take turns to read out the sentences in exercise 5. Pay attention to the *r* sounds. Then, using the expressions from exercise 2, discuss the pros and cons of solar and wind energy.

The consonantal **r** is a rolled sound at the back of the throat:
*spa**r**en, funktionie**r**en, P**r**oblem*
The vocalic **r** sounds more like a vowel sound:
*einfache**r**, Kinde**r**, Vegane**r***
Some words contain both **r** sounds:
*besse**r**e**r**, Vegeta**r**ie**r***
Listen and repeat the words.

Lesen 7 Translate the paragraph into English.

Meiner Meinung nach ist die Umwelt wirklich wichtig. Ich denke, ich werde weniger Fleisch essen. Das wird schwierig sein, weil es so lecker ist! Ich glaube auch, dass wir zu viel Energie benutzen. Ich finde, dass Sonnen- und Windenergie gute Möglichkeiten sind. Stimmst du zu?

Hören 8 Listen to Leo answering the following questions. Make notes in English on the following points:

1 environmental problems in Leo's country
2 what actions we should take for the environment
3 something Leo has done for the environment
4 how Leo sees his future.

Schreiben 9 Write approximately 90 words about environmental issues. Include the following points:

- an environmental problem we are facing and what we should do about it
- something you did recently to help the environment
- how the future is looking for you.

Meiner Meinung nach ist … ein großes Umweltproblem.
Wir sollen für die Umwelt (Energie sparen).
Ich habe neulich (mit meinen Freunden) (Papier/Glas gesammelt).
Ich interessiere mich für …
Ich will/möchte … studieren.
Ich hoffe auf …
Ich habe Angst vor …
Ich freue mich auf …

hundertsiebenundsechzig **167**

Grammatik 1

Prepositions (Culture, page 157)

Schreiben 1 Translate the phrases into German.

Example: 1 for the environment – für die Umwelt

1 for the environment (f)
2 against world hunger (m)
3 with the organisation (f)
4 without the money (nt)
5 in the future (f)
6 from Switzerland (f)
7 to Austria
8 a year ago (nt)

Hören 2 Listen and write down the words you hear to complete the sentences.

1 Ich spreche ___ ___ Frau.
2 Er arbeitet ___ ___ Organisation.
3 Wir gehen ___ ___ Stadt.
4 Sie kommt ___ ___ Land in Europa.
5 Wir sind ___ ___ Gruppe.
6 Ich gehe ___ ___ Schule aus.

Pronouns in the accusative and dative cases (Unit 1, page 158)

Lesen 3 Translate the sentences into English.

1 Für mich ist die Gesundheit sehr wichtig.
2 Für ihn ist die Familie wichtiger.
3 Was ist für dich wichtig?
4 Für uns sind Freunde total wichtig.
5 Ist Geld wichtig für Sie, Herr Schmidt?
6 Für euch ist die Umwelt wichtiger, oder?
7 Und die Kinder? Was ist wichtiger für sie?
8 Meine Schwester liebt ihre Arbeit. Die Arbeit ist wichtig für sie.

Schreiben 4 Complete the sentences with the correct dative pronoun.

1 Freunde sind ___ wichtig. (to me)
2 Sind Tiere ___ wichtig, Mia? (to you)
3 Die Natur ist ___ sehr wichtig. (to him)
4 ___ ist die Arbeit wirklich wichtig. (to her)
5 Das Studium ist ___ ganz wichtig. (to us)
6 Die Freiheit ist ___ wichtiger. (to them)
7 Ist das Geld ___ wichtig, Frau Thomas? (to you, formal)
8 Jan und Mia, ist Familie ___ wichtig? (to you, plural)

Kapitel 7

Verbs followed by prepositions (Unit 1, page 159)

Lesen 5 Write the correct letter to match each preposition to the correct verb.
Example: 1 b

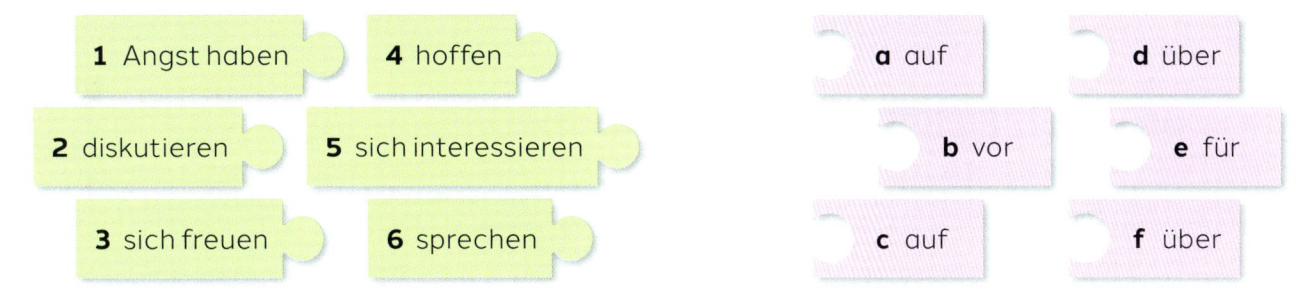

1 Angst haben
2 diskutieren
3 sich freuen
4 hoffen
5 sich interessieren
6 sprechen

a auf
b vor
c auf
d über
e für
f über

Schreiben 6 Copy and complete the sentence with the correct preposition. Then rewrite sentences 1–4 using *da(r)…*

Example: 1 Ich hoffe **auf** gute Noten. – Ich hoffe **darauf**.

1 Ich hoffe ___ gute Noten.
2 Freust du dich ___ die Zukunft?
3 Er interessiert sich ___ Menschenrechte.
4 Sie warten ___ bessere Zeiten.
5 Ich habe Angst ___ meinen Prüfungen.
6 Wir diskutieren ___ die Umwelt.

Sprechen 7 In pairs, play noughts and crosses. Complete the sentence with your own idea to win the square.

Ich spreche …	Du freust dich …	Wir hoffen …
Sie interessieren sich …	Er diskutiert …	Hast du Angst …?
Sie freut sich …	Wir sprechen …	Ich interessiere mich …

Expressions with *haben* (Unit 1, page 159)

Schreiben 8 Copy and complete the sentences with words from the cloud. Then make a sentence with the remaining word.

1 Ich kaufe eine Flasche Wasser. Ich habe ___.
2 Hilfe! Ich habe ___ vor meinen Prüfungen.
3 Ich möchte etwas essen. Ich habe ___.
4 Das stimmt! Du hast ___!

Angst   Durst
Recht   Lust
Hunger

hundertneunundsechzig

Grammatik 2

Modal verbs (Unit 2, page 160)

Hören 1 Listen and write down the answers to the questions. (1–6)

Example: 1 *Ich kann mit dem Fahrrad zur Schule fahren.*

Umweltfreundlich in der Schule

1 Was kannst du machen, Lea?
2 Was darfst du nicht machen, Tim?
3 Was sollst du machen, Mia?
4 Was sollen die Lehrer machen?
5 Was können die Kinder machen?
6 Was müssen die Eltern machen?

Schreiben 2 Translate the sentences into German.
1 I should recycle paper.
2 We can buy green school things.
3 They should use glass bottles.
4 We want to protect the environment.
5 I want to save more energy.
6 We must go into town by bike.
7 You can go to school on foot.
8 I am not allowed to buy paper.

Compound nouns (Unit 2, page 161)

Lesen 3 Create <u>five</u> compound nouns by combining nouns from the word cloud. Then translate them into English.

Example: das Umweltproblem – environmental problem

(das) Glas
das Problem
das Unterwasser
die Flasche
die Gesundheit
die Umwelt
der Streik
die Welt
das System
die Schule

> Remember that some **compound nouns** lose or add an extra letter in the middle, and the second noun changes to lower case when combined into the compound noun. The compound noun takes the same gender as the final noun in the word.
> *Schule + Buch* ⟶ *das Schulbuch*

170 hundertsiebzig

Kapitel 7

Using the perfect tense (Unit 3, page 163)

4 In pairs, ask and answer the questions about what you did last week for the environment. Use verbs in the perfect tense.
- *Hast du Wasser gespart?*
- *Ja, ich habe …*
- *Bist du mit dem Fahrrad zur Schule gefahren?*
- *Nein, ich bin nicht …*
- *Hast du neue Kleidung gekauft?*
- *…*
- *Hast du Papier recycelt?*
- *…*

Using *man* (Unit 4, page 164)

5 Translate the sentences into English.

Example: 1 One/People/You should not buy new clothes so often.

Was kann man machen?
1. Man soll nicht so oft neue Kleidung kaufen.
2. Man muss weniger Energie benutzen.
3. Man soll Energie sparen.
4. Man kann öfter zu Fuß gehen.
5. Man kann Windenergie benutzen.
6. Man darf kein Papier kaufen.

Los geht's!

6 Write down the words you hear to complete each sentence.
1. Ich ___ kein schmutziges Wasser ___.
2. Du hoffst ___ gute Noten.
3. Ich ___ ___ eine ___.
4. Ich wohne ___ ___.
5. Das sind ___ ___.
6. Ich ___ ___ ___.
7. Man ___ ___ ___.
8. ___ ___ ___ mit dem ___.

7 Copy and complete the paragraph with words from the box.

Die Umwelt ist **1** sehr wichtig. Ich habe Angst **2** der Zukunft und ich freue mich nicht **2** . Ich **4** die Natur schützen und ich denke, **5** soll sich **6** die Umwelt kümmern.

| vor | will | um |
| darauf | mir | man |

hunderteinundsiebzig **171**

Kapitel 7 Lese- und Hörtest

Reading

Lesen 1

What is important. Some German students are discussing what is important to them and why. Write the correct name to answer each question. Write **P** for Paula, **E** for Elias or **L** for Leonie.

Paula
Ich arbeite immer viel in der Schule und ich lerne sehr gern, weil die Ausbildung für mich wichtig ist. Nach dem Studium möchte ich später in meinem Leben einen interessanten Beruf haben.

Elias
Jedes Wochenende gehe ich mit einer Gruppe in die Natur und wir sammeln Müll. Das finde ich sehr wichtig, weil wir eine saubere Welt brauchen.

Leonie
Meiner Meinung nach ist es wirklich schlecht, wenn man kein Haus oder keine Wohnung hat. Alle Menschen sollen dieselben Chancen und Möglichkeiten haben.

1 Who helps the environment?
2 Who worries about homeless people?
3 Who studies hard?
4 Who is thinking about a future career?
5 Who spends time outside every weekend?
6 Who is concerned about equality?

> Read all of the texts before deciding on any answers and look for key words in the English questions to help you locate the answers in the texts.

Lesen 2

Being vegan. You read Tim's blog about his lifestyle. Write the correct letter, **A**, **B** or **C**, to complete each sentence.

Ich bin Veganer, weil das umweltfreundlicher und besser für die Natur ist. Meiner Meinung nach kann man auch Tiere schützen, wenn man kein Fleisch und keinen Fisch isst. Gemüse und Obst essen ist gesünder.

Meine Eltern sind nicht Veganer, weil sie das zu extrem finden. Sie denken, dass es auch nicht billig ist. Sie finden es komisch, dass veganes Essen oft wie Fleisch aussieht. Ich denke, dass man aber nur Pflanzen braucht. Meine Familie kann ohne Fleisch einfach nicht leben, weil sie **Gulasch** zu lecker findet!

1 Tim thinks that being vegan …
   A is natural.   B helps the environment.   C helps you make friends.
2 Tim also thinks that being vegan …
   A makes you hungry.   B is healthier for animals.   C helps protect animals.
3 Tim's parents think that being vegan is …
   A really amusing.   B too extreme.   C cheap.
4 Tim says that all you need is …
   A plants.   B meat.   C your family.
5 Read the last sentence again. What would you do with **Gulasch**?
   A decorate with it   B plant it   C eat it

> Sometimes words can have more than one meaning. For example, the word *komisch* can mean both 'funny' and 'strange'. These types of words are called homonyms. Use the context to help you work out the meaning of homonyms.

172 hundertzweiundsiebzig

Lesen 3

Translate these sentences into English.

Look at the component parts of a compound noun to work out its meaning.

Remember to translate intensifiers and time expressions.

1 Ich spare immer Energie.
2 Der Umweltschutz ist mir sehr wichtig.
3 Ich glaube, wir sollen alle Menschen akzeptieren.
4 Wir arbeiten für eine bessere Welt ohne Mobbing.
5 Letztes Jahr bin ich zu oft mit dem Auto gefahren.

Can you remember what the dative pronoun *mir* means?

Which tense is this?

Watch out for false friends.

When you translate into English, you may need to change the word order. Think about what sounds natural in English. For example, time phrases are often in a different position in English.

Listening

Hören 4

Being environmentally friendly. You hear Milan talking about what he does for the environment. What does he say? **Listen to the recording** and answer the questions in English.

1 How do Milan's family normally travel?
2 How do they travel when they go abroad?
3 Which **three** actions does Milan say his family takes at home? Write the **three** correct letters (**A–E**).

A	save water
B	use glass bottles
C	grow their own fruit
D	eat meat
E	recycle everything

Use the context to help you anticipate the vocabulary and structures you might hear and try to recall some of the more technical vocabulary you have learned relating to this topic.

You will hear the recording twice. Make notes the first time, then use the pause between the first and second to work out your answers. Use the second listening to complete and check your answers.

All of the answer options may be mentioned on the recording, so you need to listen carefully for negatives and other language that will help you discount the incorrect options.

Dictation

Hören 5

You will hear four short sentences. Write down exactly what you hear in German.

Think carefully about how these sounds and letters are pronounced when writing down what you hear:
-tion
-er
r

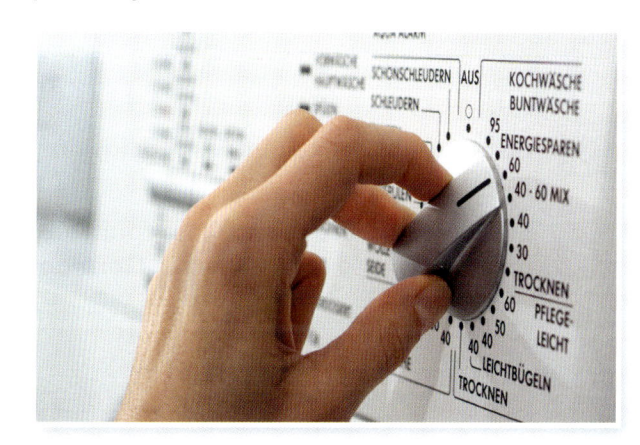

hundertdreiundsiebzig **173**

Kapitel 7 Mündlicher Test

Role-play

1 Look at the role-play card and prepare what you want to say.

> You are talking to your Swiss friend about where you live.
> 1 Say where you live. (Give **one** detail.)
> 2 Say **one** thing you do to help the environment.
> 3 Say **one** social issue where you live.
> 4 Say how you travel into town. (Give **one** detail.)
> 5 **?** Ask your friend a question about the environment.

Remember that your response to each task must contain a verb.

You could use *Man kann (nicht) …, Es gibt (viel/kein) …, Die Menschen können (nicht) …*

You will need to use *mit* + dative with transport or *zu Fuß* if you walk. Also think about which verb you will need: *gehen* or *fahren*?

Remember, to form a question you can either use a question word (e.g. *Wie oft …? Was …?*) or use subject–verb inversion (*Sparst du …? Fährst du …?*).

2 Practise what you have prepared. Then, using your notes, listen and respond to the teacher.

3 Listen to Taylor's answers and make a note of:
  a how he answers the questions for points 1–4
  b what question he asks for point 5.

Reading aloud

4 Look at this task. With a partner, read the sentences aloud, paying attention to the underlined letters.

> Ich bin eine nichtbinäre Person.
> Manchmal gibt es Mobbing.
> Wir sollen Leute akzeptieren und unterstützen.
> Ich arbeite für Menschenrechte, denn ich will diese Situation verbessern.
> Information und Aktion sind wichtig für eine bessere Welt.

Think carefully about how to pronounce these sounds and letters:
-tion
-er
r

Remember that the stress falls on the first syllable of a compound noun like *Menschenrechte*.

5 Listen and check your pronunciation.

6 Listen to the teacher asking four follow-up questions. Translate each question into English and prepare your own answers in German. Then listen again and respond to the teacher.

174 hundertsvierundsiebzig

Kapitel 7

Photo card

Hören 7 — Listen to Taylor describing the photos and answer the questions.
1. Where does Taylor say the people in the first photo are? (Give **two** details.)
2. What does he say they are doing?
3. What does he say about the weather? (Give **two** details.)
4. Which **three** modes of transport does Taylor mention in relation to the second photo?
5. Which mode of transport does he say is more environmentally friendly?

You will be asked to talk about the content of these photos. You must say at least one thing about each photo.

After you have spoken about the content of the photos, you will be asked questions related to any of the topics within the theme of **Communication and the world around us**.

Your responses should be as **full and detailed** as possible.

Sprechen 8 — Prepare your own description of both photos. Then, with a partner, take turns describing them.

> Auf dem ersten Foto gibt es …

Hören 9 — Listen to the teacher's first follow-up question, *Was hast du letzte Woche für die Umwelt gemacht?*, and Taylor's response. Write down <u>three</u> actions Taylor mentions.

Hören 10 — The teacher then asks Taylor, *Was wirst du in der Zukunft für die Umwelt machen?* Write down <u>three</u> positive actions Taylor plans to take.

> You may be asked similar questions in different tenses, such as *Was **hast** du letztes Wochenende gemacht?* (past tense) and *Was **wirst** du nächstes Wochenende **machen**?* (future tense). You could just give the same answer and change the verb tense: *Ich habe Energie gespart* and *Ich werde Energie sparen*. However, it's better to avoid repetition, by using different vocabulary or persons of the verb, and adding subordinate clauses. For example, *Letztes Wochenende haben meine Familie und ich Wasser gespart* and *Nächstes Wochenende werden meine Schwester und ich kein Fleisch essen, weil es besser für die Umwelt ist.*

Sprechen 11 — Listen to two more follow-up questions and prepare your answers. Then respond to the recording.

Sprechen 12 — Prepare your own answers to as many of the Module 7 questions on page 227 as you can. Then practise with a partner.

hundertfünfundsiebzig **175**

Kapitel 7 Schreibtest

Translation

Schreiben 1 Read the English sentences and correct the mistakes in Cara's translations.

1. I am a vegan.
2. We want to save endangered animals.
3. I am interested in a better world.
4. Unfortunately there are not enough buses in my village.
5. Last week we saved energy.

1. Ich bin keine Veganerin.
2. Ich will Tiere in Gefahr retten.
3. Ich interessiere mich für Menschenrechte.
4. Leider gibt es nicht genug Busse im Stadtzentrum.
5. Gestern haben wir Wasser gespart.

Schreiben 2 Translate these sentences into German.

Take care with this irregular verb. *Ich will* is 'I want', but how will you translate 'We want'?

Remember that this is a reflexive verb.

1. I am a vegetarian.
2. We want to recycle paper.
3. I am interested in the environment.
4. Unfortunately there is too much rubbish in the town centre.
5. Last week I saved energy.

Which preposition do you need here?

Remember, 'there is' and 'there are' are the same in German.

Think about the tense you need to use here.

90-word writing task

Schreiben 3 Look at this writing exam task and then, for each bullet point:

1. think about the vocabulary and structures you have learned which you could use in your answer. For example:
   - **nouns**, **verbs** and **adjectives** to write about the importance of friends
   - **verbs of opinion** and **adjectives** to give reasons
   - language for **narrating a story** about a friend's problem
   - how to explain **what your plans are** and **why**
   - connectives and intensifiers you would like to use.
2. write down three or four ideas for what you could write about.
3. identify which tense(s) you could use in your answer.

You are writing to your German friend about issues facing young people today.

Write approximately **90** words in **German**.

You must write something about each bullet point.

Describe:
- the importance of friends
- a problem a friend had recently
- how you want to help with local issues in the future.

176 *hundertsechsundsiebzig*

Kapitel 7

Lesen 4 Read Cara's answer to the exam task. Answer the questions in the coloured boxes (1–5).

1 This is an example of **complex language**. What does it mean? Find two more examples of complex language in the text.

2 Cara uses several **cognates or near-cognates**. What do these words mean? Find two more examples.

> Meine Freunde sind mir sehr wichtig. Wir gehen oft in die Stadt und haben viel Spaß. Ich kann immer mit ihnen sprechen. Wir diskutieren über die Ausbildung, unsere Interessen und Mobbing. Viele Jugendliche haben Angst vor Mobbing.
>
> Letzte Woche hat meine Freundin keinen Sport gemacht, weil sie keine Freizeit hatte. Wir hatten viele Hausaufgaben und sie war traurig, denn es gab eine Prüfung. Das war total langweilig!
>
> In der Zukunft möchte ich für die Umwelt arbeiten. Ich interessiere mich total für die Natur. Ich werde auch mehr recyceln und Energie sparen.

3 Which **tense** is this? Find three more examples.

4 How could Cara **avoid repetition** here?

5 Which connective could you use here to form an **extended sentence**? What other connectives does Cara use?

Lesen 5 Read Cara's answer again and complete the sentences.

1 … are very important to Cara.
2 Many teenagers are worried about …
3 Cara's friend didn't have any … last week, because they had a lot of …
4 Cara's friend was sad about …
5 Cara is really interested in …

Lesen 6 Prepare your own answer to the task.

- Look back at your notes from exercises 3 and 4.
- Think about how you can develop your answer for each bullet point.
- Use the 'Challenge checklist' and consider how you can show off your German!
- Write a **brief** plan and organise your answer into paragraphs.
- Write your answer and then carefully check for accuracy.

Challenge checklist

🥨	✓ Connectives (*und, aber, oder, denn*) ✓ Some extended sentences (*Ich spare Energie und ich gehe zu Fuß.*) ✓ An opinion (*Ich finde die Umwelt sehr wichtig.*)
🥨🥨	✓ The imperfect tense (*ich hatte, es gab, sie waren*) ✓ Different persons of the verb (*wir haben, die Umwelt ist*) ✓ Past, present and future time frames ✓ Use of negatives (*keine, nie, ohne*) ✓ Expressions with *haben* (*ich habe Angst, Lust, Hunger, Durst*) ✓ More interesting vocabulary (*umweltfreundlich, weniger, Tiere retten, die Luft*)
🥨🥨🥨	✓ Conjunctions which change the word order (*weil, da, dass, wenn, obwohl, als*) ✓ Use of *man* + infinitive (*man muss/soll/kann Wasser sparen*) ✓ Subject–verb inversion (*hier kann man, manchmal recycle ich, dann möchte ich, später werden wir*) ✓ Use of the dative (*ich helfe der Umwelt, das ist mir wichtig*) ✓ Complex structures (*ich habe Angst vor, ich interessiere mich für*) ✓ Using two tenses (*Ich habe schon Papier recycelt, aber ich werde auch weniger Fleisch essen.*)

hundertsiebenundsiebzig 177

Kapitel 7 Wörter

Key:
bold = this word will appear in higher exams only
* = this word is not on the vocabulary list but you may use it in your own sentences

Wir verbessernn die Welt! (pages 156–157):

Wir verbessern die Welt!	We're improving the world!
der Blog	blog
der Kontakt	contact
der Mensch	person
der Ort	place
die Aktion	action, campaign
die Angst	fear, anxiety
die Erfahrung	experience
die Geschwister	brothers and sisters, siblings
die **Organisation**	organisation
die **Regierung**	government
das *Zuhause	home
die Drogen	drugs
die Jugendliche	young people
akzeptieren	to accept
*identifizieren	to identify
bauen	to build
gründen	to start, found, establish
informieren	to inform
sicher	safe
nicht binär	non-binary
die *Transphobie	transphobia
die *Diskriminierung	discrimination
*xier	they

Was ist dir wichtig? (pages 158–159):

Wichtige Themen in der Welt	Important topics in the world
der Computer	computer
die Ausbildung	education, training
die Arbeit	work
die Familie	family
die Freiheit	freedom
die Freizeit	free time
die Freunde	friends
die **Generation**	generation
die Gesundheit	health
die *Individualität	individuality
die Interessen	interests
die Prüfung	exam
die Umwelt	environment
die Welt	world
das Geld	money
das Studium	studies

Was ist dir wichtig im Leben? — What is important to you in life?
Mir ist (die Familie) wichtig. — (Family) is important to me.
(Die Gesundheit) ist mir auch wichtig. — (Health) is also important to me.
Ist (die Arbeit) wichtig für dich? — Is (work) important to you?
Für mich ist (die Arbeit) (nicht/ziemlich/sehr) wichtig. — (Work) is (not/rather/very) important to me.
Ich habe Angst vor …
  (dem) Mobbing. — bullying.
  der Zukunft. — the future.
Ich freue mich auf …
  die Ferien. — the holidays.
  bessere Zeiten. — better times.
Ich hoffe auf …
  eine bessere Zukunft. — a better future.
  gute Noten. — good grades.
Ich interessiere mich für … — I'm interested in …
  mein Studium. — my studies.
  die Umwelt. — the environment.
  Menschenrechte. — human rights.
Ich diskutiere/spreche über … — I discuss / talk about …

Unser armer Planet (pages 160–161):

Umweltprobleme	Environmental problems

Meiner Meinung nach ist (das extreme Wetter) ein großes/wichtiges Problem. — In my opinion, (the extreme weather) is a big/important problem.

Meiner Meinung nach sind (die *steigenden Temperaturen) ein großes/wichtiges Problem. — In my opinion, (rising temperatures) are a big/important problem.

Ich *stimme nicht zu. — I do not agree.
Das stimmt (nicht). — That is (not) correct/right.
Du hast Recht. — You are right.
Was sollen wir machen? — What should we do?
Ich glaube, wir sollen … — I believe we should …
Wir können auch … — We can also …

der Umweltschutz	environmental protection
der Verkehr	traffic
der Wind	wind
die Energie	energy
die Gefahr	danger, risk
die Kleinstadt	small town
die Luft	air
die Temperatur	temperature
die Umwelt	environment
das Land	country
das Trinkwasser	drinking water
das Umweltproblem	environmental problem
das Verkehrsmittel	means of transport
das Wasser	water
das Wetter	weather
extrem	extreme
frisch	fresh
sauber	clean
schmutzig	dirty
wärmer	warmer
wichtig	important

Jeder kann was tun! (pages 162–163):

Persönliche **Verantwortung** für die Umwelt	*Personal responsibility for the environment*
Was machst du (normalerweise) für die Umwelt?	*What do you (usually) do for the environment?*
Ich kaufe ...	*I buy ...*
*umweltfreundliche Sachen.	*eco-friendly things.*
neue Kleidung.	*new clothing.*
*Plastikflaschen.	*plastic bottles.*
Ich spare ...	*I save ...*
Energie.	*energy/power.*
Wasser.	*water.*
Ich recycle ...	*I recycle ...*
Ich sammle ...	*I collect ...*
Papier.	*paper.*
Glas(flaschen).	*glass (bottles).*
Ich spare Energie.	*I save energy.*
Ich benutze weniger Energie.	*I use less energy.*
Ich gehe zu Fuß.	*I walk.*
Ich fahre mit dem Fahrrad.	*I cycle.*
Was hast du letzte Woche für die Umwelt gemacht?	*What did you do for the environment last week?*
Was wirst du in der Zukunft machen?	*What will you do in the future?*
benutzen	*to use*
können	*to be able to*
müssen	*to have to*
schützen	*to protect*
sollen	*to be supposed to*
sammeln	*to collect*
verbessern	*to improve*
wegwerfen	*to throw away*

Wir wollen eine bessere Welt! (pages 164–165):

Internationale Verantwortungen	*International responsibilities*
der **Bürger**	*citizen*
der Mensch	*person*
der Naturschutz	*protection of nature*
der Welthunger	*world hunger*
die **Organisation**	*organisation*
das Kind	*child*
das Leben	*life*
Auf dem Foto gibt es (vier) Personen.	*In the photo there are (four) people.*
Sie sind ungefähr (zwanzig) Jahre alt.	*They are around (twenty) years old.*
Der Mann trägt ...	*The man is wearing ...*
Die Frau trägt ...	*The woman is wearing ...*
Der Junge trägt ...	*The boy is wearing ...*
Das Mädchen trägt ...	*The girl is wearing ...*
einen Rock.	*a skirt.*
eine Jacke.	*a jacket.*
eine Hose.	*a pair of trousers.*
ein T-Shirt.	*a t-shirt.*
ein Hemd.	*a shirt.*
Schuhe.	*shoes.*
Sie sind ...	*They are ...*
draußen / zu Hause / in der Schule.	*outside / at home / at school.*
am Strand / an der Küste.	*on the beach / at the coast.*
in der Straße / im Park / in der Stadt.	*in the street / in the park / in town.*
Im Hintergrund sieht man ...	*In the background you can see ...*
einen See.	*a lake.*
einen Fluss.	*a river.*
Bäume.	*trees.*
Berge.	*mountains.*
Felder.	*fields.*
Häuser.	*houses.*
Leute.	*people.*
das Meer.	*the sea.*
Sie sammeln Papier/Glas.	*They are collecting paper/glass.*

Dialog ist wichtig! (pages 166–167):

*Meinungsäußerung	*Expressing opinions*
Meiner Meinung nach ist ... ein großes Umweltproblem.	*In my opinion, ... is a big environmental problem.*
Wir sollen für die Umwelt (Energie sparen).	*We should (save energy) for the environment.*
Ich habe neulich (mit meinen Freunden) (Papier gesammelt).	*I have recently (collected paper) (with my friends).*
Ich interessiere mich für ...	*I'm interested in ...*
Ich will/möchte ... studieren	*I want / would like to study ...*
Ich hoffe auf ...	*I hope for ...*
Ich habe Angst vor ...	*I'm afraid of ...*
Ich freue mich auf ...	*I'm looking forward to ...*
dafür	*for it*
dagegen	*against it / on the other hand*
Das stimmt, aber ...	*That's right, but/however ...*
also	*well, ...*
auch	*also*
bestimmt	*definitely, certainly*
Ich glaube ...	*I believe ...*
Ich finde (aber) ...	*(But) I find/think ...*
Ich denke (auch) ...	*I think (also) ...*
Du hast Recht.	*You are right.*

Kapitel 8

Wie sieht die Zukunft aus?

Ich will helfen
- Learning about military and civilian service
- Using *möchten* and *wollen*

a) Immer beliebter: ein Freiwilliges Soziales Jahr

In Deutschland, Österreich und der Schweiz gibt es ein **F**reiwilliges **S**oziales **J**ahr (**FSJ**). Wenn junge Leute das möchten, können sie nach der Schule ein Jahr lang anderen Menschen helfen. Rund 47 000 Jugendliche machen jedes Jahr ein FSJ in Deutschland.

Warum soll man ein Freiwilliges Soziales Jahr machen?
Man macht ein Freiwilliges Soziales Jahr, …

1 … denn man will praktische Dinge lernen.
2 … denn man möchte einen Arbeitsalltag erleben.
3 … denn man will unabhängig sein.
4 … denn man möchte anderen Menschen helfen.
5 … denn man möchte sich selbst besser kennenlernen.
6 … denn man will 500 Euro pro Monat verdienen.

Welche Arbeiten kann man machen?
Man kann …

A älteren Menschen helfen.

B mit Kindern arbeiten.

C Tieren helfen.

D der Umwelt helfen.

E Menschen ohne Zuhause helfen.

F im Krankenhaus arbeiten und kranken Menschen helfen.

Freiwilliges Soziales Jahr — voluntary year of social work or service

b) Warum möchtest du ein FSJ machen?

Silvia: Ich will **praktische Dinge lernen und neue Leute treffen**. Ich kann auch anderen Menschen helfen. Das finde ich wichtig! Es gibt so viele Menschen, die Hilfe brauchen!

Malik: Was möchte ich in meinem Leben machen? Soll ich ein Studium machen? Soll ich eine Ausbildung machen? Ich muss noch nicht wählen und das finde ich gut!

Katharina: Ich will in meinem Beruf vielleicht mit **Kindern arbeiten**, aber ich weiß es noch nicht. Vielleicht werde ich nach dem Freiwilligen Sozialen Jahr eine bessere Idee haben.

Robin: Ich liebe Tiere, aber ich darf keine Tiere zu Hause haben, weil meine Mutter Angst vor Tieren hat. Im FSJ kann ich aber mit Tieren arbeiten. **Vielleicht möchte ich auch in der Zukunft mit Tieren arbeiten**. Mal sehen!

> Remember to use the following when you want to say what you **would like to** do or **want to do**:
> *Ich möchte* + infinitive (= I would like to …)
> *Ich will* + infinitive (= I want to …, and **not** I will!)
> Look for examples of this in the numbered sentences in part (a) of the text.

180 *hundertachtzig*

Kulturzone — Kapitel 8

Lesen 1 Read the first part of the article (**a**). Find the German for the phrases below.
1. You would like to help other people.
2. You would like to experience everyday working life.
3. You would like to get to know yourself better.
4. You want to learn practical things.
5. You want to earn 500 euros a month.
6. You want to be independent.

> In Germany, compulsory military service (*Wehrpflicht*) was abolished in 2011. However, Austria and Switzerland still require most adult male citizens to do the equivalent of a few months of military service.
>
> Conscientious objectors (i.e. people who don't want to be trained for war) can choose civilian service (*Zivildienst*) instead of military service. Women in all three countries are allowed to join the armed forces (or the civilian service), but they are not obliged to do so. In Germany, Austria and Switzerland a *Freiwilliges Soziales Jahr* is also a possibility for school leavers.

Lesen 2 Read the texts in section (**b**) about why Silvia, Malik, Katharina and Robin want to do an FSJ and answer the questions with **S, M, K** or **R**.

Who …?
1. is not allowed to have animals at home
2. cannot decide between studying and training
3. finds it important that they can help other people
4. thinks the year will help them decide what they want to do later
5. says that there are so many people who need help
6. is happy that they don't have to choose what they want to do yet

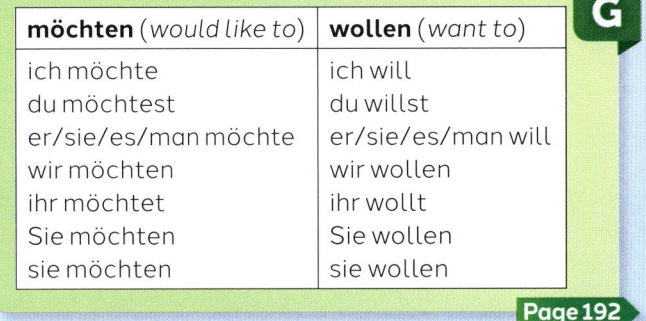

G

möchten (would like to)	wollen (want to)
ich möchte	ich will
du möchtest	du willst
er/sie/es/man möchte	er/sie/es/man will
wir möchten	wir wollen
ihr möchtet	ihr wollt
Sie möchten	Sie wollen
sie möchten	sie wollen

Page 192

Lesen 3 Translate the sentences in **bold** in Silvia, Malik, Katharina and Robin's texts into English.

Hören 4 Listen to people talking about what they would like to do for their FSJ and write the letter of the correct area of work from part (**a**) for each person. (1–6)

Hören 5 Listen and write down the sentence you hear. Be careful with the *j* sound.

> **j** is pronounced like the English 'y' in '**y**es'.
> Listen and repeat the words.
> **j**edes **J**ahr, **j**etzt, **J**uli, **J**ugendliche
> However, how is the letter *J* in *FSJ* pronounced?

Sprechen 6 In pairs, write down a sentence in secret, with one phrase from each column below. Take turns to guess the sentence. You can only say how many parts your partner got right, not <u>which</u> parts! Keep trying until all three parts are guessed correctly.

- *Ich möchte im Sommer eine interessante Arbeit machen.*
- *Zwei richtig.*
- *Ich möchte nach der Schule eine interessante Arbeit machen.*
- *Ja, richtig!*

Ich möchte	im Sommer	alten/kranken Menschen helfen.
Ich will	nächstes Jahr	Menschen ohne Zuhause helfen.
Mein Freund möchte	nach den Prüfungen	mit Kindern/Tieren arbeiten.
Meine Freundin will	in der Zukunft	der Umwelt helfen.
Wir möchten	nach der Schule	eine interessante Arbeit machen.
Wir wollen		praktische Dinge lernen.
		einen Arbeitsalltag erleben.
		unabhängig sein.

hunderteinundachtzig **181**

1 Was wirst du nach deinen Prüfungen machen?

- Discussing plans for after exams
- Using reflexive verbs
- Revising ways to refer to the future

Hören 1 Listen to and read the forum posts. Find the German for the phrases below.

Was wirst du nach deinen Prüfungen machen?

Chris: Nach meinen Prüfungen werden wir längere Ferien als normal haben. **Ich treffe mich gern mit meinen Freunden** und wir werden viel Spaß zusammen haben.

Alina: Nach meinen Prüfungen werde ich zuerst einmal nichts machen und **ich freue mich sehr auf die Freiheit!** Ich werde viel Kunst machen, denn ich bin sehr kreativ.

Elias: Nach meinen Prüfungen werde ich in den Urlaub fahren. Ich werde mit meinen Freunden nach Wales fahren. **Ich verstehe mich total gut mit meinen Freunden**, und wir werden wandern gehen. Das wird lustig sein.

Layla: Nach meinen Prüfungen werde ich zuerst Spaß haben. Danach werde ich wahrscheinlich eine Arbeit suchen. **Ich interessiere mich sehr für Kleidung** und muss Geld verdienen, weil ich neue Sachen möchte.

1 after my exams
2 we will have a lot of fun together
3 I will do lots of art
4 I will go on holiday
5 we will go hiking
6 After that I will probably look for a job

> In German, you form the future tense with the correct form of **werden** and the <u>infinitive</u>, which goes to the end of the sentence.
> Ich **werde** Spaß <u>haben</u>.   I **will** <u>have</u> fun.

Lesen 2 Translate the sentences in **bold** in the forum posts into English.

Hören 3 Listen to the plans for next year. Write down <u>two</u> details in English for each person. (1–6)

Ich werde	zuerst dann danach	viel schlafen. nichts tun. nach (Deutschland) fahren. reisen.
		weiterstudieren. nur (drei) Fächer haben. eine Ausbildung machen.
		an meiner Schule bleiben. auf eine neue Schule gehen. nicht mehr in die Schule gehen.
		eine Arbeit/Stelle suchen. einen Job suchen. in einer Firma arbeiten. in einem Geschäft/Büro arbeiten.

> **G**
> **Reflexive verbs** are used with a pronoun which usually goes straight after the verb.
> ich interessiere **mich**   wir interessieren **uns**
> du interessierst **dich**   ihr interessiert **euch**
> er/sie/es/man interessiert **sich**   Sie interessieren **sich**
>   sie interessieren **sich**
>
> After subordinating conjunctions like **dass** (that) and **weil** (because) the **reflexive pronoun** comes after the subject (e.g. ich, wir) and the <u>verb</u> goes to the end.
>
> Ich gehe gern einkaufen, **weil** ich **mich** für Kleidung <u>interessiere</u>.
> I like going shopping because I'm interested in clothes.
>
> Ich hoffe, **dass** wir **uns** <u>treffen</u>.
> I hope that we meet (each other).
>
> Page 192

182 hundertzweiundachtzig

Sprechen 4 — In pairs, replace the words in **bold** with one of the ideas in brackets (or your own idea). Your partner should then translate your sentence into English.

1 Ich interessiere mich sehr für **Musik**. (Kochen, Fußball, Geschichte)
2 Ich kümmere mich um **die Tiere**. (meine Großeltern, meine Schwester, die Umwelt)
3 Ich freue mich auf **nächstes Wochenende**. (meinen Geburtstag, den Sommer, die Schulferien)
4 Ich entscheide mich für **das Studium**. (eine Arbeit, ein FSJ, ein Jahr im Ausland)
5 Ich treffe mich mit **meiner Tante**. (meiner Freundin, meinem Freund, meinen Schwestern)
6 Ich verstehe mich gut mit **meinem Bruder**. (meiner Schwester, meinen Eltern, meinem Onkel)

Schreiben 5 — Write a short paragraph about what you are going to do after the exams. Use the key language box on page 182 to help you.

> You can use sequencers to extend your answers but remember that the first verb must always be in second place.
> **Zuerst** werde ich viel schlafen und **dann** werde ich … **Danach** werde ich …
> **First of all** I will sleep a lot and **then** I will … **After that** I will …

Hören 6 — Listen to and read the interview. Copy and complete the sentences in English.

Gespräch mit einem Berufscoach

Coach: Hallo, Finn, wie geht's? Was wirst du nach deinen Prüfungen machen?

Finn: Ich weiß es noch nicht genau. Ich möchte nicht auf die Universität gehen, aber ich interessiere mich für einen gut bezahlten Job. Ich habe aber Angst. Vielleicht werde ich ohne Ausbildung nicht sehr viel Geld verdienen.

Coach: Welche Arbeit interessiert dich denn?

Finn: Hm, ich bin mir nicht so sicher, aber ich denke, dass ich lieber mit Menschen als mit Computern arbeite. Ich kann nicht lange am Computer arbeiten, denn ich muss mich oft bewegen! Ich möchte gern neue Dinge lernen. Ich will auch neue Leute kennenlernen, und ich möchte bestimmt nicht immer dieselbe Arbeit machen.

1 Finn is interested in a … job.
2 He is worried that he won't earn well without …
3 He is interested in working with …
4 He cannot work … on computers.
5 He would like to learn …
6 He would not like to always do … work.

Sprechen 7 — In pairs, talk about your own plans for the future using longer sentences.

Was möchtest du nächstes Jahr machen?
Was wirst du nach der Schule machen?
Was willst du in der Zukunft machen?

Nächstes Jahr Nach der Schule Nach den Prüfungen In der Zukunft Zuerst Dann Danach	möchte ich werde ich will ich	an meiner Schule bleiben, auf eine neue Schule gehen, eine Ausbildung / einen Kurs machen, auf die Universität gehen, (eine) Arbeit / einen Job finden, reisen,	denn ich mag meine Lehrer. denn ich möchte neue Leute kennenlernen. denn ich möchte mehr lernen. denn ich möchte studieren. denn ich will Geld verdienen. denn ich will die Welt sehen.
Ich weiß noch nicht, Ich bin nicht sicher,	aber vielleicht werde ich …		

Schreiben 8 — Translate the sentences into German.

1 Next year, I would like to go to a new school.
2 In the future, I would like to find a job.
3 I don't know yet, but perhaps I will stay at my school.
4 After school, I want to do some training.
5 After my exams, I will travel a bit.

> There are several ways to talk about your plans for the future:
> - present tense with a future time phrase
> - Ich möchte …   I would like to …
> - Ich werde …   I will …
> - Ich will …   I want to …

hundertdreiundachtzig

2 Was ist dein Traumberuf?

- Discussing what jobs you would like to do in the future
- Using *werden* (to become)
- Forming past participles of *-ieren* verbs

Lesen 1 Read the survey results. Write the correct letter to match each picture (a–h) to the types of work.

Was für eine Arbeit möchtest du in der Zukunft machen?

1 Ich möchte als Lehrer*in arbeiten.
2 Ich möchte einen Computer benutzen.
3 Ich möchte mit Tieren arbeiten.
4 Ich möchte die Umwelt schützen.
5 Ich möchte in einem Büro arbeiten.
6 Ich möchte Menschen in einem Café helfen.
7 Ich möchte Künstler*in werden.
8 Ich möchte Fußballspieler*in werden.

Hören 2 Listen. Copy and complete the sentences in English.

1 Lukas would like to work with …
2 Hanna likes …
3 Lara is not interested in …
4 Elif would like to be …
5 Max finds … very important.

> **G** The verb **werden** can be used in different ways in German:
> - to form the future tense: *Ich werde morgen ins Kino gehen.*
> - to mean 'to become' (or 'get/turn into something'):
> *Ich möchte Arzt werden.*   I would like to **become** a doctor.
> *Das Essen wird kalt.*   The food **is getting** cold.
> *Die Kinder werden müde.*   The children **are getting/becoming** tired.
>
> Page 193

Sprechen 3 In pairs, ask and answer questions about what you would like to do in the future. Use the phrases from exercise 1.

- Möchtest du vielleicht (einmal) mit/als … arbeiten?
- Nein, ich denke nicht.
- Was ist dein Traumberuf?
- Mein Traumberuf ist Fußballspielerin.

Möchtest du vielleicht (einmal) mit/als … arbeiten?	Ja, sehr gern. 👍👍
Möchtest du in der Zukunft vielleicht (in einem Geschäft arbeiten)?	Ja, gern. 👍
	Das ist möglich. 🤔
	Nein, ich denke nicht. 👎
	Nein, ganz sicher nicht! / Nein, gar nicht! 👎👎
Was möchtest du in der Zukunft werden?	Ich möchte in der Zukunft vielleicht (Arzt) werden.
	Ich weiß es noch nicht.
Was ist dein Traumberuf / deine ideale Arbeit?	Mein Traumberuf / Meine ideale Arbeit ist (Sänger*in).

Remember that **ä, ö, ü** are pronounced differently from **a, o, u**.

Listen and repeat the words.
Arzt   **Ä**rztin
m**o**chte   m**ö**chte
Sch**u**tz   sch**ü**tzen

hundertvierundachtzig

Kapitel 8

Hören 4 Listen to and read the texts. Which statements are true?

Hast du schon einmal gearbeitet? Wie war es?

Layla
Ich habe letzten Sommer als Verkäuferin in einem Geschäft gearbeitet. **Ich habe mich für einen Job in einem Café interessiert**, aber es gab keine Cafés in meiner Stadt. Als Verkäuferin muss man immer pünktlich sein und das war schwierig für mich. Trotzdem war es eine gute Erfahrung.

Charlotte
Ich habe nicht so viele Jobs gemacht, aber letzten Sommer habe ich als DJ gearbeitet. **Ich habe sieben Partys organisiert** und es hat total viel Spaß gemacht!

Es war aber nicht immer einfach. **Manchmal haben die Lautsprecher nicht funktioniert, aber das ist nicht oft passiert**.

Matteo
Ich habe einige Jobs mit meinen Eltern diskutiert. Ich wollte etwas Geld verdienen, aber **sie haben das nicht akzeptiert**. Sie haben gesagt, ich soll mich besser um meine Schularbeit kümmern, weil gute Noten die Berufschancen verbessern. **Sie haben beide an der Universität studiert**, aber das will ich nicht.

1 Layla always wanted to work in a shop.
2 She found it difficult to be on time.
3 Charlotte has done lots of jobs.
4 She enjoyed organising parties.
5 Matteo's parents didn't want him to find a job.
6 He is concerned about his school work.

G -*ieren* verbs follow a different pattern in the perfect tense. To form the past participles:
- you don't add *ge-*
- but you do take off the *-en* and add *-t*, as for normal regular past participles.

infinitive	past participle	example
diskutier**en**	(habe) diskutier**t**	*Ich habe es mit meinen Eltern diskutiert.* I discussed it with my parents.
studier**en**	(habe) studier**t**	*Sie hat in Berlin studiert.* She studied in Berlin.
akzeptier**en**	(habe) akzeptier**t**	*Er hat meine Entschuldigung akzeptiert.* He accepted my apology.
passier**en**	(ist) passier**t**	*Was ist passiert?* What happened?

Page 193

Lesen 5 Translate the sentences in **bold** in exercise 4 into English.

Schreiben 6 Copy the paragraph and replace the underlined phrases with your own ideas.

Ich möchte in der Zukunft <u>Menschen helfen, die krank sind</u>. Ich denke, dass das <u>interessant</u> ist. Vielleicht werde ich auch <u>die Umwelt schützen</u>, aber ich möchte ganz sicher nicht <u>als Lehrerin arbeiten oder in einem Geschäft arbeiten</u>. Persönlich finde ich das sehr langweilig. Mein Traumberuf ist <u>Sängerin, weil ich Musik liebe</u>.

G Jobs and roles in German are expressed in male and female forms.

Add **-in** at the end of the male form to create the female version. Some nouns also add an umlaut in the female version.
Arzt → Ärzt**in**
Lehrer → Lehrer**in**
Verkäufer → Verkäufer**in**
Sänger → Sänger**in**
Student → Student**in**

Page 194

hundertfünfundachtzig **185**

3 Was kannst du gut?

- Discussing characteristics and skills
- Revising subordinating conjunctions
- Extending your written work

Hören 1 Listen to six young people. Write down the letters of the strengths and skills (a–j) each person mentions. Then write down which job you think best suits each person. (1–6)

Was kannst du gut? Was für Qualitäten hast du?

a	Ich bin freundlich und geduldig.
b	Ich kann gut organisieren und planen.
c	Ich kann immer ruhig bleiben.
d	Ich kann andere Menschen gut verstehen.
e	Ich arbeite gern und bin gut mit meinen Händen.
f	Ich bin sportlich und sehr aktiv.
g	Ich arbeite gut in einem Team.
h	Ich schreibe sehr gern und ich habe viele Ideen.
i	Ich bin gut mit Sprachen.
j	Ich habe gute Qualifikationen.

Lehrer*in
Polizist*in 
Verkäufer*in 
Arzt/Ärztin 
Journalist*in 
Betreuer*in 

Sprechen 2 In pairs, choose a photo each from exercise 1. Then take turns to ask and answer questions and try to guess which job your partner has chosen.

- *Was kannst du gut?*
- *Ich bin sportlich und aktiv. Ich arbeite auch gut in einem Team.*
- *Bist du Polizist/Polizistin?*
- *Ja, richtig! / Nein. Das ist falsch.*

qu is pronounced like 'kv' in English.
Listen and repeat the words.
*Qu*iz, be*qu*em, Konse*qu*enz, *Qu*elle, *Qu*alifikation

Schreiben 3 Write a few extended sentences about your own strengths and skills.

Ich bin der Meinung, dass ich sportlich und aktiv bin. Mein Lehrer sagt, dass ich gut in einem Team arbeite, aber ich schreibe nicht gern.

Try to extend your written work by using **conjunctions**, **expanding** your information and including **opposites**.
- **Conjunction:** *Ich bin freundlich.* → *Ich bin der Meinung, dass ich freundlich bin.*
- **Expand:** *Ich denke auch, dass … Meine Eltern/Lehrer sagen auch, dass …*
- **Opposite:** *Aber ich kann nicht gut planen und ich bin nicht sehr praktisch. Ich bin nicht immer sehr geduldig, aber ich möchte mich verbessern.*

Kapitel 8

Hören 4 Listen to and read the text. Answer the questions below in English.

Mein Berufsweg

Lea

Schon als ich klein war, wollte ich immer mit Tieren arbeiten. Ich wollte auch ein gutes Leben haben. **Weil mein Bruder Angst vor Tieren hatte**, konnte ich aber keine Tiere zu Hause haben. **Als ich 15 war**, habe ich aber einen Job als Katzensitterin gefunden und viel über Katzen gelernt. Nach der Schule habe ich Tiermedizin studiert. **Obwohl das Studium sehr lange dauert**, ist das eine sehr wichtige Qualifikation. Ich habe einen Hund und auch zwei Katzen, **da ich beide Tiere liebe**. **Wenn ich genug Geld habe**, werde ich auch ein Pferd kaufen.

die Tiermedizin — veterinary medicine

1 Why could Lea not have pets when she was young?
2 What does she say about the course in veterinary medicine?
3 Does she prefer cats or dogs?
4 When is she going to buy a horse?

Lesen 5 Translate the phrases in **bold** in the text in exercise 4 into English.

Lesen 6 Now read the text in exercise 4 again and find:
- three verbs in the perfect tense
- three verbs in the imperfect tense
- three verbs in the present tense
- one verb in the future tense (with *werden*).

G All **subordinating conjunctions** link sentences together and send the verb to the end of the clause.

als	when (in the past)	obwohl	although
dass	that	weil	because
da	because, since	wenn	if, when

Ich war klein. → *Ich wollte immer Ärztin werden, als ich klein war.*
I always wanted to become a doctor, **when** I was little.

When you start with the subordinating conjunction, the verbs of both parts meet in the middle, separated by a comma. This is called a 'verb-**comma**-verb-structure'.
***Als** ich klein war, wollte ich immer Ärztin werden.*
When I was little, I always wanted to become a doctor.

Page 194

G You have already seen verbs in the **imperfect tense**, for example:
*Ich **war** sechzehn Jahre alt.* — I **was** sixteen years old.
*Ich **hatte** einen Hund.* — I **had** a dog.
*Es **gab** drei Personen im Zug.* — **There were** three people on the train.

You can also use **modal verbs** with an infinitive in the imperfect tense:
*Ich **wollte** in einem Team arbeiten.* — I **wanted** to work in a team.
*Ich **musste** studieren.* — I **had** to study.
*Ich **konnte** keine Tiere zu Hause haben.* — I **couldn't / wasn't able** to have any animals at home.
*Ich **durfte** eine Ausbildung machen.* — I **was allowed** to do a training course.

Schreiben 7 Rewrite the sentences using the conjunction in brackets. Then, in pairs, take turns to read out the sentences you have written.

Example: 1 *Ich habe viele Katzen, **da** ich Tiere liebe.*
1 Ich habe viele Katzen. Ich liebe Tiere. (*since*)
2 Ich habe meine Prüfungen gemacht. Ich möchte einen guten Job. (*because*)
3 Ich werde an der Uni studieren. Ein Studium ist sehr teuer. (*although*)
4 Ich werde einen Job suchen. Ich brauche Geld für Kleidung. (*when, whenever*)
5 Es ist wichtig in vielen Jobs. Man arbeitet gut in einem Team. (*that*)
6 Ich hatte einen Samstagsjob. Ich war 14 Jahre alt. (*when*)

hundertsiebenundachtzig

4 Ein Zwischenjahr? Warum nicht?

- Discussing gap years
- Revising relative clauses
- Asking questions

Hören 1 Listen and write down the percentages you hear.

Was machen die deutschen Jugendlichen in ihrem Zwischenjahr?

1. Arbeiten und Reisen: ___ %
2. Freiwilligenarbeit: ___ %
3. Beruf im Ausland: ___ %
4. Urlaub: ___ %
5. als Au-pair arbeiten: ___ %
6. Sprachreise: ___ %

Gap years originated in the 1960s, but some say that they are a longstanding tradition that dates back to the 13th century, when craftspeople travelled around the world to perfect their skills (*Wanderjahre*). The modern gap year is a recent phenomenon in Germany and there is no direct translation. Some people say: *ein Jahr aussetzen*. Others call it *ein Sabbatjahr* or *ein Zwischenjahr*. An *FSJ (Freiwilliges Soziales Jahr)* is something that some young people undertake during their gap year. (See the culture box on page 181.)

Hören 2 Listen to and read the texts. Write down two reasons in English why each person chose a gap year.

Möchtest du ein Zwischenjahr machen?

Paul: Warum möchte ich ein Zwischenjahr machen? Weil ich eine Pause brauche. Ich habe so hart gearbeitet und ich bin müde nach den vielen Prüfungen! **Ich möchte in einem fremden Land wohnen, das total anders ist.** Vielleicht werde ich nach China fahren. Ich habe gehört, dass das Essen dort wunderbar ist!

Hanna: Ich möchte in meinem Zwischenjahr einige Jobs machen und Geld verdienen. Arbeite ich lieber draußen oder in einem Büro? Mit älteren Menschen oder mit Kindern? Ich weiß es noch nicht! **Viele Firmen wollen Leute, die schon viel Berufserfahrung haben**, und ich glaube auch, dass das wichtig ist.

Tim: **Ich möchte in meinem Zwischenjahr einen Job machen, der mir Spaß macht.** Geld ist mir im Moment nicht so wichtig. Ich will nur etwas lernen und etwas Positives machen. Wenn jeder junge Mensch für einige Monate anderen Menschen hilft, dann wird die Welt besser sein.

etwas Positives — something positive

Lesen 3 Translate the sentences in **bold** in exercise 2 into English. Be careful – each of the sentences contains a relative pronoun that translates as **who**, **which** or **that**.

Schreiben 4 Translate the sentences into German. Use the language in the texts from exercise 2 to help you.

1. I am tired and need a break.
2. I would like to earn money in my gap year.
3. I would like to do a few jobs.
4. I want to live in a world that is better.

G Remember that **relative pronouns** (who, which, that) refer back to someone or something. They send the verb to the end of the clause, and they always come after a comma in German.
*ein Job, **der** mir Spaß macht*
a job **which** is fun
Page 194

188 *hundertachtundachtzig*

Kapitel 8

Lesen 5 Match the questions and answers about Yannie's gap year.

1 Hast du ein Zwischenjahr gemacht, Yannie?
2 Wohin bist du gefahren?
3 Warum bist du nach Österreich gefahren?
4 Wie waren die Leute in Österreich?
5 Wie war es am Anfang?
6 War alles positiv am Ende?

a Sie waren alle sehr nett und haben mir immer geholfen.
b Ich wollte mein Deutsch verbessern, denn ich will Deutsch an der Uni studieren.
c Am Anfang war es schwierig, denn ich habe die Sprache nicht gut verstanden.
d Ja, ich habe mein Zwischenjahr im Ausland gemacht.
e Ich bin nach Österreich gefahren.
f Ja, es war toll, und mein Deutsch ist jetzt viel besser!

verstanden understood

Hören 6 Listen to the dialogue and see whether you have matched the sentences in exercise 5 correctly. Then read out the dialogue with a partner.

Hören 7 Listen to Mohammed, Kim and Arda talking about their gap year experiences. Copy and complete the table.

	where?	why?	activities	opinions
Mohammed				

Sprechen 8 Take turns to ask and answer questions about Emily's gap year using the questions and answers in exercise 5 and the notes below.

Zwischenjahr: Ja, im Ausland

Wo: Großbritannien

Warum: Englisch lernen

die Leute: freundlich und lustig

☺ : toll, Englisch ist besser

☹ : schwierig, keine Freunde

G Remember that there are two ways to form a question in German.
- Invert the **verb** and the subject of the sentence:
  Warst du im Ausland?
- Use a **question word**:
  Wo warst du?

Page 195

hundertneunundachtzig 189

5 Meine Träume für die Zukunft

- Discussing hopes for the future
- Dealing with unfamiliar vocabulary
- Consolidating key language and grammar points

Lesen 1 Read the texts and match the sentences below to the correct person: Lara (**L**), Martin (**M**) or Toni (**T**).

Worauf hoffst du?

Ich hoffe auf eine interessante Arbeit und ich will viel Geld verdienen. Ich möchte auch viel reisen und im Ausland arbeiten, vielleicht in der Türkei, weil die Kultur dort mich total interessiert. Eine gute Work-Life-Balance ist mir auch wichtig. Es gibt viele Sachen, die ich gern in meiner Freizeit mache. **Lara**

Ich hoffe, dass ich später eine gute Partnerin finde. Ich muss nicht heiraten – eine zivile Partnerschaft ist auch eine Möglichkeit. Einfach zusammenleben ist auch schön, aber ich will ganz sicher Kinder haben. Ich habe viele Geschwister, und ich will bestimmt eine große Familie haben. **Martin**

Ich hoffe auf ein Leben in der Zukunft mit wunderbaren Freunden. Für mich sind Freunde und ihre Unterstützung extrem wichtig und ich will meine Freizeit mit ihnen verbringen. Heiraten ist mir auch wichtig, aber vielleicht später. Ich bin im Moment ledig und ich möchte zuerst auch eine interessante Arbeit finden. **Toni**

1 I want to have children.
2 I would like to travel.
3 I would like to get married in the future.
4 I want to spend time with friends.
5 I want to earn well.
6 I am not certain about getting married.

> **Worauf hoffst du?** What are you hoping for?
>
> - Ich hoffe auf + noun = I'm hoping for…
>   Ich hoffe auf eine gute Arbeit.
> - Ich hoffe, dass … = I'm hoping that …
>   Ich hoffe, dass die Arbeit interessant ist.

Hören 2 Listen to Mila, Felix, Robin and Jana talking about what is and isn't important to them for their future plans. Copy and complete the table in English. (1–4)

	important	not so important
1		

There are often several ways of expressing the same ideas:

Für mich ist	ein Partner / eine Partnerin viel Geld verdienen eine interessante Arbeit ein netter Chef / eine nette Chefin eine gute Work-Life-Balance Heiraten	(nicht) wichtig. (sehr) wichtig.
Für mich sind	gute Freunde nette Kollegen/ Kolleginnen Kinder	
Für mich ist es (nicht) wichtig,	dass ich viel Geld verdiene. dass ich gute Freunde habe. dass ich Spaß habe. dass ich in einem Team arbeite.	

Sprechen 3 In pairs, take turns to ask and answer these questions.

- Was ist für dich wichtig im Beruf?
- Was ist für dich nicht so wichtig im Beruf?
- Was ist für dich wichtig im Leben?
- Was ist für dich nicht so wichtig im Leben?

Kapitel 8

Hören 4

Listen to and read the opinions below and write down **two** ideas from each text about what the world could be like in 20 years' time. Then translate the words in **bold** into English and decide whether they are cognates, compound nouns or words that can be worked out from the context.

Wie wird die Welt in 20 Jahren aussehen?

1 Das ist eine schwierige Frage, aber Technologie wird immer wichtiger werden, glaube ich. **Künstliche Intelligenz** wird eine größere Rolle im Unterricht und am Arbeitsplatz spielen.

2 Ich denke, es wird mehr **Naturkatastrophen** geben. Vielleicht werden wir in der Zukunft mehr Wälder und **Tierarten** verlieren.

3 Ich glaube, die Zukunft wird einfacher sein. **Roboter** werden uns mehr helfen. Sie werden vielleicht für uns in Geschäften einkaufen und große Gebäude sauber machen. Die Zukunft wird besser als heute sein!

> Reading texts sometimes contain words you may not have seen before, but there are a number of ways to work out their meaning:
> - Does the word look very similar to a word in English? There are a lot of **cognates** in German.
> - Is the word made up of two or more words? **Compound nouns** are very common, and breaking them down into words you know helps.
> - What is the sentence containing the word about? Use the **context** to work out the meaning.

Hören 5

Listen to two students and copy and complete the table in English. (1–2)

	strengths	what is important	what they wanted to be as a child	the future
1				

Schreiben 6

Write approximately 90 words in German about career options and the future. Include the following points:
- your qualities and what is important to you
- what you wanted to be when you were younger
- how you think the future will be.

Ich kann … Ich bin …
Für mich ist/sind … wichtig.
Als Kind wollte ich … werden.
In der Zukunft wird es vielleicht … geben.

hunderteinundneunzig **191**

Grammatik 1

Möchten and wollen (Culture spread, page 181)

1 Translate the sentences into English.

1. Ich **will** ein Freiwilliges Soziales Jahr machen.
2. Viele Jugendliche **wollen** das machen.
3. Meine Freundin **möchte** anderen Menschen helfen.
4. **Willst** du den Arbeitsalltag erleben?
5. Ich **will** noch nicht arbeiten, weil ich noch sehr jung bin.
6. Meine Freunde und ich **möchten** im Ausland leben.

2 Copy and complete the sentences with the correct form of the modal verb in brackets.

Example: 1 Er **will** kein FSJ machen.

1. Er ___ kein FSJ machen. (*wollen*)
2. Ich ___ an der Uni Medizin studieren. (*möchten*)
3. Wir ___ gut verdienen. (*wollen*)
4. ___ Sie praktische Dinge lernen? (*wollen*)
5. Mia ___ eine interessante Arbeit machen. (*möchten*)
6. Toni und ich ___ mit Tieren arbeiten. (*möchten*)

3 Translate the sentences from exercise 2 into English.

Reflexive verbs (Unit 1, page 182)

4 Put the words in order to make sentences.

Example: 1 *Ich interessiere mich sehr für Musik.*

1. interessiere für sehr Musik Ich mich.
2. auf mich Ich Wochenende nächstes freue.
3. nicht kümmert um Er die sich Schularbeit.
4. verstehen gut Wir Lehrer uns unserem mit.
5. Am trifft Wochenende mit sich Freunden sie.
6. Geschenk das Freut euch ihr über?

	reflexive pronouns
ich	mich
du	dich
er/sie/es/man	sich
wir	uns
ihr	euch
Sie	sich
sie	sich

sich freuen über: to be happy about
sich freuen auf: to look forward to

5 Listen and check your answers to exercise 4. (1–6)

6 Translate the corrected sentences from exercise 4 into English.

Schreiben 7 Complete the sentences using the correct form of the reflexive verb in brackets.
Example: 1 Ich freue mich auf die Sommerferien.
1 Ich ___ auf die Sommerferien. *(sich freuen)*
2 Ich ___ gut mit meinen Eltern. *(sich verstehen)*
3 Wir ___ mit unseren Freunden. *(sich treffen)*
4 Charlotte ___ für ein Jahr im Ausland. *(sich entscheiden)*
5 Mein Vater ___ für Sport. *(sich interessieren)*
6 Ich ___ über die Arbeit. *(sich freuen)*

> Check whether you know the correct preposition for each verb. They are sometimes different in English: I am interested **in** …
> ⟶ Ich interessiere mich **für** …

Using *werden* (Unit 2, page 184)

Lesen 8 Translate the sentences into English.
Example: 1 After the exams he will take a gap year.
1 Nach den Prüfungen wird er ein Zwischenjahr machen.
2 Sie möchte Ärztin werden.
3 Im Sommer werde ich eine Reise machen.
4 Dein Kaffee wird kalt.
5 Wir werden viel Spaß haben.
6 Ich denke, ich werde krank.

	werden
ich	werde
du	wirst
er/sie/es/man	wird
wir	werden
ihr	werdet
Sie	werden
sie	werden

The irregular verb *werden* is used in different ways in German:
To become:
Ich werde krank.
I **am becoming/getting** ill.
Future tense:
Ich werde auf die Uni gehen.
I **will** go to university.

Schreiben 9 Translate the sentences into German.
1 After school we will take a gap year.
2 My friend will work in London.
3 I will first travel and then work.
4 I get tired when I work a lot.
5 I would like to become a teacher.
6 My parents will be happy.

Sprechen 10 In pairs, take turns to ask and answer the questions.
• Was wirst du nächstes Jahr machen?
• Was möchtest du werden?
• Wann wirst du müde?

Past participles of *-ieren* verbs (Unit 2, page 185)

Hören 11 Listen and fill the gaps with the words you hear.
1 Meine Oma hat mich immer ___.
2 Er hat mit seinen Eltern ___.
3 Heute ist nicht viel ___.
4 Sie hat eine Reise nach Italien ___.
5 Ich habe ein Jahr in Berlin ___.
6 Das WLAN hat in den Ferien nicht ___.

Grammatik 2

Adding -in to male person nouns (Unit 2, page 185)

1 Copy and complete the sentences with the correct form of the noun.
1. Meine Schwester ist ___. (*doctor*)
2. Mein Freund möchte als ___ arbeiten. (*teacher*)
3. Meine Mutter war früher ___. (*singer*)
4. Mein Halbbruder ist ___ in einem Geschäft. (*sales assistant*)
5. Meine Freundin will ___ werden. (*police officer*)
6. Meine Stiefschwester arbeitet als ___. (*artist*)

Subordinating conjunctions (Unit 3, page 187)

2 Choose the correct subordinating conjunction from the box for each gap.
1. Ich denke, ___ ich gut mit Sprachen bin.
2. ___ sie einen Job hat, hat sie kein Geld.
3. Er hat einen Samstagsjob und spart Geld, ___ das Studium sehr viel Geld kostet.
4. Ich will im Ausland arbeiten, ___ ich Sprachen liebe.
5. ___ er jünger war, wollte er Arzt werden.
6. Wir werden im Ausland leben, ___ wir älter sind.

als   dass   da   obwohl   weil   wenn

3 Listen and check your answers to exercise 2.

> Remember that these subordinating conjunctions send the verb to the end of the clause.

4 Translate the sentences into German.
Example: 1 *Ich weiß, dass ich Tiere mag.*
1. I know that I like animals.
2. I want to go to Austria in winter because I like snow.
3. When I have more time, I will do more sport.
4. Although the lessons are boring, I like going to school.
5. I want to carry on studying since I love maths.
6. When I was six years old, I wanted to become a police officer.

Relative clauses (Unit 4, page 188)

5 Listen and write down the missing relative pronouns: *der, die, das.*
1. Ich möchte eine Arbeit, ___ interessant ist.
2. Ich will in einem Büro arbeiten, ___ sehr modern ist.
3. Ich möchte einen Chef, ___ mich gut versteht.
4. Ich will Kollegen haben, ___ nett sind.
5. Ich arbeite mit Tieren, ___ nicht immer sehr freundlich sind!
6. Ich will einen Job finden, ___ mir eine gute Work-Life-Balance gibt.

Kapitel 8

Asking questions (Unit 4, page 189)

Lesen 6 Match the German and English question words.

1 warum?
2 was?
3 was für?
4 wer?
5 wie?
6 wo?
7 woher?
8 wohin?

a where from?
b how?
c why?
d where to?
e what kind of?
f who?
g what?
h where?

Schreiben 7 Translate the questions into German.
1 Who is Mr Schmidt?
2 Where do you live?
3 What do you think?
4 Where are you going to?
5 Where do you come from?
6 Do you come from Germany?
7 Do you have a job?
8 How do you find your job?

> 💡 Remember that questions start either with a verb or a question word.
> *Hast du einen Bruder?*
> *Wo wohnst du in der Schweiz?*

Los geht's!

Sprechen 8 Read the sentences out and translate them into English. Then listen to the recording to see whether you have pronounced the words correctly. Afterwards, read the sentences out once more.

> Wir wollen die Natur schützen!
> Das Mädchen möchte später Ärztin werden.
> Er wollte Kunst studieren und Künstler werden.

Hören 9 Listen and write down the missing words (1–8).

> Ich möchte ein Zwischenjahr **1** und in einem Krankenhaus arbeiten. Ich möchte **2** später Arzt werden. Nach meinen **3** werde ich aber zuerst Urlaub machen, weil ich **4** bin. Ich habe das Hotel schon **5** und ich freue mich sehr darauf. Ich **6** mich sehr für andere **7**, die gutes Wetter haben. Ich mag Sonne und **8**. Was magst du?

hundertfünfundneunzig 195

Kapitel 8 Lese- und Hörtest

Reading

Lesen 1

After the exams. You read Alina's blog about what she will do after her exams.

> There are three different types of question in this task. Use the skills you have learned during the course to help you approach each part effectively.

Jetzt mache ich meine Prüfungen. Nach meinen Prüfungen werden wir längere Ferien als normal haben. Zuerst möchte ich viel schlafen und nichts machen. Danach werde ich Urlaub mit meiner Familie machen. Ich habe es verdient, denn ich habe viel gearbeitet.

Nach den Ferien werde ich an meiner Schule bleiben, denn ich möchte hier weiterlernen. Ich will nicht in eine neue Schule gehen, denn ich will meine Freunde nicht verlieren. Ich hoffe, dass ich einen Samstagsjob finde. Ich möchte Geld sparen, denn ich will in der Zukunft ein Jahr im Ausland verbringen.

1 Write **P** for something Alina has done **in the past**, **N** for something she does **now** or **F** for a plan for something **in the future**.
   (i) exams
   (ii) going on holiday
   (iii) working hard

> Use tenses and time expressions to help you decide which time frame applies to each aspect.

2 Write the correct letter, **A**, **B** or **C**, to complete each question.
   (i) After the holidays, Alina wants to …
      A stay at home.   **B** carry on studying.   **C** start her career.
   (ii) Alina does **not** want to …
      A make new friends.   **B** lose her friends.   **C** work at the weekend.

> The incorrect answer options will often be in the text too, so read carefully to discount them.

3 Answer the following questions in English.
   a What does Alina hope to find?
   b What does Alina want to do in the future?

> You don't need to write in full sentences when you answer open questions.

> ⭐ Don't worry if there is a word you don't recognise. Focus on what you do understand and then use the context and your wider knowledge of German grammar and vocabulary to help you work out the meaning of unfamiliar words.

Lesen 2

The future. You read these online forum posts. What is the opinion of each teenager about the future? Write **P** for a **positive opinion**, **N** for a **negative opinion** and **P + N** for a **positive and negative** opinion.

Nadia: Ich glaube, Computer werden unsere Arbeit machen. Ich habe Angst vor der Zukunft, denn ich will nicht arbeitslos sein.

Jonas: Ich denke, die Technologie wird eine größere Rolle im Unterricht spielen. Vielleicht werden wir nicht in die Schule gehen. Vielleicht werden wir zu Hause lernen, wo es wirklich ruhig ist. Ich kann zu Hause besser lernen.

Lara: Meiner Meinung nach werden wir mehr gegen Umweltprobleme machen und das freut mich. Es wird aber vielleicht zu spät sein und das macht mich traurig.

1 Nadia   2 Jonas   3 Lara

Lesen 3 Translate these sentences into English.

1 Ich bin sehr höflich.
2 Mein Bruder ist gar nicht geduldig.
3 Wir verstehen uns gut in unserer Schule.
4 Wenn ich älter bin, will ich an der Universität studieren.
5 In den Ferien hat meine Schwester in einem Geschäft gearbeitet.

Make sure you translate every word and don't overlook any 'little' words like this one.

Watch out for false friends like *will* when translating, but also use cognates and near-cognates to help you.

Focus carefully on verb tenses and make sure your English translation matches the German.

Listening

Hören 4 *Job skills.* You hear Julian, Hanna and Noah talking about their job skills. What do they say? Listen to the recording and write the correct letter, **A**, **B** or **C**, for each question.

1 Julian always …
  A keeps calm.
  B relies on other people.
  C changes his plans.

2 Julian has …
  A a well-paid job.
  B nice colleagues.
  C good ideas.

3 Hanna likes …
  A her college.
  B languages.
  C meeting new people.

4 Noah is …
  A a team player.
  B disorganised.
  C sporty.

Hören 5 *Work experience.* You hear Yasmin, Lukas and Paula talking about work experience. For each person, write down in English what work they chose and what the disadvantage was.

Listen carefully when answering open-ended questions like this. Try to anticipate areas of work you might hear mentioned. Listen out for negative adjectives and verbs connected to dislikes, to help you identify the disadvantage each person mentions.

Dictation

Hören 6 You will hear <u>four</u> short sentences. Write down exactly what you hear in German.

In the dictation task, there will always be some words that are not on the vocabulary list. You may not have come across them before, so listen carefully and think about the sounds you hear when you transcribe (write down) these words.

Think carefully about how these sounds are pronounced when you write down what you hear:
j
qu
a, ä, o, ö, u, ü

hundertsiebenundneunzig

Kapitel 8 Mündlicher Test

Role-play

Sprechen 1 Look at the role-play card and prepare what you want to say.

> You are talking to your German friend about your part-time job.
> 1 Say how old you are.
> 2 Say where you work. (Give **one** detail.)
> 3 Give **one** opinion about your job.
> 4 Say **one** quality or skill you have.
> 5 ? Ask your friend a question about work.

Work with the vocabulary you know: for example, 'in a shop', 'in a restaurant'.

You could use an adjective to explain a quality or use *Ich kann* + verb to explain what you can do.

You could use a question word here (*wo, was, wie*) or subject–verb inversion for a question like 'Do you have a job?'

Sprechen 2 Practise what you have prepared. Then, using your notes, listen and respond to the teacher.

Hören 3 Listen to Farah's response. Make a note of:
  a how she answers the questions for points 1–4
  b what question she asks for point 5.

Reading aloud

Sprechen 4 Look at this task. With a partner, read the sentences aloud, paying attention to the underlined letters.

> Ich bin geduldig.
>
> Ich arbeite gern mit meinen Händen und kann gut organisieren.
>
> Nach meinen Prüfungen im Juli will ich bequem zu Hause bleiben.
>
> Nächstes Jahr muss ich eine Ausbildung wählen.
>
> Meine Brüder möchten Ärzte werden.

Think carefully about how to pronounce these sounds and letters:
j
qu
a, ä, o, ö, u, ü

Hören 5 Listen and check your pronunciation.

Sprechen 6 Listen to the teacher asking four follow-up questions. Translate each question into English and prepare your own answers in German. Then listen again and respond to the teacher.

hundertachtundneunzig

Photo card

7 **Listen to Farah describing the photos and answer the questions.**
1. Where does Farah say the people in the first photo are?
2. What does she say about the man in the middle? (Give **three** details.)
3. What does she say about the weather? (Give **two** details.)
4. What job does Farah say the people in the second photo do?
5. Where does she say they work?
6. What does she say they are doing? (Give **two** details.)

> You will be asked to talk about the content of these photos. You must say at least one thing about each photo.
>
> After you have spoken about the content of the photos, you will be asked questions related to any of the topics within the theme of **People and lifestyle**.
>
> Your responses should be as **full and detailed** as possible.

8 **Prepare your own description of both photos. Then, with a partner, take turns to describe them.**

> Auf dem ersten Foto gibt es …

9 **Listen to the teacher's first follow-up question, *Was für Arbeit hast du schon gemacht?*, and Farah's response. Answer the questions in English.**
1. Why did Farah want to earn some money?
2. Name **one** of Farah's strengths.
3. Name **one** task Farah did in the park.
4. What did Farah enjoy doing?

10 **The teacher then asks Farah, *Was möchtest du nach deinen Prüfungen machen?* Listen to Farah's response and complete the sentences in English.**
1. Farah is going to do nothing, because …
2. Then Farah will have fun with …
3. Farah would like to find a job to pay for her …
4. Farah and her family will travel to …

11 **Listen to two more follow-up questions and prepare your answers. Then respond to the recording.**

> Remember to expand your answers to the follow-up questions, adding descriptions, opinions and reasons. Using words like *aber*, *denn*, *weil* and other connectives will help you to develop your answers.

12 **Prepare your own answers to as many of the Module 8 questions on page 227 as you can. Then practise with a partner.**

hundertneunundneunzig **199**

Kapitel 8 Schreibtest

Describing a photo

Schreiben 1 Look at this writing exam task and Liam's response. Correct the mistake in each sentence.

1 Es gibt keine Leute auf dem Foto.
2 Sie sind in einem Restaurant.
3 Im Hintergrund gibt es eine Tür.
4 Die Leute tanzen.
5 Niemand trägt ein T-Shirt.

> Keep your sentences short in the photo-description task and describe what you see. You must include a verb in each sentence, and they can all be in the present tense.

You see this photo on Instagram.

What is in the photo?

Write **five** sentences in **German**.

Schreiben 2 Prepare your own answer to the task.

Grammar task

Schreiben 3 Using your knowledge of grammar, select the correct option to complete each sentence.

> Is *wir* a singular or plural pronoun? The verb needs to agree with it.

> Is *hat* a singular or plural part of the verb *haben*? The pronoun needs to match it.

1 **Ich / Er / Wir** hat Angst vor der Zukunft.
2 **Wir** interessiere / interessieren / interessiert uns für Weltprobleme.
3 Meine Gesundheit ist **wichtig / wichtigen / wichtiger** als das Geld.
4 **Seinen / Seine / Sein** ältere Schwester studiert an der Uni.
5 In den Sommerferien habe ich im Geschäft viel Geld **verdient / verdienen / verdiene**.

> Use the gender of the noun and the adjective ending to help you here.

> Two things are being compared here. How do you form comparisons in German?

> Which tense is used in this sentence?

90-word writing task

Schreiben 4 Look at this writing exam task and then, for each bullet point:
1 think about the vocabulary and structures you have learned which you could use in your answer. For example:
   - **nouns** and **adjectives** to write about the topic of work
   - **verbs of opinion** and **adjectives** to give your opinions
   - language for **narrating a story** about what you did after your exams
   - how to explain **what you want to do in the future**
   - connectives and intensifiers you would like to use.
2 write down three or four ideas for what you could write about.
3 identify which tense(s) you could use in your answer.

You are writing to your Austrian friend about work and plans.

Write approximately **90** words in **German**.

You must write something about each bullet point.

Describe:
- your opinions of work
- what you did after your exams last year
- your career plans for the future.

200 *zweihundert*

Kapitel 8

Lesen 5 — Read Liam's answer to the exam task. Answer the questions in the coloured boxes (1–5).

1 Liam uses a variety of **modal verbs**. What do these verbs mean? Find <u>two</u> more examples.

2 This is an example of **complex language**. What does it mean? Find <u>three</u> more examples of complex language in the text.

3 What **grammatical structure** is this? Find <u>two</u> other examples.

Man muss eine Stelle haben. Man braucht Geld. Die Arbeit soll nicht langweilig sein. Ich helfe gern anderen Menschen und ich bin sehr geduldig. Ich schreibe auch sehr gern und habe oft gute Ideen. Ich will in einem Team arbeiten, obwohl ich gut allein arbeite.

Nach meinen Prüfungen, als ich Zeit hatte, habe ich mich oft mit meinen Freunden getroffen. Ich bin auch mit meiner Familie ins Ausland gefahren.

In der Zukunft werde ich oft einen Computer benutzen. Ich liebe Mathe. Vielleicht sollte ich Mathelehrer werden, aber das weiß ich noch nicht.

4 Which connective could you use here to form an **extended sentence**? What other connectives does Liam use?

5 How could Liam **avoid repetition** here?

Lesen 6 — Read Liam's answer again and complete the sentences.

1 Liam feels a job should not be …
2 Liam likes helping …
3 After his exams, Liam went … with his family.
4 In the future, Liam will work with …

Schreiben 7 — Prepare your own answer to the task.

- Think about how you can develop your answer for each bullet point.
- Look back at your notes from exercises 4 and 5.
- Use the 'Challenge checklist' to help you show off your German!
- Write a **brief** plan and organise your answer into paragraphs.
- Write your answer and then carefully check for accuracy.

Challenge checklist

🥨
- ✓ Connectives (*und, aber*)
- ✓ Some extended sentences (*Ich bin unabhängig und immer freundlich.*)
- ✓ An opinion (*Ich finde die Arbeit schwierig.*)

🥨🥨
- ✓ Different persons of the verb (*die Arbeit ist, meine Kollegen waren, ich wollte, es gab, man kann*)
- ✓ Past, present and future time frames
- ✓ Compound nouns (*der Traumberuf, der Arbeitsplatz*)
- ✓ More interesting vocabulary (*der Beruf, die Karriere, der Chef, meine Träume*)
- ✓ Imperfect tense (*ich hatte, sie waren, es gab*)
- ✓ Different ways of expressing opinions (*ich meine, ich denke, ich glaube, meiner Meinung nach*)

🥨🥨🥨
- ✓ man + modal + infinitive (*Man muss/soll hart arbeiten.*)
- ✓ möchte + infinitive (*Ich möchte Geld verdienen.*)
- ✓ Reflexive verbs + pronouns (*ich interessiere mich für, ich freue mich auf, ich treffe mich mit*)
- ✓ Dative (*in einem Team, mit Freunden, macht mir Spaß*)
- ✓ Subordinating conjunctions + verb at the end (*weil, dass, da, als, wenn, obwohl*)
- ✓ Modals in the past (*ich wollte, ich musste, ich mochte*)
- ✓ Relative pronouns (*eine Arbeit, die interessant ist*)

zweihunderteins 201

Kapitel 8 Wörter

> **Key:**
> **bold** = this word will appear in higher exams only
> * = this word is not on the vocabulary list but you may use it in your own sentences

Ich will helfen (pages 180–181):

Ich will helfen	I want to help
Ich möchte …	I would like to …
Ich will …	I want to …
Mein Freund möchte …	My friend would like to …
Meine Freundin will …	My friend wants to …
Wir möchten …	We would like to …
Wir wollen …	We want to …
im Sommer	in (the) summer
nächstes Jahr	next year
später	later (on)
nach den Prüfungen	after the exams
in (der) Zukunft	in (the) future
nach der Schule	after school
mit Kindern arbeiten.	work with children.
eine interessante Arbeit machen.	do an interesting job.
alten/kranken Menschen helfen.	help old/ill people.
Menschen ohne *Zuhause helfen.	help people without a home.
Tieren / der Umwelt helfen.	help animals / the environment.
praktische Dinge lernen.	learn practical things.
einen *Arbeitsalltag erleben.	experience a working day.
unabhängig sein.	be independent.
mich selbst besser kennenlernen.	get to know myself better.
Geld verdienen.	earn money.
der *Zivildienst	civilian service
die Ausbildung	training, education
die *Wehrpflicht	compulsory military service
das Krankenhaus	hospital
das Leben	life

Was wirst du nach deinen Prüfungen machen? (pages 182–183):

Pläne für die Zukunft	Plans for the future
Was möchtest du nächstes Jahr machen?	What would you like to do next year?
Was wirst du nach der Schule machen?	What will you do after school?
Was willst du in der Zukunft machen?	What do you want to do in the future?
Ich werde …	I will …
Ich will …	I want to …
Ich möchte …	I would like to …
eine Ausbildung machen.	do an apprenticeship / some training / a course.
(eine) Arbeit / einen Job finden.	find employment / a job.
nach (Deutschland) fahren.	travel to (Germany).
reisen.	travel.
weiter studieren.	carry on studying.
nur (drei) Fächer haben.	only have (three) subjects.
an meiner Schule bleiben.	stay at my school.
auf eine neue Schule gehen.	go to a new school.
auf die Universität gehen.	go to university.
nicht mehr in die Schule gehen.	no longer attend school.
eine Arbeit/Stelle suchen.	look for a job/position.
einen Job suchen.	look for a job.
in einer Firma arbeiten.	work at a company.
in einem Geschäft/Büro arbeiten.	work in a shop/business/office.
denn ich mag meine Lehrer.	because I like my teachers.
denn ich möchte neue Leute kennenlernen.	because I would like to meet new people.
denn ich möchte mehr lernen.	because I would like to learn more.
denn ich möchte studieren.	because I would like to study.
denn ich will Geld verdienen.	because I want to earn money.
denn ich will die Welt sehen.	because I want to see the world.
Nächstes Jahr …	Next year …
Nach der Schule …	After school …
Nach den Prüfungen …	After the exams …
In der Zukunft …	In the future …
Zuerst …	First of all …
Dann …	Then …
Danach …	After that …

Was ist dein Traumberuf? (pages 184–185):

Über Jobs reden	Talking about jobs
Was für eine Arbeit möchtest du in der Zukunft machen?	What kind of work would you like to do in future?
Ich möchte …	I would like to…
als Lehrer*in arbeiten.	work as a teacher.
einen Computer benutzen.	use a computer.
mit Tieren arbeiten.	work with animals.
die Umwelt schützen.	protect the environment.
in einem Büro arbeiten.	work in an office.
Menschen in einem Geschäft helfen.	help people in a shop.
Fußballspieler*in werden.	become a football player.
Künstler*in werden.	become an artist.
Möchtest du vielleicht (einmal) mit/als … arbeiten?	Would you perhaps (one day) like to work with/as …
Möchtest du in der Zukunft vielleicht (in einem Geschäft arbeiten)?	In the future would you perhaps like to (work in a shop)?
Ja, sehr gern.	Yes, very much.
Das ist möglich.	It is possible.
Nein, ich denke nicht.	No, I don't think so.
Nein, ganz sicher nicht!	No, definitely not!
Nein, gar nicht!	No, not at all!
Was möchtest du in der Zukunft werden?	What would you like to become in the future?
Ich möchte in der Zukunft vielleicht (Arzt/Ärztin) werden.	In the future, I would perhaps like to become (a doctor).
Was ist dein Traumberuf / deine ideale Arbeit?	What is your dream job / your ideal work?

Mein Traumberuf / Meine ideale Arbeit ist (Sänger).	My dream job / My ideal work is as a (singer).
akzeptieren	to accept
diskutieren	to discuss
sich kümmern um	to take care of
passieren	to happen
studieren	to study
verdienen	to earn

Was kannst du gut? (pages 186–187):

Was kannst du gut?	What can you do well?
Ich bin der Meinung, dass ich (geduldig) bin.	I am of the opinion that I am (patient).
Ich denke auch, dass …	I also think that …
Meine Eltern/Lehrer sagen auch, dass …	My parents/teachers also say that …
Aber …	But/However, …
Ich kann gut …	I am good at …
organisieren.	organising.
planen.	planning.
Ich bin freundlich und geduldig.	I am friendly and patient.
Ich kann immer ruhig bleiben.	I can always stay calm.
Ich kann andere Menschen gut verstehen.	I can understand other people well.
Ich arbeite gern und bin gut mit meinen Händen.	I like working and am good with my hands.
Ich bin sportlich und sehr aktiv.	I am sporty and very active.
Ich arbeite gut in einem Team.	I work well in a team.
Ich schreibe sehr gern und ich habe viele Ideen.	I like writing very much and have lots of ideas.
Ich bin gut mit Sprachen.	I'm good at languages.
als	when
dass	that
obwohl	although
weil	because
wenn	when/if
Ich war …	I was …
Ich hatte …	I had …
Es gab …	There was/were …
Ich wollte …	I wanted…
Ich musste …	I had to…
Ich konnte …	I could …
Ich durfte …	I was allowed to …

Ein *Zwischenjahr? Warum nicht? (pages 188–189):

Ein *Zwischenjahr	A gap year
Möchtest du ein *Zwischenjahr machen?	Would you like to take a gap year?
Ich weiß noch nicht.	I do not know yet.
Ich möchte …	I would like to …
in meinem *Zwischenjahr Geld verdienen.	earn money in my gap year.
einige Jobs erleben.	experience a few jobs.
in einer Welt wohnen, die besser ist.	live in a world which is better.
in einem fremden Land leben.	live in a foreign country.
in die Türkei fahren.	travel to Turkey.
anderen Menschen helfen.	help other people.
mein (Deutsch) verbessern.	improve my (German).
einen Job machen, der mir Spaß macht.	do a job which is fun (for me).
arbeiten.	work
lernen.	learn.
reisen.	travel.
anders	other
etwas **Positives**	something positive
freiwillig	voluntarily / without pay / as a volunteer

Meine Träume für die Zukunft (pages 190–191):

Hoffnungen für die Zukunft	Hopes for the future
Was ist für dich wichtig (im Beruf)?	What is important to you (at work)?
Was ist für dich nicht so wichtig (im Beruf)?	What is not so important to you (at work)?
Ich hoffe auf …	I hope for …
Ich hoffe, dass …	I hope that …
Für mich ist … (nicht/sehr) wichtig. /	For me, … is (not/very) important. /
ein Partner / eine Partnerin	a partner
viel Geld	a lot of money
eine interessante Arbeit	an interesting job
ein netter Chef / eine nette Chefin	a nice boss
eine gute *Work-Life-Balance	a good work-life balance
Heiraten	marriage
Für mich ist es (nicht) wichtig, …	To me, it is (not) important …
dass ich viel Geld verdiene.	that I earn a lot of money.
dass ich gute Freunde habe.	that I have good friends.
dass ich Spaß habe.	that I have fun.
dass ich in einem Team arbeite.	that I work in a team.
Als Kind wollte ich … werden.	As a child, I wanted to be …
In der Zukunft wird es vielleicht … geben.	In the future, there may be …
die *Naturkatastrophe	natural disaster
die zivile Partnerschaft	civil partnership
bestimmt	definitely, certainly
künstlich	artificial
ledig	single, unmarried
vielleicht	perhaps

Kapitel 1–8 Grammatik: Wiederholung

Compound nouns

Schreiben 1 Combine words from both boxes to form ten compound nouns. Write the words out with the correct article (*der, die, das*) and English meaning. Start each word with a noun from box A. Can you make more than ten words?

A		B	
der Lehrer	das Fastfood	das Restaurant	der Kuchen
die Stadt	der Fußball	das Geschäft	die Schmerzen
der Rücken	das Haus	die Flasche	der Plan
die Speise	der Sport	das Zimmer	die Spielerin
das Wasser	der Geburtstag	die Aufgaben	die Karte

Which of these compound nouns needs to have a combining letter?

> Remember compound nouns take their gender (*der, die, das*) from the final element. They sometimes also need a 'combining letter' such as *n* or *s*.

Adjective endings

Lesen 2 Select the adjectives with the correct ending in each sentence. Use the table on page 205 for reference.

1 Das **blaue** / **blaues** Buch (*nt*) ist in meiner **roten** / **rotem** Schultasche (*f*) auf dem **großer** / **großen** Tisch (*m*).
2 Sein **kleine** / **kleiner** Bruder (*m*) trägt eine **schwarzen** / **schwarze** Jacke (*f*) und **schöne** / **schönen** Schuhe (*pl*).
3 Das **nettes** / **nette** Mädchen (*nt*) hat ein **neuen** / **neues** Handy (*nt*) in ihrer **alter** / **alten** Schultasche (*f*).
4 Für mich ist **heiße** / **heißer** Kaffee (*m*) immer besser als **kaltes** / **kalter** Wasser (*nt*).
5 Unsere **neuer** / **neue** Wohnung (*f*) liegt in einem **ruhiges** / **ruhigen** Dorf (*nt*) neben einem **breiten** / **breitem** Fluss (*m*).
6 Ich habe ein **billige** / **billiges** Hotel (*nt*) für unseren **nächsten** / **nächster** Urlaub (*m*) gefunden. Leider sind **gute** / **guten** Hotels (*pl*) sehr teuer.
7 Wir recyceln immer **alte** / **alten** Flaschen (*pl*), weil **recyceltes** / **recycelte** Glas (*nt*) sehr nützlich ist.
8 Die **junge** / **jungen** Schüler*innen (*pl*) brauchen **gute** / **guten** Noten (*pl*) für die **beste** / **besten** Karrieren (*pl*).

Schreiben 3 Copy and complete the sentences with the correct form of the adjectives in brackets.

1 Ich trage heute die ▇ Hose. (*grün*)
2 Sofie hat einen ▇ Freund. (*neu*)
3 Er hat ▇ Augen und ▇ Haare. (*braun, kurz*)
4 Alle wollen eine ▇ Umwelt. (*sauber*)
5 Heute gibt es ein ▇ Fest in der ▇ Stadt. (*interessant, klein*)
6 Das ▇ Restaurant hat ▇ Essen. (*neu, lecker*)
7 Wir haben keine ▇ Pläne für die ▇ Sommerferien. (*gut, lang*)
8 Der ▇ Mann will in Zukunft in einem ▇ Büro arbeiten. (*jung, modern*)

Grammatik: Wiederholung — Kapitel 1–8

Using interrogative and demonstrative adjectives

Schreiben 4 Write down the words *welch*… (for the questions) and *dies*… (for the answers) with the correct endings in the accusative case.

1 Welcher Beruf (*m*) ist der beste? — Dies___ Beruf ist toll!
2 Welch___ Geschäfte (*pl*) sind in der Stadtmitte? — Diese Geschäfte sind in der Stadtmitte.
3 Welchen Computer (*m*) kaufst du? — Ich kaufe dies___ Computer.
4 Welch___ Farbe (*f*) hast du lieber? — Ich mag diese Farbe.
5 Welches Buch (*nt*) liest du? — Ich lese dies___ Buch.
6 Welch___ Fächer (*pl*) wirst du nächstes Jahr lernen? — Ich werde diese Fächer lernen.

Reflexive verbs

Lesen 5 Match up the sentence halves.

1 Im Winter freue ich
2 Die Schüler bewegen
3 Kinder, wo werdet ihr
4 Mit seinen Eltern versteht
5 Meine Schwester und ich interessieren
6 Vor dem Frühstück musst du

a Jan sich schlecht.
b dich anziehen.
c uns für die Natur.
d mich auf den Urlaub.
e euch treffen?
f sich in der Sportstunde.

Lesen 6 Translate the sentences from exercise 5 into English.

Adjectives used with the **definite article** follow this pattern:

	nominative	accusative	dative
masc	der gut**e** Freund	den gut**en** Freund	dem gut**en** Freund
fem	die gut**e** Freundin	die gut**e** Freundin	der gut**en** Freundin
neut	das gut**e** Kind	das gut**e** Kind	dem gut**en** Kind
pl	die gut**en** Kinder	die gut**en** Kinder	den gut**en** Kinder**n**

Adjectives used with the **indefinite article**, *kein* and **possessive adjectives** follow this pattern:

	nominative	accusative	dative
masc	ein gut**er** Freund	einen gut**en** Freund	einem gut**en** Freund
fem	eine gut**e** Freundin	eine gut**e** Freundin	einer gut**en** Freundin
neut	ein gut**es** Kind	ein gut**es** Kind	einem gut**en** Kind
pl	keine gut**en** Kinder	keine gut**en** Kinder	keinen gut**en** Kinder**n**

Adjectives used with **no article** follow this pattern:

	nominative	accusative	dative
masc	heiß**er** Kaffee	heiß**en** Kaffee	heiß**em** Kaffee
fem	kalt**e** Milch	kalt**e** Milch	kalt**er** Milch
neut	gut**es** Wasser	gut**es** Wasser	gut**em** Wasser
pl	kein**e** Kinder	kein**e** Kinder	kein**en** Kinder**n**

zweihundertfünf

Kapitel 1–8 Grammatik: Wiederholung

Word order in main clauses

Schreiben 1 Beginning with the word in **bold**, write out the sentences using correct word order.
1 **Wir**   mit dem Zug   <u>im Sommer</u>   fahren   in die Schweiz
2 **Mein Bruder**   eine Reise   durch Deutschland   mit seiner Freundin   <u>jetzt</u>   macht
3 **Samira**   mit Kindern   <u>in Zukunft</u>   will   arbeiten   in einem Krankenhaus
4 **Ich**   <u>in den Ferien</u>   schwimme   im See   mit meiner Familie
5 **Die Schüler*innen**   in der Kantine   <u>in der Mittagspause</u>   essen   mit ihrem Lehrer

Schreiben 2 Rewrite the sentences in exercise 1 beginning with the <u>underlined</u> time phrase.

> In main clauses the conjugated verb must be the **second** idea. Remember the '**time – manner – place**' rule. Any elements which show time, manner or place must come in this order in the sentence.

Word order in subordinate clauses

Schreiben 3 Link the two sentences by using the conjunction in brackets. The second sentence will become the subordinate clause.
1 Wir lernen Deutsch. Die Sprache ist nützlich. (*weil*)
2 Ich möchte dieses neue Handy. Es ist ziemlich teuer. (*obwohl*)
3 Meine Familie und ich essen Frühstück zusammen. Wir haben Zeit. (*wenn*)
4 Viele Jugendliche glauben jetzt. Rauchen ist gefährlich. (*dass*)
5 Lukas durfte nicht fernsehen. Er war jünger. (*als*)
6 Der Lehrer hat mich gefragt. Ich arbeite gern in einem Team. (*ob*)

> The verb goes to the end in a subordinate clause. If there are two verbs, it is the conjugated verb which goes to the end. If the sentence begins with the subordinate clause, the first word in the main clause will be the verb. Think about the '**verb-comma-verb**' rule.

Schreiben 4 Rewrite the sentences in exercise 3, beginning with the subordinate clause.

Relative pronouns

Lesen 5 Select the correct relative pronoun to complete the sentence.
1 Ich habe einen Freund, **der / die / das** Paul heißt.
2 Ich besuche meine Oma, **der / die / das** in Österreich wohnt.
3 Ich mag das Haus, **der / die / das** groß und weiß ist.
4 Der Lehrer, **der / die / das** sich für Geschichte interessiert, ist nett.
5 Englisch und Sport sind die Fächer, **der / die / das** interessant sind.

> The relative pronoun must be the same gender as the noun to which it refers. As relative clauses are also subordinate clauses, the conjugated verb goes to the end of the clause. The relative clause can come in the middle of the main clause, in which case the main clause verb comes immediately afterwards.

206 zweihundertsechs

Grammatik: Wiederholung — Kapitel 1–8

Relative clauses

6 Translate the sentences into German.
1. I have a sister who is called Mia.
2. I have a brother who is called Noah.
3. Dr Thomas is a doctor who works in the hospital.
4. My parents, who are called Anna and Max, are funny.
5. The book which I am reading is good.

Verbs with prepositions

7 Copy and complete the sentences with a preposition from the box.
1. Die faulen Schüler hoffen ___ gute Noten.
2. Im Unterricht diskutieren wir ___ Menschenrechte.
3. Felix interessiert sich ___ Geschichte.
4. Ich habe keine Angst ___ Hunden.
5. Die Kinder freuen sich ___ ihren nächsten Urlaub.
6. Die Lehrerin spricht mit der Klasse ___ die Prüfung.

> auf   auf   für   über   über   vor

Personal pronouns

8 Copy and complete the table with the correct pronouns in the accusative and dative.

Nominative	Accusative	Dative
ich	mich	1
du	2	dir
er	3	ihm
sie	sie	4
es	es	5
wir	6	uns
ihr	euch	7
Sie	8	Ihnen
sie	sie	9

9 Read this sentence about presents and translate it into English.

Mein Freund hat ein Geschenk für mich gekauft und dann hat er es mir gegeben.

Then use the structure of the example sentence and the pronouns from the table above to translate the following sentences into German.
1. He bought a present for you (sg) and then he gave it to you.
2. She bought a present for him and then she gave it to him.
3. We bought a present for her and then we gave it to her.
4. I bought a present for them and then I gave it to them.
5. You (sg) bought a present for us and then you gave it to us.
6. They bought a present for you (familiar, pl) and then they gave it to you.

Kapitel 1–8 Grammatik: Wiederholung

Question words

Lesen 1 Select the correct word or phrase from the word cloud to complete the questions. There are more words than you need.

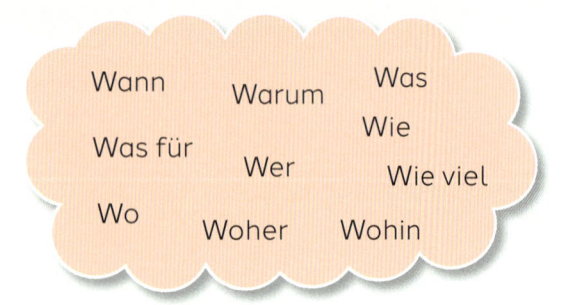

> Wann, Warum, Was, Was für, Wie, Wer, Wie viel, Wo, Woher, Wohin

Take care not to confuse wer (who) and wo (where).

1 ___ wohnst du?
2 ___ kommst du? Aus England?
3 ___ ist dein Lieblingssänger?
4 ___ Geld hast du?
5 ___ kommt der Bus an?
6 ___ einen Beruf möchtest du?

Word order in questions

Schreiben 2 Rewrite the statements as questions by changing the word order.

Example: 1 *Hast du Mathe in der nächsten Stunde?*

1 Du hast Mathe in der nächsten Stunde.
2 Wir gehen am Nachmittag ins Kino.
3 Milan kauft eine Flasche Wasser.
4 Es gibt ein Problem mit dem Hotel.
5 Sie möchten etwas trinken.
6 Die Kinder wollen schwimmen gehen.

To form questions without a question word, invert the subject and verb:
Er ist … → Ist er …?

Sentences with a question word follow normal word order, so the verb must be the second idea.

Identifying tenses

Lesen 3 Look at the tense used in each sentence and select the correct time phrase.

1 **Morgen / Gestern / Später** bin ich mit dem Fahrrad gefahren.
2 **Gestern / Morgen / Heute** ist es warm.
3 **Normalerweise / Gestern / Letzte Woche** trinken wir Tee zum Frühstück.
4 **Vor zwei Jahren / In Zukunft / Heute** möchte ich Tierärztin werden.
5 **Dieses Jahr / Nächstes Jahr / Letztes Jahr** durften wir einen Laptop in der Prüfung benutzen.
6 **Jetzt / Letzten Samstag / Früher** will ich nach Hause gehen.
7 **Heute / Morgen / Gestern** wird mein Vater seinen Geburtstag feiern.
8 **Nächste Woche / Vor einem Jahr / Jetzt** habe ich meinen Opa besucht.

Lesen 4 Translate the sentences in exercise 3 into English.

Grammatik: Wiederholung — Kapitel 1–8

The perfect tense

Schreiben 5 Copy and complete the table, writing the past participles of the verbs from the word cloud in the correct column.

besuchen, fahren, gehen, hören, kaufen, kommen, nehmen, studieren, reisen, sehen, spielen, verstehen

> The past participle usually begins with *ge-* unless there is an inseparable prefix such as *be-* or *ver-* or if the infinitive ends in *-ieren*.
> - The ending is usually *-t* for regular verbs and *-en* for irregular verbs.
> - Some irregular verbs also have a change to the stem.
> - Remember that verbs indicating movement or a change of state take *sein*, otherwise the auxiliary verb is *haben*.

Ich habe …	Ich bin …
besucht	gefahren

Past, present and future tenses

Schreiben 6 Copy and complete the sentences in three tenses using the verb in brackets.

1 Heute ___ ich Wurst zu Mittag. Gestern ___ ich Pommes ___. Morgen ___ ich Pizza ___. (*essen*)

2 Jetzt ___ ich ins Museum. Letzten Sonntag ___ ich in die Kirche ___. Nächsten Samstag ___ ich ins Theater ___. (*gehen*)

3 Diese Woche ___ wir Volleyball. Letzte Woche ___ wir Tennis ___. Nächste Woche ___ wir Basketball ___. (*spielen*)

4 Dieses Jahr ___ ich nach Deutschland. Letztes Jahr ___ ich nach Österreich ___. Nächstes Jahr ___ ich in die Schweiz ___. (*fahren*)

5 Mein Freund ___ jetzt in Köln. Früher ___ er in München ___. In Zukunft ___ er in London ___. (*studieren*)

6 Am Samstag ___ wir die Seifenoper im Fernsehen. Letztes Wochenende ___ wir einen Krimi ___. Nächstes Wochenende ___ wir eine Komödie ___. (*sehen*)

Words that are easily confused

Lesen 7 Translate the sentences into English, paying particular attention to the words in **bold**.

1 Mein Bruder **wird** immer müde, wenn er Fußball spielt.
2 Mein Bruder **wird** nächste Woche Fußball spielen.
3 Ich **werde** in Zukunft heiraten.
4 Ich **will** in Zukunft heiraten.
5 **Man** soll Wasser sparen.
6 Der **Mann** trinkt viel Wasser.
7 Du **darfst nicht** ins Kino gehen, weil es spät ist.
8 Du **musst nicht** ins Kino gehen, wenn du nicht willst.
9 Kennst du meine Schwester? **Sie** ist 10 Jahre alt.
10 Kennst du meine Geschwister? **Sie** sind 10 Jahre alt.

> - Remember *werden* can mean 'to become' as well as being used to form the future tense. *Ich werde* should not be confused with *ich will* (I want).
> - The pronoun *man* should not be confused with the noun *der Mann*.
> - The modal verb *müssen* can be translated as 'must' or 'have to'. You should use the second option to translate it when it is negative.
> - Although the pronoun *sie* means both 'she' and 'they', look carefully at whether the verb ending is singular or plural.

zweihundertneun

Kapitel 1 Wiederholung

1 *Refresh your memory!* Match the word halves to create six adjectives.

1 interes
2 kompli
3 prak
4 ein
5 lang
6 schwier

a weilig
b ig
c sant
d ziert
e tisch
f fach

2 *Refresh your memory!* Unjumble the second part of each sentence.

1 Ich lerne Englisch, weil das ist sehr interessant .
2 Ich mag Kunst, weil ist es einfach .
3 Sie findet Handball toll, weil sportlich sie ist .
4 Wir glauben nicht, dass ist diese Regel richtig .
5 Er mag Sport nicht, weil er langweilig findet das .
6 Meine Freunde denken, dass schwierig ist Geschichte .

> Remember that both *weil* and *dass* change the word order in the second part of the sentence.

3 *Refresh your memory!* Listen and write down the missing modal verbs. Then translate the sentences into English.

1 Ich ___ für den Test lernen.
2 Ich ___ meine Hausaufgaben machen.
3 Wir ___ das Handy nicht benutzen.
4 Man ___ im Unterricht nicht reden.
5 Wir ___ im Klassenzimmer ruhig sein.
6 Wir ___ gut lernen.

4 *School life.* Jana is talking about school. What does she say? Listen to the recording and write **A**, **B** or **C** for each question.

1 Jana likes …
   A history.   B sciences.   C art.
2 Jana chats to her friends …
   A at breaktime.   B at lunchtime.   C after school.
3 Jana wears a blue …
   A blazer.   B skirt.   C shirt.
4 Jana has lots of …
   A friends.   B homework.   C subjects.

> Don't worry if you hear an unfamiliar word. You may be able to work out its meaning from the context or the questions. You may not even need to know the word to answer the questions.

210 zweihundertzehn

Kapitel 1

Lesen 5

School life. Translate these sentences into **English**.
1. Ich gehe jeden Tag in die Schule.
2. Es gibt viele Schüler in meiner Klasse.
3. Wir essen und trinken in der Pause.
4. Ich mag Kunst, aber ich finde Mathe kompliziert.
5. Letzte Woche bin ich mit der Schule ins Kino gegangen.

Lesen 6

School life. You read some online posts about life at school. Write the letter of the correct statement that matches each topic. (1–3)

A	Ich mag viele Schulfächer, aber ich habe kein Lieblingsfach.
B	Letztes Jahr bin ich mit meiner Klasse nach England gefahren.
C	Ich finde die Schuluniform praktisch, aber unbequem.
D	Jeden Abend muss ich zu Hause arbeiten. Das finde ich so langweilig!
E	Es gibt zwei Pausen und sechs Stunden.

1. The school day
2. A school trip
3. Homework

Schreiben 7

Complete the photo-description task.

You see this photo on Instagram.

What is in the photo?

Write **five** sentences in **German**.

- Keep your sentences simple to avoid making mistakes. Remember to include a verb in each sentence.
- Only write about what you can see in the picture. Don't invent things and don't say what you can't see.

Sprechen 8

Read the text aloud and prepare responses to the follow-up questions. Then listen to check your pronunciation and respond to the teacher.

Ich lerne Mathe und Theater.

Meine Uniform ist praktisch.

Ich trage eine rote Hose und weiße Sportschuhe.

Ich mache Sport mit meinem Freund.

Wir müssen Englisch und Wissenschaften lernen, weil sie wichtig sind.

Be careful with cognates as they are not pronounced exactly the same way in German. Think carefully about how to pronounce the cognates and these sounds:
o, ö, u, ü, w

Follow-up questions:
- Was lernst du in der Schule?
- Beschreib deine Schule.
- Wie findest du Deutsch?
- Was machst du in der Pause?

zweihundertelf **211**

Kapitel 2 Wiederholung

Lesen 1 *Refresh your memory!* Match up the English and German question words.

what   when   why   how
who   which   where

wo   wann   wer   was
wie   warum   welch…

Lesen 2 *Refresh your memory!* Find six intensifiers in the word snake and translate them into English.

wirklichsehrsozuziemlichbesonders

Schreiben 3 *Refresh your memory!* Copy and complete the future tense sentences with the correct form of *werden* from the box.

1 Wir ___ in die Stadt gehen.
2 Ihr ___ morgen Basketball spielen.
3 Ich ___ heute Abend fernsehen.
4 Das ___ toll sein!
5 Du ___ allein einen Film sehen.
6 Meine Freunde ___ ins Kino gehen.

wird   werden
wirst   werde
werden   werdet

> In sentence 6, the subject of the verb is a noun (*Meine Freunde*) rather than a pronoun. Think about which pronoun would replace it, to help you decide which part of *werden* to use.

Hören 4 *Free time.* Four German teenagers are talking about their free time. What do they like doing? Listen to the recording and write the correct letter (A–F) for each person.

1 Kai   2 Robin   3 Sara   4 Aïsha

A	visiting friends
B	calling friends
C	shopping
D	hiking
E	listening to music
F	downloading music

> Always read the instructions carefully to make sure you know exactly what to do. Here, you need to choose the four options that are mentioned in the recording. The incorrect options will not be mentioned.

Hören 5 You will hear <u>four</u> short sentences. Write down exactly what you hear in German.

> Think carefully about how these sounds are pronounced, when writing down what you hear:
> a, ä, o, ö
> ei, ie, i, eu
> sp, st, sch

> There will be some words in the dictation task that are not on the vocabulary list, but don't panic: use your knowledge of sound–spelling links to help you transcribe these words accurately.

212 zweihundertzwölf

Kapitel 2

Lesen 6
Life as a famous actor. You read this interview with Zita, an actor.

Interviewer: Was für Filme machst du am liebsten?

Zita: Ich finde Horrorfilme super! Ich habe auch einige Fernsehsendungen gemacht, aber Gameshows und Seifenopern finde ich blöd.

Interviewer: Willst du immer Schauspielerin sein?

Zita: Im Moment liebe ich mein Leben! Aber Musik ist für mich auch wichtig und ich möchte Lieder schreiben und singen. Das wird besonders spannend sein.

Interviewer: Wie wichtig ist Kleidung für dich?

Zita: Ich gehe gern einkaufen und kaufe sehr gern neue Kleidung. **Schmuck** mag ich aber nicht, weil ich ihn schön, aber zu teuer finde.

How does Zita feel about these aspects of her life? Write **P** for a **positive** opinion, **N** for a **negative** opinion or **P+N** for a **positive and negative** opinion.

In question 4, you must work out the meaning of a word that you might not have met before (**Schmuck**). Read Zita's last response carefully for clues to help you.

1 Game shows
2 Writing songs
3 Going shopping
4 Read the last sentence again. What would you do with **Schmuck**? Write the correct letter.
   A watch it   **B** eat it   **C** wear it

Sprechen 7
Complete the role-play task.

You are talking to your Austrian friend.
1 Say how often you use your mobile phone.
2 Give **one** opinion about your mobile phone.
3 Say what you do online. (Give **one** detail.)
4 Describe your favourite influencer. (Give **one** detail.)
5 ? Ask your friend a question about social media.

Remember to include a verb in each of your responses.

You can add *Lieblings-* to the start of any noun.

You could ask your friend's opinion, or ask about how often they use social media.

Schreiben 8
Translate these sentences into German.

Use a verb + *lieber*.

1 I prefer reading books.
2 My friend sometimes writes emails.
3 The cinema is good but very expensive.
4 I go swimming with my brother at the weekend.
5 Last weekend I played on the computer.

Remember: Time – Manner – Place.

Remember to invert the subject and the verb if you use the time expressions at the start of the sentence.

Which tense do you need to use here?

zweihundertdreizehn

Kapitel 3 Wiederholung

1 *Refresh your memory!* Copy and complete the table. Write the words in the correct column.

positive adjectives	negative adjectives	intensifiers and qualifiers
kreativ	böse	ziemlich

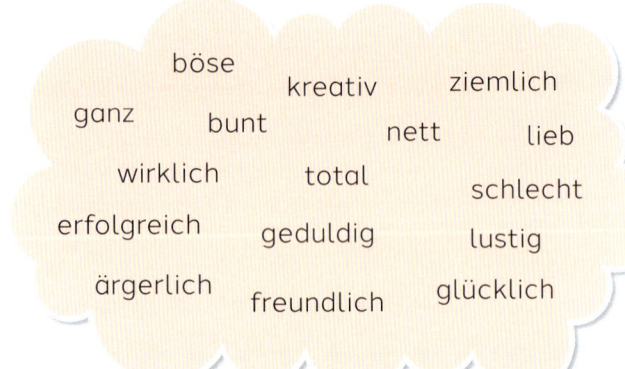

böse   kreativ   ziemlich
ganz   bunt   nett   lieb
wirklich   total   schlecht
erfolgreich   geduldig   lustig
ärgerlich   freundlich   glücklich

2 *Refresh your memory!* Decide if these opinions are positive (**P**) or negative (**N**).
1 Dieses Fest interessiert mich nicht.
2 Das finde ich wirklich ärgerlich.
3 Ich trage gern lustige Kleidung.
4 Die Musik gefällt mir.
5 Das macht keinen Spaß.
6 Ich glaube, dass der Weihnachtsmarkt immer schön ist.

3 *Refresh your memory!* Listen to Max talking about his family. Write down the words you hear to fill in the gaps.

Es gibt drei Personen in meiner Familie. Ich **1** mich sehr gut mit meinem **2** . Er unterstützt mich und hat immer **3** für mich. Ich verstehe mich nicht so gut mit meiner Schwester, **4** Katja heißt. Sie kann **5** sein, aber sie ist **6** ungeduldig.

4 *Birthdays.* You hear Zara talking about three celebrations. Write **P** if she is talking about a celebration **in the past**, **N** if it is something happening **now** or **F** if it is something she is planning to do **in the future**.
1 sister's party
2 dad's birthday
3 Zara's birthday

> Listen carefully for different tenses. There could also be clues in time phrases, such as *letzte Woche*.

5 Translate these sentences into English.

1 Meine Tante ist ziemlich sportlich.
2 Er hat einen Stiefbruder, der Karl heißt.
3 Wir besuchen jede Woche unsere Großeltern.
4 Ich verstehe mich nicht gut mit meiner Mutter.
5 Letzte Woche haben wir Silvester gefeiert.

> How will you translate this relative pronoun?

> Reflexive pronouns are not always needed in English.

> Time phrases give a clue to the tense.

Kapitel 3

Lesen 6

My uncle. Read Mesut's post on an internet forum. Write the correct letter, **A**, **B** or **C**, to complete each sentence.

> Mein Onkel hat vor fünf Jahren meine Tante geheiratet und jetzt haben sie drei Kinder, die zwei, vier und fünf Jahre alt sind. Meine Tante ist in ihrer Arbeit sehr erfolgreich und manchmal muss sie ins Ausland fahren.
>
> Mein Onkel arbeitet nicht. Er bleibt zu Hause und kocht oft **Sauerbraten** für die Kinder. Das finden sie echt lecker. Ich kann ihn besuchen und dann bin ich glücklich, denn mein Vater hat keine Zeit für mich. Aber mein Onkel unterstützt mich immer und das finde ich sehr lieb von ihm. Ich besuche auch gern meine Cousins. Wir spielen zusammen und sehen fern.

1 Mesut's uncle …
  A lives abroad.   B is successful.   C is married.

2 Mesut's uncle and aunt have …
  A three children.   B two children.   C four children.

3 Mesut likes his uncle because he …
  A always has time for him.   B supports him.   C works hard.

4 Read the last paragraph again. What would you do with **Sauerbraten**? Write the correct letter, **A**, **B** or **C**.
  A play with it   B watch it   C eat it

Schreiben 7

Complete the 50-word writing task.

> Try to add variety to your written work:
> - Give opinions in different ways: *ich liebe/mag, gefällt mir, ich (+ verb) gern/lieber, Meiner Meinung nach, Ich glaube, dass …*
> - Use adjectives and qualifiers to describe people.
> - Vary the conjunctions you use and check your word order: *denn, weil, dass, aber.*

Your German friend asks you about your relationships.

Write a description of your friends and family.

Write approximately **50** words in **German**.

You must write something about each bullet point.

Mention:
- your personality
- your relationship with a family member
- a description of your best friend
- how often you see your friends
- activities you do with friends.

Sprechen 8

Read the text aloud and prepare responses to the follow-up questions.

> Mein Br__u__der ist __w__irklich positi__v__ und geduldig.
> Er hat k__u__r__z__e, sch__w__ar__z__e Haare und grüne Augen.
> Meine Familie __u__nd ich gehen oft __z__usammen __w__andern.
> __W__ir __v__erstehen __u__ns __z__iemlich g__u__t.
> Ich mag Partys, __w__eil sie Spaß machen.

Think carefully about how to pronounce these sounds:
v, w, z
u, ü

Follow-up questions:
- Beschreib dich!
- Wie verstehst du dich mit deiner Familie?
- Wie ist ein guter Freund oder eine gute Freundin?
- Wie findest du Feste?

Kapitel 4 Wiederholung

Lesen 1

Refresh your memory! Copy and complete the sentences.

1 Du darfst ▢ rauchen.
2 Sie trinkt ▢ Kaffee.
3 Er isst ▢ pro Tag Käse mit Brot.
4 Ich verbringe ▢ Zeit auf meinem Handy.
5 Ich möchte ▢ spazieren gehen.
6 ▢ einer Woche habe ich Fußball gespielt.

- never
- mostly
- three times
- less
- more often
- ago

Hören 2

Refresh your memory! Listen to six people talking about health problems. Copy and complete the table. (1–6)

	health issue	advice
1		

Listen carefully for negatives – the answer may be something they should **not** do.

Lesen 3

Refresh your memory! Match up the sentence halves.

1 Wenn das Wetter schön ist,
2 Wir haben Tennis
3 Ich werde am Wochenende
4 Ich finde Basketball gut, aber
5 Meine Familie und ich fahren
6 Mein Lieblingsessen ist Pommes, weil

a Fußball ist besser.
b sie lecker sind.
c im Park gespielt.
d ab und zu Fahrrad.
e gehe ich schwimmen.
f spazieren gehen.

Use your knowledge of German grammar and word order to help you. Think about how past and future tenses are structured and what happens to the verb in sentences containing *weil* or *wenn*.

Hören 4

Priorities in life. Noah, Arda and Lena are talking in a podcast. What do they say? Listen to the recording and write **A**, **B** or **C** to complete each sentence.

1 Noah only wants to be …
  A happy.   B healthy.   C wealthy.
2 Arda thinks that his … is more important.
  A career   B family   C happiness
3 What Lena finds boring is …
  A her family.   B work.   C school.
4 What is important to Lena is …
  A her health.   B her family.   C her health and her family.

Hören 5

Dictation. You will hear <u>four</u> short sentences. Write down exactly what you hear in German.

Think carefully about how these sounds are pronounced when writing down what you hear:
a, ä   s, schw
au, äu   -ig
o, ö
u, ü

Lesen 6

Life changes. Read Lara's blog post about her life and answer the questions **in English**.

> 31. Dezember
>
> Im Moment bin ich mit meinem Leben ganz glücklich, aber ich möchte einige Sachen verbessern. Zuerst möchte ich ein bisschen mehr Energie haben. Ich will früher ins Bett gehen – um 22 Uhr. Leider habe ich das gestern nicht gemacht und deswegen bin ich heute Morgen immer noch sehr müde.
>
> Ich möchte auch mehr Zeit mit meiner Familie verbringen. Meine Karriere und meine Freizeitaktivitäten sind mir wichtig, aber meine Familie ist mir noch wichtiger.
>
> Meine Freunde sind mir auch sehr lieb. Wir können nicht immer zusammen ausgehen, aber ich werde sie öfter anrufen.
>
> Lara

Remember that you do not need to understand every word of a text to be able to answer the questions. You might not have come across lieb (kind, dear) before, but you don't need to know it to respond to the question about friends. Focus on the language you do know!

1 Complete the sentences below. Write the correct letter, A, B or C, for each question.
  (i) Lara is quite … with her life at the moment.
   A happy   **B** unhappy   **C** disappointed
  (ii) Lara would like to …
   A improve a few things.   **B** keep everything the same.   **C** change lots of things.
  (iii) Yesterday, Lara went to bed …
   A early.   **B** later than planned.   **C** at 10 p.m.

2 Answer the following questions **in English**. You do not need to write in full sentences.
  (i) What is Lara's second aim?
  (ii) What will Lara do with regard to her friends?

Sprechen 7

Complete the photo-card task.

You will be asked to talk about the content of these photos. You must say at least one thing about each photo.

After you have spoken about the content of the photos, you will be asked questions related to any of the topics within the theme of **People and lifestyle**.

Your responses should be as **full and detailed** as possible.

You only need to give a brief description of the photos. Try to give longer, more detailed responses to the conversation questions that follow and remember to include opinions and reasons.

Schreiben 8

Translate these sentences into German.

Use a verb + *gern*.

1 I like playing football.
2 My family is sporty and we eat healthily.
3 My friends are very important to me.
4 I find cycling more interesting than hiking.
5 Yesterday we went swimming.

'Healthy' and 'healthily' are the same word in German.

Remember, there are two ways of saying this in German.

Think carefully about how to translate this verb of movement in the perfect tense.

This is a comparative adjective and will be one word in German.

zweihundertsiebzehn

Kapitel 5 Wiederholung

Lesen 1

Refresh your memory! Copy and complete the table with the missing adjectives and comparatives.

adjective	comparative
klein	
	größer
jung	
	später
alt	
hoch	

> Remember that some adjectives add an umlaut in the comparative. *Hoch* is irregular. Can you remember how to spell its comparative form?

Schreiben 2

Refresh your memory! Rewrite the sentences, changing the nouns in brackets to the plural form.

1 In meinem Dorf gibt es keine (Geschäft).
2 Finn hat zwei (Haus).
3 Meine Tante hat zwei (Kind).
4 In den (Straße) gibt es viele (Auto).
5 Ich habe neue (Schuh) gekauft.
6 Mein Haus hat fünf (Zimmer).

Lesen 3

Refresh your memory! Match the word halves to form compound nouns. Then translate the new words into English.

Groß — tür
Einkaufs — zimmer
Schlaf — geschäft
Kranken — stadt
Haus — straße
Kleidungs — haus

> Do you remember how to find the gender of a compound noun? Make sure you learn the gender and plural form of nouns, irregular verb forms and how to pronounce the new words you come across.

Hören 4

My house. Listen to Elias describing his house. Which rooms does he **like** and **not like**, and why? Answer **both** parts of each question in **English**.

1 a Elias' favourite room to spend time in is the …
  b Reason: …
2 a Elias **doesn't** like the …
  b Reason: …

> Listen out for words that can change the meaning of a sentence such as *nicht*, *kein* and *aber*. Verbs of like and dislike can alter the meaning too.
>
> Don't write down the first thing you hear. Listen to each extract to the end first, discount any irrelevant information and listen for key words.

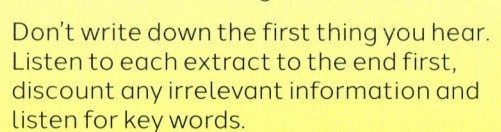

218 *zweihundertachtzehn*

Kapitel 5

Lesen 5 — *My home town.* Read Charlotte's blog post about where she lives and answer the questions in **English**.

> Als ich jung war, haben meine Familie und ich in Österreich und in der Schweiz gelebt. Jetzt wohne ich im Osten von Deutschland in einer Kleinstadt, die in der Nähe von der Hauptstadt Berlin liegt. Viele Menschen besuchen die Stadt, weil es alte Häuser und ein großes Schloss gibt. Hier findet man auch viele Geschäfte und Cafés, aber kein Kino. Es gibt einen kleinen Park in der Nähe vom Bahnhof. Ich möchte gern ein **Freibad** haben, weil ich sehr gern draußen schwimme, wenn das Wetter schön ist.

1. Where did Charlotte live when she was young? (Give **two** details.)
2. Where does Charlotte now live? (Give **two** details.)
3. Why do people visit her town? (Give **two** details.)
4. What does Charlotte's town **not** have?
5. Read the last sentence again. What would you do in a **Freibad**?
   - **A** have a coffee
   - **B** sunbathe
   - **C** swim

> Use the language in the rest of the sentence to help you work out the meaning of the unknown word in question 5.

Schreiben 6 — Complete the 50-word writing task.

> Some young German visitors are coming to your town.
> Write a short description of where you live.
> Write approximately **50** words in **German**.
> You must write something about each bullet point.
> Mention:
> - the town
> - the shops
> - what there is to do
> - transport
> - your home.

> For the 50-word writing task, you can write everything in the present tense. Think about including descriptions and opinions. Remember to build complete sentences, each containing a correct verb. Try to use varied language, such as adjectives, intensifiers and connectives.

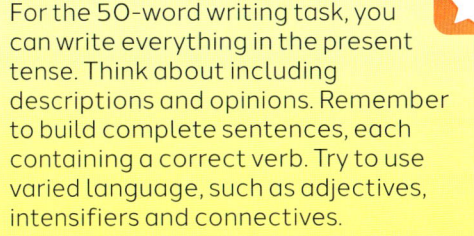

Lesen 7 — Translate these sentences into English.

1. Meine Gegend ist ziemlich ruhig.
2. In der Stadt gibt es viele alte Häuser.
3. Wir fahren mit dem Fahrrad ins Stadtzentrum.
4. Ich lebe lieber an der Küste, da sie schön ist.
5. Als ich jünger war, habe ich im Ausland gelebt.

Sprechen 8 — Read the text aloud and prepare responses to the follow-up questions.

> Ich wohne in einer großen Wohnung mit einem Spielzimmer.
> Diese Gegend ist wirklich sauber und sicher.
> Es gibt Geschäfte und ein Sportzentrum, aber keinen Fluss.
> Das alte Schloss ist sehr schön und liegt in der Stadt.

Think carefully about how to pronounce these sounds:
s, ss, ß
sp, st, sch
w

Follow-up questions:
- Sag mir etwas über dein Haus oder deine Wohnung.
- Was machst du mit deiner Familie zu Hause?
- Wie findest du die Geschäfte in deiner Gegend?
- Was gibt es für junge Leute in deiner Gegend?

zweihundertneunzehn

Kapitel 6 Wiederholung

Lesen 1 *Refresh your memory!* Read the notes about the weather forecast. Copy and complete the table in English.

An der Küste: kalt, Wind
Im Osten: es regnet
Am See: Sonne
In der Schweiz: Sonne, warm
Im Süden: sehr heiß
In Österreich: Schnee

place	forecast
	sunny
In the south	
	rainy
	sunny and warm
In Austria	
	cold and windy

Hören 2 *Refresh your memory!* Listen and write the correct letter to match each item (1–6) to its problem (a–f).

1 bag
2 laptop
3 room
4 money
5 bed
6 Wi-Fi

a uncomfortable
b forgotten
c lost
d doesn't work
e broken
f dirty

Lesen 3 *Refresh your memory!* Match up the German and English negatives.

ohne   kein   niemand   nichts   nie   nicht

no one   not   never   no   without   nothing

Lesen 4 *My Swiss holiday.* Mesut is writing about his holiday in his blog. What does he say? Write **P** for something he did **in the past**, **N** for something he is doing **now** and **F** for something he wants to do **in the future**.

Ich bin in der Schweiz und sitze in meinem Hotelzimmer! Normalerweise fahren wir im Herbst in die Schweiz, aber dieses Jahr sind wir im Frühling hier. Nächstes Jahr möchte ich lieber im Sommer nach Österreich fahren!

Wir sind mit der Bahn zum Ferienhaus gefahren, weil es billiger war. Die Ferien machen Spaß, aber es hat fast jeden Tag geregnet. Nur gestern war es **trocken**, obwohl es keine Sonne gab.

1 Staying at a hotel
2 Going to Austria
3 Travelling by train
4 Rainy weather
5 Read the last two sentences again. What would you do on a day that is **trocken**?
   A use an umbrella   B go out for a walk   C wear a raincoat

Kapitel 6

Hören 5

My summer holiday. Listen to Aïsha talking about her last summer holiday. What does she think about these aspects? Write **P** for a **positive** opinion, **N** for a **negative** opinion or **P+N** for a **positive and negative** opinion.

1 Visiting the mountains
2 Holidays in cities
3 Travelling by car
4 Shopping

Sprechen 6

Complete the role-play task.

> This could be a compass point ('in the north') or vocabulary like 'near' or 'not far from'.

> This could be any kind of sporting activity, such as swimming, football or walking. Work with the vocabulary you know best. You can use the German for 'one/you can …'.

You are talking to your German friend about your local area.

1 Say **where** your town is situated. (Give **one** detail.)
2 Give your opinion of your local area.
3 Say what **sport you can do** in your local area. (Give **one** detail.)
4 Say **one** thing about the **shops** in your town.
5 **?** Ask your friend a **question** about restaurants.

> You could say what type of shops there are or describe what the shops are like.

> Use a question word (*Wo …?, Wann …?*, etc.) or subject–verb inversion (*Gibt es …?* or *Kann man …?*).

Schreiben 7

Translate these sentences into German.

1 I like the holidays.
2 We go walking on the beach.
3 I like swimming in the sea with my brother.
4 I visit the beautiful mountains in the summer.
5 Last year we went to Austria by train.

> In English we use 'I like' a lot, but in German *ich mag* is not used as often. German speakers prefer to use a conjugated verb + *gern*: for example, *Ich lese gern* ('I like reading'). However, when there is no suitable action verb, use *ich mag* + a noun: for example, *Ich mag Musik* ('I like music').

Hören 8

Dictation. You will hear <u>four</u> short sentences. Write down exactly what you hear in German.

> Think carefully about how these sounds are pronounced when you write down what you hear:
> long *a*, short *a* and *ä*
> long *e* and short *e*
> long *o*, short *o* and *ö*
> -*b*, -*d*, -*g*
> *w* and *v*
> *s*, *ss* and *ß*

zweihunderteinundzwanzig

Kapitel 7 Wiederholung

Lesen 1 — *Refresh your memory!* Match up the words to form compound nouns. There may be more than one correct answer.

- Groß
- Umwelt
- Menschen
- Welt
- Tier
- Trink

- schutz
- wasser
- stadt
- rechte
- hunger
- problem

Hören 2 — *Refresh your memory!* Listen and write down the words you hear to fill the gaps. Then translate the sentences into English.

1 Das ist ▢ wichtig.
2 Das ist nötig für ▢.
3 Das ist ein großes Problem für ▢.
4 Das war sehr interessant für ▢.
5 Das war langweilig für ▢.
6 Das ist ▢ viel wichtiger.

> In this task, you are filling in missing pronouns like 'me', 'him', 'you', 'her', 'us' and 'them'. You will need a mixture of accusative and dative pronouns.

Schreiben 3 — *Refresh your memory!* Copy and complete the German translations with the correct form of *haben* and the correct noun.

1 Ich ▢ immer ▢. — I am always hungry.
2 Er ▢ nie ▢. — He is never right.
3 Wir ▢ manchmal ▢. — We are sometimes thirsty.
4 Ich ▢ heute keine ▢. — I don't feel like it today.
5 Meine Schwester ▢ oft ▢. — My sister is often scared.

> Think carefully about the form of *haben* you need to use. Which person of the verb is *Meine Schwester*?

Hören 4 — *A podcast.* You hear a German podcast that discusses the findings of a survey about what is important to young people. Listen to the recording and write the correct letter, **A**, **B** or **C**, to complete each sentence.

1 The survey questioned 3,000 …
  A schools.   B pupils.   C university students.

2 For 30%, … was an important issue.
  A education   B sports facilities   C health

3 40% are anxious about …
  A protecting animals.   B their careers.   C drinking water.

4 90% hope for a better …
  A future.   B job.   C education.

> In tasks like this, the incorrect options are often mentioned in the recording too, so you need to listen carefully to the surrounding language to help you identify the correct answers.

5 Lesen

World issues. You see some headlines in an Austrian newspaper. Which headline matches each issue? Write the correct letter (A–E).

A	Schüler in Österreich: Ausbildung ist uns sehr wichtig
B	Tiere in Gefahr: Wollen wir sie retten?
C	Soziale Inklusion: Aktion für eine bessere Welt
D	Umweltprobleme an der deutschen Nordseeküste
E	Angst vor Gesundheitsproblemen

1 Endangered animals
2 Pollution
3 Education

6 Schreiben

Complete the 90-word writing task.

You are writing to a Swiss friend about the environment.

Write approximately **90** words in **German**.

You must write something about each bullet point.

Describe:
- the environment where you live
- what you did last week to help the environment
- what you will do to be greener in the future.

> Plan your answer before starting to write. Think about the structures and vocabulary you want to use for each bullet point and remember to vary your vocabulary to avoid repetition. Using synonyms (words that have a similar meaning) is a good way of doing this. Aim to use as many complex structures (modal verbs, prepositions, conjunctions, word order, adverbs) and verb formations (perfect, imperfect, future, conditional, present) as you can. Once you have finished writing, remember to check your work for any mistakes.

7 Lesen

Translate these sentences into English.

Remember to translate mir in this sentence.

How will you translate man here?

How will you translate wenn here?

1. Saubere Luft ist mir wichtig.
2. Man muss Energie und Wasser sparen.
3. Meine Freunde haben Angst vor ihrer Ausbildung.
4. Wenn ich älter bin, möchte ich ein umweltfreundliches Auto kaufen.
5. Letzte Woche sind wir zu Fuß zur Schule gegangen.

How should you translate haben here?

Which tense is this?

8 Sprechen

Read the text aloud and prepare responses to the follow-up questions.

Man muss mehr Energie und Wasser sparen.
Mir sind aber Aktion und Information wichtiger.
Man sollte immer Tiere in Gefahr retten.
Umweltschutz und Welthunger sind große Probleme.
Wir müssen Respekt vor Menschenrechten haben und alle akzeptieren.

Follow-up questions:
- Wie fährst du zur Schule?
- Was ist dir wichtig?
- Wie hilfst du anderen Menschen?
- Sollte man Veganer*in sein?

> Think carefully about how to pronounce these sounds:
> -tion
> -er
> r
> Remember where the stress falls on a compound noun.

zweihundertdreiundzwanzig

Kapitel 8 Wiederholung

Lesen 1

Refresh your memory! Copy and complete the sentences with the correct verb from the box.

1 Ich ___ Lehrer*in werden. (*would like*)
2 Er ___ eine Ausbildung machen. (*must*)
3 Sie ___ in einem Krankenhaus arbeiten. (*wanted*)
4 Ich ___ anderen Menschen helfen. (*will*)
5 Er ___ seine Arbeit sehr. (*likes*)
6 Sie ___ die Umwelt schützen. (*wants*)

> will   mag   möchte
> wollte   muss   werde

Hören 2

Refresh your memory! Listen to six young people explaining what their plans are for next year. Write down the correct letters for **what** they plan to do and **why** (1–6).

What?
a I would like to work in a hospital.
b I will do some training.
c I will stay at school.
d I will study at university.
e I hope to find a job.
f I want to spend a gap year abroad.

Why?
i I'd like to earn some money.
ii I don't want to lose my friends.
iii I want to improve my languages.
iv I want to help others.
v I'd like to be a doctor.
vi I like learning practical things.

Lesen 3

Refresh your memory! Find the verbs ending in *-ieren* in the word snake and match them to the English translations in the box.

verlieren passieren akzeptieren organisieren studieren diskutieren

> to accept   to organise   to lose   to study   to discuss   to happen

Hören 4

A gap year. You hear Felix and Samira talking about their work experience and future plans. Which **two** aspects does each person mention? Write the **two** correct letters (A–F) for each person.

A	university
B	work experience
C	learning new things
D	choosing a career
E	learning about yourself
F	travelling

Hören 5

Dictation. You will hear **four** sentences. Write down exactly what you hear in German.

> Think about how these sounds are pronounced when writing down what you hear.
> j
> qu
> a, ä, o, ö, u, ü

224 zweihundertvierundzwanzig

Kapitel 8

Lesen 6
My skills. You read this discussion on an online forum. Complete the sentences below. Write the correct letter, **A**, **B** or **C**, for each question.

Lara ▸ Ich arbeite gern mit meinen Händen. Ich habe es immer sehr leicht gefunden. Leider bin ich gar nicht gut mit Sprachen. Ich finde es schwierig, wenn man kein Deutsch versteht oder spricht.

Joe ▸ Ich kann die Leute gut verstehen und es gefällt mir sehr, wenn ich mit anderen Menschen zusammen arbeite. Ich mag es nicht, wenn ich allein bin oder wenn es einfach zu ruhig ist.

Elif ▸ Ich bin der Meinung, dass ich geduldig bin. Ich helfe gern anderen Menschen und ich mag praktische Arbeit. Eine schlechte Sache ist, wenn ich viel schreibe. Ich benutze nicht gern meinen **Füller** – ich arbeite lieber am Computer.

1 Lara finds working with her hands …
  A difficult.   **B** easy.   **C** boring.
2 Joe finds it easy to understand …
  A people.   **B** other languages.   **C** German.
3 Joe likes working …
  A alone.   **B** in a quiet environment.
  C with other people.
4 Elif likes …
  A creative tasks.   **B** helping others.   **C** writing.
5 Read Elif's paragraph again. What would you do with a **Füller**?
  A write with it   **B** type on it   **C** read it

> In question 5, look carefully at the verbs to work out what Elif does and doesn't like doing. This will help you work out what a *Füller* can be used for.

Sprechen 7
Complete the photo-card task.

You will be asked to talk about the content of these photos. You must say at least one thing about each photo.

After you have spoken about the content of the photos, you will be asked questions related to any of the topics within the theme of **People and lifestyle**.

Your responses should be as **full and detailed** as possible.

Schreiben 8
Translate these sentences into German.

> Remember that some German verbs are followed by a preposition.

> How will you translate 'you' in this context?

> Think carefully about word order with modal verbs.

1 I am working on Sunday.
2 At nine o'clock, I meet my colleague.
3 I look forward to my job.
4 You can learn lots of practical things.
5 Last weekend I earned lots of money.

> Which preposition should you use when talking about days of the week and the time?

> Which reflexive verb do you need to use here?

> Which tense do you need to use here?

zweihundertfünfundzwanzig **225**

Conversation questions

You can use these questions to help you prepare for two different sections of the speaking test:
- the questions which follow on from the **reading aloud task**.
- the questions that you will be asked during the **photo card task**.

In the **reading aloud task** there are four follow-up questions. All four questions are in the present tense and are focused on the same topic as the reading aloud task.

In the **photo card task**, there is an unprepared conversation relating to the theme of the photos in which you have the opportunity to show the examiner that you know a range of structures and tenses in German.

Kapitel 1 (pages 6–29)

Theme 1: People and lifestyle
1. Magst du (Deutsch)? Warum (nicht)?
2. Was ist dein Lieblingsfach? Warum?
3. Beschreib einen typischen Schultag!
4. Was machst du in der Pause/Mittagspause?
5. Was hast du gestern im Unterricht gemacht?
6. Was trägst du in der Schule?
7. Wie findest du die Schuluniform?
8. Wie findest du die Schulregeln in deiner Schule?
9. Hast du letztes Jahr eine interessante Aktivität in der Schule gemacht?
10. Wie findest du Hausaufgaben?

Kapitel 3 (pages 56–79)

Theme 1: People and lifestyle
1. Beschreib deine Familie!
2. Wie bist du? (Wie siehst du aus? Wie ist dein Charakter?)
3. Wie sieht dein (Bruder) / deine (Schwester) aus?
4. Beschreib einen guten Freund / eine gute Freundin!
5. Verstehst du dich gut mit deinem (Stiefvater) / deiner (Großmutter)?
6. Wer ist dir wichtig? Warum?

Theme 2: Popular culture
7. Hast du ein Lieblingsfest?
8. Hast du schon ein deutsches Fest erlebt? (Wie war es?)
9. Wie hast du deinen letzten Geburtstag gefeiert?
10. Wie wirst du das Schuljahresende feiern?

Kapitel 2 (pages 30–53)

Theme 2: Popular culture
1. Was ist deine Lieblingsmusik? (Wer ist dein Lieblingssänger / deine Lieblingssängerin?)
2. Wie findest du (klassische Musik)?
3. Was machst du gern in deiner Freizeit?
4. Was hast du letztes Wochenende gemacht?
5. Was wirst du nächstes Wochenende machen?
6. Was hast du neulich im Kino / online gesehen? (Wie war es?)
7. Wer ist dein Lieblingsstar? Warum?

Theme 3: Communication and the world around us
8. Was machst du online?
9. Was sind die Vor- und Nachteile von Technologie, deiner Meinung nach?
10. Was hast du gestern online gemacht?

Kapitel 4 (pages 80–103)

Theme 1: People and lifestyle
1. Was ist dein Lieblingssport? (Wie oft machst du das?)
2. Welchen Sport machst du nicht so gern?
3. Wie findest du Teamsport?
4. Was machst du für deine Fitness?
5. Was machst du, wenn du schlechte Laune hast?
6. Was hast du neulich für deine Gesundheit gemacht?
7. Wie wichtig ist deine Gesundheit für dich?
8. Isst du gesund?
9. Wie findest du Rauchen?
10. Was wirst du nächstes Wochenende für deine Gesundheit machen?

Speaking test revision

How to prepare:
- Read through the questions to check you understand them. Focus on the question words (like *Was …? Wo …? Wie … ?* etc).
- Check the verbs and time phrases to understand which time frame the question is about.
- Then practise answering the questions using full sentences.
- Think about how you could extend your answers using more complex structures, particularly for answering questions during the **photo card task** conversation.

Ways to extend your answers:
- Join together ideas with connectives: *und, aber, auch …*
- Add in opinions and justify them: *ich mag … (nicht) / ich … (nicht) gern, weil …*
- Use opposing arguments: *Auf der einen Seite … auf der anderen Seite … jedoch …*
- Add in examples of recent activities in the past tense.
- Add in examples of different tenses.

Kapitel 5 (pages 104–127)

Theme 3: Communication and the world around us

1. Wie ist deine Stadt / dein Dorf?
2. Magst du es, wo du wohnst?
3. Wie war deine Stadt / dein Dorf früher?
4. Wie fährst du am liebsten zur Schule? Warum?
5. Kaufst du lieber online oder in einem Einkaufszentrum ein? Warum?
6. Was hast du letztes Wochenende in der Stadt gemacht?
7. Beschreib mir dein Haus / deine Wohnung!
8. Wie ist dein idealer Wohnort?
9. Ist deine Gegend gut für junge Leute / Touristen? Warum (nicht)?
10. Wo möchtest du in der Zukunft wohnen?

Kapitel 6 (pages 132–155)

Theme 3: Communication and the world around us

1. Was machst du gern in den Ferien?
2. Wie findest du Urlaube am Strand / in den Bergen?
3. Wie findest du Ferienparks?
4. Was machst du in den Ferien zu Hause?
5. Was denkst du über Urlaube im Ausland?
6. Was hast du in den letzten Ferien gemacht?
7. Gab es ein Problem?
8. Verbringst du lieber Zeit mit deinen Freunden oder deiner Familie in den Ferien?
9. Welches Land möchtest du besuchen? Warum?
10. Was wirst du in den nächsten Ferien machen?

Kapitel 7 (pages 156–179)

Theme 1: People and lifestyle

1. Vor wem hast du Respekt?
2. Was ist dir wichtig im Leben?
3. Wie wichtig ist dir deine Familie?
4. Hast du im Moment Angst?

Theme 3: Communication and the world around us

5. Was ist ein großes Umweltproblem, deiner Meinung nach?
6. Bist du umweltfreundlich? (Was machst du?)
7. Was hast du neulich für die Umwelt gemacht?
8. Was wirst du in der Zukunft für die Umwelt machen?
9. Bist du für oder gegen grüne Energien?
10. Sollte man Veganer*in sein?

Kapitel 8 (pages 180–203)

Theme 1: People and lifestyle

1. Was wirst du nach deinen Prüfungen machen?
2. Wirst du an deiner Schule bleiben? Warum (nicht)?
3. Willst du einen Sommerjob finden?
4. Hast du schon einmal gearbeitet? (Wie war es?)
5. Was ist dein Traumberuf?
6. Was ist für dich wichtig im Beruf?
7. Was kannst du gut?
8. Wie wichtig ist dir das Geld?
9. Möchtest du in der Zukunft heiraten?
10. Wie sieht die Zukunft aus, deiner Meinung nach?

zweihundertsiebenundzwanzig

German phonics

Here is a list of all the sounds that you need to understand and produce.
The **SSCs** (sound-symbol correspondences) will be assessed in the **reading aloud** and **dictation** tasks.

The **reading aloud task** will be the second task in your speaking test. You will have **15** minutes' preparation time for the whole speaking test. The task will contain around **five** sentences (35 words minimum) from a specific theme.

The **dictation task** will form part of your listening paper. You will have to transcribe a minimum of **20** words (in four sentences). Some of the words will not be on the vocabulary lists. Practising the sounds on these pages will help with both the **reading aloud** and **dictation** tasks.

Sounds	Key words and other examples	Pages with a focus on this sound	Further examples to practise
long a / ah / aa	Tag / Jahr / Haar	pages 33, 133	Ich habe lange Haare.
short a	kalt / alle / zusammen	pages 33, 87, 133, 184	Am Anfang hatte ich Angst.
long e / eh / ee	lesen / nehmen / leer	pages 8, 134	Ich nehme Tee am Meer.
short e	wenn / denn / denken	pages 8, 134	Meine Eltern sprechen Englisch.
ei / ai	Polizei / Mai / frei	page 31	Ich weiß, wir drei sind meistens frei im Mai.
z	Zeit / Zimmer / zu	page 66	Es gibt zwanzig Zuschauer im Zimmer.
w	schwer / Welt / wieder	pages 15, 66, 112, 142	Werden wir wirklich im Winter wandern?
ie	lieben / spielen / Energie	page 31	Sieben Mitglieder singen viele schwierige Lieder.
long o / oh	Person / ohne / Sohn	pages 37, 87, 133	Das Kino, wo ich wohne, ist so groß.
short o	Kopf / soll / obwohl	pages 37, 133, 184	Die Sonne im Oktober ist oft nicht im Osten.
long i / ih	wir / ihr / ihn	page 31	Interessiert ihr euch für Musik?
short i	bitte / wissen / Himmel	page 31	Sie ist nicht im Zimmer.
hard ch	machen / mochte / Buch	page 136	Ihre Tochter sucht auch ein Buch.
soft ch	Mädchen / möchte / euch	pages 8, 136	Vielleicht sprechen die Mädchen über Bücher?
long u / uh	Buch / Zug / Uhr	pages 7, 59, 87	Er hat einen Stuhl, eine Uhr und einen Kuchen.
short u	Grund / und / Hunger	page 59	Die Umwelt in seiner Umgebung ist schmutzig.
long ü / long y / üh	Tür / früh	pages 7, 8, 59, 87, 184	Die grünen Türen und Stühle sind überall berühmt.
short ü / short y	Stück / fünf / Typ	pages 7, 59	Ich bin glücklich, dass es fünf typische Brücken gibt.
long ä / äh	spät / Mädchen / wählen	pages 41, 184	Das Mädchen isst regelmäßig europäischen Käse.
short ä	Geschäft / lächeln / kälter	pages 41, 87, 133, 184	Die Länder haben viele Städte und Geschäfte.
long ö / öh	Größe / höher / schön	pages 37, 87, 133	Die Berge sind größer und höher in Österreich.
short ö	zwölf / können / Töchter	pages 37, 184	Zwölf Schlösser öffnen für die Öffentlichkeit.
äu	läuft / träumen / Gebäude	page 87	Sie träumt von Gebäuden und Bäumen.

zweihundertachtundzwanzig

Speaking test revision

Sounds	Key words and other examples	Pages with a focus on this sound	Further examples to practise
sch	schnell / schreiben / schwimmen	pages 35, 81, 108	Man lernt schnell Schwimmen in britischen Schulen.
sp-	sportlich / Spaß / spannend	pages 8, 35, 108	Sport treiben ist spannend und macht Spaß.
st-	stehen / Stadt / studieren	pages 35, 108	Er stand eine Stunde am Strand und in der Straße.
s- / -s-	singen / sind / lesen	pages 85, 108, 143	Diese Sänger singen sofort sieben Lieder am See.
ß / ss / -s	Fuß / dass / blaues	pages 108, 143	Ein schönes großes Schloss liegt am Fluss.
er	er / erst / Erfolg	page 163	Er ist ernst, erfolgreich und hat Energie.
unstressed -er	Zimmer / Vater / Theater	page 163	Sie hat nur eine Schwester, aber vier Brüder.
v	Vater / viel / vergessen	pages 66, 142	Mein Vater verdient viel als Verkäufer..
au	auch / auf / Haus	page 87	Die Frauen laufen gern im August.
consonantal r	Problem / reden / richtig	page 167	Der Lehrer hat ein rotes Fahrrad im Raum.
vocalic r	klar / Uhr / Meer	page 167	Nur am Morgen gibt es mehr Verkehr.
eu	Euro / heute / neulich	page 39	Eure neuen Freunde sprechen heute kein Deutsch.
th	Thema / Theater / Mathe	page 8	Er hat Mathe und Theater studiert.
unvoiced -b / -d / -g	halb / Land / Weg	page 143	Im Urlaub hat er sein Geld im Zug verloren.
-ig	wenig / wichtig / zwanzig	page 88	Ich bin lustig, ruhig, oft schwierig, aber nie traurig.
j	jemand / ja / jede	page 181	Jedes Jahr macht Jana im Juni oder Juli Urlaub.
-tion	Situation / Information / Tradition	page 157	Man braucht Information in dieser Situation.
qu	bequem / Quelle	page 187	Das Wasser von der Quelle schmeckt gut, aber der Weg ist nicht bequem.

Hören 1 Listen to and repeat each sound, example word and practice phrase. Make a list of the sounds or words you find most challenging and keep practising them. Then find other words for each sound to test your pronunciation.

zweihundertneunundzwanzig 229

Role-play skills

What do I need to know about the role-play?
- It is an imagined conversation with a friend about a topic.
- It is the <u>first</u> part of the speaking test (before the **reading aloud** task).
- The teacher speaks first.
- You will say something for each of the **five** bullet points.
- You should speak in the present tense for all bullet points.
- You will need to ask **one** question.
- Three of the bullet points will require one detail.
- One bullet point will require an opinion or a description.

Themes and topics

There are three themes and nine subtopics. Look back at these modules for some role-play or conversation examples. There are also role-play cards on the exam pages at the end of each module, and in the revision module.

Themes and topics	Module
Theme 1 – People and lifestyle	
1 Identity and relationships with others	Modules 3 and 7
2 Healthy living and lifestyle	Module 4
3 Education and work	Modules 1 and 8
Theme 2 – Popular culture	
1 Free-time activities	Modules 2 and 4
2 Customs, festivals and celebrations	Module 3
3 Celebrity culture	Modules 2 and 3
Theme 3 – Communication and the world around us	
1 Travel and tourism, including places of interest	Module 6
2 Media and technology	Module 2
3 The environment and where people live	Modules 5 and 7

> ⭐ In order to score full marks, you will need to give a verb in your answer. Make sure you give an opinion when asked to.
> For example, if you are asked to **give an opinion about school uniform**
> Don't say: *Schlecht.*
> Instead say: *Ich finde die Schuluniform schlecht.*

> ⭐ Make sure you use the *du* form of the verb when you have to ask a question. For example if you have to **ask a friend a question about a sport**, you could say:
> *Spielst du Tennis?*
> or
> *Magst du Basketball?*

Useful words and phrases

Meiner Meinung nach	In my opinion
Ich finde … (nicht) (so) (gut)	I find … (not) (so) (good)
Ich spiele (gern)	I (like to) play
Ich esse (gern)	I (like to) eat
Ich gehe/fahre (gern)	I (like to) go
Ich höre (gern)	I (like to) listen to
Mein Lieblings… ist	My favourite … is
Das Wetter ist	The weather is
Mein Haus ist in	My house is in
Meine Schule liegt in	My school is in
Es gibt	There is/are

> ⭐ **Learn these key phrases for the following questions:**
> <u>How often:</u>
> *Ich spiele/höre/gehe jede Woche / einmal/zweimal pro Woche / jeden Tag …*
> I play/listen to/go … every week / once/twice a week / every day.
>
> <u>When:</u>
> *Ich esse / sehe fern / fahre … am Morgen / am Abend / am Montag / am Wochenende / um (fünf) Uhr …*
> I eat / watch TV / go … in the mornings / in the evenings / on Monday / at the weekend / at (5) o'clock.
>
> <u>Where:</u>
> *Ich spiele/höre … im Park / in meinem Zimmer / in der Stadt / in der Schule / im Wohnzimmer / zu Hause.*
> I play / listen to … in the park / in my room / in town / at school / in the living room / at home.
>
> **Learn these useful second-person verbs**
> *Magst du …?* — Do you like …?
> *Wie findest du …?* — What do you think of …?
> *Spielst/Isst/Hörst du (gern) …?* — Do you (like to) play / eat / listen to …?

Questions

The last bullet point requires you to ask a question. This is a key part of the task and you should practise asking questions for every topic.

Role-play example topics	Example questions
Free-time activities Ask your friend a question about hobbies.	*Hörst du* gern Musik? *Was ist* dein Lieblingssport?
The environment and where people live Ask your friend a question about their local area.	*Gibt es* ein Schwimmbad in deiner Gegend? *Was machst du gern* in deiner Gegend?
Education and work Ask your friend a question about school.	*Wie findest du* deine Schule? *Was denkst du über* die Schulregeln?
Healthy living and lifestyle Ask your friend a question about food.	*Was isst du* zum Frühstück? *Bist du* Vegetarier?
Customs, festivals and celebrations Ask your friend a question about celebrations.	*Wie feierst du* deinen Geburtstag? *Wie findest du* Silvester?
Travel and tourism, including places of interest Ask your friend a question about holidays.	*Was machst du* in den Sommerferien? *Wohin möchtest du* in Urlaub fahren?
Media and technology Ask your friend a question about social media.	*Welche* sozialen Medien benutzt du? *Wie findest du* Instagram?

Example role-play

Look at the example role-play card below and the model conversation on the right.

- You are talking to your German friend.
- Your teacher will play the part of your friend and will speak first.
- You should address your friend as *du*.
- When you see this – **?** – you will have to ask a question.

In order to score full marks, you must include at least one verb in your response to each task.

1 Say **one** activity you do at school at break time.
2 Say where you do this activity.
3 Say what you think of your school uniform.
4 Say what you like to eat.
5 **?** Ask your friend a question about a school subject.

Teacher: Was machst du in der Pause?
Student: Ich spreche mit meinem Freund.
Teacher: Und wo machst du das?
Student: Ich spreche in der Kantine.
Teacher: Wie findest du deine Schuluniform?
Student: Ich finde meine Schuluniform nicht bequem.
Teacher: Was isst du gern?
Student: Ich esse gern Hähnchen mit Reis.
Teacher: Interessant.
Student: Wie findest du Englisch?
Teacher: Ich finde es toll.

Practice role-play

Look at the role-play card and prepare your answers to the numbered points.

- You are talking to your Austrian friend.
- Your teacher will play the part of your friend and will speak first.
- You should address your friend as *du*.
- When you see this – **?** – you will have to ask a question.

In order to score full marks, you must include at least one verb in your response to each task.

1 Say **one** activity you do in your free time.
2 Say how often you do sport.
3 Say what music you like to listen to. (Give **one** detail.)
4 Give **one** opinion about TV.
5 **?** Ask your friend a question about hobbies.

> Remember to use a verb in every answer. Look at the 'useful words and phrases' box on page 230 to help you with your answers.

> Remember to use the *du* form when asking a question. Start with the verb if asking a yes/no question or start with a question word if you are seeking specific information.

Photo card task

The **photo card task** is the final part of your speaking test and is made up of **two** parts:

The photo card contains two photos relating to one of the three themes:
- **Theme 1 – People and lifestyle**
- **Theme 2 – Popular culture**
- **Theme 3 – Communication and the world around us**

Each theme is made of three topics (see page 230).

1 Response to the two photos *(one minute)*
Give a detailed description of both photos on the photo card.

2 Unprepared conversation *(three to four minutes)*
Take part in a conversation on one or more topics from the theme specified on the photo card.

Response to the two photos

During your preparation time, **PLAN** how you are going to respond to the content of the two photos. Prepare a detailed description of both photos. This could include, for example, **People/things**, **Location** and **Activities**.

People/things
Who/What can you see?

Location
Where are they?

Activities
What are they doing?

Now check your accuracy carefully.

Check:
- verbs
  - regular / irregular
  - correct verb ending
- adjective agreements
- word order

To gain top marks you must give a full, detailed description of both photos using **accurate language** and **correct pronunciation**.

Auf dem ersten Foto	gibt es	(vier) Personen/Kinder/Erwachsene.
Auf dem zweiten Foto	sieht man	einen Jungen / ein Mädchen.
Es gibt auch		ein Auto / einen Bahnhof / eine Straße.
Man sieht auch		viele Geschäfte/Häuser/Bäume.
Ich denke, dass sie		eine Familie / Freunde sind.
		Schüler und Schülerinnen sind.
Die Person auf der linken/rechten Seite		ist (groß/klein) und hat (kurze/lange) Haare.
		trägt Jeans / eine schwarze Hose / ein weißes T-Shirt.
Das Essen	sieht	lecker
Die Leute/Gebäude	sehen	glücklich/schön/alt/modern

...aus.

Die Personen/Leute/ Menschen	sind in	einem Park / einem Bahnhof. einer Schule / einer Stadt. einem Geschäft / einem Restaurant / einem Hotel. auf Urlaub / am Strand / in den Bergen.
Ich denke, dass		es Sommer/Winter ist. / die Leute glücklich aussehen.
Das Wetter ist		schön/schlecht/gut/warm/kalt.
Im Hintergrund sieht man		Häuser / Gebäude / viele Menschen / Berge / einen Garten.
Sie / Die Leute/Personen		spielen / essen / kaufen / sitzen / lernen / hören / gehen / fahren / tanzen …
Die Person in der Mitte / auf der linken/rechten Seite		spielt / isst / kauft / sitzt / lernt / hört / geht / fährt / tanzt …

To say what people are doing, use the **present tense**. There is no present continuous in German.
Das Mädchen **spielt** *Fußball.* The girl is playing / plays football.
Die Schüler **lesen** *ein Buch.* The students are reading / read a book.

232 *zweihundertzweiunddreißig*

Example photo card task (Theme 3: Communication and the world around us)

During your preparation time, look at the two photos. You may make as many notes as you wish and use these notes during the test.

Your teacher will ask you to talk about the content of these photos. The recommended time is approximately **one** minute. You must say at least **one** thing about each photo.

After you have spoken about the content of the photos, your teacher will ask you questions related to any of the topics within the theme of **Communication and the world around us**.

> Sag mir etwas über die Fotos.

Example answer:

Auf dem ersten Foto gibt es fünf Personen: drei Mädchen und zwei Jungen. Ich denke, dass sie Freunde sind. Sie sind in einem Bus und ich denke, dass sie auf Urlaub sind. Die Sonne scheint. Sie tragen alle Sommerkleidung. Sie haben Spaß.

Auf dem zweiten Foto sieht man drei Personen: zwei Mädchen und einen Jungen. Ich denke, sie sind in einem Flughafen. Sie machen ein Foto. Sie sehen glücklich aus.

Unprepared conversation

You will then take part in an unprepared conversation on one or more of the three topics from the theme stated on the photo card.

- Listen carefully to the questions and take care with how you start each answer. Are you using the correct tense?
- If you make a mistake, just correct yourself. If you want the teacher to repeat a question, ask: *Können Sie das bitte wiederholen?*
- Use the example questions on pages 226–227 to practise answers to the questions you might be asked. This is an opportunity to show off your German!

To gain more marks, you need to develop your sentences. This means that you need to give extra details. You could use longer sentences containing conjunctions, such as *weil, wenn, aber* or *obwohl*, and talk about someone else.

For example: *Ich spiele gern Tennis, **aber** ich mag Hockey nicht. Ich finde Hockey langweilig, **obwohl** mein Freund Hockey liebt. Wir spielen am Wochenende Fußball, **wenn** wir Zeit haben.*

Examples of varied vocabulary and structures:

- opinion phrases: *ich liebe, ich mag, ich ... (nicht) gern, ich hasse*
- opinion words: *blöd, schlecht, schlimm, schrecklich, schön, spannend, toll, wunderbar*
- qualifiers and intensifiers: *echt, extrem, ganz, sehr, total, wirklich, ziemlich*
- comparatives: *besser, billiger, interessanter, kleiner*
- conjunctions: *aber, denn, oder, obwohl, weil, wenn*

To gain higher marks, make sure you:
- answer the question
- develop your ideas
- use varied vocabulary
- use conjunctions
- use all three tenses
- are accurate

Verb tables

Key:
* = this verb form won't appear in exams, but you may use it in your own work.

Regular verbs

Infinitive	Present tense	Perfect tense	Future tense
Regular verbs			
wohnen *to live*	ich wohn**e** du wohn**st** er/sie/es wohn**t** wir wohn**en** ihr wohn**t** Sie/sie wohn**en**	ich habe … **ge**wohn**t**	ich werde … wohnen
arbeiten *to work*	du arbeit**est** er/sie/es arbeit**et** ihr arbeit**et**	ich habe … **ge**arbeit**et**	ich werde … arbeiten
Reflexive verbs with accusative			
sich freuen *to be happy, look forward to*	ich freue mich du freust dich er/sie/es freut sich wir freuen uns ihr freut euch Sie/sie freuen sich	ich habe mich … **ge**freut	ich werde mich … freuen
Separable verbs			
einkaufen *to shop*	ich kaufe ein	ich habe … ein**ge**kauft	ich werde … einkaufen

Key irregular verbs

Infinitive	Present tense	Perfect tense	Future tense
haben *to have*	ich habe du hast er/sie/es hat wir haben ihr habt Sie/sie haben	ich habe … gehabt	ich werde … haben
sein *to be*	ich bin du bist er/sie/es ist wir sind ihr seid Sie/sie sind	ich bin … gewesen	ich werde … sein
werden *to become*	ich werde du wirst er/sie/es wird wir werden ihr werdet Sie/sie werden	ich bin … geworden	ich werde … werden
wissen *to know*	ich weiß du weißt er/sie/es weiß wir wissen ihr wisst Sie/sie wissen	ich habe … gewusst	ich werde … wissen

Verbs with changes in the *du* and *er/sie/es* stems

Infinitive	Present tense	Perfect tense	Future tense
abnehmen *to lose weight, decrease, reduce*	du nimmst ab er/sie/es nimmt ab	ich habe ... abgenommen	ich werde ... abnehmen
anfangen *to start*	du fängst an er/sie/es fängt an	ich habe ... *angefangen	ich werde ... anfangen
ansehen *to watch*	du siehst ... an er/sie/es sieht ... an	ich habe ... angesehen	ich werde ... ansehen
brechen *to break*	du brichst er/sie/es bricht	ich habe ... gebrochen	ich werde ... brechen
empfehlen *to recommend*	du empfiehlst er/sie/es empfiehlt	ich habe ... empfohlen	ich werde ... empfehlen
essen *to eat*	du isst er/sie/es isst	ich habe ... gegessen	ich werde ... essen
fahren *to go, drive*	du fährst er/sie/es fährt	ich bin ... gefahren	ich werde ... fahren
fallen *to fallen*	du fällst er/sie/es fällt	ich bin ... gefallen	ich werde ... fallen
geben *to give*	du gibst er/sie/es gibt	ich habe ... gegeben	ich werde ... geben
gefallen *to please*	du gefällst er/sie/es gefällt	es hat ... gefallen	es wird ... gefallen
heißen *to be called, mean*	du heißt er/sie/es heißt	ich habe ... geheißen	ich werde ... heißen
helfen *to help*	du hilfst er/sie/es hilft	ich habe ... geholfen	ich werde ... helfen
lassen *to let, allow*	du lässt er/sie/es lässt	ich habe ... gelassen	ich werde ... lassen
laufen *to run, walk*	du läufst er/sie/es läuft	ich bin ... gelaufen	ich werde ... laufen
lesen *to read*	du liest er/sie/es liest	ich habe ... gelesen	ich werde ... lesen
nehmen *to take*	du nimmst er/sie/es nimmt	ich habe ... genommen	ich werde ... nehmen
schlafen *to sleep*	du schläfst er/sie/es schläft	ich habe ... geschlafen	ich werde ... schlafen
sehen *to see, watch*	du siehst er/sie/es sieht	ich habe ... gesehen	ich werde ... sehen
sprechen *to speak*	du sprichst er/sie/es spricht	ich habe ... gesprochen	ich werde ... sprechen
sterben *to die*	du stirbst er/sie/es stirbt	er/sie/es ist ... gestorben	er/sie/es wird ... sterben
tragen *to carry, wear*	du trägst er/sie/es trägt	ich habe ... getragen	ich werde ... tragen
treffen *to meet*	du triffst er/sie/es trifft	ich habe ... getroffen	ich werde ... treffen
vergessen *to forget*	du vergisst er/sie/es vergisst	ich habe ... vergessen	ich werde ... vergessen
werfen *to throw*	du wirfst er/sie/es wirft	ich habe ... geworfen	ich werde ... werfen

Verb tables

Key:
* = this verb form won't appear in exams, but you may use it in your own work.

Other useful verbs

Infinitive	Present tense	Perfect tense	Future tense
akzeptieren to accept	ich akzeptiere	ich habe … akzeptiert	ich werde … akzeptieren
anrufen to ring, phone	ich rufe … an	ich habe … angerufen	ich werde … anrufen
antworten to answer	ich antworte	ich habe … geantwortet	ich werde … antworten
anziehen to attract, put on	ich ziehe an	ich habe … *angezogen	ich werde … anziehen
bauen to build, construct	ich baue	ich habe … gebaut	ich werde … bauen
beginnen to begin	ich beginne	ich habe … begonnen	ich werde … beginnen
bekommen to receive, get	ich bekomme	ich habe … bekommen	ich werde … bekommen
benutzen to use	ich benutze	ich habe … benutzt	ich werde … benutzen
bestellen to order, reserve	ich bestelle	ich habe … bestellt	ich werde … bestellen
besuchen to visit	ich besuche	ich habe … besucht	ich werde … besuchen
bleiben to stay	ich bleibe	ich bin … geblieben	ich werde … bleiben
brauchen to need	ich brauche	ich habe … gebraucht	ich werde … brauchen
bringen to bring	ich bringe	ich habe … gebracht	ich werde … bringen
denken to think	ich denke	ich habe … *gedacht	ich werde … denken
diskutieren to discuss	ich diskutiere	Ich habe … diskutiert	ich werde … diskutieren
entscheiden to decide	ich entscheide	ich habe … entschieden	ich werde … entscheiden
(sich) entschuldigen to excuse, apologise	ich entschuldige (mich)	ich habe (mich) … entschuldigt	ich werde (mich) … entschuldigen
(sich) erinnern to remind, remember	ich erinnere (mich)	ich habe (mich) … erinnert	ich werde (mich)… erinnern
erklären to explain	ich erkläre	ich habe … erklärt	ich werde … erklären
erlauben to allow, permit	ich erlaube	ich habe … erlaubt	ich werde … erlauben
erleben to experience	ich erlebe	ich habe … erlebt	ich werde … erleben
erreichen to achieve, reach	ich erreiche	ich habe … erreicht	ich werde … erreichen
erzählen to tell	ich erzähle	ich habe … erzählt	ich werde … erzählen
fehlen to lack, be missing, be absent	ich fehle	ich habe … gefehlt	ich werde … fehlen

zweihundertsechsunddreißig

Verb tables

Infinitive	Present tense	Perfect tense	Future tense
feiern *to celebrate, party*	ich feiere	ich habe ... gefeiert	ich werde ... feiern
finden *to find*	ich finde	ich habe ... gefunden	ich werde ... finden
fliegen *to fly*	ich fliege	ich bin ... geflogen	ich werde ... fliegen
folgen *to follow*	ich folge	ich bin ... gefolgt	ich werde ... folgen
fragen *to ask*	ich frage	ich habe ... gefragt	ich werde ... fragen
gehen *to go*	ich gehe	ich bin ... gegangen	ich werde ... gehen
gehören *to belong*	ich gehöre	ich habe ... gehört	ich werde ... gehören
genießen *to enjoy*	ich genieße	ich habe ... genossen	ich werde ... genießen
gewinnen *to win*	ich gewinne	ich habe ... gewonnen	ich werde ... gewinnen
glauben *to believe, think*	ich glaube	ich habe ... geglaubt	ich werde ... glauben
heiraten *to marry*	ich heirate	ich habe ... geheiratet	ich werde ... heiraten
holen *to get, fetch*	ich hole	ich habe ... geholt	ich werde ... holen
kennen *to know*	ich kenne	ich habe ... *gekannt	ich werde ... kennen
kommen *to come*	ich komme	ich bin ... gekommen	ich werde ... kommen
kriegen *to get*	ich kriege	ich habe ... gekriegt	ich werde ... kriegen
lächeln *to smile*	ich läch(e)le	ich habe ... gelächelt	ich werde ... lächeln
lachen *to laugh*	ich lache	ich habe ... gelacht	ich werde ... lachen
leiden *to suffer*	ich leide	ich habe ... *gelitten	ich werde ... leiden
liegen *to lie, be lying down*	ich liege	ich bin ... *gelegen	ich werde ... liegen
meinen *to think, have an opinion*	ich meine	ich habe ... gemeint	ich werde ... meinen
öffnen *to open*	ich öffne	ich habe ... geöffnet	ich werde ... öffnen
passen *to fit, suit*	ich passe	ich habe ... gepasst	ich werde ... passen
retten *to save, rescue*	ich rette	ich habe ... gerettet	ich werde ... retten
schließen *to close, shut*	ich schließe	ich habe ... geschlossen	ich werde ... schließen

zweihundertsiebenunddreißig **237**

Verb tables

Infinitive	Present tense	Perfect tense	Future tense
schreiben *to write*	ich schreibe	ich habe ... geschrieben	ich werde ... schreiben
schwimmen *to swim*	ich schwimme	ich bin ... geschwommen	ich werde ... schwimmen
singen *to sing*	ich singe	ich habe ... gesungen	ich werde ... singen
sitzen *to sit*	ich sitze	ich habe/bin ... *gesessen	ich werde ... sitzen
sorgen *to care, worry*	ich sorge	ich habe ... gesorgt	ich werde ... sorgen
spielen *to play*	ich spiele	ich habe ... gespielt	ich werde ... spielen
springen *to jump*	ich springe	ich bin ... gesprungen	ich werde ... springen
stehen *to stand*	ich stehe	ich bin ... gestanden	ich werde ... stehen
steigen *to climb, rise, increase*	ich steige	ich bin ... gestiegen	ich werde ... steigen
teilen *to share, divide*	ich teile	ich habe ... geteilt	ich werde ... teilen
träumen *to dream*	ich träume	ich habe ... geträumt	ich werde ... träumen
treiben *to do (sport)*	ich treibe	ich habe ... getrieben	ich werde ... treiben
trinken *to drink*	ich trinke	ich habe ... getrunken	ich werde ... trinken
tun *to do*	ich tue	ich habe ... *getan	ich werde ... tun
üben *to practise*	ich übe	ich habe ... geübt	ich werde ... üben
übersetzen *to translate*	ich übersetze	ich habe ... übersetzt	ich werde ... übersetzen
verbringen *to spend (time)*	ich verbringe	ich habe ... verbracht	ich werde ... verbringen
verlieren *to lose*	ich verliere	ich habe ... verloren	ich werde ... verlieren
verstehen *to understand*	ich verstehe	ich habe ... verstanden	ich werde ... verstehen
wählen *to choose, elect, vote, select*	ich wähle	ich habe ... gewählt	ich werde ... wählen

Verb tables

Modal verbs

Infinitive	Present tense	Imperfect tense	Perfect tense	Future tense
dürfen *to be allowed*	ich darf du darfst er/sie/es darf wir dürfen ihr dürft Sie/sie dürfen	ich durfte du durftest er/sie/es durfte wir *durften ihr *durftet Sie/sie *durften	ich habe ... *gedurft	ich werde ... dürfen
können *to be able to, can*	ich kann du kannst er/sie/es kann wir können ihr könnt Sie/sie können	ich konnte du konntest er/sie/es konnte wir *konnten ihr *konntet Sie/sie *konnten	ich habe ... *gekonnt	ich werde ... können
mögen *to like to*	ich mag du magst er/sie/es mag wir mögen ihr mögt Sie/sie mögen	ich mochte du mochtest er/sie/es mochte wir *mochten ihr *mochtet Sie/sie *mochten	ich habe ... *gemocht	ich werde ... mögen
müssen *to have to, must*	ich muss du musst er/sie/es muss wir müssen ihr müsst Sie/sie müssen	ich musste du musstest er/sie musste wir *mussten ihr *musstet Sie/sie *mussten	ich habe ... *gemusst	ich werde ... müssen
sollen *to ought to, be supposed to*	ich soll du sollst er/sie/es soll wir sollen ihr sollt Sie/sie sollen	ich sollte du solltest er/sie/es sollte wir *sollten ihr *solltet Sie/sie *sollten	ich habe ... *gesollt	ich werde ... sollen
wollen *to want*	ich will du willst er/sie/es will wir wollen ihr wollt Sie/sie wollen	ich wollte du wolltest er/sie/es wollte wir *wollten ihr *wolltet Sie/sie *wollten	ich habe ... *gewollt	ich werde ... wollen

Imperfect tense

haben	sein	es gibt
ich hatte du hattest er/sie/es hatte wir hatten ihr hattet Sie/sie hatten	ich war du warst er/sie/es war wir waren ihr wart Sie/sie waren	es gab

Conditional

mögen
ich möchte du möchtest er/sie/es möchte wir möchten ihr möchtet Sie/sie möchten

zweihundertneununddreißig

Derivational morphology

Prefixes and suffixes are used to change the meanings of words. In your reading exam, you will come across words which are based on words from the vocabulary list but used with prefixes and suffixes.

The prefixes *Lieblings-* and *Haupt-*

Lesen 1

Translate the nouns into English.

1 der Lieblingssport
2 der Lieblingsort
3 das Lieblingszimmer
4 die Lieblingsfarbe
5 die Hauptstraße
6 die Hauptperson
7 die Hauptstadt
8 der Hauptbahnhof

> The prefix *Lieblings-* can be added to describe your favourite item, and the prefix *Haupt-* can be added to describe the main item.

The prefix *un-*

Lesen 2

Translate the adjectives into English.

1 unmöglich
2 unglücklich
3 unsicher
4 unhöflich
5 unsportlich
6 unruhig
7 unwichtig
8 unehrlich

> The prefix *un-* is added to an adjective to make the opposite meaning.

Ordinal numbers

Lesen 3

Read out the phrases and translate into English.

1 der erste Mai
2 am dritten März
3 Mein Geburtstag ist am zwanzigsten Januar.
4 Heute ist der siebte April.
5 Silvester ist am einunddreißigsten Dezember.
6 Die Ferien beginnen am vierzehnten Juli.

> Cardinal numbers are: one, two, three, etc. Ordinal numbers indicate a position in a series, e.g. first, second, third, etc. In German, ordinal numbers are made by adding *-ten* to the numbers 4–19 and *-sten* to the numbers 20 and above. Some ordinal numbers are irregular. Can you find three of these in this list of dates?

The suffixes *-ung* and *-er*

Schreiben 4

Write out the verbs these nouns have come from.

1 die Öffnung
2 die Bedeutung
3 die Veränderung
4 die Einladung
5 der Arbeiter
6 der Spieler
7 der Fahrer
8 der Besucher

> The suffix *-ung* can be added to the verb stem to change a verb into a noun with an equivalent meaning. The suffix *-er* can be added to the verb stem to create male people nouns.

The suffix *-s*

Lesen 5

Translate the words into English.

1 Dienstag
2 dienstags
3 nachmittags
4 am Morgen
5 morgens
6 abends

> The suffix *-s* can be added to the nouns for days and times of day to change them into adverbs. For example, *Montag* means 'Monday', but *montags* means 'on Mondays' (in general).

Oxford International Primary History

Workbook

3

Pat Lunt

OXFORD

OXFORD
UNIVERSITY PRESS

Great Clarendon Street, Oxford, OX2 6DP, United Kingdom

Oxford University Press is a department of the University of Oxford. It furthers the University's objective of excellence in research, scholarship, and education by publishing worldwide. Oxford is a registered trade mark of Oxford University Press in the UK and in certain other countries.

© Pat Lunt 2017

The moral rights of the author have been asserted.

All rights reserved. No part of this publication may be reproduced, stored in a retrieval system, or transmitted, in any form or by any means, without the prior permission in writing of Oxford University Press, or as expressly permitted by law, by licence or under terms agreed with the appropriate reprographics rights organization. Enquiries concerning reproduction outside the scope of the above should be sent to the Rights Department, Oxford University Press, at the address above.

You must not circulate this work in any other form and you must impose this same condition on any acquirer.

British Library Cataloguing in Publication Data
Data available

ISBN: 978-0-19-841817-7

5 7 9 10 8 6

Paper used in the production of this book is a natural, recyclable product made from wood grown in sustainable forests. The manufacturing process conforms to the environmental regulations of the country of origin.

Printed in Great Britain by Bell and Bain Ltd, Glasgow

Acknowledgements

Cover illustration: Carlo Molinari

Illustrations: Aptara

Photos: p19 & p61: David Noton Photography/Alamy;
p33 (T): Fedor Selivanov/Alamy; **p33 (M):** Peter Horree/Alamy;
p33 (B): Peter Horree/Alamy; **p57:** Everett Collection/Shutterstock;
p62 (T): Christopher Godfrey/Alamy; **p62 (B):** Ancient Art and Architecture: Alamy; **p63:** Granger Historical Picture Archive/Alamy

Although we have made every effort to trace and contact all copyright holders before publication this has not been possible in all cases. If notified, the publisher will rectify any errors or omissions at the earliest opportunity.

Links to third party websites are provided by Oxford in good faith and for information only. Oxford disclaims any responsibility for the materials contained in any third party website referenced in this work.

Contents

1 From hunter-gatherers to village people

- **1.1** Life in the Stone Age — 6
- **1.2** Food and shelter in the Stone Age — 8
- **1.3** Stone Age art and craft — 10
- **1.4** Farming changes the world — 12
- **1.5** Living in one place — 14
- **1** Thinking about my learning — 16

2 The Metal Ages

- **2.1** Technology in the Bronze Age — 20
- **2.2** Towns, trade and travel — 22
- **2.3** Life and death in the Iron Age — 24
- **2.4** Iron Age settlements — 26
- **2.5** Fighting tribes or traders? — 28
- **2** Thinking about my learning — 30

3 Early civilisations

- **3.1** Early civilisations — 34
- **3.2** Farming and food — 36
- **3.3** City life in the early civilisations — 38
- **3.4** Writing and number systems — 40
- **3.5** Trade and war — 42
- **3** Thinking about my learning — 44

4 A history of communication

- **4.1** Writing and writing tools — 48
- **4.2** Printing — 50
- **4.3** Staying in touch — 52
- **4.4** Telecommunication — 54
- **4.5** Mass communication — 56
- **4** Thinking about my learning — 58

Glossary — 60

1 From hunter-gatherers to village people

What do I already know?

What do you think are good answers to the questions in the speech bubbles? Discuss your answers with some friends. Write your answers in a notebook. Your teacher will ask you to look back at your answers when you have completed the unit.

> When was the Stone Age?

> Why is that time in history called the Stone Age?

> What evidence is there about life in the Stone Age?

> What did people in the Stone Age eat?

> What were Stone Age homes like?

Things I would like to know about the Stone Age

_____

_____

Life in the Stone Age

1. Look at the image of cave art on page 6 of your Student Book. Stone Age people could not write. They drew pictures on cave walls. What do these drawings tell us about life in the Stone Age?

   _____

   _____

   _____

2. Stone Age people made weapons, musical instruments and tools. What do you think these objects tell us about life in the Stone Age?

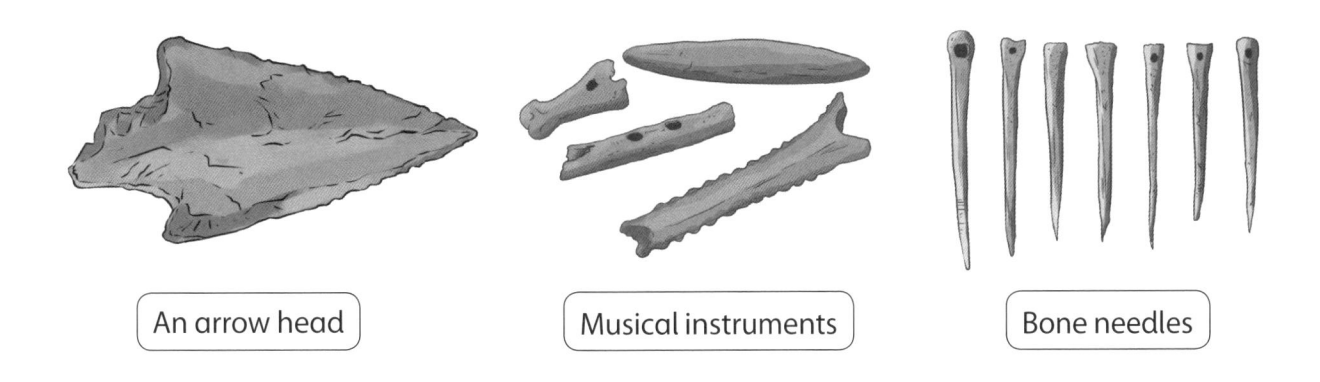

   | An arrow head | Musical instruments | Bone needles |

   _____

   _____

   _____

3. The Stone Age objects we find help us know about life in the Stone Age. What other evidence did Stone Age people leave behind?

   _____

   _____

   _____

1.1 Life in the Stone Age

Stone Age food

1. Write the letters of the pictures to answer questions **a** and **b**.

   a Which of these foods were available to people in the Stone Age?

   _____

   b Which of these foods are only available today?

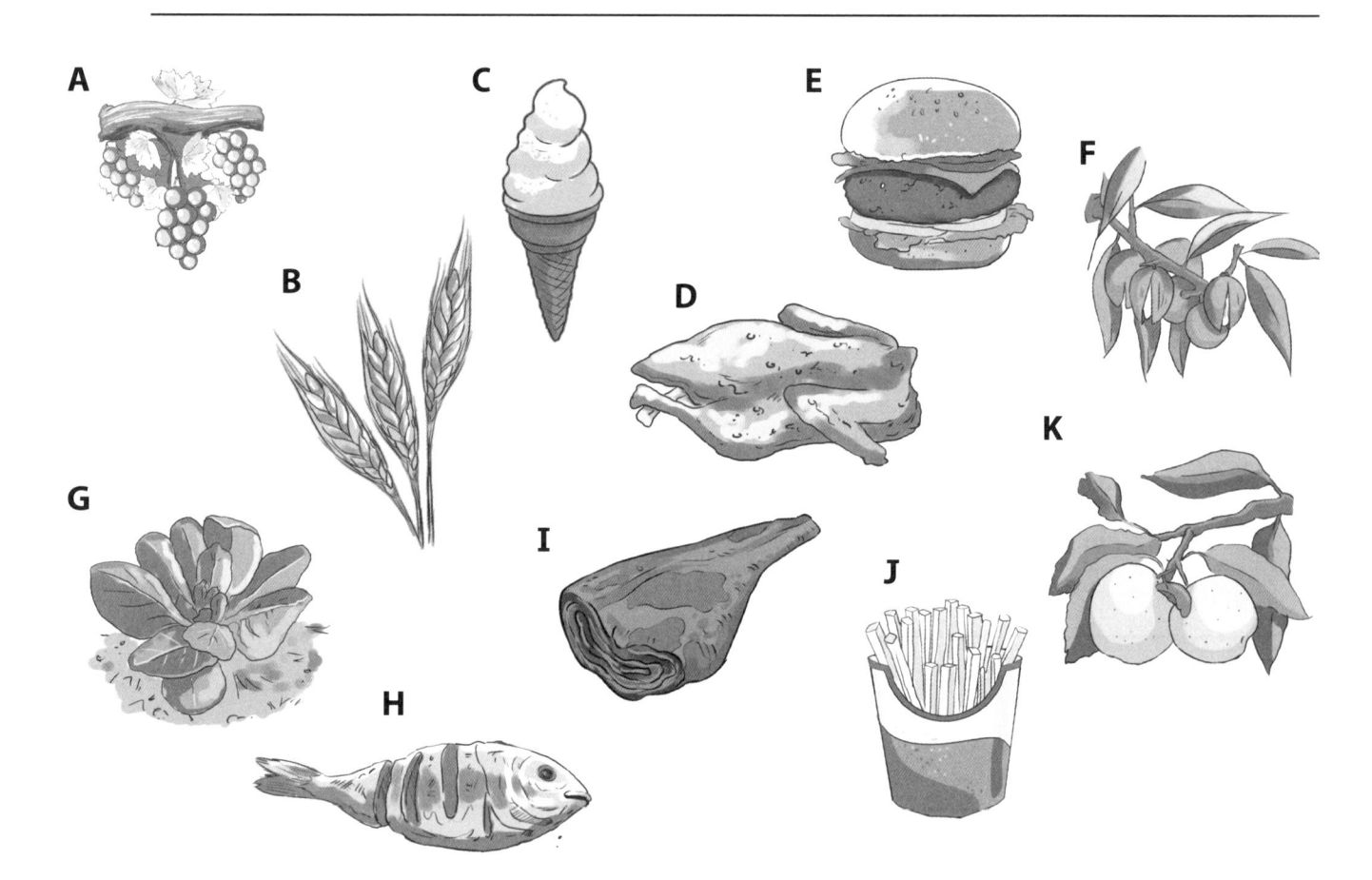

   _____

A
B
C
D
E
F
G
H
I
J
K

2. How do you think people cooked food in the Stone Age?

   _____

   _____

   _____

Where does food come from?

1 Write down three ways in which Stone Age people got their food.

_____
_____
_____
_____
_____
_____
_____

2 Write down two places where people buy food today. Where does this food come from?

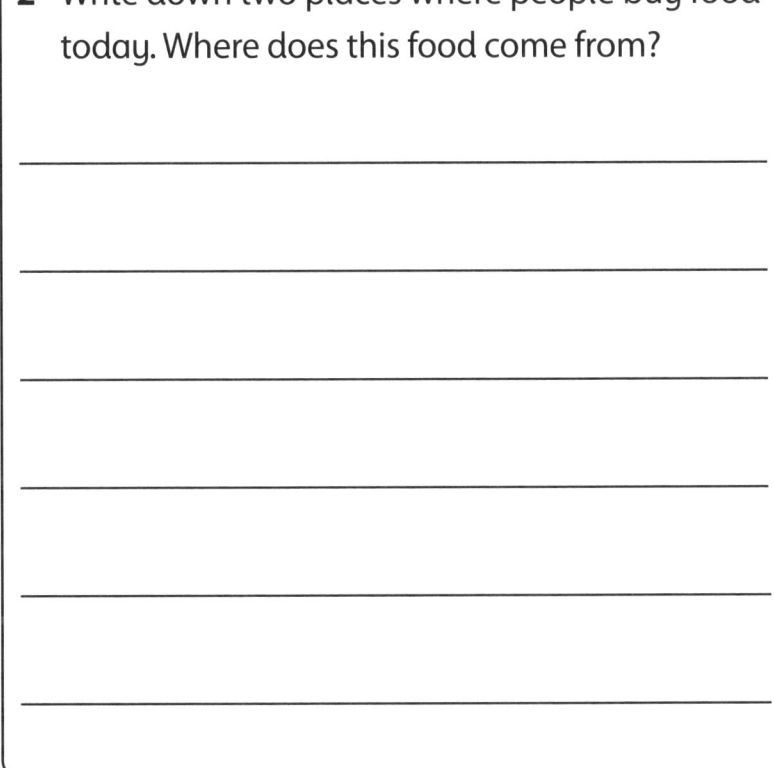

_____
_____
_____
_____
_____
_____
_____

1 From hunter-gatherers to village people

7

1.2 Food and shelter in the Stone Age

Ice Age animals

1 All these objects are the remains of animals that lived in the Ice Age. Draw lines to join each object to the correct animal.

This tooth came from an animal that lived in a cave.

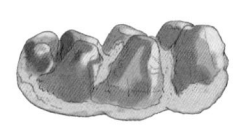

This tooth came from a large animal with long tusks.

This horn came from an animal with two horns on its head.

This skull is from an animal that hunted its prey.

A woolly rhinoceros

A cave bear

A sabre-toothed tiger

A woolly mammoth

2 Do you think these objects were found lying on the ground? If not, where do you think they were found?

_____

_____

3 How does this evidence help us know what Ice Age animals were like?

_____

_____

Stone Age shelter

1 Early people sometimes made shelters from the bones of woolly mammoths. Label the parts of the shelter with the correct letter. The first one has been done for you.

> a Large leg bones
> b Tusks
> c Fire
> d Animal skin covering
> e Frame for stretching skin
> f Bones tied together

2 Why did people need to build shelters like this one?

_____

_____

_____

3 Remains of huts like this one are sometimes found in groups. What does this tell us about how early people lived?

_____

_____

_____

1.3 Stone Age art and craft

Stone Age art

Stone Age cave drawings show many different things. We can see people, animals and boats. Some drawings show objects from the sky such as the sun and the moon.

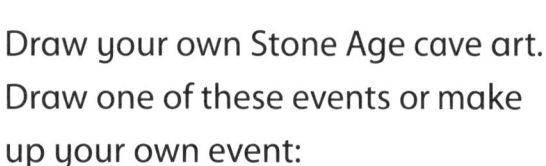

Draw your own Stone Age cave art. Draw one of these events or make up your own event:

- We went hunting and chased a mammoth.
- We went spear fishing in a river full of big fish.
- I found a cave near some trees on a big hill.
- We saw a sabre-toothed tiger chasing a deer.

For more ideas, look at the pictures on pages 6 and 10 of your Student Book, in reference books and on the Internet.

Stone Age craft

This picture shows jewellery that people wore in the Stone Age. Answer the questions about Stone Age jewellery. Use the words in the box to help you.

teeth	shells	bone needle
small bones	hair	plant fibres

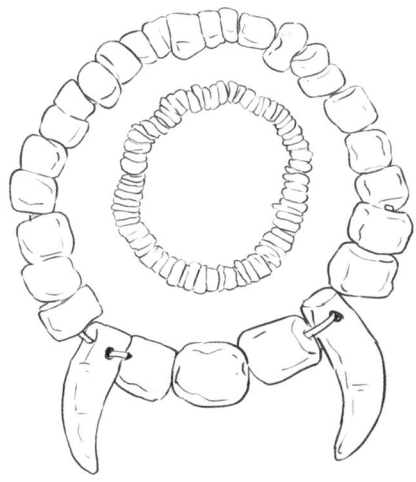

1 This piece of jewellery is made from beads. What do you think the beads are made from?

   _____

   _____

2 The beads are on a cord. What do you think the cord is made from?

   _____

   _____

3 Which tool do you think people used to thread the beads onto the cord?

   _____

   _____

4 Why do some people today like to wear jewellery? Do you think Stone Age people wore jewellery for the same reasons? Explain your answer.

   _____

   _____

1.4 Farming changes the world

Early farming

trees	dam
grains	fertile
water	wool
vegetables	barley
linen	wheat
plough	reeds
water channels	

Starting a farm in the Neolithic period was hard work.

Read this description of starting a Stone Age farm. Fill in the gaps. Use the words in the box to help you. You may use more than one word to fill some gaps.

We must choose a good site. It should be near some fresh _____.

The soil must be _____. We will have to clear away

_____. We will have to prepare the land

for sowing seeds. We will use a _____. We will plant different crops

such as _____. To help us water the

crops we will dig _____. To help store water

we will build a _____ to block the river. To make the flour for our bread

we grind _____. We need clothes to wear.

These are made from _____.

New jobs

1 Draw a piece of Neolithic pottery. Use reference books and the Internet to help you.

2 What do you think people used this pottery for?

_____

_____

Local history study

Find out the nearest place to you where pieces of Neolithic pottery have been found. Use reference books and the Internet to help you. In your notebook:

- write the name of the place where the pottery was found
- write about what was found.

Challenge

What did archeologists say about the pottery? What did the pottery tell the archeologists about life in Neolithic times in that place? Write your answers in your notebook.

1.5 Living in one place

Settling down

This map shows places where people settled and farmed in Neolithic times. Complete these tasks. Use an atlas to help you.

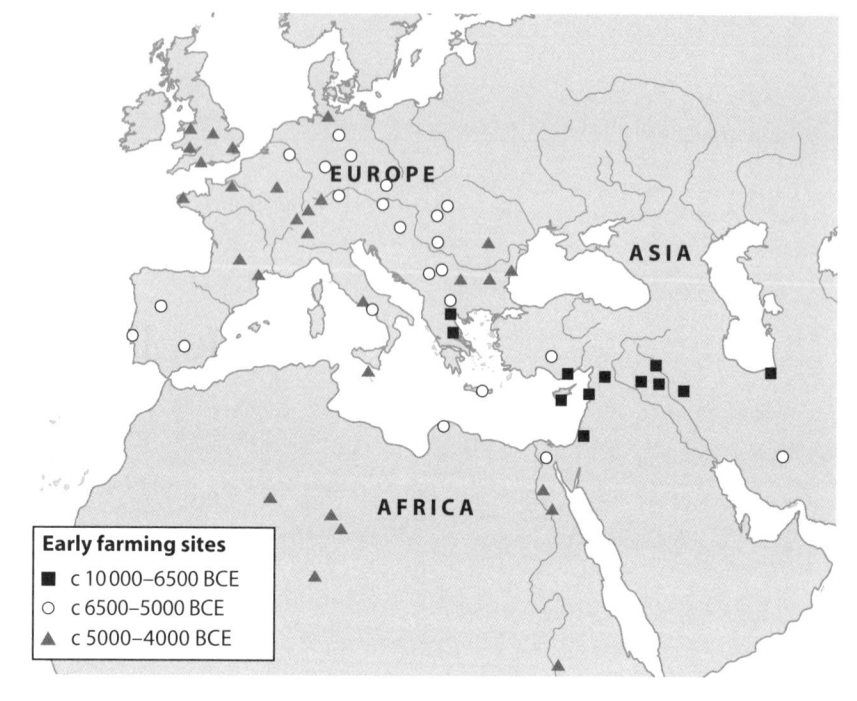

Early farming sites
- ■ c 10 000–6500 BCE
- ○ c 6500–5000 BCE
- ▲ c 5000–4000 BCE

1 Write the names of two modern countries where farming started in each of the different time periods.

between about 10 000 BCE and 6500 BCE	between about 6500 BCE and 5000 BCE	between about 5000 BCE and 4000 BCE

2 The map shows how farming spread to different places over time.

   a In which part of the world did farming start?

   b In which general direction did farming spread?

   c How long did it take for farming to reach Britain?

3 Some of the early settlements in Africa are in places that are desert today. How do you think farming was possible in these places in Neolithic times?

_____

_____

_____

Choosing where to build a Neolithic village

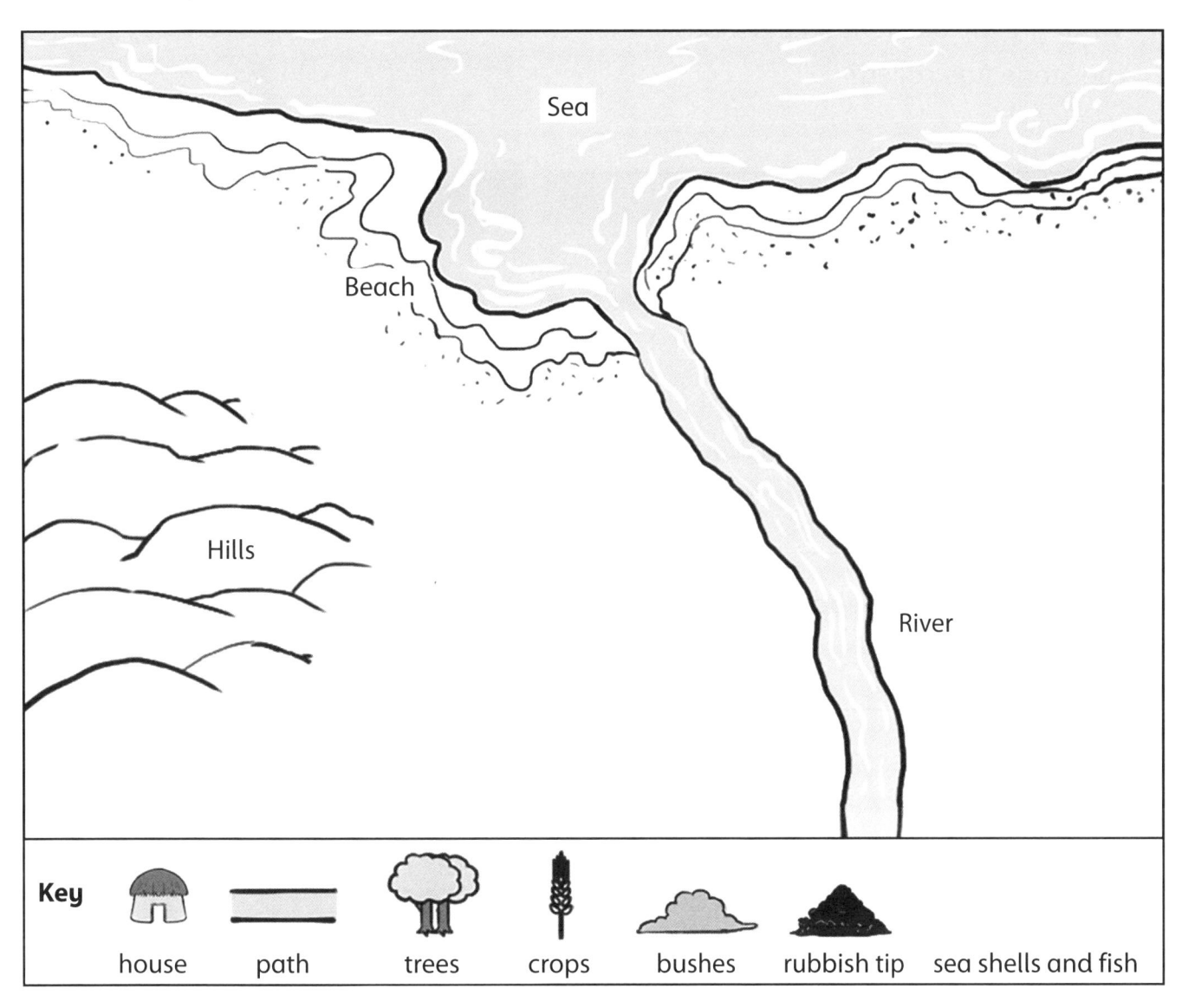

Key: house, path, trees, crops, bushes, rubbish tip, sea shells and fish

1 Draw a plan of a Neolithic village on the map above, using the symbols from the key. You can use each symbol as many times as you like.

2 Draw a symbol for sea shells and fish in the key. Add this symbol to your map to show where the villagers can find sea shells and fish.

1 Thinking about my learning

Stone Age times

Find your answers to the questions in speech bubbles on page 4 at the beginning of the unit. Use a different colour to add to your answers or rewrite them. Include any new information you have learned while studying this unit.

How did life change during the Stone Age?

1   What are the different time periods within the Stone Age called?

　_____

　_____

　_____

　_____

2   How did tools and weapons change during the Stone Age?

　_____

　_____

　_____

3   How did many people's lives change towards the end of the Stone Age?

　_____

　_____

　_____

Thinking about my learning

☺ I understand and can do this well.
😐 I understand but I am not confident.
☹ I don't understand and find this difficult.

Learning outcome	☺	😐	☹
Discuss how people lived long ago.			
Explain how people first began farming.			
Discuss similarities and differences between life in the past and life now.			
Explain how we use evidence to find out about Stone Age people.			

One thing I learned about how Stone Age people lived is…

_____

_____

One difference between life in the Stone Age and life today is…

_____

_____

The best fact I know about the Stone Age is…

_____

_____

One thing I would still like to know about the Stone Age is…

_____

_____

2 The Metal Ages

What do I already know?

What do you think are good answers to the questions in the speech bubbles? Discuss your answers with some friends. Write your answers in a notebook. Your teacher will ask you to look back at your answers when you have completed the unit.

> What are bronze and iron?

> What was life like in the Bronze Age?

> When were the Bronze Age and the Iron Age?

> What was life like in the Iron Age?

> What did people make from bronze and iron?

Things I would like to know about the Bronze Age and the Iron Age

_____

_____

_____

Evidence from the past

1 Look at this photo of a hill fort. Some people in the past built hill forts to protect themselves. Who or what might they need to protect themselves from? Why did they build these forts on the top of a hill?

_____

_____

_____

_____

2 The pottery objects on page 18 of your Student Book are from different periods of time. Which pottery object do you think is older? How did you decide? What clues did you see?

_____

_____

_____

3 What does the older pottery object tell us about life at the time when it was made?

_____

_____

_____

2.1 Technology in the Bronze Age

What is bronze?

1 Match the pictures of the tool (A) and the weapon (B) shown below with how they were made. Write the two pairs of letters that go together.

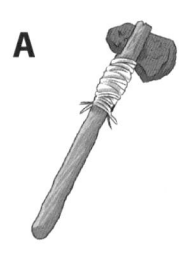

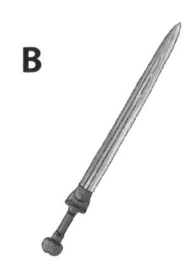

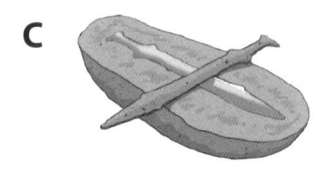

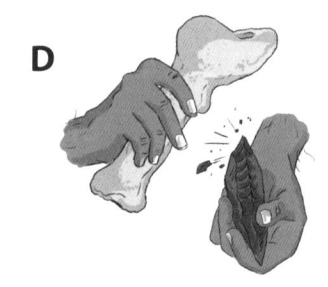

A   B   C   D

_____

2 Describe how people made tools in the Stone Age. Use the words in the box to help you. Use the words as many times as you like.

| stone | hit | hammer | sharp edge |

_____

_____

_____

3 Describe how people made tools in the Bronze Age. Use the words in the box to help you. Use the words as many times as you like.

| copper | tin | liquid metal | mould | poured |

_____

_____

_____

Farming technology

1 Write the phrases in the box in the correct column of the table. Then draw a line to link each job with the tool or equipment used.

pottery jars	plough fields	a cart	store food
potter's wheel	harvest crops	an axe	make pots
take food to market	a plough	clear trees	a scythe

Jobs on a Bronze Age farm	Tools and equipment

2 Archeologists often find stone or bronze objects that were made in the Stone Age or the Bronze Age. Many objects were also made from wood in those times. Why don't archeologists find so many of the wooden objects?

_____

_____

_____

2.2 Towns, trade and travel

Where were the first cities?

1 Label the drawing of the Bronze Age city with the correct letters from the box.

   a outer walls   **b** inner walls   **c** palace   **d** steep slope   **e** river   **f** houses

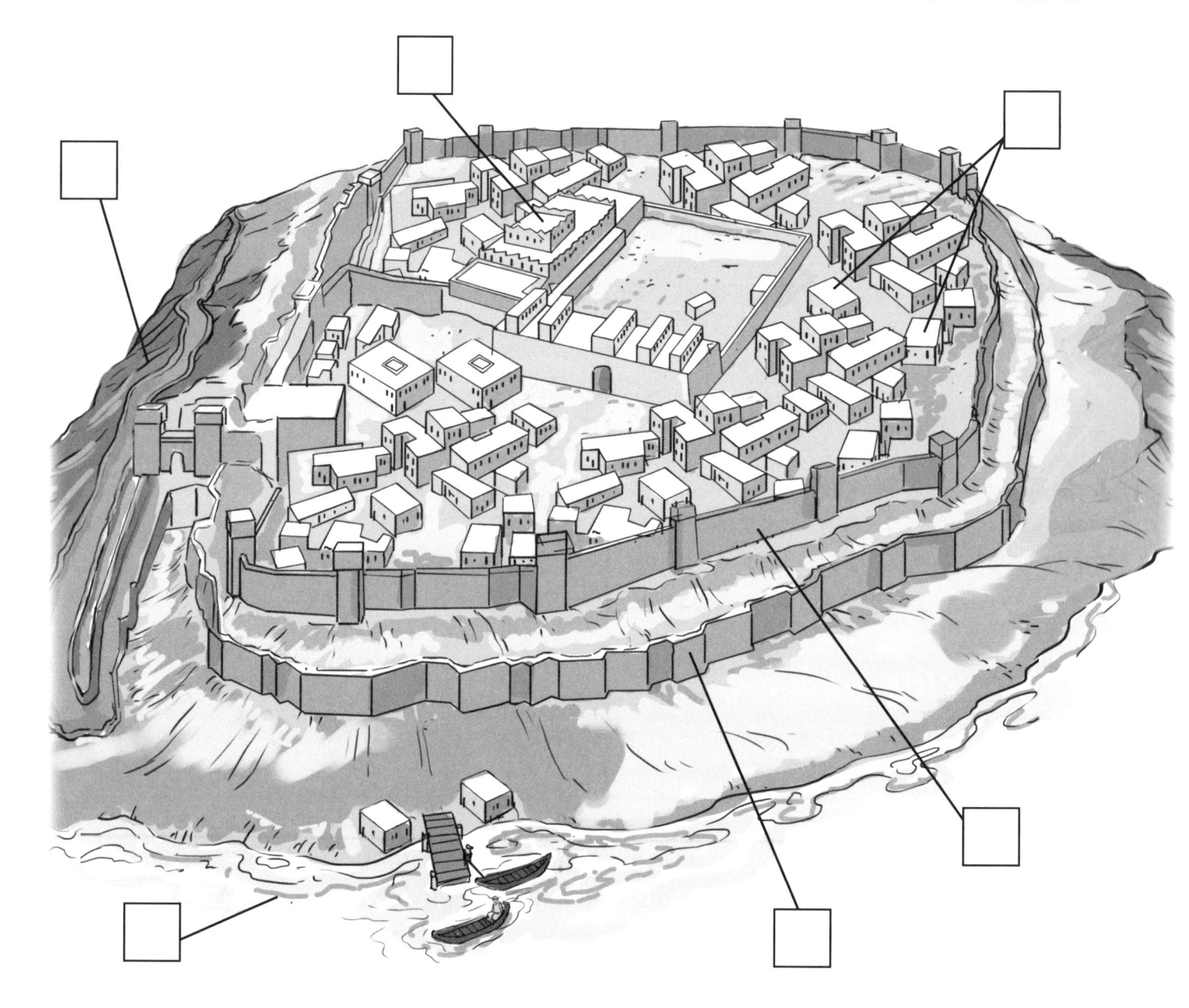

2 Explain why the people who built this city chose this site.

_____

_____

Bronze Age jobs

Read what the people in the pictures say about their work. Using the words in the box, write the job that each person does. Use your Student Book page 24 and a dictionary to help you.

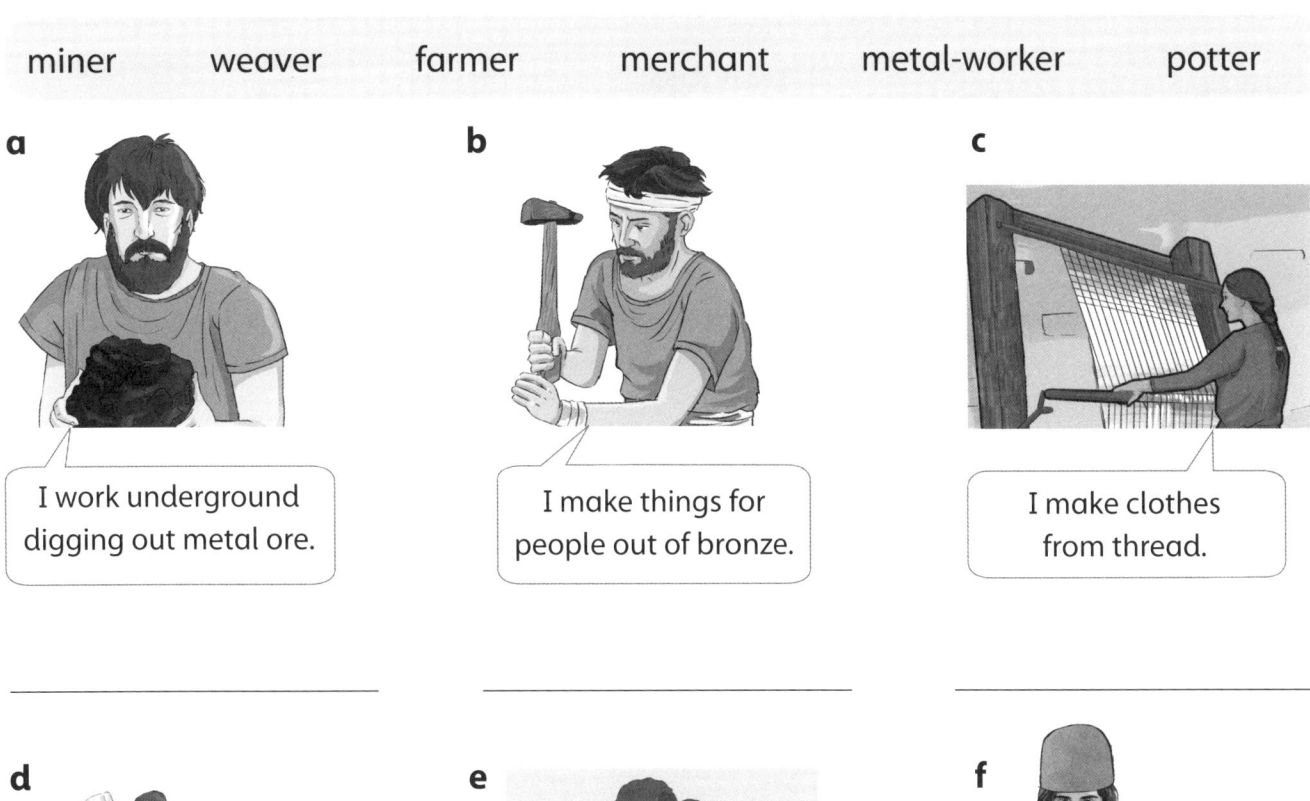

| miner | weaver | farmer | merchant | metal-worker | potter |

a — I work underground digging out metal ore.

b — I make things for people out of bronze.

c — I make clothes from thread.

d — I grow food to bring to the city.

e — I make vases and bowls from clay.

f — I buy and sell goods in different places.

Challenge

In your notebook explain how we know that Bronze Age cities looked like the one shown on page 22. What historical evidence do you think we have?

2 The Metal Ages

2.3 Life and death in the Iron Age

Iron tools

1 Complete each box in the table with a drawing and a short sentence.

Today	Iron Age
Ploughing Farmers today plough fields using a tractor.	Farmers in the Iron Age…
Harvesting Farmers today harvest crops using a combine harvester.	Farmers in the Iron Age…

2 Iron Age people used iron to make swords, knives, and the blades for ploughs, scythes and sickles. Why was iron a good material for these things?

_____

_____

Special objects

Long, narrow straps used to control horses are called reins. The picture shows a rein ring from the Iron Age. Two rein rings were attached to a chariot. The horse's reins were passed through the rings. The ring shown here is made from bronze and has red and blue glass set into it.

1 Colour the rein ring to match the labels. Choose other colours to colour the rest of the design.

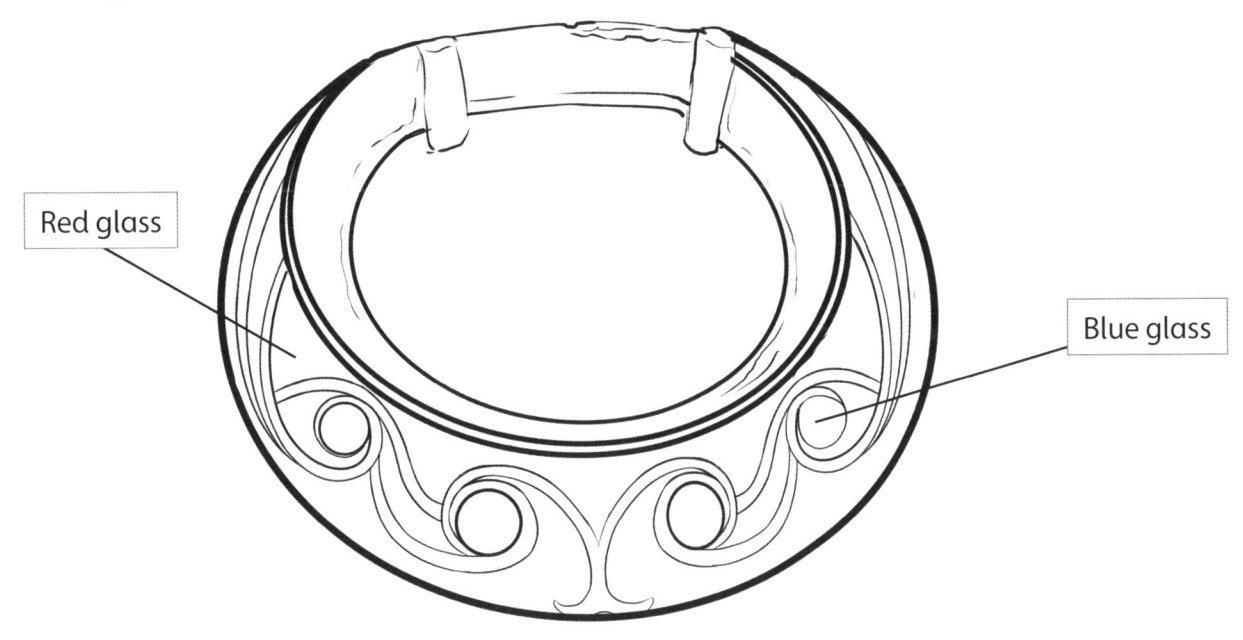

Red glass

Blue glass

2 The rein rings are beautiful and took a lot of skill to make. Who do you think the rein rings belonged to?

_____

_____

3 Objects such as rein rings are sometimes found where Iron Age people were buried. Why do you think these objects were buried with the people who owned them?

_____

_____

_____

2.4 Iron Age settlements

Village life

1 In an Iron Age village most people worked on farms, but there were other jobs.

   a Work for men included…

   _____

   b Work for women included…

   _____

   c Children in an Iron Age village had to…

   _____

2 Write some jobs that people do where you live today.

   _____

   _____

3 Write some things that children do where you live today.

   _____

   _____

A roundhouse

1 Describe what it was like inside an Iron Age roundhouse.

_____

_____

_____

2 Describe what it is like inside your home.

_____

_____

_____

3 Write three things you do in your home that Iron Age people did in their houses.

_____

_____

_____

2.5 Fighting tribes or traders?

Iron Age warriors

Objects from the Iron Age provide the best evidence about Iron Age warriors.

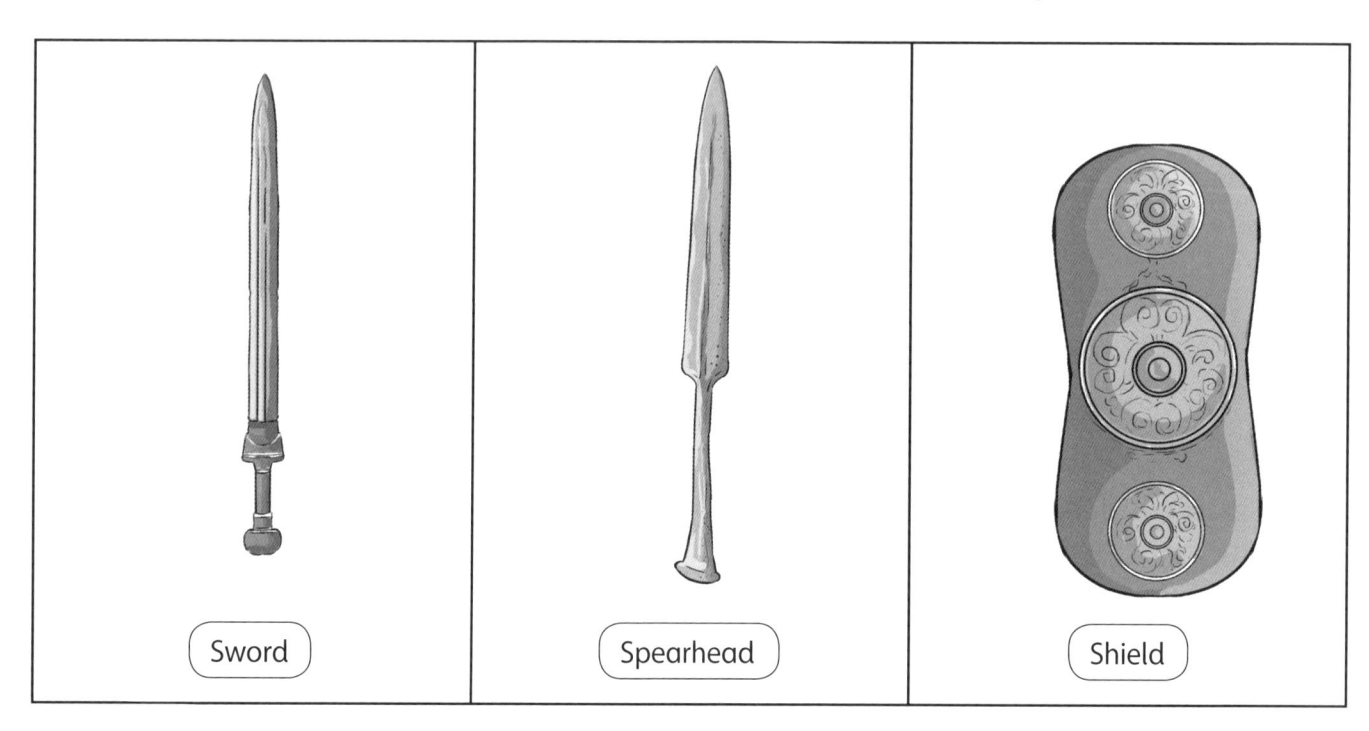

| Sword | Spearhead | Shield |

1 What does each of these objects tell us about how Iron Age warriors fought?

   _____

   _____

2 What does each of these objects tell us about the skills of Iron Age metal-workers?

   _____

   _____

3 Why do you think people were sometimes buried with objects like these?

   _____

   _____

Iron Age trade

1 Look at this map. Colour the boxes in the key. Colour the numbered areas on the map, using the correct colours.

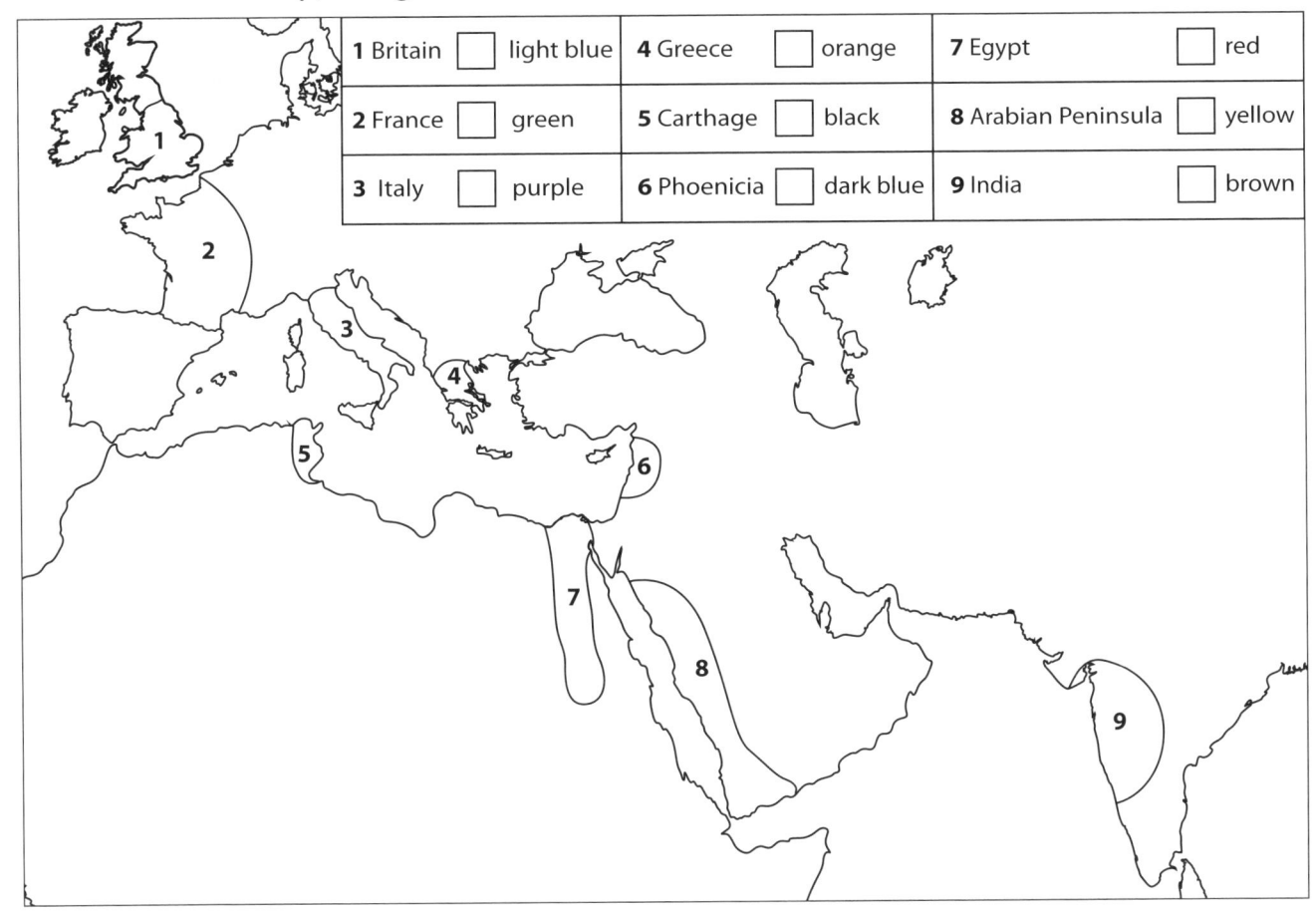

1 Britain	☐ light blue	4 Greece	☐ orange	7 Egypt	☐ red
2 France	☐ green	5 Carthage	☐ black	8 Arabian Peninsula	☐ yellow
3 Italy	☐ purple	6 Phoenicia	☐ dark blue	9 India	☐ brown

Archeologists have found items from the Iron Age, including:

- pottery from Italy in north-west France and Britain
- tin from Britain in southern France and Greece
- jewellery from Egypt in the Arabian Peninsula
- spices from India in Phoenicia.

2 Explain what the list of items tells us about trade in the Iron Age.

_____

_____

_____

3 Draw arrows on the map to show how the items in the list may have travelled between the different places.

2 Thinking about my learning

The Metal Ages

Find your answers to the questions in speech bubbles on page 18 at the beginning of the unit. Use a different colour to add to your answers or rewrite them. Include any new information you have learned while studying this unit.

The Bronze and Iron Ages

1 Many changes happened when people learned how to make bronze. Describe how bronze tools changed farming.

   _____
   _____
   _____
   _____
   _____

2 Write two reasons why people stopped using bronze and started using iron instead.

   _____
   _____
   _____
   _____

Local history study

In your notebook create a timeline that shows some places, events or people from the Bronze Age and the Iron Age in your country. Use reference books and the Internet to help you.

Thinking about my learning

☺ I understand and can do this well.
😐 I understand but I am not confident.
☹ I don't understand and find this difficult.

Learning outcome	☺	😐	☹
Talk about how people lived in the Bronze Age and the Iron Age.			
Describe how people first began making things from metal.			
Discuss similarities and differences between life in the past and life in the present day.			
Explain how we use evidence to find out about people from prehistoric times.			

One thing I learned about the Bronze Age or Iron Age is…

One difference between life in the Bronze Age or Iron Age and today is…

The best fact I know about the Bronze Age or Iron Age is…

One thing I would still like to know about the Bronze Age or Iron Age is…

3 Early civilisations

What do I already know?

What do you think are good answers to the questions in the speech bubbles? Discuss your answers with some friends. Write your answers in a notebook. Your teacher will ask you to look back at your answers when you have completed the unit.

> What is a civilisation?

> Where in the world did early civilisations begin?

> Why did people create civilisations?

> Did people from different early civilisations meet?

> Was life the same in all the different civilisations?

> Why did the civilisations end?

Things I would like to know about the Ancient Sumer civilisation, the Indus Valley civilisation and the Shang Dynasty civilisation

_____

_____

_____

_____

1 Look at this image of a carving showing men rowing a boat. The carving is from the ancient civilisation in Sumer. What does the carving tell us about how people made their boats move?

_____

_____

_____

2 Why do people use boats today? Write a list of reasons. Put ✓ next to all the reasons that you think were the same for people in Ancient Sumer.

_____

_____

_____

_____

3 a What materials do you think these objects are made from?

_____

_____

   b Can you describe the craftspeople who made these objects? You can use the words in the box to help you.

   | clever   creative   skilful   artistic   patient |

_____

_____

_____

3.1 Early civilisations

Facts about three early civilisations

1. Use the timeline on page 35 of your Student Book and the maps on pages 34–35 to help you fill in the table. Two answers have been done for you.

Civilisation name	Location	Began	Ended	Important rivers	Three important towns
Ancient Sumer					
					Harappa

2. Complete these sentences about the three civilisations, using information from the maps and the timeline.

   a The earliest civilisation was _____.

   b Two civilisations that might have traded with each other are

   _____ and _____.

   c The _____ was the latest civilisation of the three.

Feeding people in the cities

1 Fill in the gaps in these sentences. Use the words in the box to help you.

| food | rivers | settlements | fertile |

In early civilisations more people began to live in larger

_____ called towns and cities. The civilisations were

based near _____. The soil near the rivers was very

_____. Farmers could grow lots of _____.

2 Explain how the people living in the towns and cities got the food they needed.

    a Write about what farmers and farm workers did on the farms.

    _____

    _____

    _____

    _____

    b Write about how farmers got food to the towns and cities.

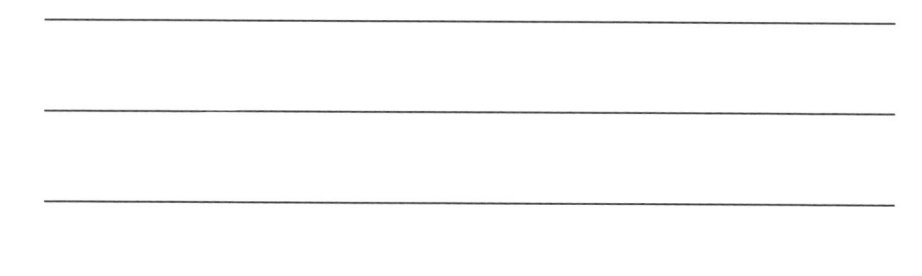

_____

_____

_____

_____

Challenge

Ancient records from Sumer tell us that people bought many kinds of food in the towns. Some people sold fresh food and others cooked food to sell.

Find out about some types of food available in Ancient Sumer. Write a list in your notebook. How are food markets where you live the same as or different from food markets in Ancient Sumer?

3.2 Farming and food

Farming and technology

Complete the table. Write the name of each invention in the box.
Write about how the invention helped with farming and the supply of food in the box next to the picture.

Invention	How the invention helped with farming or supplying food

Clothes in ancient civilisations

Use page 37 of your Student Book and the Internet to help you with the activities on this page.

1 Complete the table. The first one has been done for you.

Source	What material is made from this source?	Which civilisations used this material?	Is it used today?
Cotton plant	Cotton	Indus Valley	Yes
Flax plant			
Sheep			
Silkworm			

2 Look at the labels in some of your clothes. Write a list of the materials that your clothes are made from. Put ✓ next to all the materials that people in early civilisations used to make clothes.

_____

_____

_____

3.3 City life in the early civilisations

Early city fact file

Eridu and Ur were important cities in Sumer. Harappa and Mohenjo-Daro were important cities in the Indus Valley. Xibo (present-day Luoyang) and Yin (present-day Anyang) were important cities in the Shang Dynasty civilisation.

1 Choose one city. Find out all you can about the city and fill in the fact file.

City name	Civilisation	City population	Dates of the city

Famous sites and interesting facts

Three archeological finds from the city

1 _____

2 _____

3 _____

2 Houses in the Sumerian and Indus Valley civilisations were made from mud bricks. Houses in the Shang Dynasty civilisation were made from a wooden frame. Explain why people in Sumer and the Indus Valley used mud bricks and did not use wood.

_____

_____

Jobs in early civilisations

1 Write down connections between these people. The first one has been done for you.

a (a farmer growing flax) (a woman spinning thread) (a child wearing clothes)

A farmer grows flax. A woman spins the fibres from the flax plant to make thread. She weaves the thread to make cloth. She makes clothes for her child from the cloth.

b (a merchant trading copper) (a metal-worker) (a farmer harvesting crops)

_____

_____

_____

_____

c (a potter) (a woman cooking food) (a family eating a meal)

_____

_____

_____

_____

d (a merchant trading gem stones) (a skilled craftsperson) (a princess wearing a necklace)

_____

_____

_____

_____

2 In early civilisations people did many jobs apart from farming. Write a list of jobs from early civilisations that people still do today.

_____

_____

_____

3.4 Writing and number systems

Writing

The people of Ancient Sumer developed a writing system called cuneiform. These are some symbols that the Sumerian people used.

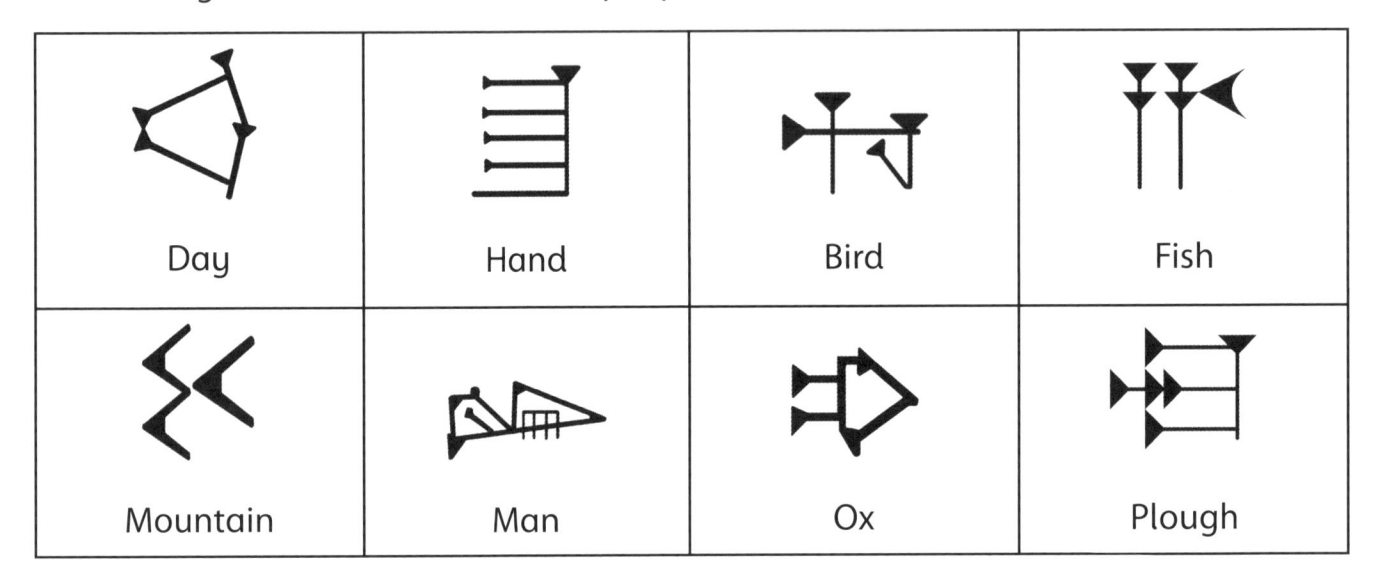

Day	Hand	Bird	Fish
Mountain	Man	Ox	Plough

1 Use the cuneiform symbols to complete these sentences.

   a The sun rises at the start of the _____ .

   b We agreed and I shook him by the _____ .

   c She said she saw a _____ fly out of the tree.

   d If we can catch one, we will have _____ to eat tonight.

   e The _____ said he travelled over the _____ .

   f I will use an _____ to pull my _____ .

2 Write a sentence for a partner to complete with a Sumerian symbol.

Number systems

Solve these calculations using the Sumerian number system.

1. Write the numbers you normally use under each symbol. Look at page 41 of your Student Book to help you.

   3 + 5 = 8

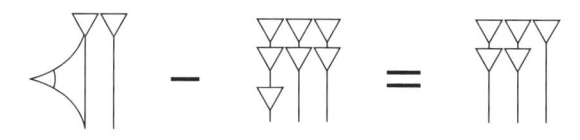

   _ × _ = _

   _ − _ = _

   _ ÷ _ = _

   _ + _ = _

2. Fill in the missing numbers and symbols in these two questions.

3.5 Trade and war

Trading peoples

Use the trade route map from page 42 of your Student Book to help you complete these tasks.

1 Colour the seas blue.

2 Draw a possible route for trade by sea between the Indus Valley civilisation and the Ancient Sumerian civilisation.

3 Draw a possible overland route for trade between Sumer and Egypt.

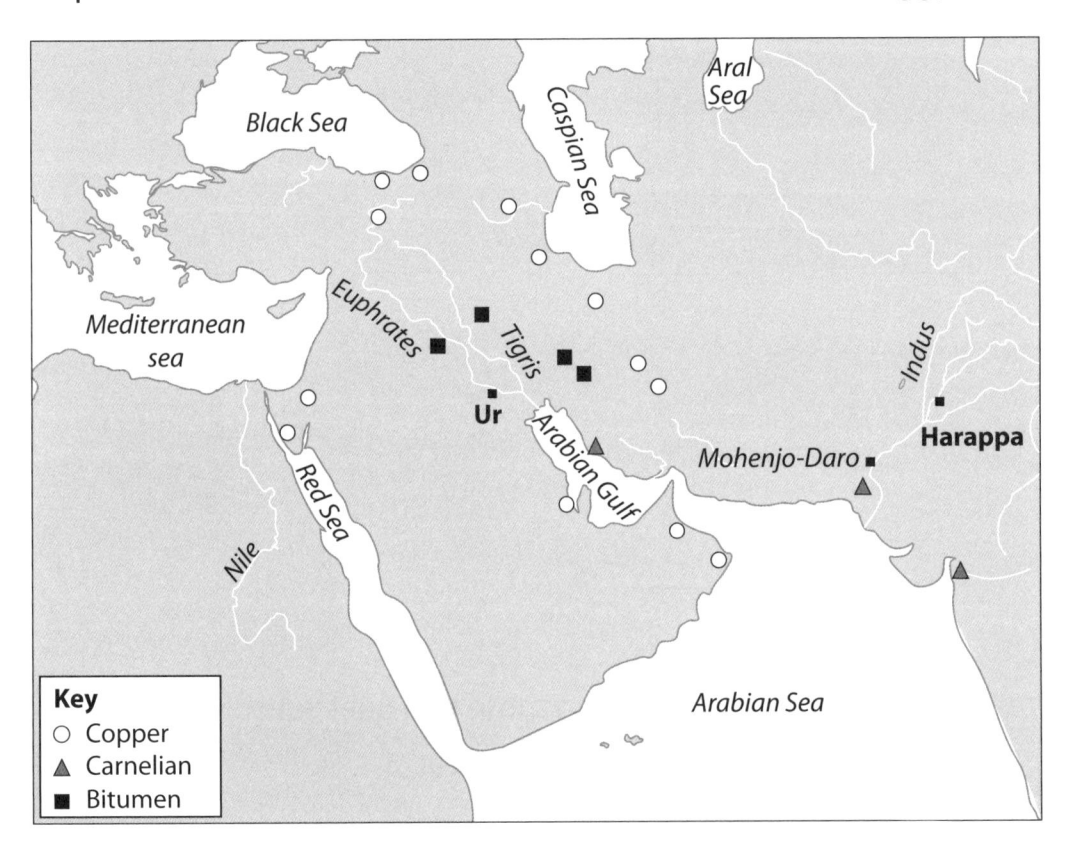

Key
○ Copper
▲ Carnelian
■ Bitumen

Challenge

Write the answers to these questions in your notebook.

1 Which resource from the Indus Valley was used to make jewellery to trade with the Sumerians?

2 Which resource from the Arabian Peninsula was useful for both the Indus Valley and the Sumerian civilisations? What might people have used this resource for?

Trade or war?

Read the speech bubbles. Each bubble contains a reason for the ruler of an early civilisation to go to war with a neighbour. Why does the ruler think these are good reasons to go to war? Write your answer next to each speech bubble. The first one has been done for you.

> We need more food to feed the people living in our city.

If the ruler can capture more land, his people will be able to grow more food for themselves.

> We have to sail our trading ships down the river past the neighbouring city-state.

_____

_____

_____

> The ruler of the neighbouring city-state is becoming too powerful.

_____

_____

_____

> We need more workers to do the hard work in the fields.

_____

_____

_____

3 Thinking about my learning

Early civilisations

Find your answers to the questions in speech bubbles on page 32 at the beginning of the unit. Use a different colour to add to your answers or rewrite them. Include any new information you have learned while studying this unit.

Life in early civilisations

1 Farming techniques improved in the early civilisations so fewer people were needed to produce a good supply of food. This meant that more people could do other types of work. Write some examples of the work that people did.

   _____

   _____

2 Write some examples of items made by workers who were not farmers.

   _____

   _____

3 Write some examples of important inventions that helped early civilisations to develop.

   _____

   _____

4 Write some reasons why early civilisations traded with each other. Give some examples of the goods they traded.

   _____

   _____

Thinking about my learning

☺ I understand and can do this well.
😐 I understand but I am not confident.
☹ I don't understand and find this difficult.

Learning outcome	☺	😐	☹
Describe some inventions from early civilisations.			
Talk about how people lived in early civilisations.			
Discuss similarities and differences between life in early civilisations.			
Describe some evidence that helps us know about early civilisations.			

One thing I learned about early civilisations is…

_____

_____

One difference between life in early civilisations and life today is…

_____

_____

The best fact I know about early civilisations is…

_____

_____

One thing I would still like to know about early civilisations is…

_____

_____

4 A history of communication

What do I already know?

What do you think are good answers to the questions in the speech bubbles? Discuss your answers with some friends. Write your answers in a notebook. Your teacher will ask you to look back at your answers when you have completed the unit.

- What is communication?
- Why do people need to communicate?
- How do people communicate today?
- Have people always communicated in the same way?
- How has technology affected the way we communicate?
- What difference does modern communication make to the world?

Things I would like to find out about the history of communication

_____

_____

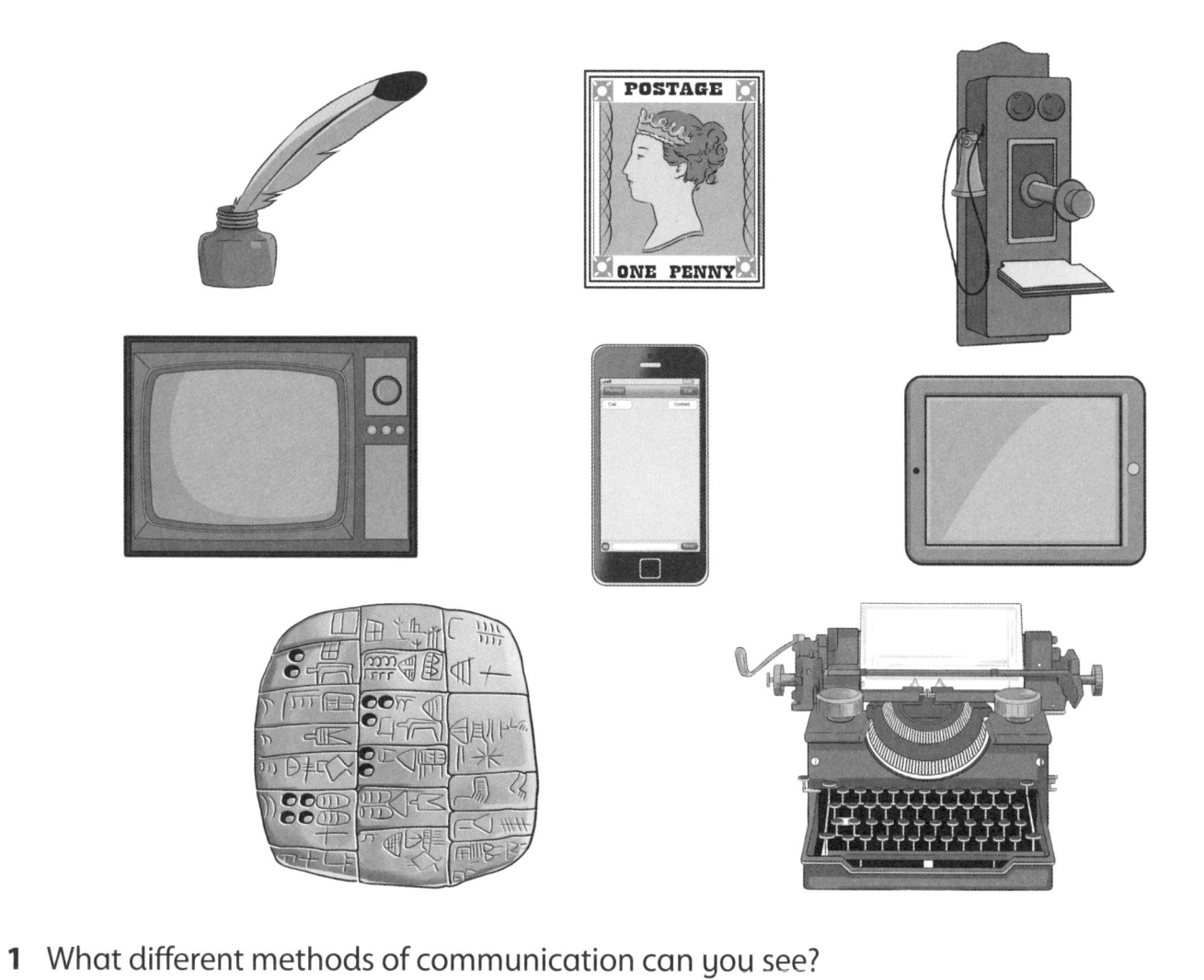

1 What different methods of communication can you see?

   _____

   _____

2 Which do you think are old methods and which are modern methods?

   _____

   _____

3 What discoveries and inventions allowed these forms of communication to exist?

   _____

   _____

   _____

4 A history of communication

47

4.1 Writing and writing tools

The invention of writing

Look at the map and examples of ancient writing, then answer the questions below.

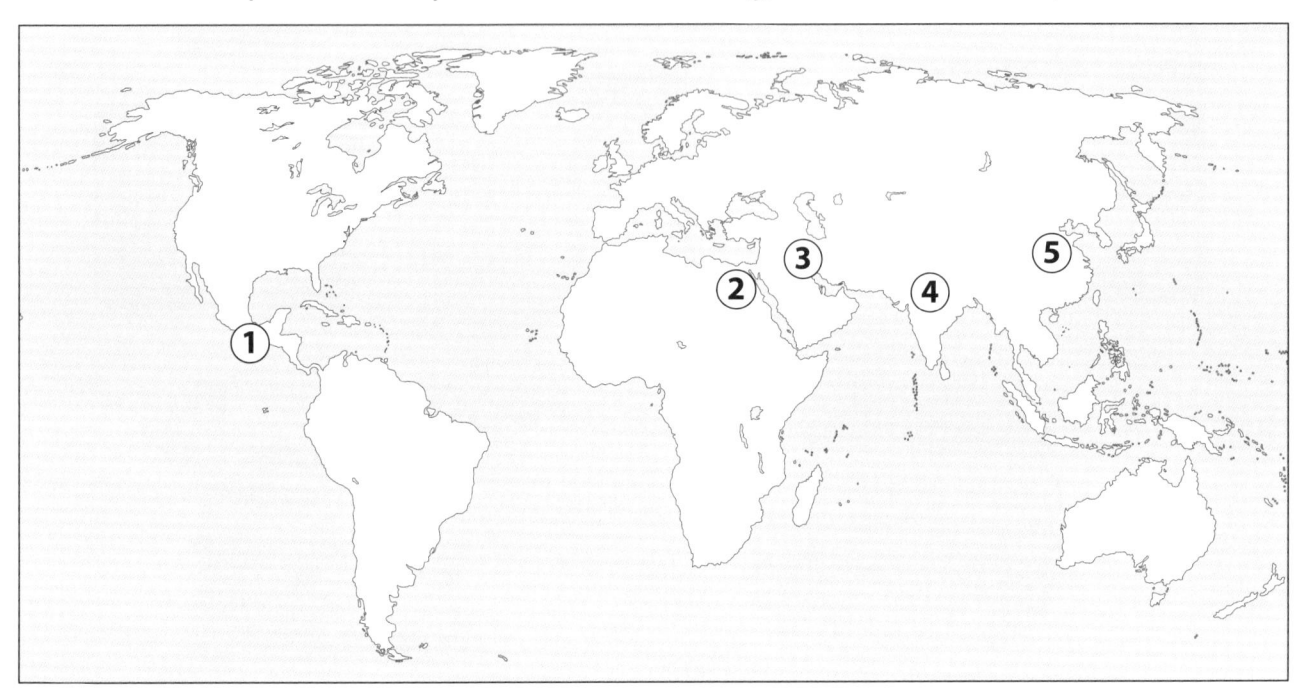

1 Write the name of the civilisation below each example of ancient writing.

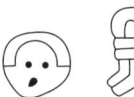

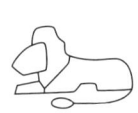

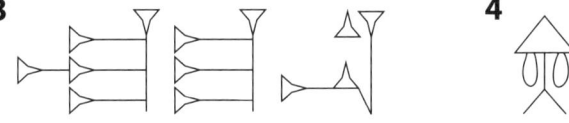

1 Meso____ - America____

2 A_____ E_____

3 A_____
  S_____

4 I_____
  V_____

5 S_____
  D_____

2 Which new language was invented in the last 50 years? Here is a clue:

```
<html xmlns="http://www.w3.org/1999/xhtml" lang="en" xml :
lang="en">…

</html>
```

_____

48

Writing tools

Put these events from the history of writing tools on the timeline. Write the letters A–G in the correct places. Draw a small picture next to each letter on the timeline.

A Wooden pencil invented: about 1560 CE

B Ancient Sumerians pressed shapes into clay tablets: about 3200 BCE

C Word processing using computer with keyboard: 1970s

D Ancient Greeks used wax tablets: 750 BCE

E First cheap ballpoint pen available: 1938

F Quill pens were first used: about 600 CE

G First successful typewriter: 1867

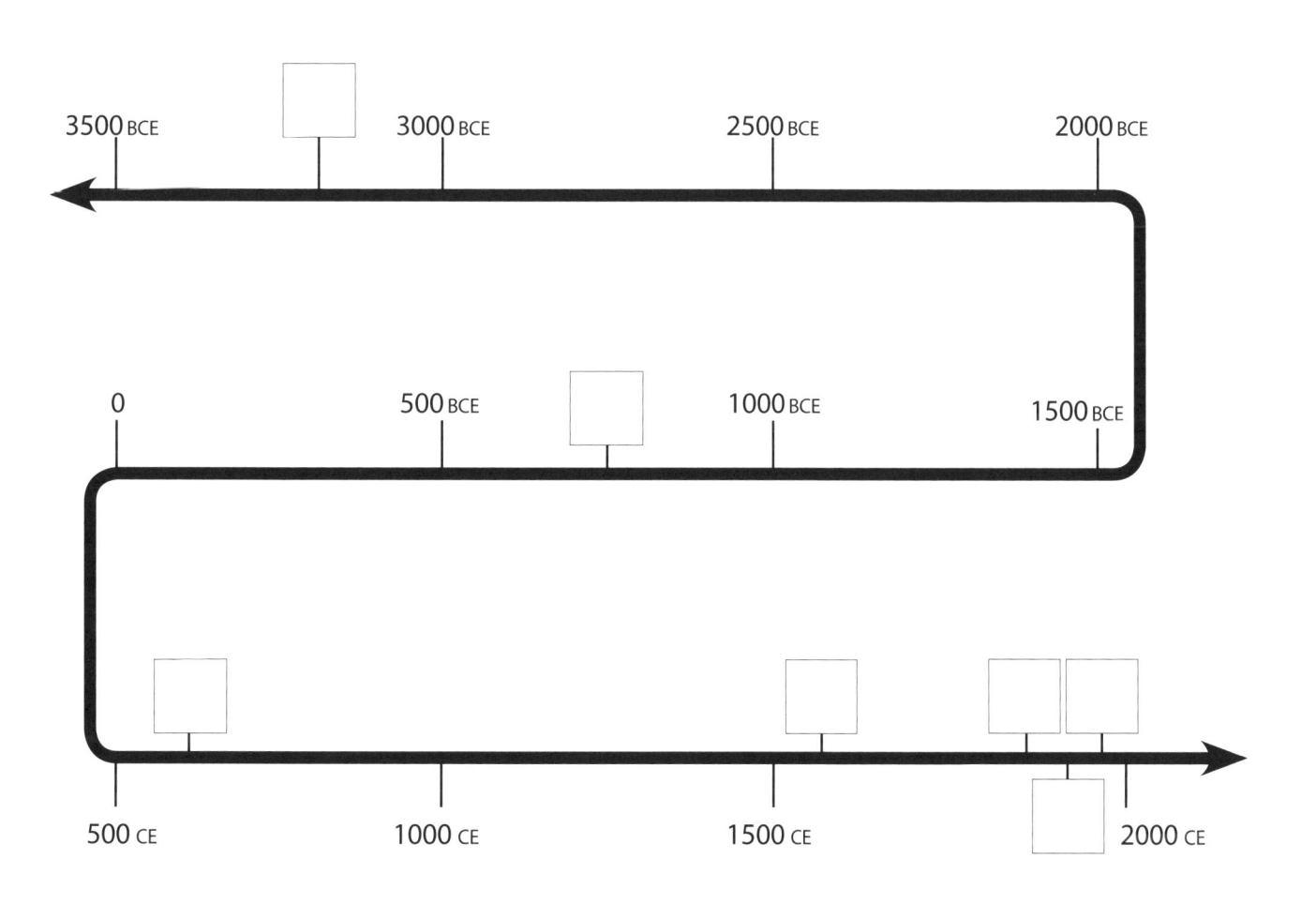

4.2 Printing

Johannes Gutenberg

Make a fact file about Johannes Gutenberg. Use page 51 of your Student Book and the Internet to help you.

Johannes Gutenberg Fact File	
Year of birth	Place of birth
Year of death	Father's occupation
How books were made before Gutenberg's printing press	
Two special things about how Gutenberg's printing press worked	
How Gutenberg's printing press affected the price of books	
How Gutenberg's printing press affected the number of people who could read	
How Gutenberg's printing press helped spread information, knowledge and ideas	

Printing

1 Make a list of three items in your home that include printed text. One item should provide information, one item should give instructions and one item should be for entertainment. Draw a picture of each item in your list.

Name of item	Purpose of the text	Drawing

2 Imagine that the printing press has never been invented. Discuss in pairs how the world would be different. What things would not exist? What events would not have happened? Be ready to share your ideas with the class.

4.3 Staying in touch

Postal transport

Find out about two different types of postal transport from different times in history. Use pages 52 and 53 of your Student Book and the Internet to help you.

1 Type of transport:

_____

Draw a picture of the transport in the box.

Write two facts about the transport.

_____

_____

Write one advantage of the transport.

_____

2 Type of transport:

_____

Draw a picture of the transport in the box.

Write two facts about the transport.

_____

_____

Write one advantage of the transport.

Oxford International Primary History

Workbook

3

OXFORD University Press

ASPIRE SUCCEED PROGRESS

Oxford International Primary for enquiring minds

OXFORD

Thinking about my learning

- 😊 I understand and can do this well.
- 😐 I understand but I am not confident.
- ☹️ I don't understand and find this difficult.

Learning objective	😊	😐	☹️
Describe how different forms of communication have changed over time.			
Explain how different forms of historical evidence are used.			
Examine significant people and events in the history of communication.			
Analyse and describe important changes in communication and their effects.			

One thing I learned about the history of communication is…

_____

_____

One difference between communication in ancient times and communication today is…

_____

_____

The best fact I know about the history of communication is…

_____

_____

One thing I would still like to know about communication is…

_____

Glossary

Using your own words, explain what these words mean.

Bronze Age

civilisation

communication

hill fort

hunter-gatherers

invention

Iron Age

postal service

pottery

prehistoric

printing

roundhouse

satellite

Glossary

settlement

society

Stone Age

Postage stamps

Find out when the countries listed in this table first used postage stamps. Write the year in the table. Add three more countries to the table. One of these should be the country you live in.

Country	Year postage stamps first used
Brazil	
China	
France	
India	
Russia	

Local history study

Find out about the history of postage stamps in your country. Use reference books, the Internet and ask older members of your family to help you.

a   How has the cost of postage stamps in your country changed over time?

b   Which people, objects, animals or flowers have been pictured on postage stamps in your country? Give three examples.

4.4 Telecommunication

Telegraphy

Telegraphy was an early way of sending messages down wires. The messages used Morse code. The code was sent by pressing a special key. At the other end of the wire another machine turned the signals into marks on paper. A quick tap on the key made a dot on the paper. A longer press made a dash.

A	•—	J	•———	S	•••	1	•————
B	—•••	K	—•—	T	—	2	••———
C	—•—•	L	•—••	U	••—	3	•••——
D	—••	M	——	V	•••—	4	••••—
E	•	N	—•	W	•——	5	•••••
F	••—•	O	———	X	—••—	6	—••••
G	——•	P	•——•	Y	—•——	7	——•••
H	••••	Q	——•—	Z	——••	8	———••
I	••	R	•—•	0	—————	9	————•

This is the Morse code for the alphabet and the numbers 0–9.

1 Use the code to write:

   a your name:

   b your age:

   c today's date:

   d the time:

2 Decode this Morse code message. When you have finished, follow the instruction you have written.

−/•−/•−−• −•−−/−−−/••−/•−− ••••/•/•−/−•• •−−−−/••−−− −/••/−−/•/•••

_____

_____

3 Write your own Morse code instruction for a friend.

_____

_____

Telephones

1 Carry out a survey of how people in your home use telephones.

Family member	Uses home phone landline Y/N	Uses own mobile phone Y/N	Uses phone for social calls Y/N	Uses phone for business calls Y/N	Time spent on phone each day (hours or minutes)	When first used a phone (year)
Me						

2 How has the way your family uses telephones changed over time?

_____

_____

_____

4.5 Mass communication

Technology and mass communication

1. A long time ago, news was spread by messengers riding horses. Draw a picture of a messenger on a horse.

2. Today, news is spread using communications satellites. Draw a picture of a modern communications satellite.

3. Create a timeline that shows at least seven people or events from the history of mass communication. Use pages 56 and 57 of your Student Book, other reference books and the Internet to help you.

⟵─────────────────────────────⟶

4. Explain how technology has changed the way we hear news from around the world.

_____

_____

Mass media in the home

We can record information about the past by listening to people talk about their experiences. This is called oral history.

Use oral history to find out how your family uses mass communications. The main forms of mass communication today are newspapers, radio, television and the Internet.

In the 1920s, some families and friends gathered round the radio set to listen.

Challenge

Carry out a survey at home

Find out:

- how members of your family use different types of mass communication today
- how members of your family used these forms of communication in the past
- the experiences of family members of different ages.

In your notebook write some questions that you can ask different members of your family. Here are some questions you could include.

- What types of mass communication do you use today (for example, newspapers, radio, television, computer, smart phone)?
- Why do you choose that form of mass communication?
- Did you use any of these forms of communication in the past?
- Was mass communication different when you were younger?

Ask at least five different family members of different ages. Bring your findings back to the class to share.

4 Thinking about my learning

Communication

Find your answers to the questions in speech bubbles on page 46 at the beginning of the unit. Use a different colour to add to your answers or rewrite them. Include any new information you have learned while studying this unit.

Ways of communicating

Look at the list of ways of communicating that people could use at the end of 1950.

> Ways of communicating by the end of 1950 included:
> - face-to-face conversations
> - messages written on paper
> - printed books
> - printed magazines and newspapers
> - telegrams
> - telephones
> - radio broadcasts and television broadcasts.

1. Decide which of these ways of communicating people could use 100 years before, at the end of 1850. Write them here.

   _____

   _____

   _____

2. New ways of communicating have been developed since 1950. Write three new ways of communicating.

   _____

   _____